RIC VIERS

THE LOCATION SOUND BIBLE

How To Record Professional Dialog for Film and TV

Published by Michael Wiese Productions
12400 Ventura Blvd. #1111
Studio City, CA 91604
tel. 818.379.8799
fax 818.986.3408
mw@mwp.com
www.mwp.com

Cover design: Johnny Ink *www.johnnyink.com*
Interior book design: Gina Mansfield Design
Editor: Gary Sunshine

Printed by McNaughton & Gunn, Inc., Saline, Michigan
Manufactured in the United States of America

Library of Congress Cataloging-in-Publication Data
Viers, Ric.
The location sound bible : how to record professional dialog for film and TV / Ric Viers.
p. cm.
Includes index.
ISBN 978-1-61593-120-0 (pbk.)
1. Sound--Recording and reproducing. 2. Television broadcasting--Sound effects. 3. Sound in motion pictures. 4. Dialog in motion pictures. I. Title.
TK7881.4.V539 2012
777'.53--dc23

2012016109

CONTENTS

ACKNOWLEDGMENTS

Since I never got a chance to become a rock star, here is my equivalent of liner notes:

To Bill Kubota and Dave Newman of KDN for hiring a cocky, long-haired kid who was fresh out of film school…

To my friends Gary Allison, Scott Clements, Fred Ginsburg, Colin Hart, Michael Orlowski, and Jamie Scarpuzza for professional advice, fact-checking and cool ideas for this book…

To my editor, Gary Sunshine, for all his work to make sure I sounded smarter than a 5th grader…

To my mom and dad for their continued support, even though they still have no idea what I do for a living…

To my best friend (who also happens to be my wife), Tracy, for putting up with my neurotic tendencies and craziness on a daily basis…

To my son, Sean, for foolishly believing that I'm the coolest dad in the world…

And to all the fans of *The Sound Effects Bible* who encouraged me to do another book…

Thanks for making a positive impact on my life. You guys rock!

FOREWORD

When Ric Viers first asked me to write the Foreword for *The Location Sound Bible,* my reaction was that he should have an actual location sound person write it. My days as a sound designer are spent largely on my own, whether making new sounds at a DAW, or out recording new sounds in the field, which will come back and be twisted into something else (hopefully interesting).

So my time is spent mostly as a hermit, tucked away in my own world. When I record in the field, it's not because of a call sheet for the entire crew. I generally get to pick my own locations, and I usually pick them for their sonic quality, not what they will look like on camera. I don't have to deal with super-early call times, or complex setups that have to work around sets and sight lines. I don't have to wait around for hours while the lighting gets set up. I don't have to worry about keeping my mic out of the shot. I don't have to wait around to record at a moment's notice when everyone else is ready. I don't have to pick my battles about what noises to bring to the director's attention (which will slow the production down). I don't have to be perfectly meticulous with file names and on-site metadata so that the track matches the shot/take in post. My gear is usually light and portable, not a cart filled with mixers and various taps for whoever needs to monitor the takes. I don't have to take what is usually the worst-case scenario for recording audio and try to make sure it turns out a take that will hold up in the final mix. If I blow a take, no worries, I haven't just ruined a shot that took a team of people hours to prepare.

And above all, given all these factors, I don't have the pressure of capturing an actor's performance. With all the production and crew, actors generally are the most "on" or "in character," on set at the time of the shot. I don't have to capture a clean whisper over the fan noise, while remaining invisible to the camera.

No, I don't have to do those things. Or maybe a better phrasing is that I don't get to do those things. Working under challenges is regarded as most rewarding, and I'd say location sound certainly qualifies. It's also the one part of Sound for Picture that gets to see and experience the scope of the production first-hand.

Location sound is vital to the flow of the final track. Whether it's capturing audio that gets used in the final mix, or if it lays out a guide track for sound to be replaced, it is a critical component of the project. I tip my hat to the brave women and men who take on this task. You have to be on your game to get a good location sound track, and *The Location Sound Bible* is a great start.

David Farmer
Sound Designer, *Lord of ohe Rings* Trilogy, *King Kong*, *Cowboys and Aliens*

PREFACE

Sound is not important to a production; it's vital to a production.

The majority of first-time directors (and unfortunately some seasoned directors) do not understand how important sound is to a film. Some do believe that sound matters, but assume that the important sound comes from post. That could not be further from the truth. While postproduction is where the magic happens in a film, plenty of magic needs to be captured on-set when the actors are in the moment delivering the performance of their lives. It is very difficult to recapture that moment during ADR. Therefore, directors need to realize that production sound is more than just a utility function. The sound mixer uses different microphones to capture different qualities and distances of sound much in the same way that the director of photography (DP) composes a shot and uses various lenses on the camera. The sound mixer is essentially the director of sonic photography.

I've yet to meet or work with a first-time independent filmmaker whose first question wasn't "Can you fix my production sound?" This question is usually followed up with a sob story about how the budget was tight and they couldn't afford a good sound mixer on set. I believe in independent films. I believe that independent films can, are, and will continue to thrive. I also believe that independent films can have great sound.

Good location sound is possible, no matter what the budget. Even with a modest level of equipment, you can use certain techniques to capture stunning soundtracks that can make a production stand apart from the rest. Those techniques are found in the pages of *The Location Sound Bible*; however, the purpose of this book is not to teach you what to do in every single situation, but rather to show you the formula to use in any situation. Every production is unique. While you will probably encounter most of the situations given in this book, it's likely that you will come across situations that are not included in these pages. You might even find yourself with a challenge that no other sound mixer has faced before. If you understand the fundamentals of the process and how to best use the tools at your disposal, you will be able to get the best sound possible.

Let's start by getting something out of the way. Sound is not "easy." If it were, then every production would have great sound! Unfortunately, most independent films (and by most, I mean 90% of them) have poor sound. The idea of "all you have to do is turn the mic channel up and make sure the levels aren't in the red" is a myth. It would be the same as suggesting that anyone who can press the shutter button on a camera is a photographer. Nope. Sorry. It's just not true. And no, the microphone on the camera isn't an option either...

But don't fret. There is hope! In your hands you hold a guide that will help you achieve better sound results immediately. Whether you are looking to start a career as a sound mixer or if you're an independent filmmaker who is going to shoot and gather sound all by yourself, this book will help you achieve Hollywood-level sound. Use it as a foundation for recording better location sound. Keep it with you in your production bag or on your sound cart. With that out of the way, let's roll (pun intended).

CHAPTER 1

WHAT IS LOCATION SOUND?

Location sound is the process of gathering sound for a production in the field. This is usually dialog, although there are other sound elements that may need to be gathered. These sound elements are collectively referred to as *production sound* and will be used by the editor or postproduction sound team to make the soundtrack for the production. Production sound is any sound that is captured during the filming or taping of a production. This could be as simple as getting "nat sound" (short for *natural sound*) for B-roll, a reporter delivering a standup for the evening news, or dialog for a feature film.

The goal of location sound is to capture clean, consistent, and intelligible audio. While there are dozens of applications for field audio, each with a different variation on priorities and protocol, the purpose of location sound is to provide dialog that can be understood. If the audience cannot understand the dialog, then there was no reason for having a sound mixer on the set!

The audience should never have to strain to hear what the actors are saying. Sometimes it's impossible to gather usable audio during production. In these cases, the production will need to have the actors re-record the dialog in a controlled environment, such as a studio. This re-recording process is called *ADR* (Automated Dialog Replacement*). For example, if the production is shooting a scene that involves special effects like wind machines, the dialog is going to be unusable. However, the actors will need a reference track of what was said so that they can replace those lines during the ADR sessions. There are times when a director intends for the audience to strain to hear the dialog for effect. In these cases, the location sound should still be recorded as clean as possible as this effect is best achieved in postproduction.

While location sound equipment has certainly changed since it was first used in the late 1920s, the art of recording quality dialog on location is pretty much the same. Don't let new gadgets and equipment distract you from your goal: clean, consistent, and intelligible dialog. While new gear may take the

**There are several possible definitions of ADR including Automatic Dialog Replacement, Automatic Dialog Recording, etc. However, the meaning is always the same: to replace dialog that was recorded during the production.*

place of some of the equipment mentioned in this book, the techniques offered in the chapters that follow will long outlast the technology.

Remember: Technique will always trump technology!

Good audio cannot improve the story or subject matter, but bad audio will pull the audience out of the story or make it difficult to focus on the subject matter. The audience should be wowed and amazed by the cinematography and performances, but if someone notices the sound work in a film, then the sound department did its job incorrectly. The sound should be transparent. The audience should feel as though they are standing in the room with the actors during the scene, not listening through microphones.

The person responsible for gathering the location sound is called the *sound mixer*, although there are a host of other pseudonyms that they work under: production sound mixer, sound recordist, location sound recordist, location sound mixer, mixer, recordist, audio operator, sound man, sound woman, sound guy, sound dude, sound chick, etc. In short, they're called anything but their first name. In fact, most people will never even learn or ask for your name. I worked with a woman on several productions over the years and ran into her at a store. She started to say hi, but realized that she didn't even know my name. She said, "Hey…" After a brief pause, she conceded defeat and simply said, "… sound guy!" We both chuckled. It happens a lot.

Many consider the sound mixer's job to be pretty easy: just point the mic at the person talking. Nothing could be further from the truth. The sound mixer faces far more obstructions than the camera operator, but because these obstacles are actually invisible sound waves, no one notices them. That is, until people listen back to the scene. They'll notice your work, but only if there is a problem.

It's impossible to make poor sound better in post. You can correct the sound, but you cannot improve it. If it sounds bad on the set, it will sound bad in post. So, the sound mixer must deliver the best sound from the set. Location sound is considered a technical job,

The author on location at Tiger Stadium, circa 1998

but there's definitely an art behind the craft. Anyone can record good audio in the studio, but it takes skill and experience to record good audio in the field. Studios are controlled environments. The field is the untamed, Wild West! Anything that can go wrong will go wrong. Location sound is about delivering the best soundtracks in the worst-case scenarios.

There are many different applications for location sound and they each have unique techniques and procedures associated with them. These include news reporting, live shots, commercials, documentaries, corporate videos, YouTube videos, and feature films. In short, any media that plays on a screen with speakers needs some type of location sound work.

Actors brave the hot Florida sun while the equipment tries to keep up with the humidity!

In this book, we will discuss the three main types of location sound productions: ENG, EFP, and feature films.

ENG stands for Electronic News Gathering. ENG work is known as "running and gunning" and involves a fast-paced workflow. The crew is usually a three-person team consisting of a producer, camera operator, and sound mixer.

EFP stands for Electronic Field Production and involves more elaborate setups for concerts, sports events and video productions shot film-style. EFP work can be a mix between ENG and high-end television production using video equipment and involves larger crews. The pace can be fast like ENG work, but is generally more planned and predictable. The focus is quality, not speed. Sporting events, political events, corporate videos, broadcast news remotes, and infomercials fall into this category. Today, the term "video production" refers to either ENG or EFP, although ENG is a much more common term.

Television production started off as strictly video production, but some productions were shot on film and converted to video for broadcast, such as news reports. As television production evolved, more productions were shot on film, such as episodic television shows. With the advent of digital filmmaking, these lines have been blurred and there is some crossover. Digital-film cameras are now so affordable that they can be used to shoot videos for YouTube or an independent feature film.

For the sake of clarification, we will use ENG to describe any video production that is not considered a dramatic production. EFP will be denoted for specific applications. *Feature films* or *features* will refer specifically to any type of film production, short narrative or full length, independent or big-budget, as well as episodic television. In Chapter 18, we will break these types of productions down even further to discuss the differences, the types of setups, and the various equipment involved.

Regardless of what type of production you are shooting or how big or small the budget is, your goal as the sound mixer will remain the same: **capture clean, consistent, and intelligible audio**.

CHAPTER EXERCISE Learn to *listen* to films, not just watch them. Listen to a high-budget feature film, a low-budget independent film, a local news broadcast, and a YouTube video. Obviously, there will be huge differences, but can you tell what those differences are? What could be done to improve the quality of sound in the various examples? Write down your results. Once you've finished the book, come back to this exercise and try again! Your skills should be much sharper and your ears more attuned to sound quality.

CHAPTER 2

SOUND BASICS

Sound isn't rocket science, but it is a science. There are mathematical equations involved and most of them include fractions. But, don't sweat it. The science in this book will only be used when necessary. You'll never find a sound mixer on location using a calculator to figure out reverb or phasing problems. Once you understand the basics of how sound works, the rest of the craft will be technique. The important thing is to understand the animal called sound, for this is what you are essentially hunting in the field.

SOUND WAVES

Sound is vibrations in the air or other mediums such as water. These vibrations arrive at the ear and are interpreted as sound. A sound event, such as a handclap, disturbs the air molecules. Like the effect of dropping a rock in a pond, the air molecules create waves of movement in the air that radiate from the point of the disturbance.

There are two parts to a sound wave: a *compression* and a *rarefaction*. A compression occurs when the air molecules are forced together and a rarefaction occurs when the air molecules move away from each other. When there is neither a compression nor a rarefaction, the air molecules are at rest. This is known as *silence*. Silence is like a still pond. There are no waves. When a rock is dropped in the pond, the water molecules are forced to displace. The

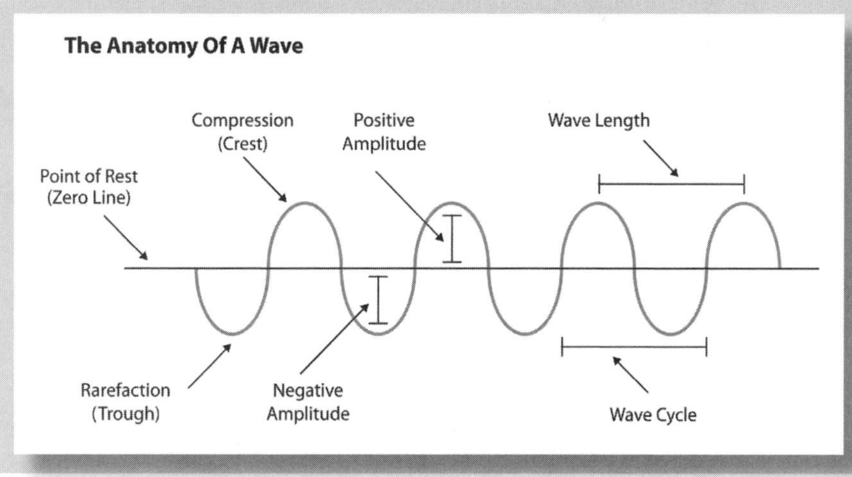

point of impact forces the water down and causes the surrounding water molecules to rise. This is the creation of the wave. In an effort to find rest again, the water molecules ripple in waves away from the source of impact. Compressions occur when the water rises above the surface. Rarefactions occur when the water sinks below the surface. A wave cycle consists of one compression and one rarefaction.

Sound waves are measured in two ways: amplitude and frequency.

FREQUENCY

Frequency refers to the number of complete wave cycles (one compression and one rarefaction) that occur in a second. Frequency is measured in *hertz (Hz)*. The more wave cycles, the higher the frequency will be. A sound that consists of 100 wave cycles per second is written as 100Hz. A sound that consists of 1,000 cycles per second is written as 1KHz (K is for "kilo," or 1,000). The hearing range of the human ear is 20Hz – 20KHz. This is a textbook number. In the real world, the hearing response of the average male is 40Hz – 18KHz. Women have a slightly better hearing response for higher frequencies than men do, which is yet another reason why girls are cooler than boys. Cats have a hearing range of 45Hz – 64KHz, which is why they're cooler than all of us combined.

The average frequency range for human speech is 100Hz – 3KHz, although harmonics can far exceed this range. Some males can produce speech frequencies as low as 60Hz. Higher frequencies are perceived as being higher in pitch. Lower frequencies are perceived as being lower in pitch.

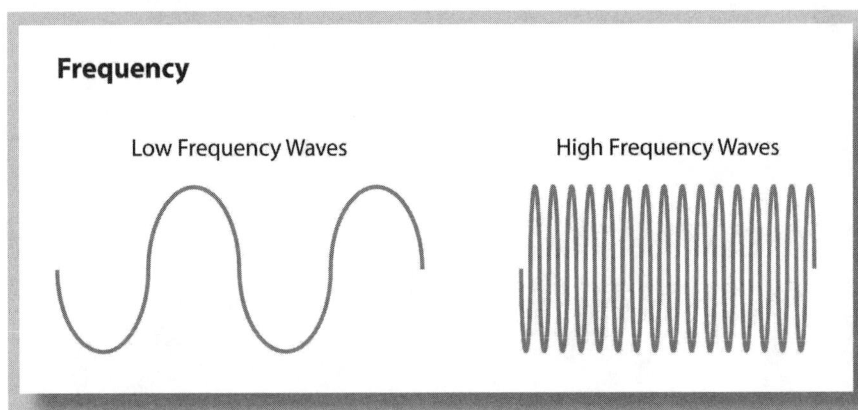

There are three main ranges of frequencies within the audible frequency range:

- Low Range or "Low End": 20Hz – 200Hz
- Mid Range or "Mids": 200Hz – 5KHz
- High Range or "High End": 5KHz – 20KHz

Sometimes the mid frequencies are broken down even further:

- Low Mid Range: 200Hz – 1KHz
- High Mid Range: 1KHz – 5KHz

Sound waves can transmit through objects such as walls. This transmission will weaken the sound waves. Lower frequencies are stronger and can pass through objects much more easily than weaker higher frequencies. An example of transmission would be a car radio blaring down the street. In your house, you probably would hear only the thumping bass of the sound system. Most of the higher frequencies wouldn't make it out of the car, let alone be able to pass through a brick wall; however, the lower frequencies are much stronger and would transmit through the car and past a brick wall. This makes sense when you realize that great energy must be exerted in order to create low frequencies. Remember, the waves in the pond will be bigger and stronger if the rock is heavy and thrown at a great rate of speed. It's easier to control, reduce, or eliminate high frequencies than low frequencies. Of course, the amount of control and reduction greatly depends on the amplitude of these frequencies, which nicely segues us to our next topic: amplitude.

AMPLITUDE

Amplitude refers to the amount of energy present in a wave. The human ear perceives this amplitude as *volume*. With a heavy rock, the splash is deeper and the waves have more energy and are larger as a result. The same is true with sound sources. Loud sounds occur when there is a greater force behind the disturbance in air molecules. The amplitude of sound waves is measured in *decibels*.

DECIBELS

Decibels are a logarithmic unit used for measuring the amplitude of a sound wave. The term "decibel" is named after Alexander Graham Bell (*bel*) and the Latin word for "ten" (*deci*). It literally means "one tenth of a bel" and is written as *dB*. The more amplitude a sound wave has, the larger the number will be in dB. A sound wave that is ten times more powerful than 0dB is written as 10dB. A sound wave that is one hundred times more powerful than 0dB would be written as 20dB.

SOUND PRESSURE LEVEL

In the real world, decibels are used to measure *sound pressure level* (*SPL*). This measurement tells us how loud a sound wave is in relation to perceived silence (0dB). The range of human hearing is amazing. Gently sliding your finger across a sheet of paper might produce an audible sound that is only a few decibels. The threshold of pain for the average human ear is 140dB. This is an astonishing one trillion times louder than the threshold of hearing!

Here are some examples of common sound pressure levels:

- Threshold of Hearing: 0dB
- Pin Drop: 10dB
- Whisper: 35dB
- Speech: 65dB
- Traffic: 85dB
- Rock Concert: 115dB*
- Jet Takeoff: 135dB
- Threshold of Pain: 140dB
- Gunshot: 145dB
- Rocket Launch: >165dB

The human ear has a *dynamic range* of 140dB. Dynamic range refers to the difference between the quietest sound and the loudest possible sound before noticeable distortion. After 140dB, the human ear experiences pain and can become permanently damaged. Longterm exposure to high SPL can and will damage your ears. According to generally-accepted practice, you should only expose yourself to SPL of 85dB for less than eight hours each day. This is the recommended highest level of SPL for studio monitors.

SIGNAL MEASUREMENT

For the human ear, 0dB represents the threshold of hearing. On audio equipment, 0dB represents the maximum amount of amplitude that can be received without distortion. The measurements on this scale are relative to

**Sorry to be the adult in the situation, but if you plan on having a long career in audio engineering, you should never attend a rock concert without earplugs.*

this level and, therefore, the scale is reversed.

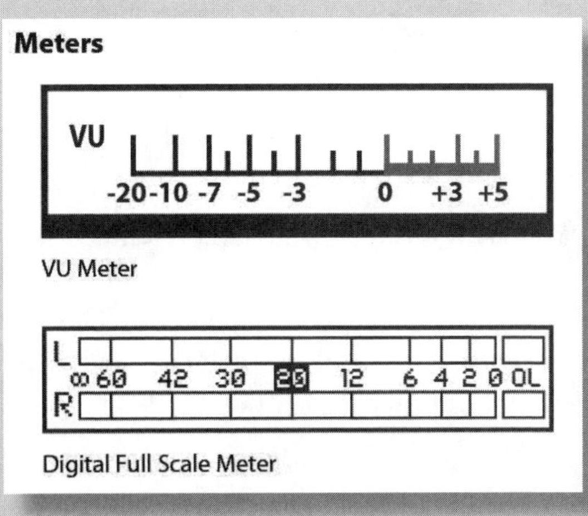

VU Meter

Digital Full Scale Meter

In analog equipment, a VU meter typically begins at -20dB and increases to as high as +6dB. A peak meter may begin at -60dB and increase to as high as +12dB in some equipment. This overage is permitted because most analog equipment can function above 0dB without noticeable distortion. Digital equipment, however, has an absolute ceiling for the amount of amplitude it can receive without a type of digital distortion known as *clipping*. Digital equipment will have a scale that begins at infinity and measures amplitude up to 0dBFS (*FS* stands for "full scale"). 0dBFS is the maximum amount of measurable amplitude in a digital sound wave. Digital audio is further explained in Chapter 11.

In signal measurement, sounds read differently than SPL levels. Here are some common sounds and their relative signal measurement:

- Silence/System Noise: -95dBFS
- Night Ambience (rural): -60dBFS
- Footsteps: -50dBFS
- Night Ambience (urban): -40dBFS
- Dialog: -20dBFS
- Car Pass-By (close range): -10dBFS
- Door Slam: 0dBFS
- Gunshot: Clipped at 0dBFS

**Note: These examples are only for reference. Different mixers, recorders, microphones, and distances to the sound sources will greatly affect these numbers.*

When monitoring signals, you will notice that a 6dB increase of amplitude will be perceived as double the volume. A decrease of 6dB (or -6dB) will be perceived as half the volume.

Audio equipment uses three levels of signal:

- Professional Line Level: +4dBu
- Consumer Line Level: -10dBv
- Professional Mic Level: -60dBu

As you can see, line level is a much stronger signal than mic level. Mic level signals require an amplifier to boost the signal up to line level so that it can be used in audio equipment. This amplifier is called a *preamplifier,* or *preamp* for short. All microphones send a mic level signal. Professional audio equipment usually provides switches to let the user select what type of signal is sent and received.

AMPLITUDE VERSUS VOLUME

It should be noted that amplitude is often confused with volume. While there is a direct correlation, it is not always an accurate one. A study by scientists Harvey Fletcher and Wilden Munson revealed that there is a curve in the human ear's perception of volume at different frequencies. This contour is known as the *Fletcher-Munson Curve*. This curve shows that humans perceive different frequencies of equal amplitude as being different in volume. In short, higher frequencies appear louder than lower frequencies even when heard at the same amplitude. For example, if a 1KHz sound wave measures 40dB SPL, a 20Hz sound wave would need to measure 90dB SPL to sound equally loud. That's an amazing 100,000 times greater in amplitude to be perceived as equal in volume! This demonstrates why amplitude and volume are not the same thing.

PHASE

When multiple sound waves are combined they create a single wave called a *complex wave*. When two waves of equal amplitude and frequency are combined, the result is a wave that is double in amplitude. In the event that waves of equal amplitude and frequency are combined but have opposite states of pressure (compression versus rarefaction), the waves can cancel each other out. The result is a thin, weak sound or no sound at all. This is called *phase cancellation*. To oversimplify this concept, take the example of adding 2 plus 2. The sum is 4. If you add -2 plus 2, the sum is 0. This is because -2 and 2 cancel each other out when added together.

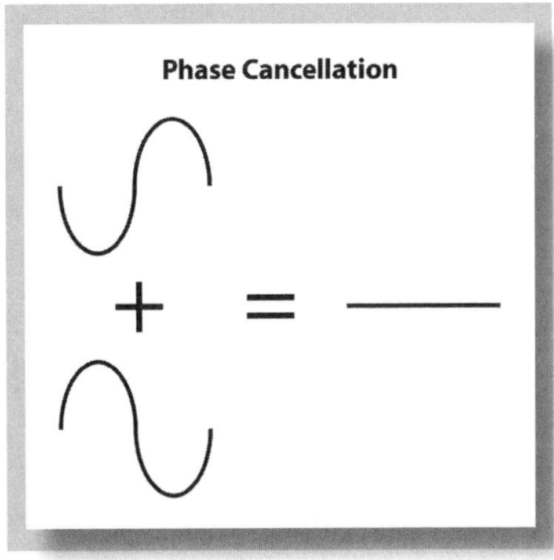

Multiple microphones recording the same source can produce sounds that are out of phase when combined together. If these mics were combined onto one channel of a recorder, they would become a single wave. The new sound wave would be the sum of the two waves. In drastic situations, this wave might contain little or no amplitude at all. Once separate sounds are combined onto one track of a recorder, the sounds cannot be separated. Therefore, if phase cancellation occurs, the effect cannot be reversed. However, if each mic is recorded to a separate track of a recorder, the effect can be repaired during editing/mixing by equalizing or inverting the phase of one of the tracks.

ECHOES AND REVERBERATION

Sound waves continue to move away from the sound source until they either lose energy or they encounter a surface. Upon encountering a surface, the energy of the wave will bounce off the surface and continue in the opposite direction. When a sound wave bounces off a surface it is called an *echo*. The echo does not have as much energy as the original wave because some energy is lost upon impact. To understand this, imagine throwing a racquetball at the side of a building. As the racquetball hits the building's wall, the energy redirects in the opposite direction. Now consider the matter of angle trajectory. If we throw the racquetball perpendicular to the wall, the racquetball will return to us. If we throw the racquetball at a 45-degree angle, it will continue in a 45-degree angle in the opposite direction.

Reverberation is the continuation of echoes in an enclosed space. If we take the same racquetball into a racquetball court, we can watch reverberation work in slow motion. Throwing the racquetball at a high rate of speed will cause the ball to continue to bounce off the walls multiple times. The walls of the court are made from drywall and are intended to be highly reflective.

If these walls were made from a material that absorbed the energy of the racquetball, such as carpet, the ball would lose energy upon impact and the return bounce would be of considerably less velocity. Not to mention, the game would not be nearly as fun.

Now, let's replace the racquetball with sound waves. By standing in the center of the racquetball court and clapping our hands together, we will send a sound wave toward the wall. The sound wave will strike the wall with a great amount of energy and bounce back in the opposite direction. The sound wave will strike the opposite wall with less energy than the first wall, but still with a great amount of energy. This will continue until the sound wave finally loses energy. Unlike a racquetball that moves in a single direction, sound waves move in a 360-degree radius from the sound source. Upon clapping our hands, we send the sound wave in every direction, including up and down. In a racquetball court, the flat surfaces allow the sound wave to continue to travel at a steady decline in amplitude until all of its energy is lost. In effect, the sound waves persist long after the sound event has occurred.

In short, sound is a messy, determined creature that wants to live as long as possible. To properly trap this animal, you need to use an *anechoic chamber*. These rooms are designed to eliminate any possible echoes, thus suffocating reverberation and successfully capturing the beast. Sound mixers, however, must capture sound without the use of this trap. Location sound work tasks the sound mixer with capturing sound in any given environment. It is therefore necessary to understand sound's properties and how it interacts with its environment. Herein lies the greatest challenge for the sound mixer: sound does not want to be tamed or captured. It wants to live on. In the next chapter, we'll discuss the microphone, our primary tool for capturing this creature.

CHAPTER EXERCISE Experiment with room acoustics to help familiarize yourself with how a room will sound in the recordings. Find a room and clap your hands together once. Next, say a few sentences at different volumes. Now, repeat these steps and record them. Play back the recording to see if the acoustical responses of the room match what you remember hearing. What are the differences between what your ears heard and what the microphone captured?

CHAPTER 3

MICROPHONE BASICS

The microphone converts acoustic energy into electric energy through a process called *transduction*. Sound waves enter the microphone's capsule and cause a diaphragm to move in direct relation to the change of air pressure. This works much in the same way as the human ear. Sound waves enter the ear and cause the eardrum to move in direct relation to the change of air pressure. The ear converts the acoustic energy into an electric energy known as nerve impulses. The brain understands these impulses as sound.

There are two main types of transducers for microphones: *dynamic* and *condenser*. They each use a different type of diaphragm that greatly affects the characteristics of the sounds they reproduce.

DYNAMIC MICROPHONES

Dynamic microphones use a moving coil wrapped around a magnet to convert sound waves into an electric signal. The moving coil is attached to a diaphragm. This is the same method in which a speaker converts electric signals into sound waves, but in reverse. Like speakers, they do not require external power to operate. Dynamic microphones are very rugged and can handle high SPL, making them an excellent tool for recording loud sounds such as drums, gunshots, and electric-guitar amplifiers. They require much more air movement than other microphone types, which helps reduce feedback and excessive background noise, but at the cost of having a lower *transient response* than that of condenser microphones. Transient response is the measurement of time it takes for the diaphragm to respond to air movement. The faster the response, the more accurately the signal is reproduced.

In television production, especially ENG work, reporters typically use dynamic handheld microphones during standups, man-on-the-street interviews, stage productions, and live events. For a dynamic microphone to capture speech, it needs to be very close to the mouth.

Dynamic mics are perfect solutions for ENG work where the talent is conducting interviews or reports in noisy environments (football stadiums, roadside reports, locker rooms of the World Series' winning team, etc.). These mics have a great rejection of background noise and tend to allow the reporter's voice to sit on top of any extraneous noise. Stage productions and live events with P.A. systems will often call for dynamic microphones because they have a high amount of feedback rejection.

Dynamic mics are seemingly indestructible. There is an incredible video on YouTube of Stockholm's Mats Stålbröst, who ran an extreme endurance test on a Shure SM58. This mic is arguably the most common stage microphone in the world. The video shows the SM58 being subjected to various tests to see how the microphone would hold up. After being used to hammer nails, dropped from six feet, submerged in water, placed in a freezer for an hour, having beer poured on it, put in a microwave on top of a slice of pizza, having a car drive over it twice and being buried in the ground for over a year to endure rain, snow, and a wide range of temperatures, the microphone still worked! This level of stamina is hard to find and I certainly wouldn't try this with a condenser microphone.

CONDENSER MICROPHONES

Condenser microphones use the change of a stored charge called *capacitance* to convert acoustical energy into an electric signal. A constant voltage is sent to a front plate (the diaphragm) and to a back plate. Air movement causes the front plate to vibrate toward and away from the back plate resulting in a change of capacitance. This change becomes the electric signal.

Years ago, condenser mics were considered extremely fragile. While they are not as rugged as dynamic microphones, today's condensers are much more robust than their predecessors and can handle higher SPL than ever before. A better transient response makes the condenser microphone sound clearer than a dynamic microphone. Condensers can faithfully reproduce subtleties in the sound wave's dynamics and capture higher frequencies than dynamic microphones. If you can hear the sound with your ears then you can bet that the condenser microphone can also hear it. Many times, the microphone seems to hear the sound even "louder." If you can faintly hear a cricket in the distance, it's safe to say that the microphone can hear the cricket's heartbeat. Not really, but you get the idea.

There are two types of condenser microphones: *true condenser* and *electret.*

True Condenser Microphones

A *true condenser microphone* requires external power known as *phantom power* to charge its capacitor. Phantom power is typically supplied through the same cable used to send audio from the microphone. Modern phantom power is 48 volts and indicated on microphones and other equipment by various abbreviations: PH, 48V, 48, P48, etc.

Phantom power requires a balanced cable to supply voltage. The power scheme is as follows: Pin 1 – Negative, Pin 2 and Pin 3 – Positive.

Since the voltage is consistent between Pin 2 and Pin 3, only the audio signal would be detected as sound, as this would be the only change in voltage down the cable; hence the name "phantom."

An older type of phantom power was called *T-Power* or *parallel powering* (usually indicated as 12T or 12 Volt T). This used the following powering scheme: Pin 1 – Ground/Neutral, Pin 2 – Positive, Pin 3 – Negative.

Some of the older microphones might have a red dot engraved on the side. The red dot indicates that their wiring is reversed. The reason for this dates back to the days of the old Nagra recorders that had positive grounds. Microphones were adapted to this odd standard to supply T-Power so that Pin 2 was negative and Pin 3 was positive. Normally, T-Power was configured so that Pin 2 was positive and Pin 3 was negative. For whatever reason, Nagra developed a system that went against this standard and so microphones featuring the red dot were developed to use with the Nagra.

Many manufacturers developed microphone models that came in either 12-volt T-Power or the now standard 48-volt phantom power. Examples are the Sennheiser MKH 416-P48 (phantom power) and the MKH 416T (T-Power). It is rare to come across T-powered microphones today; however, if you plan on using mics with a T-Power supply, you'll need to observe the polarity or your microphone will not work. In a pinch, you can simply reverse the polarity by soldering an XLR cable so that Pin 2 on one end connects to Pin 3 on the other end and vice versa. Beware that sending modern 48-volt phantom power to a T-Powered mic will damage the microphone.

Certain models of microphones can receive phantom power from an internal battery. You should never double-power a microphone (i.e., use an external phantom power supply in addition to a mixer's phantom power or internal batteries on the microphone in addition to a mixer's phantom power). On most mixers and recorders, if you are not using phantom power, choose the "dynamic" setting. This means that the microphone signal is accepted as is with no powering of any kind. Phantom power should be turned off when using a device that does not require phantom power. Dynamic microphones are pretty much immune to phantom power but devices, such as wireless receivers, recorders, and mixer outputs connected to the input of a device with phantom power, can be damaged or result in poor signal quality. The bottom line: if your device does not require phantom power or is already receiving phantom power, then turn the phantom power supply off.

The majority of the boom microphones used in the film and broadcast industries are true condenser microphones and will require phantom power. There are a few exceptions, but you will most certainly use phantom power every day.

Electret Condenser Microphones

The *electret condenser* has a permanently charged back plate. Phantom power is not required for the capsule to operate; however, most electret microphones use phantom power to power a preamplifier that amplifies the weaker audio signal produced by these types of capsules. This preamplifier can be powered by an internal battery or directly from phantom power supplied through the microphone cable.

Electret microphones are probably the most popular and widely used in the world. These mics can be found in nearly every cell phone, telephone, headset, and handheld recorder. While the consumer market uses relatively low-cost and low-quality electret microphones, there is a place for higher-grade electret microphones that are priced much lower than true condenser mics, but still deliver great quality. ENG-grade shotguns use electret capsules that are a low-cost solution for ENG work; however, their quality isn't high enough to meet the standards for feature films. In the film and broadcast world, the most popular use for electret microphones is *lavalier mics*. Nearly all lavaliers are electret microphones, with the exception of some that are dynamic, which are not useful for production sound.

FREQUENCY RESPONSE

The range of frequencies that a microphone can reproduce is known as the microphone's *frequency response*. In general, the wider the spectrum of frequencies reproduced, the more accurate the sound will be. If frequencies are reproduced at amplitudes different from that of the original sound, the sound is considered "colored." Audio engineers often use the term "color" to describe different frequencies within the frequency spectrum. In the light spectrum, different frequencies of light waves appear as colors. Lower-light frequencies like reds and oranges are described as warm. Higher-light frequencies like blues and greens are known to be cold. Similarly, lower-frequency sounds are described as warmer and higher-frequency ones are described as colder.

The frequency response of most professional microphones is intended to mirror the hearing range of the human ear: 20Hz – 20KHz.

In general, a *flat frequency response* is preferred for professional dialog recording. In a flat frequency response, all of the frequencies are faithfully reproduced without any colorization. None of the frequencies are artificially amplified or attenuated; rather, they are reproduced just as they were heard. Some models of microphones deliberately color their frequency response to highlight a specific band of frequencies that the sound source will produce or to correct certain frequencies that will be missing from the source. An example of this would be the TRAM TR50 lavalier microphone. Common applications for this microphone often require it to be buried under clothing to hide it from the camera's eye. In doing this, the higher frequencies are lost in the transmission through the clothing. To compensate for this loss of frequencies, the TR50 has an increase in its frequency response around 8KHz.

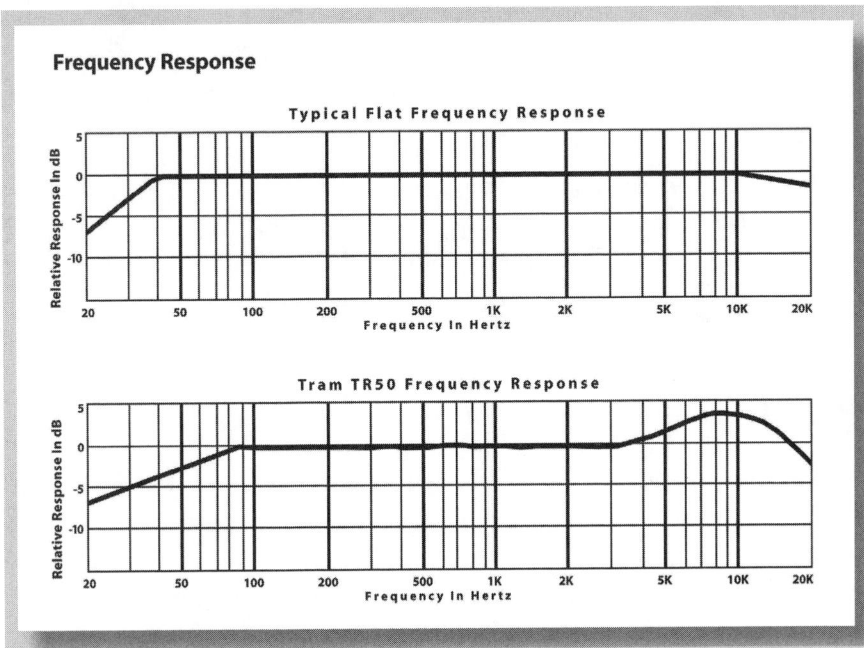

MICROPHONE POLAR PATTERNS

The directionality of a microphone is called its polar pattern. Different polar patterns will "pick up" sound from different directions. There are six polar patterns:

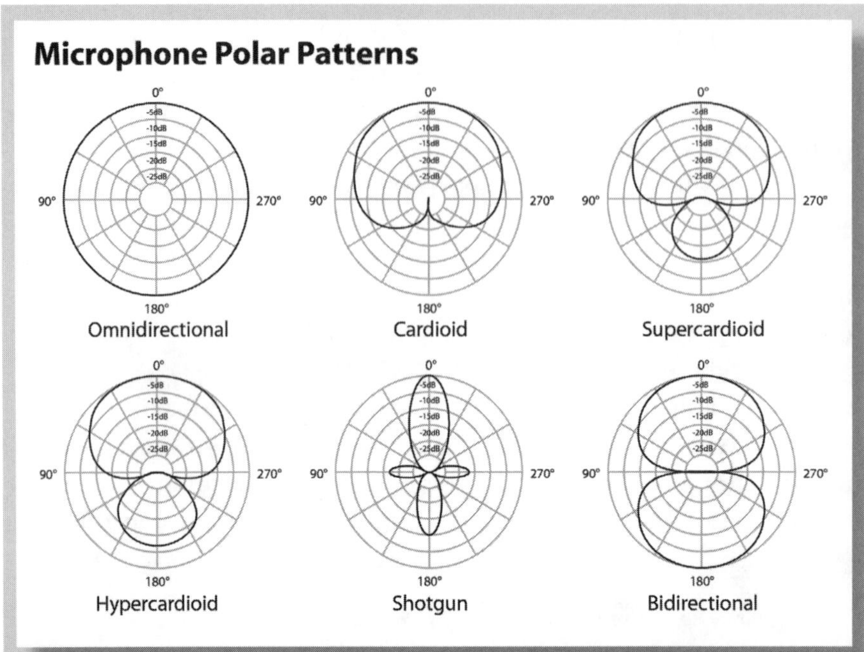

Omnidirectional

This pattern picks up sounds coming in a 360° sphere around the capsule.

Cardioid

A heart-shaped pattern gathers sound primarily from the front of the microphone, with some rejection of the sides and all of the rear.

Hypercardioid

This cardioid pattern has a tighter response in front of the mic and some sensitivity in the rear.

Supercardioid

A more focused version of the hypercardioid pattern, it features a higher rejection of the sides and rear of the capsule.

Shotgun

This is the most directional of all the polar patterns, with the highest rejection of the sides of the capsule. It should be noted that there is a rear lobe that will pick up sounds coming from directly behind the microphone.

Figure Eight or Bidirectional

This is a dual cardioid pattern that picks up sound from both sides of the microphone. Other than in the use of MS microphones, this polar pattern is not used in location sound work.

ON-AXIS/OFF-AXIS RESPONSE

When a sound occurs within the primary area of the microphone's polar pattern, it is considered *on-axis*. This is also called the "sweet spot." When a sound occurs outside of the polar pattern, it is considered *off-axis*. The off-axis part of a polar pattern is sometimes referred to as the "rejection zone" (which is also the nickname I gave my high school). On-axis sounds are bright and crisp, while off-axis sounds are more flat with less high end.

Some microphones have better off-axis sounds than others. In these mics, sounds that occur off-axis sound quieter than those on-axis. Others tend to color off-axis sounds because of a frequency-response difference between the on-axis and off-axis part of the pattern. Not only will the sound appear quieter, but will also typically sound duller as fewer higher frequencies are picked up. When using these types of microphones, it is very important to keep the sound consistently inside the polar pattern to avoid coloring the sound. A sound that drifts between on-axis and off-axis will sound weird and unnatural. The listener will realize that something doesn't sound right. This is less noticeable with wider patterns like cardioids and more noticeable with shotgun patterns.

Sometimes the background noise is so intrusive that you'll need to position the mic so that it gives the maximum rejection of the background. This might be at the expense of optimal positioning for dialog pickup, but remember, the audience needs to hear the dialog so that they can understand what is said. If you put the mic in a position that rejects the majority of the excessive background noise with the dialog slightly off-axis, it will sound better than on-axis dialog that is difficult to understand over the background noise.

During a sound effects recording expedition, I recorded fighter jets at an air show in Cocoa Beach, Florida, with my good friend, Colin Hart of Hart FX. The air show took place on the edge of the ocean, which put us close to the jets. They were so close I could've probably thrown my car keys and hit them. I might have tried, but then I would have to fish my keys out of the water.

The sounds of the fly-bys were amazing; however, it was a windy day and the waves were unusually loud. We were having a difficult time separating the end of the pass-bys with the high-end sizzle of the foamy white caps. To combat this, we were forced to position the jets slightly off-axis to reduce the sound of the ocean waves. It was a disappointing compromise, given that this was a golden opportunity to be so close to military aircraft without jumping through hoops with the military's P.R. department. I live two miles from an Air Force base and it took me ten years of phone calls to get access to be on the runway once for only a couple of hours.

We had to make do with what we had. The show was going on whether we were recording or not. Positioning the microphones slightly off-axis was not optimal, but listening back to the recordings, we realized it was the best decision. We came back with dozens of solid, ear-splitting jet engine sound effects that roared from one speaker to the other. Had we stuck with the on-axis positioning, many of those recordings would have been unusable.

Background sounds are the enemy of a good sound effect. In general, sound effects need to be isolated from the background sounds so that they can be used in more than one setting. Fortunately, dialog can be quite usable with a minimal amount of background sound, especially for ENG and documentary work. In those types of productions, the environment is part of the story. The editors probably will not have access to a sound team to rebuild the background tracks for them, so providing a little ambience in the dialog will help spice up the track and sell the story.

It's one thing to read about the polar pattern of a microphone and another to hear it in action. Experiment with different types of polar patterns. Record sounds on-axis and off-axis and play them back. Listen to the differences.

INVERSE SQUARE LAW

This concept is actually a lot simpler than its name might imply. The *inverse square law* states that volume is doubled when the distance between the microphone and the source is halved. So, when you double the distance between the microphone and the sound source, you are effectively reducing the volume in half. In cowboy terms this means the closer you get to a sound, the louder it will be. You can use this principle when trying to reduce background noise. Placing the microphone closer to the sound source will not only make the sound louder, but will reduce the sound in the background.

Always keep the mic as close to the sound source as possible. This reduces background noise and the need to increase gain on the microphone's channel, which can result in noise. However, if the microphone is too close to the sound source, it can produce the *proximity effect*, an artificial increase in low frequencies, which makes the sound deeper and bassy. This phenomenon occurs when a sound source is too close to the microphone. The result is like a deep, radio announcer's voice. This can be used for an effect, but is generally undesirable for natural-sounding dialog.

MICROPHONE ACCESSORIES

An expensive microphone can be rendered useless if you are not supporting that microphone with the right gear. The two main elements that can adversely affect a microphone are vibrations and wind noise. Most professional microphones will come with accessories to combat these elements, but they are usually not as effective as products offered by third-party manufacturers. If your budget is tight, it might make more sense to purchase a mid-priced microphone and have enough money left over for the right support gear.

SHOCK MOUNTS

Shock mount

Microphones are sensitive to vibrations. The vibrations produce an unnatural low frequency rumble in the microphone. In location sound, these vibrations are caused by handling noise from holding the boom pole. The slightest movement will induce handling noise, so the microphone must be placed in a *shock mount* to help isolate the microphone from the boom pole or mic stand. Shock mounts reduce handling noise, but do not eliminate the noise completely. Therefore, the microphone must always be handled gently.

Sometimes, the mic cable is the source of handling noise. Although the microphone may be suspended in a shock mount, the mic cable is connected to the microphone, which can transmit bumps and thumps from the cable. To correct this, leave some slack near the mic connection to help reduce handling noise.

There are three general types of shock mounts:

- Rubber Bands
- Suspended Mic Clips
- Rubber Suspension

WIND PROTECTION

Microphones are extremely sensitive to wind noise. The microphone's diaphragm is designed to respond to movement in air pressure. Wind is essentially extremely low-frequency sound waves at massive levels of amplitude. The effect is an extremely undesirable distortion of the diaphragm. It is absolutely imperative to protect the microphone from wind noise.

There are four types of wind protection for microphones:

- Foam Windscreen
- Windshield
- Furry
- Blimp

Unfortunately, there are no industry standard terms for these types of wind protection and the names are interchangeable between manufacturers. There are, however, distinct features amongst these types. The following will give an explanation and examples to clarify the differences and applications for wind protection.

Foam Windscreen

A *foam windscreen* is the most basic type of wind protection. The foam is placed over the microphone and reduces *plosives* and minor air movement. This air movement can be caused by airflow from a vent or fan as well as the actual movement of the boom pole itself. Plosives are sudden bursts of air that are produced by the mouth during the use of certain consonants such as "P's" and "B's". Wind foam is most commonly used indoors and provides the least amount of wind protection of all the designs. Wind foams should never be used outdoors.

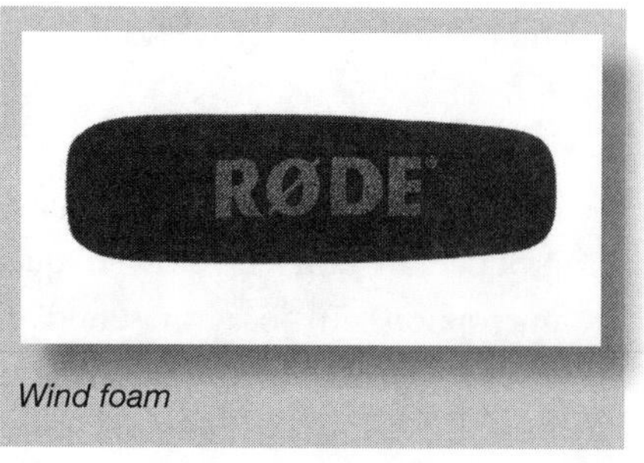

Wind foam

Wind Furry

A *wind furry* is made from artificial fur and slips over the microphone or wind foam, adding greater protection. Miniature versions of the furry are designed to be used with lavaliers. They offer the maximum amount of wind protection for a lavalier mic, but at the expense of making the mic more noticeable on camera. Different manufacturers use different names for their model of wind furry: Fur Windsock

Wind furry

(K-Tek), Furry Windjammer (Rycote), and the Dead Cat and Dead Kitten (Rode).

Windshield

Windshields have a plastic or foam mesh covered in a faux fur to reduce air movement from reaching the microphone. They slip on over the microphone, allowing for quick changes between setups, and are commonly used in ENG. Windshields are quite effective, but do not give the same amount of wind protection that a blimp system does.

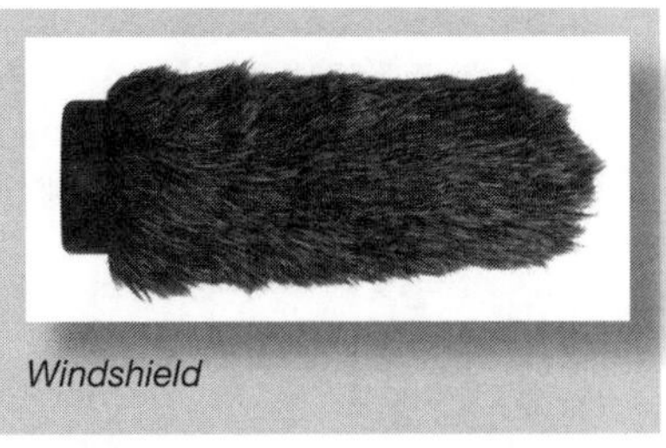

Windshield

Blimp

A tubular housing unit made from a combination of plastic and special fabrics, resembles the German dirigible and is often called a *blimp* or a *zeppelin*. A blimp consists of an outer shell that slides over a shock mount typically on a pistol grip. The pistol grip can be used to hold the microphone by hand (seldom done in location sound, but useful for sound effects recording) or mounted on the end of a boom pole. Labeling the pistol grip of a blimp with a piece of white gaffer tape can help identify which microphone is loaded inside. The blimp provides the most superior wind protection.

Blimp

Windsock

A *windsock* is essentially a large, custom furry tailored to fit a specific model of blimp. They have many nicknames, my favorite being Wookie Condom. Different manufacturers have different names for windsocks as well: Wind Muff (Sennheiser), Dead Wombat (Rode), and Windjammer (Rycote). Heavy-duty windsocks like Rycote's Hi-Wind Cover offer even greater wind reduction in extremely windy conditions. Some sound mixers will place a foam windscreen over the mic inside a blimp for additional protection if a Hi-Wind cover is not available. Remember to remove the foam windscreen at the end of the day. A colored piece of gaffer tape can help signify that a foam windscreen is in use inside the blimp.

Windsock

Anytime you put something in front of the microphone, no matter how thin, you will lose high frequencies. Wind protection will reduce some of the high frequencies your mic would normally pick up. This loss of high frequencies may be unnoticeable, but as a rule of thumb, you should only use blimps indoors when absolutely necessary. A microphone should never be used outdoors without wind protection.

RAIN PROTECTION

Rain Man

Rain is another element that a microphone might encounter. Using a boom pole in the rain will require some additional protection for the microphone. You can use hog's hair or other homemade rigs to stop the rain from hitting the blimp and making noise. Hog's hair is applied over the top of a windsock. The windsock itself will become soaked. Some sound mixers will place a non-lubricated condom over the microphone before mounting it in the blimp. This will ensure the rain doesn't damage the microphone.

Avoid pointing the mic directly at the ground, as this will amplify the sound of the rain hitting puddles below. If the project is a film production, the scene will probably be replaced with ADR and your audio will be used as a guide track. Don't assume this, however. Still try your best to deliver a clean audio track. A *Rain Man* is a special blimp covering that will keep the microphone dry and the dialog relatively clean, but the boom positioning can be a bit tricky. The typical overhead position might not work as this can block raindrops in front of the actor. Another problem is water buildup, which can form heavy streams of water from the end of the blimp in front of the actors. This is not as noticeable in heavy downpours, but will be more noticeable in light rain.

CHAPTER EXERCISE Take a microphone outdoors and record without any wind protection. Next, experiment with the different types of wind protection discussed in this chapter. Play back the recordings. What do you hear? Which type of wind protection provided the best results?

CHAPTER 4

MICROPHONES FOR LOCATION SOUND

Several kinds of microphones are used in film and television production:

- Boom Mics
- Lavaliers
- Boundary Microphones
- Plant Mics
- Handhelds
- Lip Mics
- Camera Mics

Each of these microphones has a unique way of capturing sound and each can have multiple polar patterns to choose from. It should be noted that microphones designed for production dialog are always mono. Stereo microphones have a wider field of sound that negates the isolation of dialog we fought so hard to achieve with cardioid microphones. A production's stereo image isn't created on location, but rather in postproduction where the re-recording mixer can work objectively with all of the production's sound elements as a whole. Nat sound can be recorded on a video camera using the on-board stereo mic. This sound is passable for B-roll shots, but should never be used for dialog or room tone (see page 180).

Let's take a look at different kinds of production microphones.

BOOM MICROPHONES

The word "boom" is often mistaken for a type of microphone, but there's technically no such thing as a "boom" mic. Instead, the term *boom* refers to the pole or rig to which the microphone is attached. The types of mics that are used on the end of the boom pole are *shotguns* and *cardioids*. While shotguns and cardioids produce the most natural-sounding dialog tracks, they both have advantages and disadvantages.

The go-to mic for ENG production is the shotgun. Its directionality makes it perfect for the often unplanned shooting style and various environments that the crew encounters. Shotguns work the best on exterior locations. The drawback to the shotgun microphone for interior locations is the tail in the polar pattern. This tail can artificially enhance the reverberation of a room, giving it an unnatural sound. Cardioids, on the other hand, will sound more natural for interior locations, but their open sound and wider pattern makes the shotgun a better choice for exterior locations.

Shotguns

Shotguns are line + gradient microphones. They have a pressure gradient diaphragm housed deep within an interference tube. Pressure gradient diaphragms respond to air movement from both sides of the diaphragm. *Omnidirectional microphones* use a pressure diaphragm. Pressure diaphragms work like a sealed kettledrum that only responds to air movement from one side. *Unidirectional microphones* (cardioids and shotguns) use a pressure gradient diaphragm. The tube, where the term "line" originates, has slits along the side called *phase ports*. When sound waves arrive at the microphone from all directions, the phase ports allow the waves to enter the interference tube at specific distances, which forces the waves to arrive at the diaphragm at slightly different timings. These different timings cause a sophisticated phase cancellation. The combination of a directional pressure gradient diaphragm and the phase cancellation caused by the interference tube is what gives the shotgun its tight pattern.

Shotguns have great rejection on the sides of the mic; however, there is still some sensitivity in the rear. Avoid pointing the mic directly opposite of noise, as this will still allow the sounds to be picked up by the mic. Instead, use the rejection zone of the polar pattern: the sides of the microphone. The pattern is live at twelve o'clock and six o'clock, but also notice that there is an increased sensitivity at nine o'clock and three o'clock. When working near traffic, beaches, crowds, or other consistent sources of background ambience, try positioning the mic so that it points away from these sources.

RF Bias Microphones

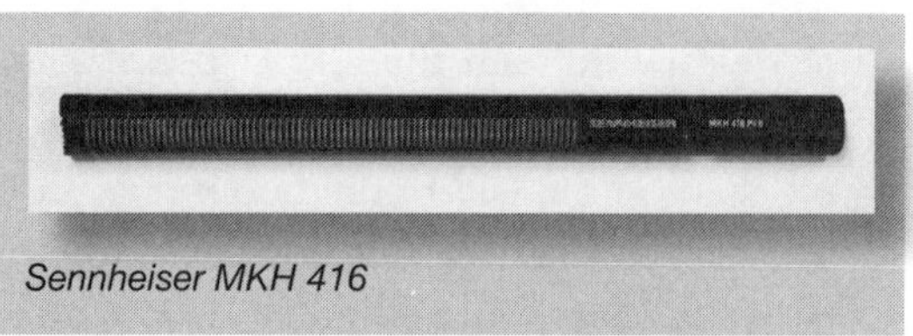
Sennheiser MKH 416

There are several shotgun mics on the market that use *RF Bias technology*. The most popular are the Sennheiser MKH 416 and the Rode NTG-3. This technology allows the microphone to be virtually immune to moisture, making RF Bias microphones the best solution when working in adverse conditions. They are often the go-to mics when looking for an "all-purpose" shotgun. While Schoeps Colette microphones are considered by many to be the Holy Grail of boom mics, they are not very useful outdoors and perform poorly in humidity.

Short Shotguns and Long Shotguns

The length of a shotgun microphone's interference tube determines the amount of rejection in the polar pattern, thus affecting the size of the pickup area. The smaller the pickup area, the more critical cueing becomes. Cueing is the process of aiming the microphone at the actor's mouth. With a wider pickup pattern, the precision of cueing is less critical because there is less chance of the voice falling off-axis. Inches can make a huge difference when cueing with an extremely narrow pickup pattern.

Long shotguns have the tightest pickup of any microphone, but at the expense of their added weight and extreme length (nearly two feet). Long shotgun mics are almost exclusively used outdoors. They can be used indoors, but only if the situation really calls for it. Large soundstages, massive sets, or other venues might provide the headroom needed to navigate the oversized shotgun, but remember that cueing needs to be precise as the pickup pattern is extremely narrow. Small moves can create big changes in the sound.

Short shotguns are more common. Their size and weight are more practical for field production. Compared to a long shotgun, the short shotgun's wider pattern is more forgiving and easier for cueing actors. Short shotguns are typically ten inches in length. The directionality of short shotguns is usually limited to mid and high frequencies. Lower frequencies are often picked up, regardless of the pattern. Long shotguns have better directionality at lower frequencies.

Examples of Short Shotgun Microphones

- Audio Technica 4073
- Beyerdynamic MC836
- Neumann KMR81IMT
- Rode NTG-2
- Rode NTG-3
- Sanken CS-1
- Sanken CS-3E
- Schoeps CMIT5U
- Sennheiser MKH 416
- Sennheiser MKH 60

Sanken CS-1

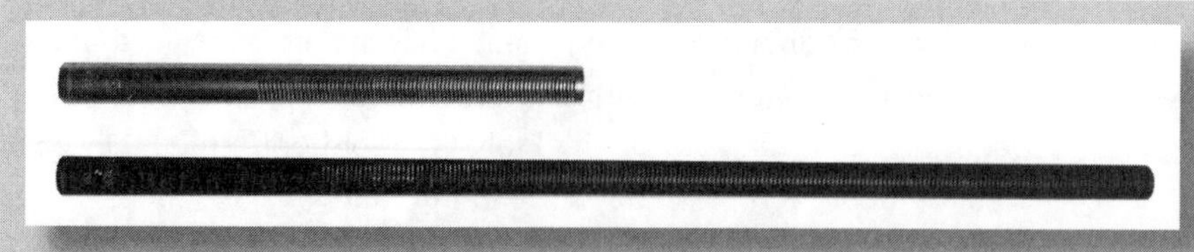

The Rode NTG-3 short shotgun (top) dwarfed by the length of the Rode NTG-8 long shotgun (bottom)

Examples of Long Shotgun Microphones

- Audio Technica 4071
- Beyerdynamic MC873
- Neumann KMR821
- Rode NTG-8
- Sennheiser MKH 70
- Sennheiser MKH 816

Electret shotgun microphones offer an economical solution to the true condenser shotguns mentioned above. They are more commonly found in ENG production and rarely used in film production. In terms of function and design, they are used in the same way as true condensers. The only difference is the type of capsule, which is found to be noisier than true condensers.

Examples of Electret Shotgun Microphones

- Audio Technica AT835b
- Audio Technica AT815b (Long Shotgun)
- Beyerdynamic MCE86
- Sennheiser ME66
- Sony ECM-674

Sennheiser ME66

Despite what you may have heard, shotgun mics do not zoom into the sound. Instead, they reduce sounds coming from the sides of the microphone. The shotgun mic does not work like a telescope; it works more like the cardboard tube from a roll of paper towels. A telescope allows you to make images from far away seem near, whereas looking through a cardboard tube simply focuses the eye on a small area by blocking out images on the periphery. However, it should be noted that the shotgun's pattern does capture a small pattern of sounds coming from the rear of the mic.

The Myth of Reach

On the subject of microphone myths, let's discuss the topic of *microphone reach.* "Reach" is the ability of a microphone to "reach" out and capture dialog at a greater distance than other microphones. This is a misleading concept and falls into the false shotgun "zoom" theory. In reality, a microphone's diaphragm is a dumb membrane that simply responds to air pressure. It cannot discern or think, it merely responds. Reach is a misnomer for directionality. *Directionality* is a microphone's ability to reject or reduce sounds that come from a specific direction. The term "reach" is commonly used in the recording world based on a simple misunderstanding.

Directional microphones sound like they are reaching and picking up a certain sound, but the opposite is what really happens. These microphones diminish sounds outside of the pickup area, making it appear to be reaching only a target sound. Case in point, the sound of a glass being set down on the counter of an empty bar can be heard from thirty feet away; however, if that bar is filled with people and music is playing over the sound system, the sound seemingly disappears. The microphone's ability to "reach" that sound has not changed. Instead, the environmental sounds have drowned out the sound from the bar glass.

Let's look at another scenario in the same crowded bar. If a person is miked from five feet away with a cardioid microphone, then the audience will struggle to hear him speaking. The result is drastically different if we replace the wide-pattern cardioid microphone with a tight-pattern shotgun microphone at the same distance. The person speaking now can be heard over the crowd. It seems as if the shotgun is reaching out and pulling the voice closer. This isn't true. Instead, the shotgun is rejecting the sounds around the sides and most of the rear of the microphone.

The bar scene is a case when shotguns work better indoors than cardioids. Rejection is key to capturing usable dialog in crowded environments such as the bar. Other indoor scenarios that call for a shotgun microphone might include locker-room interviews, concert interviews, and factories. The adverse effect of the noisy environment far outweighs the adverse reverb effect picked up by shotgun microphones in quieter environments.

To summarize, "reach" is a term that is mistaken for directionality. The microphone is not actively reaching for anything, but rather reducing the level of sounds coming from outside of its polar pattern.

Cardioid Microphones

A *cardioid mic* is the general name given to any type of cardioid pattern (cardioid, hypercardioid, and supercardioid). These wider patterns offer more natural sound than shotguns and are almost always used indoors. The physical characteristics and pickup patterns of shotguns and cardioids make it much easier to decide their best uses.

Shotguns need more headroom and can't be used in rooms with low ceilings. Cardioids are much smaller and can be easily maneuvered in cramped quarters. This works out well since cardioids sound the best when they are closest to the subject. Shotgun mics can still sound great several feet away from the subject. Cueing is less critical with wider cardioid patterns than with shotgun microphones. In addition to a wider pattern, cardioids are more forgiving with off-axis sounds that might occur with multiple actors or if the actor is moving around, making it difficult to capture with a shotgun.

Examples of Cardioid Microphones

- DPA 4011
- Neumann KM 184
- Neumann KM 185
- Rode NT5
- Rode NT6
- Schoeps MK41
- Sennheiser MKH 50

Sennheiser MKH 50

LAVALIER MICROPHONES

Lavalier microphones are extremely small electret microphones designed to be mounted on the talent. The word "lavalier" is French, meaning "a pendant worn around the neck." The first lavaliers were literally worn around the neck, which is how the microphone got its name. The modern lavalier, commonly called a "lav," is much smaller and can be hidden easily or worn by the talent without drawing too much attention. Today, nearly every news anchor, talk-show host, and reality-television star is miked with a lavalier.

Lavs do not sound as natural as boom mics. Lavs sound like lavs. These mics are devoid of perspective. In a long shot, a lav mic will make the actor seem close. Lavs are dialog focused, since they are typically mounted on the actor's chest. As a result, they sound sterile and unrealistic. Sounds that would normally be picked up by a boom mic will be missing from the track, such as interaction with props, room sound, etc. Lavs can be placed further down the chest to help compensate for this and give the voice a more open sound.

The lavalier's size makes it necessary for the diaphragm to be very small. In some cases, the lav diaphragm is as small as 1mm. This is much smaller than the 12mm shotgun diaphragm and infinitesimal next to the 25mm studio condenser. In general, larger diaphragms produce better responses than smaller diaphragms.

Omnidirectional and Unidirectional Lavs

Omnidirectional lavs are the most popular lavs. Their polar pattern allows them to capture sound from each direction. This is an important feature in a lav because the talent might turn his head or move during dialog, which would easily fall out of the pickup pattern of a unidirectional lav. Unidirectional lavs are almost always used outside of the clothes in the center of the chest and pointed at the mouth. They are most commonly used in news reporting and interview scenarios where the talent will be addressing a camera or will be less likely to turn his head. Unidirectional mics can be very useful in sound reinforcement applications because their polar pattern provides protection against feedback.

Lavs have two types of design: *side-address* and *top-address*. Side-address lavs face forward, whereas top-address lavs face the end of the body, allowing them to be positioned up, down, or to the sides. For the most part, the construction of the lav makes no major difference in the pickup pattern. The lav's construction does determine the mic's mounting ability and aesthetics. Side-address lavs tend to be square and relatively wide next to the tubular and often taller top-address lavs. Having both types of lavs will give you more options in the field, but avoid mixing different models together in the same scene. As with other types of microphones, there will be noticeable differences between the mics, specifically the background sound.

Examples of Side-Address Lavalier Microphones

- Countryman EMW
- Lectrosonics M152
- Rode Pin Mic
- SONOTRIM STR-ML
- TRAM TR50

TRAM TR50 with mounting accessories

Examples of Top-Address Lavalier Microphones

- Countryman B6
- DPA 4061
- Rode Lav
- Sanken COS11D
- Sennheiser MKE2

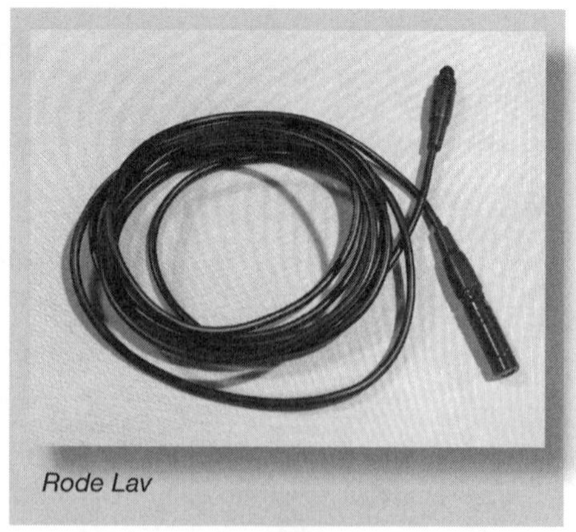
Rode Lav

Lav microphones can be phantom-powered directly through the mic cable, or internally with either AA or button batteries. Button batteries like those in the TRAM TR50 can be difficult to locate if you need to replace them. You can remove the battery and supply phantom power to the lav from an alternate source (e.g., a mixer, recorder, or camera).

Lavs don't last forever, but with care, they can endure for a long time. An electret will eventually lose its static charge and become noisy, unlike true condenser microphones that receive their charge externally, giving them a much longer shelf life. I have a couple of lavs that have lasted for more than ten years.

BOUNDARY MICROPHONES

Boundary microphones are used to capture sound from a large area such as a conference-room table. They are used on the walls of film sets and found on the floors of theatrical stages. The omnidirectional condenser mic element is elevated above the surface via the mic's housing. This allows sound to enter the mic directly, but also picks up sounds reflected off the surface. The result is a doubling in acoustic signal strength. If the surface area is less than three-foot square, lower frequencies will not be properly picked up by the mic.

Surface vibrations can affect the performance of a boundary microphone. If this is an issue, you can help isolate the mic from the surface using foam (e.g., mouse pads, or ear plugs taped to the bottom of the mic). The first boundary mic was Crown's PZM (Pressure Zone Microphone). Although the trademarked name is specific to Crown's product, boundary microphones are commonly referred to as PZMs.

Examples of Boundary Microphones

- Crown PZM-6D
- Crown PZM-30D
- DPA BLM4060
- Sanken CUB-01
- Schoeps BLM 03

Sanken CUB-01

PLANT MICS

A *plant mic* is any type of microphone that is hidden, positioned, or fixed somewhere on the set. The situation should dictate what type of mic is selected. Shotguns, cardioids, lavaliers, and boundary mics can all make useful plant mics. Plant mics can be placed virtually anywhere. This could include mounting a shotgun mic on a C-stand, gaff-taping a lav to the sun visor of a car, or hiding a cardioid on a desk behind some books. Some lavalier microphones are so tiny they can be placed in the middle of a shot and the camera would never see them. Plant mics can be used to pick up a single line or word of dialog in a scene when an actor turns his head, looks out a doorway, or leaves a room.

Rode NT3 with mic flag

HANDHELD MICROPHONES

Handheld microphones, often referred to as "reporter mics," are held by the talent as they speak. Since they will be seen on screen, many networks and shows will use a mic flag around the handle of the microphone to identify the network. As a result of this practice, many handheld mics are designed with long, skinny handles and are sometimes called "stick mics."

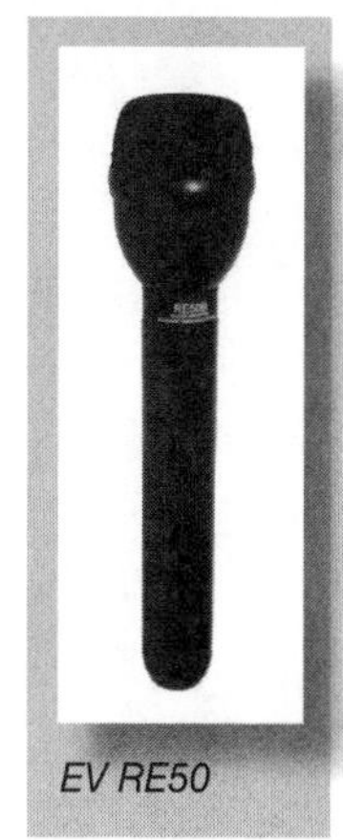

EV RE50

The EV RE50 is the industry-standard handheld microphone for reporters. The mic is extremely durable and features a dual internal pop filter that reduces plosives during speech. It has excellent rejection of background sounds and can be used to report in the middle of the loudest environments while still delivering clearly understood speech.

Handheld mics are almost always dynamic mics, so to function properly, they need to be close to the talent's mouth; four inches away is optimal. Distances further than twelve inches will start to thin out the voice. Beginners and guests will need to be instructed to avoid "talking with their hands," which causes the mic to move toward and away from their mouths, leaving the audience seasick as the reporter's voice floats from loud to soft to loud again. While holding the microphone directly over the mouth is a common practice for vocal performances, television audiences want to see the mouth of the reporter. For this reason, the reporter should avoid "eating the mic." Instead, she should keep the microphone at the base of her chin. This will produce the best sound while allowing the reporter's mouth to be seen.

Undoubtedly, reporters need to be reminded to keep the microphone close to their mouths. The same is true when a reporter holds the mic in front of the person she is interviewing. The mic needs to be close to the source to be heard. Even sound engineers can forget to do this. I always get a kick out of watching sound professionals give lectures or workshops and the audience has to remind them to speak into the microphone.

If the reporter fails to position the mic properly during a live shot, try to get her attention by using hand gestures such as mimicking holding a mic to your mouth. Be careful not to distract the reporter or throw off her concentration. Audiences are accustomed to seeing the talent using a microphone, and, on a basic level, audiences understand the recording process. Dynamic microphones are virtually useless on a boom pole or a film set. The necessary proximity to the voice is impractical for the camera and the transient response is dull in comparison to a condenser microphone.

Examples of Handheld Microphones

- Audio Technica AT8004
- EV RE50
- Rode NT3
- Shure VP64AL

LIP MICROPHONES

The *lip mic* is a unique ribbon device manufactured by Coles, used by reporters to record voiceovers on location as well as sports announcers. The microphone's construction includes a special bar that helps space the mouth of the

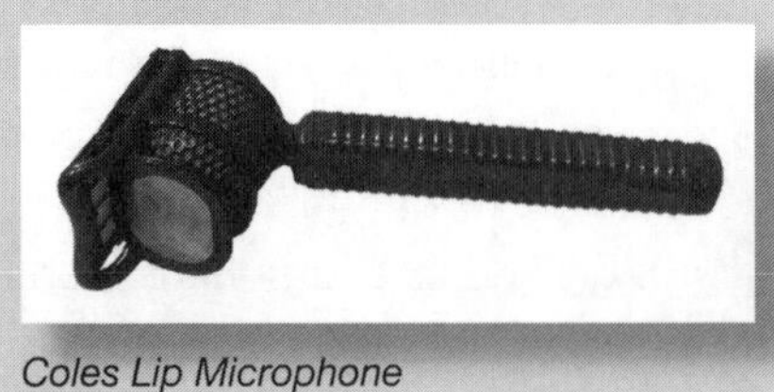

Coles Lip Microphone

reporter at the proper distance to the diaphragm. Because of this design, the reporter's mouth is completely hidden from view, making the microphone an off-camera choice. These microphones have been around for decades and have since been replaced by more modern instruments. Despite new technology, lip microphones are still found in news trucks everywhere and provide newsworthy reports every night around the world. A word of caution: applying phantom power to this microphone will cause serious damage!

CAMERA MICROPHONES

Camera microphones are mounted to the top of the camera. They can be a third-party mic or the mic that was supplied with the camera by the manufacturer. Shotgun microphones are the most common since they can easily pick up dialog and reduce background noise. Documentary productions might use a stereo camera microphone to provide better ambience tracks.

Camera mics are very subjective. They are susceptible to camera noise, handling noise, and background noise. Because they are physically mounted to the camera, they will suffer from poor mic placement most of the time. Therefore, the camera mic should only be used when necessary or when audio is not critical, such as B-roll. It is impossible to get the best audio by only using the camera mic. Boom poles will bring the microphone to places the camera cannot reach and can follow the dialog without affecting the shot.

Camera mics supplied with the camera are often electret condenser shotguns. Camera operators who want to capture the best possible audio with their camera will replace this mic with a true condenser shotgun, such as a Sennheiser MKH 416 or Rode NTG-1. When using short shotguns on the camera, zoom out the lens to a wide shot and check that the microphone is not seen.

Many moons ago, I was brought in to shoot behind the scenes footage on the music video "Nightmares" for King Gordy. The video was shot in Detroit and included special appearances by members of D-12 and Good Charlotte. Because of the celebrities involved and the fact that this was King Gordy's debut album, there was a high priority on documenting the music video. Part of my duties included interviewing the cast and crew. The shoot was low budget, so I was a one-man band. This meant that I was both the camera operator and the sound mixer.

I used a wireless lav for the interviews and mounted a Sennheiser MKH 416 as the camera mic for any improvisation, which was bound to happen. It was a long night. I easily shot five or six hours of tape. After fourteen hours of shooting, I headed home, just as the sun was rising. I was excited to see the footage that I had shot. I plugged the camera into a monitor at the studio, eager to see my stellar cinematography. Much to my dismay, I realized that the shotgun was in the upper-right-hand corner of every wide shot. This wasn't my first rodeo. I know that I had checked for the mic in the viewfinder when I mounted it to the camera. Apparently, the lens wasn't full wide or the viewfinder didn't fully display the corners of the frame. Either way, the footage still had a microphone in the shot.

I called the producer and told him about my error. Surprisingly, he had a big laugh about it. This was a much different response than I had expected. He said not to worry about it. But, he always asked me to double-check my setups on the shoots that followed. Whenever you mount a shotgun to the camera, make sure that it is out of the frame!

Examples of Third-Party Camera Microphones

- Beyerdynamic MCE86
- Rode NTG-1
- Rode Video Mic
- Rode Stereo Video Mic
- Sennheiser MKE 400
- Sennheiser MKH 416
- Sony ECM-CG50

Rode NTG-1 used as a camera microphone

A great resource for comparing microphone models and specifications is *www.microphone-data.com*. This non-biased organization gathers and stores information on virtually every microphone. The library section of the website hosts several articles that further discuss the technology and applications of microphones.

THE ALL-PURPOSE MICROPHONE

Is there such thing as an all-purpose microphone? The answer is a confusing "No, but yes." In reality, there is no single mic that will be the best choice for every situation. However, limitations such as budget, time constraints, and portability can sometimes force a sound mixer into selecting a workhorse microphone to carry around in the field. Here are the reasons why:

Budget

Microphones aren't cheap. Purchasing every possible type of microphone can cost more than $10,000! When starting off, you'll need to be more selective as to which microphone(s) you buy first.

Time Constraints

Feature-film work is much different than ENG work. In features, you have the luxury of swapping out mics to best capture the dialog for a scene. With ENG work, seconds count! Many times you'll find yourself indoors shooting interviews. Then, moments later, you'll have to race out the door to shoot a stand-up. Moments after the stand-up, you'll jump inside a car and race off to grab some man-on-the-street interviews. Realistically, you won't have time to stop the flow of production and swap out mics.

Portability

Many times ENG work requires you to travel on planes or race around town and you won't have the space you need to bring a good selection of mics. More often than not, you'll need to pick your favorite mic and make do.

There are tons of microphone types, pickup patterns, brands, and price ranges. When first starting out, these options can make your head spin, especially if you don't understand all of the technical specs. Some microphones are considered industry standards because they are popular and have proven themselves in the field. However, there may be better and/or less expensive microphones to choose from. When considering which microphone to purchase, you should always listen to the microphone first. Resist the urge to buy online without hearing and testing the microphone. If possible, borrow the mic from a friend or rent one from a local rental house. Ask around to find out other people's experience with that particular microphone. Check online forums and ask local sound mixers in your area.

So, let's sum up the all-purpose mic argument. In theory there is no such thing as an all-purpose mic. In practice, all-purpose mics do exist. The short shotgun mic offers the greatest flexibility in general fieldwork. Keep in mind: it is not the ideal mic for every situation, but if you are just starting out and can only afford one microphone, the short shotgun mic is the best choice. It is the Swiss army knife of microphones for location sound.

MICROPHONE PLACEMENT

Mic placement is just as important, if not more important, as mic selection.

An inexpensive microphone in the right place will sound better than an expensive microphone in the wrong place! Proper microphone placement is determined by two factors: distance and angle.

The closer the mic is to the sound source, the greater the rejection of reverberation and extraneous noise. If the microphone is too distant, the direct sound of the voice will be more affected by the indirect sound of the environment's acoustics and can result in unintelligible dialog. *Direct sound* means that the microphone captures the sound directly from the sound source. To achieve direct sound, the microphone needs to be either close to the sound source or in a sound-treated room. Sound treatment on location is a pipe dream, so proximity is the goal of mic placement in order to capture direct sound. *Indirect sound* refers to sound waves that are immediately bounced off nearby objects, including walls, floors, and ceilings, before they reach the microphone.

Indirect sound can be a single bounce or slap off a hard surface such as a music stand during a voiceover session or excessive buildup in the form of reverb. When a microphone is in close proximity to the sound source (e.g., the actor's mouth), more direct sound is captured. When a microphone is further away from the sound source, the more indirect sound is captured. On a primal level, humans understand this concept and use it to determine the size of the room they are in and the distance they are to a sound.

If you're struggling to understand how indirect sound will translate on screen, think of a home movie. The problem with home-movie sound is that a wide-pattern microphone on the front of the camera captures the sound. This tends to pick up more indirect sound than direct sound. There is a distinct sound or character to this effect that is not desirable. If you don't want your production sound to sound like a home movie, then you'll need to get the mic closer to the actors to capture more direct sound.

Miking at a closer distance allows you to capture more direct dialog and less indirect dialog from reverb or reflections. If you hear reflections, position the mic so that they enter through its side. The boom's pickup pattern will reduce or eliminate the reflections, leaving the direct dialog. In addition to more direct sound, the voice will be louder and require less amplification from the mixer or recorder. As a result, there will be less noise or hiss in the recording.

The angle of the microphone should match the best use of the microphone's polar pattern. For this reason, the angle of an omnidirectional microphone is not important. With unidirectional microphones, it is imperative to stay on-axis. The source of the sound, the voice, should be the focus of the microphone. Pointing the microphone directly at the feet of the person speaking will not provide the best audio. This might be obvious, but it is very common for a novice boom operator to aim the microphone at the top or side of the talent's head. The same principle as pointing the microphone at the talent's shoes applies. There is no sound coming from the shoes or the top of the head; therefore, the microphone should not be aimed toward these places. Always point the microphone at the sound source.

How you angle the microphone at the mouth depends on the camera's framing and background noise. The boom mic will always capture the most natural audio when positioned overhead and pointing downward toward the talent. Although the sound source is the mouth, most experienced sound mixers will angle the microphone at the actor's chest. This technique is called *lobing*, as the lobe of the microphone's polar pattern is used to capture the dialog.

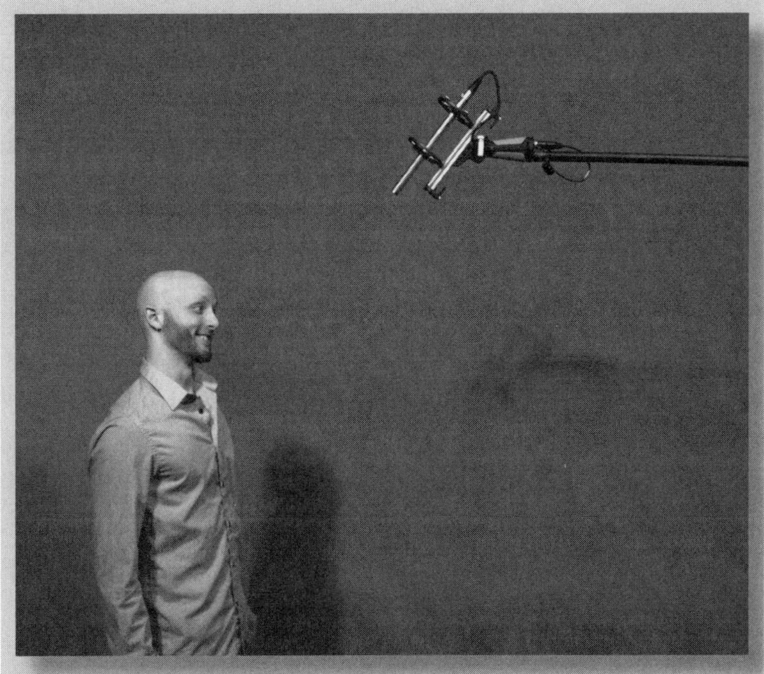

Example of proper microphone placement with a shotgun microphone

Aiming the mic at the sternum allows for a more even frequency response. Essentially, you have a larger area at which to point the boom mic. When pointing directly at the mouth, you have a target that is only the size of a golf ball. If the talent moves her head in any direction, her voice can be colored, unless the boom moves precisely in sync with her head. This is much more difficult than it might seem. With the sternum, the target is now the size of a paper plate. This larger area is more forgiving and allows the color of the voice to remain consistent. The ideal angle of the shotgun mic is thirty degrees. When pointed at the chest from overhead, this angle reduces the amount of noise in the background.

Low ceilings, obstructions, camera angles, and other factors may prevent the boom mic from being positioned overhead. If this is the case, you can use another positioning method called *scooping*. Scooping is the process of miking the actor with a boom mic from underneath. The angle is the same as from overhead, but is positioned from below. This technique reduces background noise or hard reflections from the ground, but will not deliver the same quality audio as an overhead position. The sound is mid-range heavy and lacks the higher frequencies that an overhead position captures.

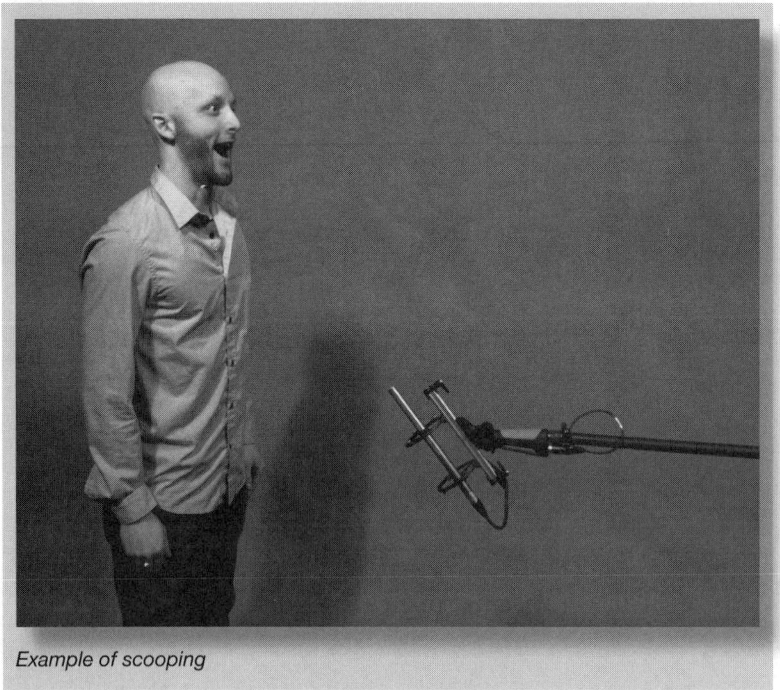

Example of scooping

As with any position, the closer the mic is to the talent's mouth, the better the quality. You can scoop as low as the knees on the talent and still get usable audio. The more distance between the subject's mouth and the mic, the thinner and weaker the sound will be. A good working range would be belt level down to the knees. If you have to go lower than the knees, you should look at other alternatives.

Boom operator Nick Schoonover works by scooping the boom outside of the frame line.

Scooping can be a lifesaver, but should only be used as a last alternative. There are several downfalls to scooping:

1. The biggest issue is that the voice can sound muddy. This position focuses on low and mid-range frequencies because the chest is a low frequency resonator for the human body. These frequencies are accentuated when the chest is closer to the mic. From an overhead position, the head is closer to the mic and the frequency response is more natural.

2. Overhead noise, such as planes, light ballasts, and ceiling reflections are introduced into the mic from the scooping position.

3. The actor's hand movements and prop handling can sound louder than the dialog, which can distort the sound perspective of the shot.

4. The boom operator will need to navigate around furniture, set pieces, and props, whereas overhead booming typically faces fewer obstacles.

5. Camera operators tend to minimize headroom, which allows for the boom to get closer to the talent when booming overhead. The caveat here is that the camera operator is more likely to widen out to reveal more of the actor's torso. This might result in moving the boom further away from the actor's mouth (e.g., booming from the thighs or knees). Be sure to communicate with the camera operator and establish a good frame line for you to work with.

The cons for scooping far outweigh the pros. Scooping may be a better option if the actor bows her head or looks down while delivering her lines; otherwise try to use an overhead position.

Angles and Distances

Here are some average angles and distances to consider with different types of microphones:

Shotguns

Short shotguns sound the best when positioned within 18" to 36" from the talent. Long shotguns can produce usable audio from 4' to 8'. If you can get closer than 4', consider switching to a short shotgun.

Lavs

Lavs should be positioned about 6" to 8" below the mouth. In general, they should be placed in the center of the sternum. This is the optimal placement for a lav. Placing a lav too high on the sternum will muffle the sound. Placing the lav too low on the sternum will result in a thin or weak sound. We will discuss dozens of placement options in Chapter 6.

Handheld Mics

Handheld mics should be placed about 4" to 12" from the mouth. The mic should be held slightly in front of the talent on an angle pointing back at the mouth. This position will allow the audience to see the performer's mouth, but will also help reduce plosives.

Microphone placement is sometimes determined by the direction of the wind or background noise. When possible, see if the camera angle can be changed to allow for optimal sound. If this is an option, try to have the talent keep their backs to the background noise when using lavs and have them face the noise when using the shotgun. If the camera angle cannot be changed, you'll have to resort to less-than-optimal microphone placement to reduce the problem.

Usable sound might come by accident, but you'll only achieve great sound by using proper techniques.

CHAPTER EXERCISE Set up a "mic shoot-out" to see which mic sounds the best. Record with a camera mic, a lavalier, a shotgun, etc. Try different placements and distances. Which one sounds the best? Next, take the best-sounding mic out of the equation and record using the remaining microphones. Try to get better results from the mics. Repeat this exercise until you are left with the worst-sounding microphone (which will undoubtedly be the camera mic). Now, experiment with the last remaining microphone and see how you can optimize its performance with placement.

CHAPTER 5

BOOM TECHNIQUES

THE BOOM OPERATOR

You can sum up great production sound gathering in two words: mic placement.

The person responsible for mic placement is the *boom operator*. They are living mic stands. Titles for this position include boom operator, boom op, boom, boomer, and boomie.

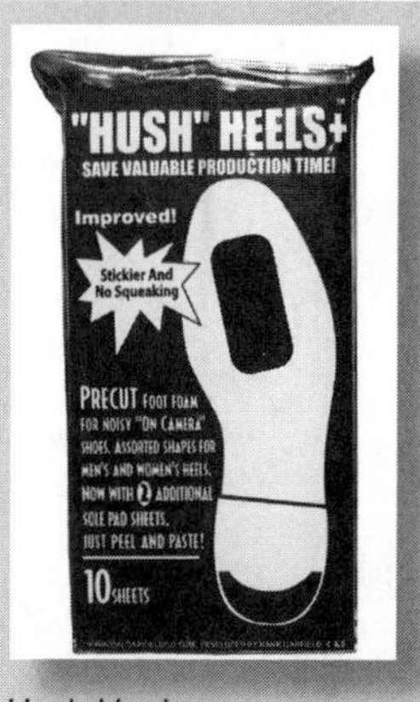

Hush Heels

Regardless of what they're called, their primary job is to position the mic so that it follows the action, often in the most uncomfortable positions. A boom operator needs to dodge props and set pieces, move quickly and quietly while maintaining perfect mic placement, and, of course, staying out of the frame. A boom operator may have to bend, reach, stretch, and even walk during the scene — all without making a sound. This means boom operators need to wear quiet clothes and should avoid dressing like Mr. T by not wearing lots of noisy jewelry. Boom operators' footsteps should be soft, so they should avoid hard sole shoes or shoes that are squeaky. If the surface they are working on is excessively noisy, they should try putting down some carpet or a sound blanket. If these are unavailable, they should try working in their socks or wearing Hush Heels.

If you're working as an ENG sound mixer, you must do double duty as both the sound mixer and the boom operator. This means you will certainly have your hands full (no pun intended). Once you set the levels on the mixer, you will need to keep your eyes glued to the mic to ensure that it is in the right position and out of the shot. You will need to use your eyes for positioning and your ears for monitoring. A trained ear will detect the slightest amount of distortion and will know when to sneak up low levels on the mixer. It is not the optimal way to record production sound, but you'll have to make it work, as you're doing the job of two crewmembers!

For productions that allow for a dedicated boom operator, it is crucial that the boom operator is qualified for the position. This is often the shortfall of independent filmmakers. There is this crazy notion that the boom operator is simply the "guy that holds the boom pole" and the only real qualification for a boom operator is having two arms. Nothing could be further from the truth.

I learned this lesson the hard way when I hired Greasy Bob to run the boom for a shoot. Greasy Bob was an old friend from high school whom I used to play in a band with. He was a great guitar player and had a really cool, raspy voice, but it was his lack of hygiene that earned him his nickname. I ran into Greasy Bob at a music store after a near decade-long hiatus of seeing each other. We caught up and shared some stories. He told me that he was in between gigs and looking for work. I told him that I'd keep him in mind.

A few days later, I got a call from a production company that needed to rent gear from me, along with a boom operator. I was already booked on another gig, so I thought of Greasy Bob. It made sense, since he had been around recording studios and understood microphones and the recording process. I booked Greasy Bob on the shoot.

Surprisingly, I received a call from the production manager after only a few hours into the shoot. He asked if I could replace Greasy Bob with someone else. As it turns out, Greasy Bob is a great musician, but a horrible boom operator. The production manager explained that during just the first few hours of the shoot Greasy Bob had raided the craft-service table, taken nearly a dozen cigarette breaks, fallen asleep twice, dipped the boom into the frame more times than he could count, and inadvertently hit the director in the head with the boom pole. The production manager was very cool about the situation and actually had a hard time explaining the day's events without laughing. I apologized profusely and found a suitable replacement, someone who knew set protocol and was actually qualified to operate the boom.

Operating the boom pole is an acquired skill. Greasy Bob had proven this to me. I never made this mistake again. My advice to independent filmmakers is to carve money out of their budget to hire a qualified boom operator. Skip the fancy gourmet sandwiches served for lunch and stick with five-dollar pizzas; find an expendable line item; plan the shooting schedule properly and cut unnecessary hours or days. In short, do whatever it takes to hire a boom operator who really knows what he's doing.

THE BOOM POLE

The *boom pole* is the boom operator's main tool. It should become part of his anatomy. The boom operator should be one with the boom pole — a single life form whose sole purpose is to gather the best dialog possible.

The purpose of the boom pole is to bring the microphone close to the talent without being seen by the camera, and therefore not seen by the audience. This gives the illusion that the camera magically records the sound. Most people do not realize that the sound they hear on television and in movies was recorded separate from the camera. Studio booms like the Fisher models are the old-style telescoping rigs still used today in TV, typically on soundstages. The advent of HD video has seen smaller, portable models of the Fisher boom used on locations to relieve boom operators from lengthy takes. The modern boom pole, sometimes referred to as a *fish pole*, is lightweight and portable, making it the perfect choice for the field.

The boom pole is comprised of sections that work like a telescope. These sections can be disassembled for cleaning and general maintenance. A locking mechanism at the end of each section, called a "knuckle," can be loosened to extend the next section. Tightening the knuckle locks the next section into place. Be sure to keep the knuckles snug to prevent the boom mic from spinning during a take and to guarantee the sections stay fully extended. Never over-tighten a knuckle. Over-tightening will not only wear the threads out, but will also make it very difficult to extend or retract a section. This can be very inconvenient if you are in a hurry!

Boom poles are constructed out of aluminum or carbon fiber. The aluminum poles are sturdier but heavier. Weight is an important factor when using a boom pole because they are deceivingly light, but quickly get heavy as the muscles fatigue. Extending the boom pole makes it seem heavier as gravity takes over. Taking advantage of the fulcrum point of the pole will help reduce the perceived weight difference. When extending the boom pole, leave a couple of inches inside the pole for each riser. This will make the boom pole sturdier, especially when the pole is fully extended. Failure to do this may cause a section to crack under the weight of the microphone.

Boom poles come in three ranges of length, each generally used for a specific application. Travel and documentary work uses a pole that is 5' to

9' in length. ENG and general video production uses a pole that is 9' to 12' in length. Film work uses a pole that is 12' to 18' in length. As the pole extends, the microphone is positioned further away from the boom operator. When extending the pole, always start with the top section first and work your way down. If you start from the bottom, you won't be able to reach the last sections as the pole is extended.

Examples of Boom Poles

- Ambient Recording QX5100
- Gitzo 3560
- K-Tek K-202CCR
- LTM Carbon Fiber
- Rode Boompole

When it comes to how much length you should extend the pole, enough isn't enough. Try to give yourself at least one to two more feet than you need. This will afford you more room to counterbalance the pole, making it easier to work with and giving your muscles a break. Keep in mind: if you are using the standard "H" position (see page 54), your arms will give you an additional reach of four feet (nearly two feet in each direction). But, don't figure that into your boom pole length. You don't want to extend your arms the entire length of the shot. Stay comfortable. Keep the additional reach as a reserve in case the actors stray from their marks.

Boom operator reaches with the pole at the beginning of the scene and pulls the pole back as the actor makes his way toward the camera.

Use common sense when working with a boom pole. When extended, the pole is an obstruction hazard — basically a weapon! Keep an eye on the pole. Set pieces, chandeliers, ceiling fans, power lines, crewmembers, and actors are all potential targets of your sonic light saber. Accidents usually happen before or after a take (just when you think it's safe to move your pole...). Stay alert and focus when using the pole. For additional safety when working with an extended pole, you could place a piece of glow-in-the-dark or neon gaffer tape on the bottom of your boom pole to help make it more visible when the pole is raised or being moved. Many stands and foreheads have fallen victim to a swinging boom pole.

Boom poles are sensitive to the slightest handling noise. Even with a shock mount, this handling noise will be transmitted through the microphone. So, the boom pole must be handled softly and gently. Many experienced boom operators will wear cotton gloves to reduce handling noise. Rode Microphones have manufactured a boom pole with the bottom section covered in soft foam to help with this noise reduction; however, this only takes care of the handling noise from one hand. The other hand will still need a glove in order to dampen handling noise. Always remove any rings from your fingers and avoid tapping your fingers against the pole.

A standard 3/8" threaded screw on the end of the boom pole is used to attach a shock mount or blimp. Nearly all blimps and shock mounts used for film work will have a 3/8" female thread to accept this screw. Should you decide to mount your blimp or shock mount to a mic stand, pick up an adaptor that will allow you to convert standard mic stands from 5/8" to 3/8".

Boom operator Dan Lorenz sports cotton gloves for the camera.

Boom poles come in one of two styles: *cabled* and *uncabled*. Cabled boom poles use either coiled cables or straight flow-through cables. Coiled cables are more ENG-friendly as the cable automatically extends and retracts inside of the pole.

Straight flow-through cables need a bit of attention when extending and retracting, as the slack will "flow through" the bottom opening of the pole. This opening is found on the side of the pole's base or butt. The advantage to having a hole in the side of the base is that it allows the pole to rest on the base when not in use. For cabled booms with an XLR jack at the bottom, a right-angled XLR cable is the best choice as it allows the pole to rest on the base.

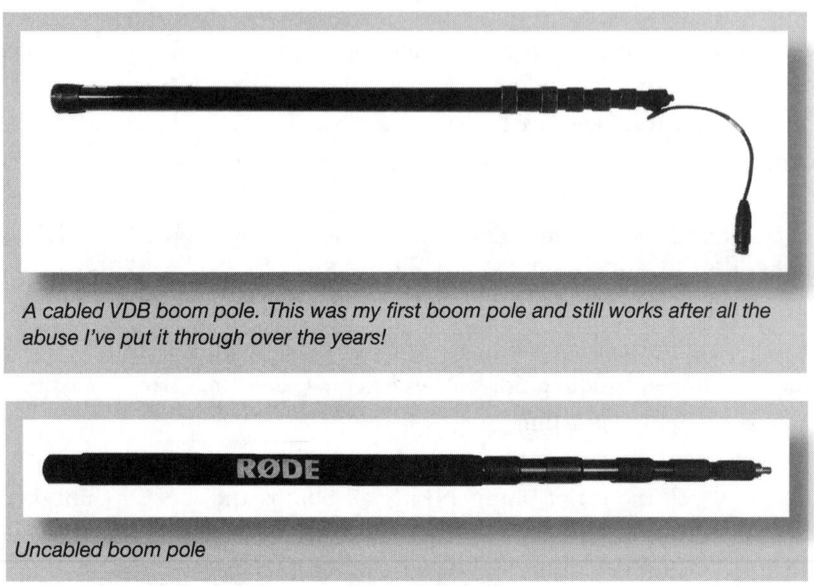

A cabled VDB boom pole. This was my first boom pole and still works after all the abuse I've put it through over the years!

Uncabled boom pole

You should always rest the connector on the top of your foot. Placing the connector on the ground will get it dirty and can also damage it over time. If you have a standard XLR connector at the bottom of the boom pole, do not rest the connector on your foot as this will bend the cable and eventually cause the wires inside to fray, resulting in intermittent crackling or loss of signal altogether. Loose XLR connections can cause intermittent noise and crackling in the track. These connections should be fixed or replaced as soon as possible. If they cannot be repaired on location, you can wrap gaffer tape around the connectors to hold them in place as a short-term fix.

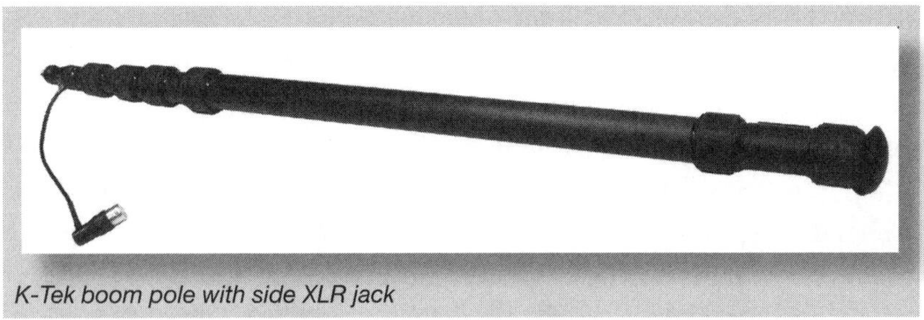

K-Tek boom pole with side XLR jack

A drawback to cabled poles is that they produce handling noise when the cable rattles inside. Take extra care so that this doesn't happen. Fast movements, specifically up and down motions, will cause the cable to smack against the sides of the pole.

Cabled boom poles are a must for ENG work. They are fast and efficient. One of the disadvantages of having a coiled internal cable is that it can easily get tangled and knotted inside the pole. This makes it difficult to fully retract the pole and can eventually cause the soldered connections to fray and short out. Routine maintenance can solve this problem by unscrewing the bottom cap, pulling the cable out, and fixing the knots.

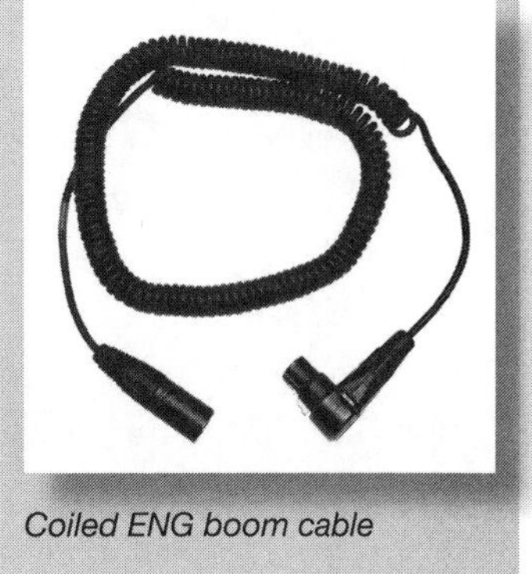

Coiled ENG boom cable

Cabled boom poles are often connected to an ENG field mixer via a short, coiled cable. This cable allows for boom pole operation without the need to manage the cable. These types of cables are a must for ENG work.

Uncabled boom poles are less expensive than cabled poles. They are simply the extending sections. The microphone cable is wrapped on the outside of the pole. This eliminates any rattling noise from inside the pole; however, loose sections of the cable can still hit the pole and create handling noise. To prevent this, the cable is snuggly wrapped and secured with *hairballs*. Hairballs are a type of rubber band with plastic balls on either side. While they are intended for use in ponytails, they are commonly

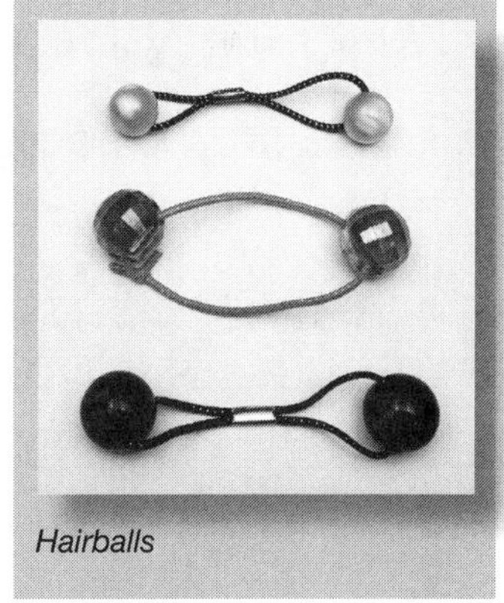

Hairballs

found on film sets and used for securing cables in place because the plastic balls allow for a quick release. Avoid using gaffer tape to secure the cable to the pole as this will not only leave a sticky residue over time, but will make extending or retracting the pole difficult.

When wrapping the cable around the pole, leave a few inches of slack between the blimp or shock mount and the end of the pole. This allows the blimp or shock mount to be angled or adjusted based on the shot and position of the actors. This also reduces additional mic-handling noise that can be produced from a taut cable. Too much slack can produce handling noise. If necessary, secure additional slack to the pole with hairballs or eliminate some of the slack.

Uncabled poles take a little finesse and preparation in extending and retracting the pole. For this reason, they are not preferred for ENG work. They are, however, better suited for feature-film work, which affords the boom operator more time to prep the pole.

Navigating around a set during a take can be tricky. There are obstacles everywhere you turn. From cables and set pieces to overhead lights and C-stands, a set can quickly turn into a minefield. The smaller the set, the worse the obstacle course can become. Experienced boom operators know to warn people when they're walking with the boom pole extended. A cautious "Boom coming through" will give the cast and crew a heads up and can avoid injuries.

When a boom pole is not in use, it should be stored in a safe place. Never leave a fully-extended boom pole leaning up against a wall unattended. On a film set, this will annoy the set department and potentially scratch the paint. If the pole falls it will not only cause damage to the pole, but could be a safety hazard for other crewmembers. If you must lean the pole against the wall, be sure to retract all of the sections first.

THE BOOMA SUTRA (BOOMING POSITIONS)

Holding the boom pole properly is a matter of leverage more than strength; however, successful boom pole operation is not for the weak. When the pole is extended, the front hand is used as the fulcrum point and the back hand steers the pole using pan, tilt, or rotation to cue the speaking actor. To angle the pole upward, push up with the front hand to support the pole and push down with the back hand. To raise the pole parallel to the floor, simply raise both the front and back hand.

There are five types of boom pole movement:

Cue

The end of the boom pole is rotated so that the boom mic can be aimed to capture the dialog from an actor.

Swing

The boom pole is move horizontally to follow the talent or to cue another actor.

Raise/Lower

The boom pole is raised or lowered parallel to the ground.

Pivot

The boom pole is raised or lowered on an angle via the fulcrum point.

Follow

The boom pole and the boom operator move together to follow the talent.

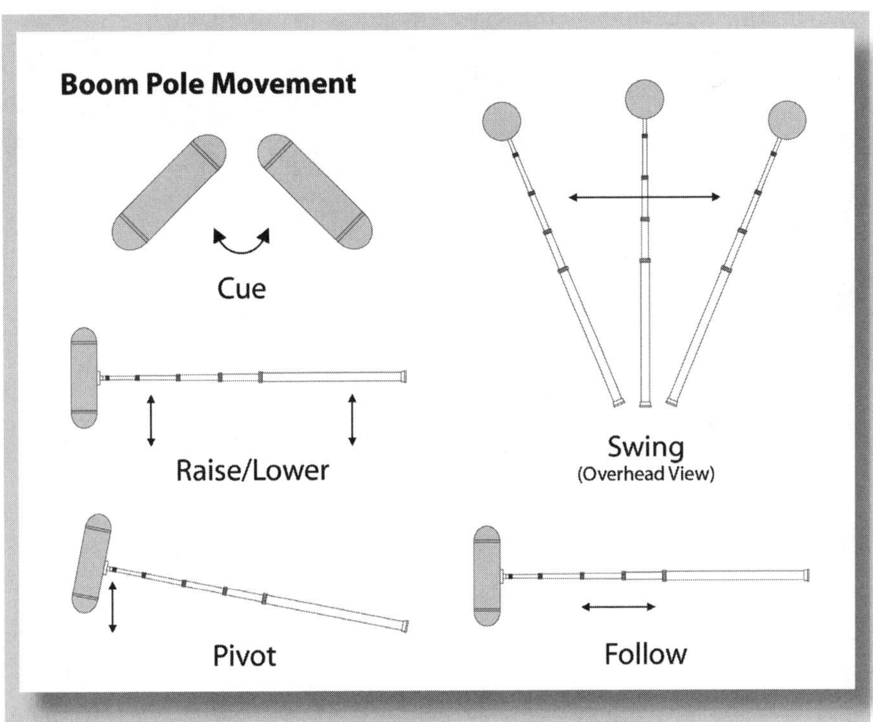

Your arms should be limber and your hands should be loose enough to allow the pole to rotate. If your hands are too firm, they will be more likely to produce handling noise. Locking your arms is a bad idea and will only cause you to start shaking uncontrollably after a minute or so. Shifting your body weight from side to side in small controlled movements can alleviate the muscles. If you stand still like a tree trunk, you'll only set yourself up for failure. Be fluid.

Here are some basic booming positions to choose from:

Standard "H" or Field Goal Position

In the standard "H" position, your arms are bent at the elbows, forming a field goal symbol. Your feet should be firmly planted for support. This position allows your arms to move a couple of feet in either direction, giving you extra reach. Avoid the "Y" position, in which you have your arms fully extended in each direction. This will eliminate the additional reach you would have with your arms. You can gain even more reach by leaning with your legs without moving your feet.

Standard "H" or field-goal position

If you are an ENG sound mixer, you can keep the pole steady with the front hand for a few seconds to make any necessary mixer adjustments with the back hand. If you must use two hands to hold the pole and the mic overloads, it will take time for you to position the pole in one hand to free up the other hand so you can adjust your levels. A quick fix is to back the mic off (move the mic away from the talent) to reduce the overload and bring the mic back into position when the loud dialog has finished. Be careful not to move the mic too far away, and avoid handling noise.

Flagpole/Lazy "H" Position

Place your hands as though you are in the field goal position; however, keep your elbows at your sides. This technique is useful as a quick break during long takes in the "H" position and also works well in close quarters with limited space, such as cramped locker rooms, small kitchens, or other rooms that restrict your movements.

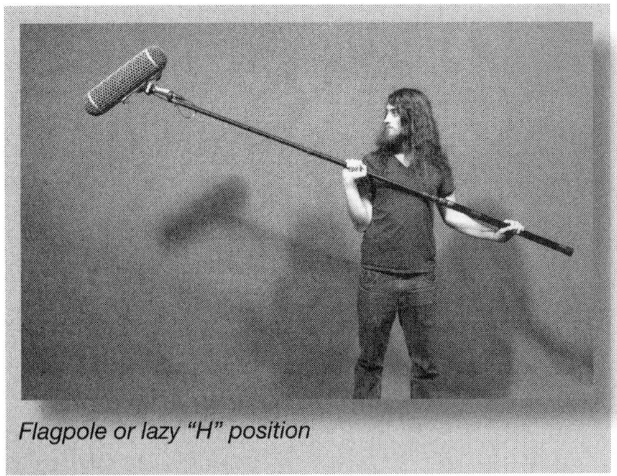

Flagpole or lazy "H" position

Crucifix Position

In this position, the boom pole rests behind your neck with both arms draped over the sides of the pole. This position is not optimal for accuracy and critical cueing, but can be a very useful trick for extremely lengthy scenes where the pole is fully extended.

Crucifix position

One-Handed Position

Between the boom pole and the mixer knobs, an ENG sound mixer can have his hands full, literally! Sometimes, both hands need to be doing different tasks. To accomplish this, use one hand to operate the mixer and the other hand to cue

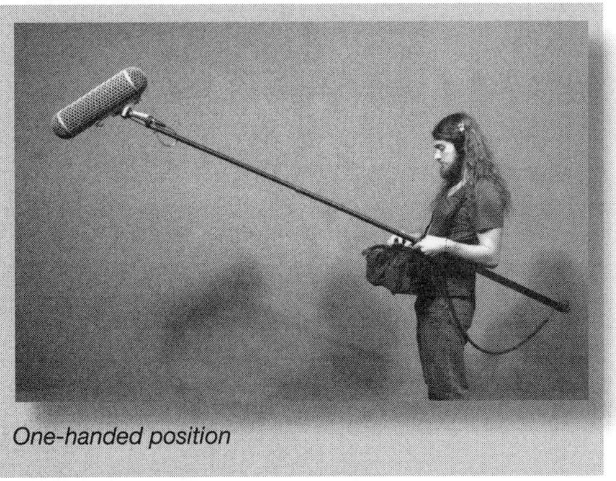

One-handed position

the pole. Rest the pole lengthwise down your forearm and grip the pole with your hand. The pole will end up on an angle, so make sure the pole does not enter the upper corners of the frame. This trick works when the pole is only extended less than nine feet. Beyond that, the pole will be too heavy to control accurately. This position is unacceptable for film work when both hands can be used easily.

Joust Position

This is an underhanded version of the one-handed position and is used for scooping.

Joust position/scooping

Head Position

Some ENG sound mixers will rest the pole on the top of the head and steer with one hand while the other hand operates the mixer. This position is not recommended, as it is very easy for the pole to slide off the head and create a hazard for the talent.

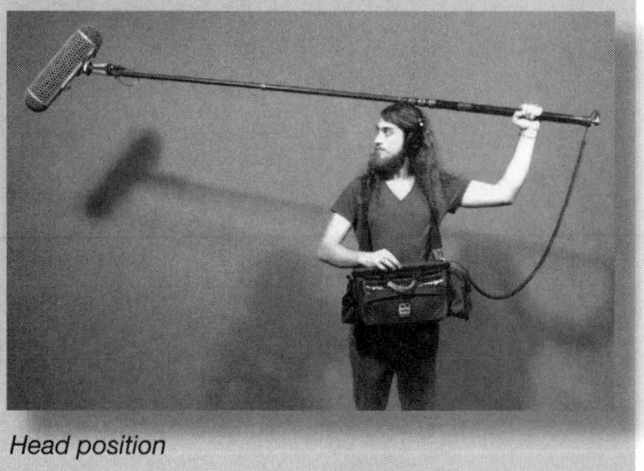
Head position

Boom Pole Holders

There are times when the talent is stationary and it makes sense to rig the boom pole on a C-stand using a *Cardellini clamp* or a boom pole holder. This setup works well and can offer great audio. On scenes or interviews where there are two stationary subjects, you can rig a separate mic for each actor on C-stands and crisscross the mics to face each actor.

Use a small sandbag to help counterbalance boom poles that are fully extended on C-stands. This ensures safety and helps the pole from bending. Standard mic stands are not very sturdy or practical for film/TV work. You can purchase boom pole

Cardellini clamp

holders or find alternatives, such as a fishing-pole holder, at your local sporting goods store. Mafer clamps can be used in a pinch, but are not recommended because they do not support the pole as well and can cause it to bend or crack.

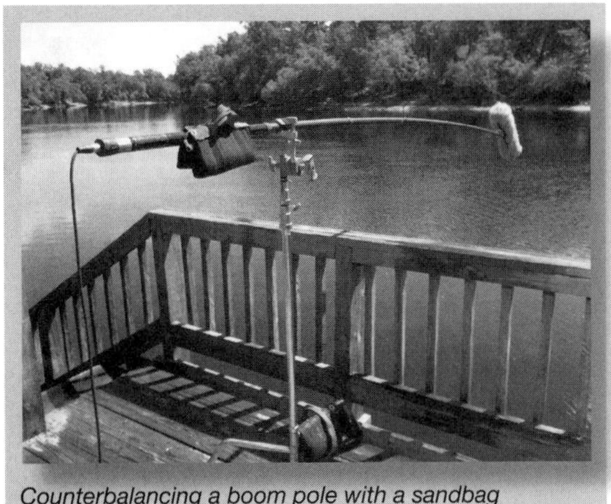

Counterbalancing a boom pole with a sandbag

Boom Pole Zen

Regardless of the position that you choose, you need to remain calm and as comfortable as possible. If you are not, the mic will dip in the shot, the pole will shake, and you'll gas out fast. Shaky arms that are weak from holding the pole can introduce handling noise. Take breaks whenever you can to give your arms a rest. The boom pole might not be heavy at the start of the day, but it only takes a few long scenes to wear your arms down. Pace yourself. Breathe deep. Relax.

BOOM OPERATION

Moving with the boom pole is an art form. Boom operation is all about using fluid movements, like a ballerina. Learn to sway your body without moving the pole. This will help relieve aching muscles and keep you prepared for sudden movements that you might need to make. I call this "The Dance of the Boom Operator," but it's more like a waltz than a slam dance. Do whatever you have to do to get the mic in the right position. Inches can make all the difference between good sound and okay sound.

The Frame Line

Once the camera operator has settled on the shot, you will need to establish a *frame line* so that you know where the boom mic can operate without being seen by the camera. The frame line is the absolute edge of the shot. Your job is to "hug the frame line," which means to stay as close to the frame line as possible. The camera operator will usually help you with this. In any case, make sure that you ask for a frame line.

"The boom's in the shot" and "mic in" are phrases that cause boom operators to break into a cold sweat. These calls indicate the end of a take. To establish the frame line, dip the mic into the center of the shot and then raise it up until it clears the frame. This is a much faster approach than starting outside of the frame and slowly lowering the mic until it enters the frame. Plus, this method will give you a true frame line, since camera operators are more focused on the shot and will undoubtedly want to play it safe. They will often tell you the boom position is fine without allowing you to get as close as possible. Instead, start with the boom in the shot and have the camera operator back you out of the frame. Sticking the mic arbitrarily above the shot will usually get a "you're fine" response, but this isn't good enough. Be dangerous and aggressive. Get the mic in there and hug the frame line!

With the frame line established, you'll need to remember where it was. Pick a spot in the background that lines up with the top of the frame line. This could be a line on a brick wall, a sign in the background, the top of a cabinet, or even a C-stand. Steadicam shots might require the boom operator to put his running shoes on. You have to keep up with the camera operator and shoot ENG-style.

Frame lines can radically change from those given during rehearsal. With the permission of the camera operator, you can place a piece of tape on the zoom ring of the lens so that you have an idea if the shot is wide or tight. This is extremely useful for ENG crews, where nothing is planned and everyone is working on the fly.

Shots that have a loose frame are extremely tough. The camera might be shooting POV or action-style where all bets are off for a frame line. In these cases, you'll need to play it safe for the sake of the frame. When in doubt, ask for playback to make sure the boom didn't dip into the shot. Some boom operators will use a thin strip of white gaffer tape on the end of the windscreen to allow the boom mic to be more visible if it dips into the frame.

White gaffer tape on the end of the windscreen

A boom operator should become familiar with *prime lenses*. Unlike a zoom lens, a prime lens has a fixed focal length commonly used on film sets. Lenses with a lower number such as 18mm will produce a wider shot, while lenses with a higher number such as 50mm will produce a tighter shot. It is helpful to understand lenses so that when the DP calls for a lens change you have a general idea of how much room you'll have to work with.

Video monitors can help establish the frame line, but be careful. Film viewfinders are different from video-camera viewfinders. To top it off, not all video monitors show everything that the camera sees. Film cameras are different. A video tap feed from a film camera allows you to see the film equivalent of underscan and will display the area outside of the film recording area. Some boom operators will strap small monitors to their arms so that they can watch the frame line while booming.

Shadows can reveal the presence of a boom mic even when the mic is out of the frame. So, you will need to become a shadow hunter. Spotting shadows can be tricky. Moving the boom pole around before the shot can easily identify shadows. Don't be subtle. That might make the shadows harder to find. Instead, be deliberate. Use exaggerated movements and watch the walls and set pieces. And for God's sake, don't hit anybody with the pole! There's nothing worse than a boom operator swinging a pole around like Curly from the Three Stooges smacking co-workers left and right.

Be proactive in solving shadow problems before bringing the issue up with the DP. It's easier to change the position of the boom operator than it is to change the position of a light. A simple trick is to try booming from the opposite side of the key light. Harsh overhead lighting that can't be relocated, such as fixed structural lights or even the sun, can make overhead booming impossible due to shadows on the actor. When this happens, you'll need to resort to scooping. If the shot is static and the boom pole doesn't move, a shadow can be camouflaged with a flag or hidden in the set to blend in. Once the boom pole moves, the game is over and the shadow is revealed.

Reflections are another enemy of the boom pole. Be aware of any reflective surfaces that might reveal the boom to the camera, such as mirrors, shiny cars, windows, or even an actor's glasses. In most cases, flags can be used to help reduce reflections. But don't be surprised if the DP is a little grumpy, especially if he has to rearrange his lighting plan "just for sound." It is very important that you correct any issues during setup or rehearsal. Noticing this problem once shooting has started can cause serious time delays and wasted shots. If the lighting department is willing to move lights on your behalf, help them by keeping your boom in place so they can correct the problem faster.

Several tricks can help you correct reflections. Dulling spray will take the sheen off of reflective surfaces. Glass can be removed from picture frames. Duvetyn or other black material can be hung outside of the frame to create a non-reflective background. Angling set pieces an inch or two will also get rid of reflections. Small movements can yield big results.

CUEING

Boom operation all comes down to mic placement. The boom operator needs to reach the actors and follow them seamlessly throughout the scene. Sometimes, this means standing on an apple box or climbing a ladder for additional reach. Other times, you may end up in a gnarly pose that looks like you are playing a vertical game of Twister. The bottom line is to do whatever it takes to get the mic close to the action!

A wide shot and unlevel ground requires the boom operator to use a ladder to stay outside the frame line.

Rehearsals are very important to a boom operator. They allow you to understand the blocking and timing of a scene. Granted, the timing and marks are never perfectly hit, but rehearsals will give you a sense of what to expect. Actors will be given marks to hit during blocking. These marks often will be marked by spike tape or gaffer tape. Regardless of what was rehearsed, you need to be prepared to go with the flow during a scene.

Ad-libbing during a scene is growing more popular with digital filmmaking. In the golden days of filmmaking, scenes were rehearsed prior to shooting. The dialog, blocking, and flow of the scene were nailed down prior to the roll. Digital videotape changed some of that. The old saying went "Tape is cheap," but nowadays, digits are virtually free!

Ad-libbing is a great way to develop a scene, making it feel more spontaneous and less rehearsed. One of my favorite lines from *The Empire Strikes Back* is Han Solo's response to Princess Leia when she professes her love to him. Han confidently replies, "I know." This was not a scripted line. The original line was, "I love you, too." I know — bad writing. Instead, the director Irvin Kershner had actor Harrison Ford give multiple responses to pull from during editing. They shot it several ways and the improvised line stayed in the picture. This is the magic that ad-libbing can bring to a scene.

Unfortunately, ad-libbing is a boom operator's nightmare. Normally, the scene has been rehearsed (hopefully) and the cues are timed in the boom operator's mind. But when a line is given and the mic is in the wrong position, the soundtrack can suffer. If this is the case, ask for another take to allow for the mic to get into position. At minimum, try to get a *wild track* of the line. A wild track is a line of dialog that is recorded without the camera rolling.

Sometimes, the director might want to shoot the rehearsal to capture a "real" performance from the actors. If possible, talk with the director to at least get an idea of where the actors might end up in the shot. For these situations, the boom operator will have to wing it and go with his gut for cueing. Other times, the director might inform the crew about shooting the rehearsal, but withhold this information from the actors so that they don't feel the pressure to perform and are more relaxed during the scene. When this happens, you won't be able to call the roll and provide sync information at the front of the take, so be sure to tail slate the scene. All of these procedures are discussed in Chapter 12. More often than not, the rehearsal will be just that: a rehearsal. The scene will likely be reshot for either performance or technical issues. If the scene will not be reshot and something went wrong for sound, be sure to let the director know.

ENG production is plagued with a similar ad-libbing situation known as "real life." When things aren't scripted, anything can happen. This is the nature of ENG work. One trick is to anticipate the subject's movements by watching their shoulders. People will often shift slightly to one direction before moving in the opposite direction. If you see a slight shift to the left, be ready for the subject to start heading to the right. Watching their eye movements may also clue you in on what they are thinking and where they might be headed.

Unpredictable scenarios with a group of people, like reality shows (although I'm not entirely convinced that reality shows aren't staged to some degree), corporate meetings, and news events require you to be on your toes when booming. Your best bet is to start in the middle of the group and see where the conversation goes. Usually, there will be one or two people who are more vocal than the others. Swinging the pole might not be practical if there's an argument or debate. People might start talking over one another and you'll need to make a snap-judgment call as to which person you cue. It can be stressful, but in these cases you need to actively engage in listening to the conversation to see where it's going. A cardioid microphone would be a good mic choice, as its wider pattern will give a little more grace on positioning. If you're using a shotgun, it's better to stay somewhere in the middle and cue from there.

If an actor turns his back to the camera, you will need to make a choice. Should the dialog sound off-mic or should the mic follow the actor? If the boom stays in its original placement (to cover another actor's dialog, for example), the audio perspective will match the shot, but if the boom follows the actor who turns, the other actor's dialog will change. This is not good. You need to have the remaining actor's dialog stay consistent throughout the shot. In this case, the best decision would be to double-mic the scene so that the actor's audio is picked up from both angles. This is extremely helpful if the camera will switch angles to cover the actor facing the camera on the reversal. The editor will have more audio to play with should they choose to have the turning actor's dialog fall off-mic. Always think coverage. If you only have one microphone available, cover the actor's dialog on-mic. In post, it's relatively easy to make a sound appear off-mic through EQ and reverb plug-ins, but it's nearly impossible to make a sound that was recorded off-mic sound as if it was recorded on-mic.

If you have a scene where one actor cuts into another actor's lines, resulting in overlapping speech, cue the second actor's dialog. Audiences are more likely to pay attention to the new dialog over the person still speaking. In general, humans don't need to hear every word that you say in order to understand the gist of what you are saying. The same is true with dialog. When an audience can't hear a new line of dialog that interrupts a previous speaker, they will feel deprived of information. If you find yourself booming a scene with intentionally interrupting actors, try to double-boom it. If you only have one boom to work with, then favor the new line of dialog.

Avoid miking from a horizontal position with the boom mic. The horizontal position has the microphone parallel to the ground and pointed directly at the subject. Shotguns compress the audio between the dialog and the background. Avoid pointing the mic straight-on at the subject as it will increase the background level, unless this is your only option for getting good audio. Above and below positions will yield better results.

If the actor starts or finishes off-camera, follow his entire action with the boom. This will provide postproduction with a consistent track to work with. If not, then the actor's voice will be off-mic and sound unnatural next to the on-mic lines. Be sure to follow the action with the boom until the director gives a "cut." Don't yank the pole out of the scene once the last line of dialog is delivered. Those quiet, subtle moments after the dialog can be used for air fills and capture prop movement or even ad-libbed lines. If a shot starts wide, the boom will need to start extremely high and lower into position as the frame tightens. The reverse might be true if the camera widens out at the end of a scene. Unless this is the case, keep the mic in position until the shot is cut.

In some situations, you might need to use two boom mics to capture the dialog. This is known as *double booming*. If you don't have a second boom operator, you can "plant" a second boom on a C-stand to pick up another actor or the same actor who has moved to a difficult position to reach. For example, if a scene takes place inside a kitchen between two actors, you should be able to boom the conversation with no problem. However, if one of the actors sticks her head outside a window or leans into a hallway to deliver a line where the boom can't reach, the line will not be picked up and will be unusable. Although the actor might be wearing a backup lav, the sound will not match the boom. So, you can place a second boom operator outside the window or in the hallway to grab the line, or at least mount a boom mic to do the job. Unless directed otherwise, the off-screen dialog should be considered just as important as the on-screen dialog. Using the same make and model of microphones will help the sound match, although this is not always exact. Many sound engineers prefer to purchase microphones with consecutive serial numbers because the sound between the microphones is more likely to match. The majority of the time, close is good enough.

Boom operator Mary Lobaugh waits outside the doorway to pick up dialog from an actor who leaves the room.

In some cases, you might boom from behind the talent with the mic angled back toward their mouth. This is helpful when an actor is shot from behind looking off a balcony while delivering dialog.

Actors wait to deliver their lines over the side of the dock as they look out onto the Suwannee River. The frame line and blocking left the sound team no choice but to place the boom poles on C-stands and boom from behind.

MIXING WITH THE BOOM POLE

The boom pole can be used as a mixing tool during ENG production. By cueing different actors or moving the pole you can effectively mix the track with the pole. During feature work, it's best to leave the mixing to the sound mixer, but in ENG you're the entire crew!

If one actor is speaking louder than another or has a stronger voice, position the mic closer to the softer actor to balance out the dialog. In effect, you're mixing the sound using microphone positioning. Cueing alone will not help as the sound mixer will be forced to adjust the level, changing the background noise/noise floor. Cue the actor speaking, but position the mic closer to the softer actor.

A similar situation involves an actor standing next to a seated actor. If the camera's frame needs to include the standing actor, then the frame line might be too high to allow the mic to pick up the seated actor properly. You have a couple of options. Assuming that both actors are wearing backup lavs, let's start with boom possibilities. You can try to position the boom to cover the standing actor and cue the seated actor from here. It may not be optimal positioning, but the boom can't break the frame line. You might consider bringing in a separate boom, especially if the standing actor walks in or out of the scene. Finally, you can try booming the standing actor and using a plant mic for the seated actor. Again, every scene is different. Experiment! Use what you know to help figure out the best mic placement.

Good boom operators are calm under fire. They know their place. They are pleasant, but not overly chatty. They are confident, but not cocky. Most important, they are alert. No one should ask where the boom operator is, because they are always standing by, paying attention. When changes are being made to the blocking of a scene, their Spidey senses tingle.

CHAPTER EXERCISE When working with a boom pole, nothing beats experience. Get a microphone on a pole and play with it. Play, play, play! Tape a flashlight to the end of the microphone. The beam of light will give you a visual representation of what the microphone's pickup pattern will be as you position the boom. A Maglite works best as you can focus the light to a narrow beam. Practice with the flashlight by following an actor or cueing between two actors to give you a sense of what positions and techniques work. Just because you can see the mic near the actors clearly doesn't mean that the microphone can hear what the actors are saying clearly.

CHAPTER 6

LAV TECHNIQUES

Lavalier microphones have their place in fieldwork. While some sound mixers might argue that their place is stored in a case somewhere and never used, the reality is they are great problem-solvers and very helpful tools. When wielded properly, a lav can offer great usable audio. While a lot of attention has been given to the boom mic, lavs are used every day for ENG work and provide nearly all of the audio for newscasts, news magazine shows like *Dateline*, game shows, reality shows, sit-down interviews, and major feature films. No matter what type of fieldwork you end up doing, you will use lav mics.

"Just slap a lav on them" is often heard from a shooter or producer in video production. Usually, they are looking for an "easy" way to capture sound, but not the best way. This is equivalent to asking a DP to just shoot everything as a close-up. And don't be lazy, either! Resist the urge to throw lavs on everyone to avoid running a boom pole.

Lavs are a necessary evil in location sound. In some cases, such as presentations, reporting, and interviews, they are the best solution. In dramatic productions lavs can be a thorn in your side. The reason for this is that lavs sound the best when they are placed on the outside of the clothes in the center of the chest. However, in dramatic productions, the lav needs to be hidden from the camera. This introduces a world of challenges including clothing noise and muffled sound. Here are some tips and tricks for getting the best sound with lavs.

LAV PERSPECTIVES

Lavs give a "close" perspective. They do not have the same quality or natural sound as a boom and can make the shot sound claustrophobic. The advantage of lav mics is that they help isolate the voice from the background. This is acceptable for ENG work, but not as useful for dramatic productions where the dialog is expected to sound natural. Placing a lav mic on the talent gets the microphone the absolute closest that it can be, but there are drawbacks when the microphone is this close. Lavs are too perfect and isolated. They don't sound natural. For features and episodic television, tracks with lavs will almost always need to be treated in postproduction. A boom will give a much more natural sound that may only need little treatment in post.

An open mic, such as a boom, can help fill in the sound of a room when using lavs as the primary mics. Some lavs blend well with different types of boom mics, but there is no such thing as a perfect match between a lav and a boom. For event coverage, such as live courtroom hearings, an open boom can help the audio sound more natural and can be used to pick up anyone who doesn't have a microphone. Of course, off-mic speaking will sound off-mic, but with live coverage anything can happen and the audience understands the news-style reporting. Open mics can be helpful in press conferences. A press box is used to split the podium mic or mics to the various news organizations. However, reporters may ask questions in random order without using a community microphone. You can use a boom mic to cover this audio. Again, these questions will sound distant, but it's better to have some audio rather than no audio at all.

My point of view during a press conference with the late Michael Jackson as I use a boom pole to capture random questions from the horde of reporters.

In some cases, lavs can be the best solution for extremely noisy locations. They can also be used to record a guide track for post. Lavs are also good solutions for locations that are difficult or impossible to boom, such as basements, tight spaceship corridors, or other sets with low ceilings. Steadicam shots that follow the action can also be challenging to boom.

However, you should try to boom before pulling out the lavs, or use lavs on the talent as a backup.

Lavs are generally omnidirectional and can act as a PZM/boundary mic using the talent's chest as the soundboard. Placing the lav lower on the actor's chest can help reduce the booming in-your-face sound and give the mic more openness. Low cuts can be used to help roll off lower frequencies on lavs that are placed on excessively bassy chests. Sometimes, you can lose the sterile effect by using the lav on another actor during dialog. For example, if two actors are positioned close together during a dialog exchange, you can use Actor #2's lav to pick up the dialog from Actor #1 and vice versa. The result can be less close sounding and more natural. This can also be useful in scenarios where the other person isn't wearing a lav (covert operations, impromptu interviews, comments from bystanders, etc.).

ACOUSTICAL CHALLENGES WITH LAVALIERS

When you place a lav on an actor's chest, you may form *acoustic shadows*. An acoustic shadow is similar to a light shadow. An object blocks the source of energy, which reduces the energy beyond the object. Placing a microphone on an actor's chest creates an acoustic shadow originating from his chin. The sound waves do not reach the lav directly. As a result, the voice will sound duller and flatter than if the lav is in direct sight of the mouth. If the lav is placed too close to the neck, the mic will sound muddy and artificially bass-heavy. If the mic is too far from the mouth, the mic can sound thin and weak.

Another challenge with lavs is when the actor turns his head to the left, right, or up. Any of these directions can cause dialog to fall off-mic. If the actor looks down at his chest, his dialog will sound like the "voice of God" as he will be speaking directly into the microphone. Hard surfaces can create harsh slap-back or echoes if the talent leans over these surfaces while wearing a lav. If the surface is out of the camera's view, such as a podium, place fabric or other absorbent material on it to reduce this effect.

HIDING/BURYING LAVS

Anytime you bury a lav under clothes, you will muffle the sound. This is because the higher frequencies are weaker than lower frequencies and are easily absorbed by the clothes. The same is true when using foam windscreens; however the foam windscreens are not nearly as dense and the reduction is hardly noticeable. Hiding lavs under clothing results in a noticeable loss of sibilance.

The sibilance range is 6KHz – 10KHz, with 8KHz the most prominent frequency. To correct this loss of sibilance, some lavs like the TRAM TR50 will have an increase in the sibilance frequencies to bring presence back to the voice.

3:1 RULE

While there is usually only one boom mic on the set, it is very common for multiple lavs to be used at the same time. This can cause phase cancellation issues. Phase cancellation sounds hollow and unpleasant. You can move mics apart to correct this, but since the lavs are mounted to the talent, you would have to move the talent as well. This is rarely an option, as it will affect blocking and shot composition. Instead of moving the talent, use the 3:1 rule. This rule states that an active mic should be at least three times louder than other mics in close proximity. In other words, decrease the level of inactive mics. For example, if Channel 1 is the active mic and the fader is at 75%, turn the inactive mics on Channel 2 and Channel 3 down to 25%. This is a failsafe method to avoid phasing problems.

LAV PLACEMENT

Lavs placed on the side the talent faces toward

The sweet spot for a lav is dead center on the sternum. The majority of the time, the center of the chest is the best placement; however, if the talent will be talking to someone on his left the entire time (for example, a guest on the *Tonight Show*), you'll get the best results by placing the lav on the talent's left side. This way, when the talent turns his head to talk, he will be on-mic. The same would be true for an actor who might be talking while looking over her shoulder or leaning her head outside of a window. Just because the sweet spot is the center of the chest, doesn't mean that it's *always* the best choice for placement. Choose a position that works best for the scene.

The way to find the best mic placement for a lav is to experiment. Unfortunately, most productions don't have time for you to experiment. You'll be lucky if they allow you to change mic placement once or twice. The first time, they'll give you a dirty look. The second time, they'll growl at you. The third time, they'll probably blow you off and give you the classic "we'll fix it in post" remark. So, it's your job to pay attention to everything that could affect your mic placement before you approach the talent.

Start with an understanding of the scene's blocking. This would include where the actors will be facing while delivering their lines. Get as much information as possible before making your decision on lav placement and mounting. You might only get one shot at it. When you need to wire talent, be sure to inform the 1st AD so that he can plan a few minutes for you to do your job.

Performances during blocking will usually be at a normal level. Most actors will hold back on their performances and save their energy during the take. This could mean that their performances will be significantly quieter than during blocking for dramatic love scenes and significantly louder than blocking during intense arguments or action sequences. Anticipate necessary adjustments for the actual take.

DOUBLE MIKING

Double miking is a lav technique in which the talent is wired with two lavaliers on the same tie bar. The purpose of this technique is redundancy during live broadcasts. Only one lav will be used; however, should that lav fail, the sound mixer would switch to the backup lav. If the talent were miked with a wireless system, this technique would require two transmitters and two receivers, one for each lav.

Double lav tie bar

PEOPLE SKILLS

No matter how you look at it, when you are wiring someone up, you are invading her personal space. A simple smile can help make the invasion a little more pleasant. Try to avoid excessive conversation. For starters, most conversations happen at a distance of two to three feet. Any conversation you have with the talent will be happening at less than a foot, which will make the interaction awkward. Besides, the talent is probably focusing on their lines or still a little shell-shocked from being on TV. Be polite and avoid telling jokes (this is very hard for me!).

When you approach the talent, introduce yourself as the sound mixer (boom operator, utility, whatever) and let them know that you are going to be miking them up. If clothing needs to be moved, removed, or otherwise navigated through, be sure to tell them before you start handling their wardrobe. This will disarm them. Most professionals are used to this process. I say most, because you do run into the occasional actor or correspondent who seems to think that there is a way to mike them up through fairy dust or some other non-physical contact. When working with nonprofessionals, remember that they probably have never done this before and the process might be a bit alarming.

Spend extra care with children who might be a little frightened at the whole ordeal of being wired. Speak slowly and friendly and if you have to navigate through their wardrobe with your hands do so in the presence of a parent or legal guardian. Obviously, tact needs to be used when mounting a lav on actors of the opposite sex, even more so when they are underage. Always have a parent or other crewmember supervise your activity with a minor. This will avoid any legal problems should an uncomfortable actor make an accusation.

CLOTHING NOISE

The greatest challenge with lavs is clothing noise. This is usually not an issue when mounting the lav on the outside of the clothes, but when a lav is hidden underneath, all sorts of problems are introduced. There are two types of clothing noise: contact noise and clothing movement.

Contact Noise

Clothes or costume pieces physically rubbing against the mic or mic cable cause contact noise. To fix this, use special mounts that shield the lav from rubbing against them and tape down the mic cable so that it doesn't transmit contact noise to the mic. Taping down loose items that might rub against the mic will also reduce contact noise. The talent should be aware of folding their arms when wearing a lav. This will create clothing rustle, muffled sound, and possibly cause the lav's mount to come loose. Patting the chest and hugging during dialog can also create problems for lavs.

Clothing Movement

Clothes or costume pieces physically rubbing against itself causes clothing movement. To prevent clothing movement, use Static Guard or water to loosen stiff fabrics. Always get permission from the wardrobe department before altering the costume. Certain types of fabrics, such as synthetics, create more contact noise than others. Ask the wardrobe department if they can use natural cloths over their noisy artificial alternatives (corduroy, rayon, vinyl, and polyester).

Jewelry, which can create intermittent and sometimes unidentifiable sounds, is another issue that falls into the clothing-movement category. Necklaces drape down to the center of the chest, right over the optimal lav position. If an actor's character wears noisy jewelry (think Mr. T's character B. A. Baracus in *The A-Team*), ask the costume department if they can supply alternatives such as rubber or plastic versions. Rubber would be better as plastic can still make noise. You never know unless you ask!

If possible, ask actors to pause dialog delivery while leaning over objects or performing actions that might cause excessive clothing noise. Another way to reduce either type of clothing noise is to check the talent's lav and costume regularly. Body moisture, movement, humidity, and excessive temperatures will cause taped rigs to lose their grip. Also, actors and wardrobe personnel will constantly adjust wardrobes. This can cause mics to fall out of their position or become loose.

STRAIN RELIEF

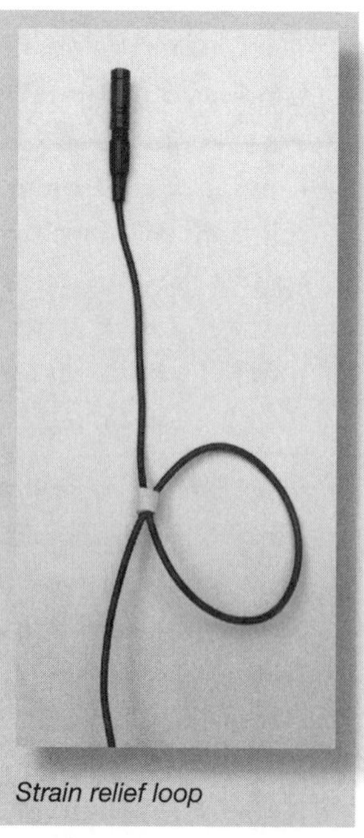
Strain relief loop

Lavs always need strain relief to protect the mic and to reduce handling noise. A piece of gaffer tape, dental floss, or string can be used to hold the cable in place. There are also several wiring tricks that you can use with various mounting accessories. The goal is to allow the cable to move if tugged on, so the loop should be loose.

The design of the lav's cable is very important. The life of a lav is quickly ended if the cable becomes separated from the capsule. Sometimes this can be repaired, but the repair would be so costly that buying a new lav might be a better choice. Stiffer cables might protect against this, but will introduce more contact noise. Other cable issues, like cuts and connector problems, can be repaired in the field.

The Lav Bullet is a handy tool for quickly running lav cables under clothing. This eliminates the mutual embarrassment out of reaching underneath the talent's clothes. They're a bit on the pricy side (just shy of $40). A homemade solution is a weighted phone plug that attaches to the lav connector with a small strip of gaffer tape. The idea is to let gravity do the work. Any weighted object that is small enough to navigate under the clothes without getting hung up will suffice. If these are not readily available, you're going to have to get your hands dirty. Professionalism is key here. If you're a practical joker or quit-witted, now is the time to bite your tongue. Breaking the ice with the talent should never be done while you have your hand up their shirt. Employ some tact and stay focused on your task. And for God's sake, use a breath mint!

Lav Bullet

LAV CONNECTORS

Lav mics can come with *connectors* to allow them to interface with specific transmitters. Others might have a standard XLR connector with a power supply for hard wiring. The new Rode

Lav has a patented "MiCon" connector that enables the user to purchase a connector for a specific transmitter. This makes their lavs more flexible in that you don't have to replace the lav if you change wireless systems. Be sure to have a convenient disconnect point so that the talent can easily unplug their microphones when they take a break or when they are finished.

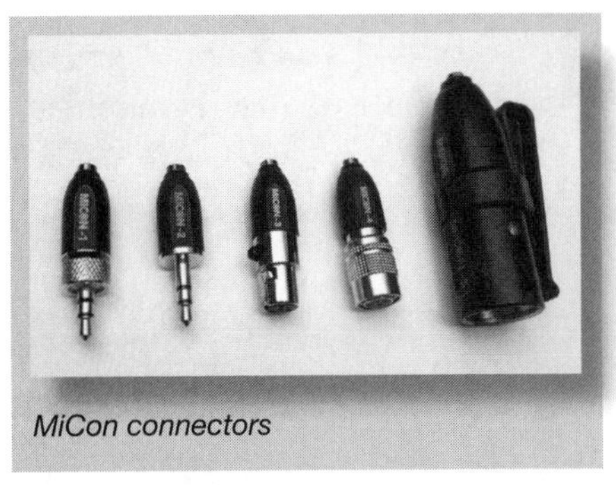
MiCon connectors

The connector is usually the weakest link in the chain and typically endures the most abuse. Although you might take good care of your gear, the life of the lav mic is often in the hands of the actors who wear them. Yanking and pulling on the cable is bound to happen. When this occurs, the connector is usually the victim of the strain. A useful trick is to loop the mic cable around a belt loop on the actor's pants before plugging the cable into the transmitter. Action sequences will require more secure mounting and strain relief for the cable.

It might be tempting to make your own adaptor cable for lavs that come prewired for a specific transmitter connector so that they can connect directly to your mixer's XLR input. However, lav microphones require a small voltage to operate (typically less than six volts). Wireless transmitters supply this voltage to the lav. Connectors that connect the lav directly to a mixer via an XLR connector will have a circuit to reduce the standard 48v phantom power down to the acceptable voltage. Others may have a power supply inside the XLR connector that is powered with a battery like the TRAM TR50. Check the manual of your microphone before attempting to make your own adaptor.

Here are some examples of lav connectors:

- XLR
- TA-3
- TA-4
- TA-5
- Lemo 3 Pin
- Hirose 4 Pin
- Mini-Plug
- Locking Mini-Plug

**Note: Not all locking mini-plug connectors use the same screw threads. Double-check the connector's specs before purchasing. Don't force the connector if it doesn't easily connect with your transmitter. This will only strip the threads.*

Lav cables and connectors should always be hidden from the camera's view, even if the lav is mounted outside of the clothes. You can run the cable under the clothes to the wireless transmitter or power supply. If the talent is wearing a jacket or coat, you can simply tuck the cable under the coat.

When hardwiring lavs, keep the power supply attached to the talent. The power supply can be clipped to a belt, tucked into a sock, or even stored in a pocket with the lav cable leading out to avoid damaging the cable. Provide strain relief when placing the power supply in the talent's pocket. For a stationary shot or a shot with limited movement, you can attach the power supply at the base of the leg. This can be done with gaffer tape around the sock, by putting the power supply inside the sock or by using a Velcro strap. If the power supply is not properly secured, you risk the chance of the lav's thin cable being yanked out if the talent walks away. With the power supply in this position, you can easily plug or unplug the XLR cable as needed.

COLORED LAVS

Most lavalier mics are black. This makes them stick out like a sore thumb when placed outside of white or light colored clothes. Audiences are used to seeing lavs on reporters and talk-show guests, so it's not the end of the world. Exposed lavs can be framed out of the shot on close-ups and are easily hidden from the audience in wide and medium shots.

In recent years, lavalier manufacturers have started to make different colored lav mics and windscreens to help hide the mic in plain sight. You can even color-coordinate mic caps and windscreens to match the talent's wardrobe. For example, on the reality show *Hell's Kitchen*, all of the contestants wear white chef-jackets. A trained eye can easily spot the white lav mics mounted just outside of the jackets. Most viewers, however, will not notice this. Colored lav mics are not required tools to have in your rental kit, but having some available might make the producers happy and, in return, make you their first call the next time they crew up for a show.

Some lav mic cables also come in different colors. If the mic cable is exposed (for whatever reason), you can try to paint the cable to match the clothes or background if used as a plant mic. Latex paint can be easily removed from the cable later without causing any damage. Never paint the grill of a lavalier. Not only will this affect the sound if the paint covers the holes in the grill, but it's possible that some of the paint may drip onto the diaphragm, which may destroy the microphone or significantly diminish its performance.

MOUNTING TECHNIQUES

You should never opt to let anyone other than a qualified member of the sound team mount a lav on the talent. This includes wardrobe personnel and experienced talent. The sound team knows all of the tricks of the trade and will always do the best job. Despite the best of intentions, the wardrobe department will be more focused on how the lav looks on the talent, not how the lav sounds. For the talent, it's a matter of perspective. It is very difficult to mount a microphone on yourself as your POV may limit your ability to see wrinkles caused by the mic cable or other visible indications of the mic. If it becomes necessary for wardrobe to disconnect the lavs from the transmitters, be sure to demonstrate how to remove the connector to prevent damaging the cable.

Mounting a directional lav is much more critical than an omnidirectional one. A directional lav needs to be pointed at the mouth. Take care so that the lav doesn't shift easily if it gets bumped. While the goal of positioning and placement of the lav is superior sound, realize that the lav must be invisible to the camera if hidden. If the lav is exposed to the camera, dress the cable of the lav so that it is presentable for the audience. There is no reason to have a sloppy lav cable appear on camera.

Lavs can be mounted just about anywhere. The ideal position is somewhere within a 12" radius of the mouth. Here are some ideas for locations:

- Inside collar
- Center button strip
- Under shirt
- Under coat
- On the ear
- Hair
- Inside shirt pocket (with inside hole cut for cable)
- Under collar
- Lapel
- Chest
- Neck of T-shirt
- Hat brim
- Sunglasses/Eyeglasses

Here are some common and crafty mounting techniques:

The cable loop held under the tie bar clip and a piece of gaffer tape holding the cable in place

Tie bar loop/"J" loop

Tie Bar Loop

This is the most popular lav mounting technique and is used for mounting a lav in a visible position outside of the clothes. The loop is sometimes referred to as a "J loop" because the cable is looped in the shape of a J and held under the tie-bar clip.

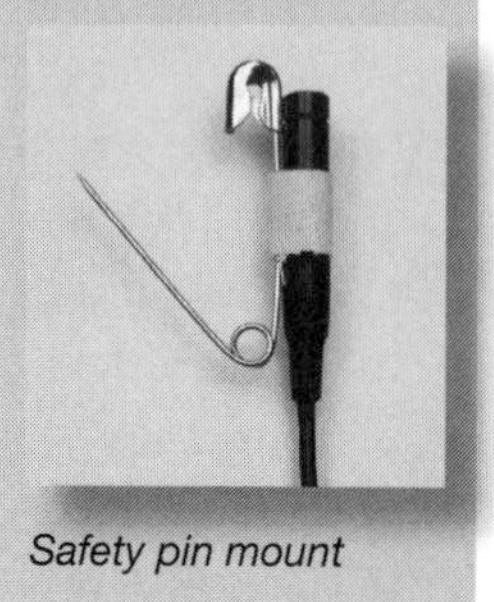
Safety pin mount

Safety Pin Mount

Top-address lavs can be easily taped to the side of a safety pin for mounting inside and underneath clothing.

Tape Triangle/Tape Football

Sandwiching a top-address lav between two tape triangles shaped like paper footballs will allow the lav to be fastened securely between layers of clothes and reduce clothing noise. Tape triangles can lose their stickiness with body moisture and humidity. Safety pins can help hold them into place.

Tape triangle before (left) and after (right)

Flat Mount

Use a 2" square of gaffer tape. Place the lav in the center of the square on the sticky side with the mic element facing away from the tape. Mount the square inside of the talent's shirt in the center of the chest area. The shirt will serve as a windscreen. Be sure to smooth out the wrinkles in the shirt that might be caused by the tape underneath. This method works best with cotton-based clothes.

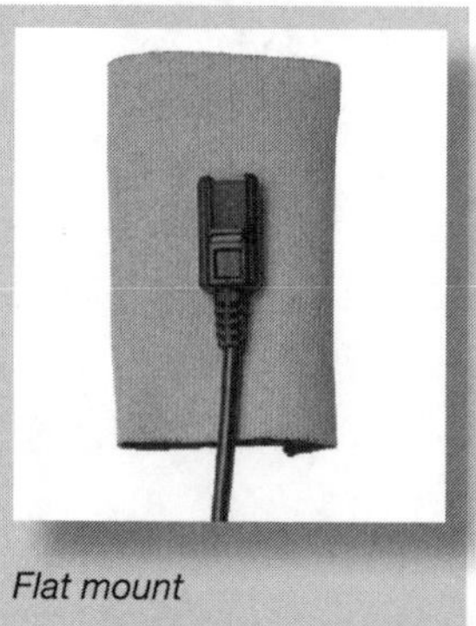
Flat mount

TRAM Mic Cage

Side-address lavs such as the TRAM TR50 should be mounted so that the diaphragm is not blocked. Tape triangles will cover the diaphragm and reduce the functionality of the mic. The TRAM Mic Cage is specifically made for the TRAM TR50. This mount has two bars on either side of the lav that help protect the mic from contact noise. The disc can be taped down or fastened with the optional vampire clip version.

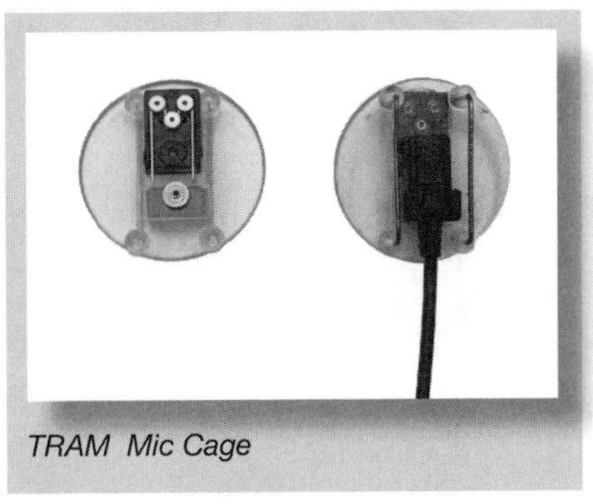

TRAM Mic Cage

Ink Pen Mount

For the spy inside just dying to use more covert methods, a hollow ink pen can serve as a perfect mounting tool to place the mic outside of the clothes. The pen cap is pointed directly at the mouth with a top-address lav inside.

Ink pen mount

Placket Mount

The placket is the front strip of buttons on a dress shirt. A lav can be mounted inside this strip between the buttons with a tape triangle or vampire clip (also called a viper clip).

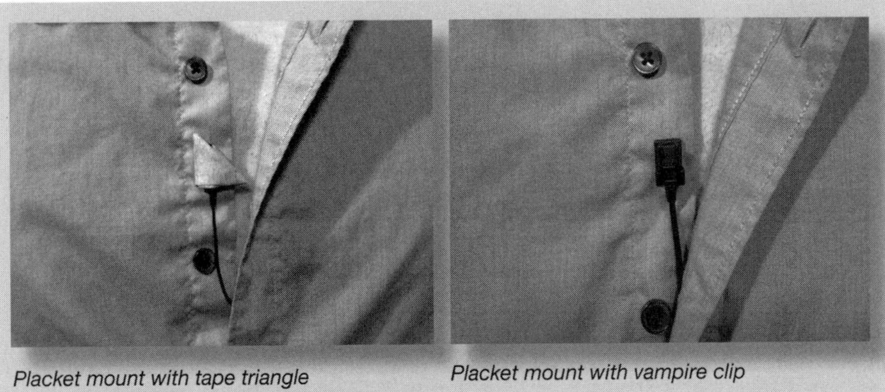

Placket mount with tape triangle

Placket mount with vampire clip

Pin Mic

Pin mics can be camouflaged easily and eliminate clothing noise completely. Rode pin mics come with different color caps. These caps can be painted or hidden.

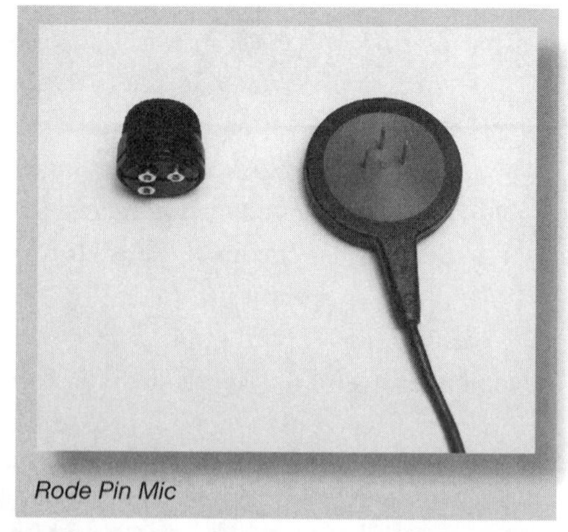

Rode Pin Mic

Chest Mounts

Mounting the lav directly on the chest works well with men who have large pectoral muscles. This allows the mic to be nestled away safely and protects the mic from clothes rubbing against it. Special adhesives like Moleskin, Transpore Surgical Tape by 3M, Topstick toupee tape, and Band-Aids will adhere to skin better than gaffer tape. Be sure to prep the skin with an alcohol wipe to remove oils, dirt, and sweat. This will give the adhesive a clean area to stick. Oils and sweat can cause adhesives to lose their stickiness, so you might need to re-clean the area in between takes and replace the adhesive. A mic cage can also help prevent clothing noise.

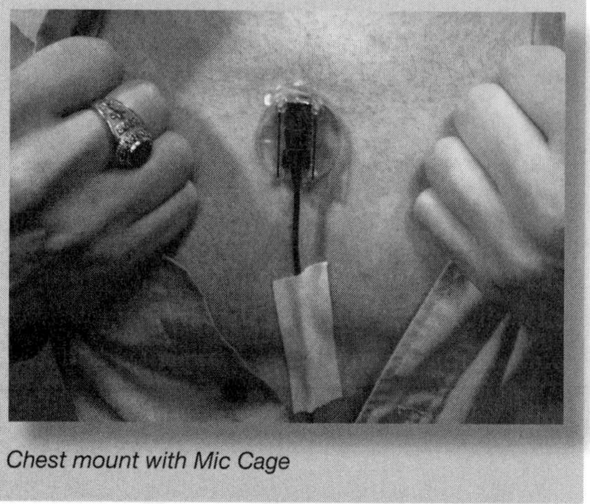

Chest mount with Mic Cage

Bra Mounts

A woman's cleavage provides the ultimate protection against contact noise. The lav can be mounted to the shirt or bra with a vampire clip and pointed toward the chest. A loop around the center bra strap will help keep the mic and cable in place and provide strain relief. Less-gifted females may require additional protection against contact noise and may benefit from a tape triangle or mic cage. If a female is uncomfortable with allowing you to place the lav on her chest, you can show her how to mount the mic and let her do it on her own in private.

Skin Mounts

Lav wires can be run down the bodies of nearly naked actors using makeup and tape to hold them in place. The lavs themselves can be placed in bikini tops or hidden on necklaces. This might work for long shots, but when the camera moves in closer, you'll need to switch to a boom to cover the dialog.

Hair, Hat, and Eyeglass Placements

Placing the lav in the actor's hair is almost exclusively done in theatre. It works well in theatre as the audience is at a distance and the lav is not noticeable. On camera, the lavs can be very easy to spot. In addition, the only place to run the lav cable is down the neck, which is easily exposed to the camera if the actor turns or the camera moves around the actor. It is, however, an option that you might want to keep in mind if you've exhausted all other resources. When placed in the actor's hair, the sound of the lav will be thinner than when placed on the actor's chest. Some sound mixers will place a mic in the brim of a hat or even on the side of a pair of eyeglasses. The challenge is how to hide the cable coming down the talent's neck. If it's a locked-off shot and the talent is perfectly still, you might get away with it. However, in most film and television productions, there is movement — either from the talent or the camera. This is especially difficult if there is more than one camera. Keep this trick in your mental toolbox. It might help you out someday.

Helmets/Masks

In some scenes, an actor may be wearing an astronaut's helmet or a mask that may make the dialog difficult to cover with a boom. In these cases, you can mount a lav inside the helmet or mask to try to pick up the dialog. More than likely, this will be a guide track for ADR, but in some cases the dialog might sound natural from this perspective. Experiment and see what you come up with.

MOUNTING ACCESSORIES

When you are ready to mount the lav, have all of your supplies with you as you approach the talent. You don't want to start undressing the talent and run cables everywhere and then realize you need to run back to your cart to get some gaffer tape. A small tackle box can hold all of the necessary mounting supplies that you'll need. At minimum, have extra strips of gaffer tape with you. You can even place the strips on your arms or pant legs to keep them out of the way. Fishing vests or camera vests can make for handy apparel when working on a set. But, be warned, you will be mocked by crewmembers who will probably take pics of you and post them on Facebook. It's your choice, but I warn you not to underestimate the power of social media.

Mounting accessories can be purchased directly from the manufacturer or improvised using common household items à la MacGyver. TRAM microphones seem to have more mounting accessories than any other lav manufacturer.

Here's a list of mounting accessories to include in your kit:

- Topstick
- Transpore
- Gaffer Tape
- Rubber Bands
- Lav Bullet
- Mic Cage
- Vampire Clips
- String
- Moleskin
- Band-Aids
- Orthodontic Rubber Bands
- Safety Pins
- Condoms
- Tie Bars
- Dental Floss
- Wireless Pouches

Lav mounting accessories

Lav adjustments between shots might be necessary, so be sure to keep an eye out for this. Hopefully, wardrobe will be looking for this as well. Check lav placement often to ensure that the mount is secure and that the fastening tape has not succumbed to moisture from body sweat. Unfortunately, lavs take a lot of abuse and are subject to all kinds of sweat and body funk. The Sanken COS-11D features a water-resistant front-mesh screen. When you have to make an adjustment, be fast and efficient in case the director wants to go again right away.

Working with lavs takes practice and creativity. There will always be curveballs thrown at you (such as an actress in a bikini or an actor in a wet suit). Understanding lav placement and having a good bag of mounting accessories will help prepare you for whatever challenge you face. Take time to practice and perfect the craft of placing and mounting lav mics.

Only allow a member of the sound team to remove lavs from the talent. The mounting techniques can have wires running throughout the costume using safety pins and other fasteners that can rip the costume. Also, the microphones and transmitters are expensive and can get damaged. No one will respect your gear the same way that you will. Lavs that get damaged by the talent or other production situations are the financial responsibility of the production. Their insurance should cover the replacement cost.

When rolling up lav mics for storage, hold the cable a couple of inches below the capsule and start there. Starting at the connector end allows the mic to dangle and bump into things that could damage the mic. Always store lavs in their cases. This will keep them safe and out of the way so that they're less likely to get tangled up together or with other gear.

WIND PROTECTION

Windscreens are a must when working outdoors. In some cases, a windscreen might be a good choice indoors as well. Try to have the talent's back to the wind in extremely windy situations to avoid wind noise whenever possible. Lav Furries, metal mesh windscreens, and foam windscreens protect from wind and air movement. Each type has its strengths and weaknesses. Furries give the best protection, but at the expense of looking like the talent is being attacked by a small forest creature. These aren't practical for dramatic productions. Windscreens may be necessary when the lav is buried under thin clothing that allows air movement to hit the mic. Rycote's Undercovers are disposable windscreen mounts that affix the lav to clothing and offer wind protection. Overcovers are a similar product, but have a small furry.

Most foam windscreens are merely pop filters and not very effective against wind noise. In high-wind situations, consider burying the lav under a coat or shirt to help prevent distortion caused by the wind. The sound will be slightly muffled but better than the awful wind rumble. Less might be more with heavier coats. Avoid burying the lav too far from the surface. Makeshift wind covers can be made from the tips of cotton gloves, cheesecloth, and dense foam.

CHAPTER EXERCISE Find a friend with an eclectic wardrobe (think Elton John) and practice mounting lavs on different outfits. Record and listen to the results. Keep in mind: on location your time will be limited. Now, go for a speed round and try to lav your friend in half the time. If the friend is your significant other, try this exercise in low lighting with romantic music. Tell your partner that this exercise will help you advance in your career. Pair this exercise with an elegant dinner and a nice Chianti. You're welcome!

CHAPTER 7

WIRELESS SYSTEMS

A *wireless system* consists of a transmitter that uses radio waves to send a signal to a receiver. In location sound, the most common use for wireless systems is to send a signal from a microphone to a recorder or mixer. These instruments are referred to as wireless mics, radio mics, wireless, and wires. Another use for a wireless system is to send a signal from the recorder or mixer to an alternate source such as a headphone feed or a primary feed from a mixer to a camera. Let's first look at wireless microphone systems.

WHY USE WIRELESS MICS?

There are three reasons to use wireless mics:

Mobility

With a wireless mic, the actor is free to move around the set without being tethered by a microphone cable. In film work, the wireless mic is typically used as a backup mic and the boom is used to provide the primary audio. In ENG work, the wireless mic can be not only the primary source of audio, but, in some cases, the only source.

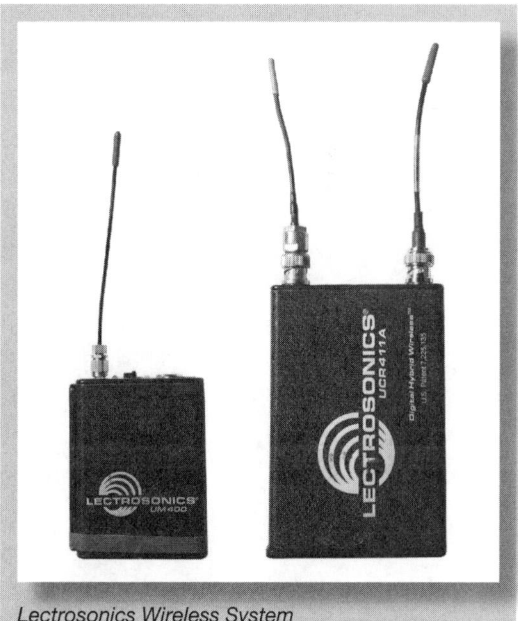

Lectrosonics Wireless System

Framing

Wide shots, locations with low ceilings, and other factors such as extreme distances may make booming impossible. Wireless systems bring the mic close to the actor without being seen by the camera.

Coverage

In some productions, such as reality shows, there are too many people to cover with one or even two boom mics. Wireless mics allow multiple actors to be recorded at the same time.

Now that we know the reason for wireless microphone systems, let's look at how they work.

RADIO WAVES

Wireless systems transmit by using radio waves. The radio frequencies used are in the megahertz range. Two main bandwidths are used in wireless systems: VHF and UHF.

VHF stands for "very high frequency." The full range for VHF is 30MHz – 300MHz; however, the part of this spectrum that the FCC (Federal Communications Commission) has reserved for wireless audio is limited to 150MHz – 216MHz.

UHF stands for "ultra high frequency." The full range for UHF is 300MHz – 3GHz. The FCC has reserved the 470MHz – 698MHz range for wireless audio. It should be noted that the UHF band used to include frequencies from 470MHz to 806MHz, but the 698MHz to 806MHz frequencies were excluded from this band and are now used for digital television transmission.

In the sound basics chapter we discussed how 1KHz represents a sound wave that repeats 1,000 times per second. A radio wave of 500MHz repeats 500,000,000 times per second. These frequencies are far above the range of human hearing, but they operate in the same fashion that sound waves do. Like sound waves, they are subject to reverberation, shadowing, and transmission through objects.

Sony Wireless System

The UHF band is preferred for professional wireless systems due to its higher output level of up to 250mW. This is up to five times stronger than VHF's maximum output level of 50mW. However, most UHF systems output at 100mW to help save battery life. VHF systems are less expensive and more commonly used for wedding videography, theatrical stage productions, DJ-ing, and houses of worship. For these applications, VHF systems can provide good results. Currently, the FCC has regulated the legal maximum output level of a wireless system to 50mW without a permit. Check the following link for more information as the regulations are subject to change: *www.fcc.gov/encyclopedia/wireless-microphones*

UHF signals are far more robust than VHF signals. Years ago, VHF wireless units were used more commonly in professional productions. I used to freelance for one company that had dozens of wireless units that the sound mixers would choose from when building their packages at the start of the day. It was always a race to see who got to the studio first to snatch up the UHF wireless units. If your call time was later in the morning, only the VHF units would be left. This meant that you were in for a rough day filled with dropouts (see below) and poor performance. Some of the sound mixers caught on to this race and would hide the UHF units in the equipment room or leave their packages built the night before along with a note that said something to the effect of "Touch this package and die!" Today, VHF units are not very common.

Radio waves, much like acoustic waves, can suffer from phase cancellation. Just as sound waves can bounce off surfaces and interact with other sound waves to increase or decrease the amplitude, radio waves act the same way. Phase cancellation in radio waves is known as a *dropout*. The *wavelengths* differ greatly between VHF and UHF. Wavelength is the distance a wave needs in order to complete one full wave cycle. A VHF wavelength measures between 4'5" and 6'5", but a UHF wavelength measures between 1'5 and 2'. If you experience dropouts due to phase cancellation of the ra waves, you will need to move a VHF receiver several feet in order to f stronger signal. With a UHF receiver, you will only have to move th a few inches to a foot to stop the phase cancellation. nin

Interference can occur through *intermodulation* of frequenc two your wireless systems. In effect, intermodulation is a combina *image* or (or more) frequencies to create a third frequency called a *freq* not occur *false frequency*. It is important to note that intermodulation when only two wireless systems are used, because intermodulation requires the combining of two or more frequencies.

While the science and mathematics behind intermodulation is far above most sound mixers' comprehension (myself included), the formula for calculating and avoiding the problem is quite simple. When working with more than two frequencies, simply subtract the lower frequency from the higher frequency. This number is now added to the higher frequency and subtracted from the lower frequency. For example, if Transmitter "A" is transmitting at 550MHz and Transmitter "B" is transmitting at 600MHz, the difference is 50MHz. By adding this number to Transmitter "B" (the higher frequency) and subtracting this number from Transmitter "A" (the lower frequency), you will arrive at intermodulation frequencies of 500MHz and 650MHz. Using a third transmitter at either of the two intermodulation frequencies will cause all kinds of problems.

The example above uses whole numbers and is relatively easy to understand; however, when working with eight wireless systems that have non-whole numbers, the math can be overwhelming. Manufacturers, such as Lectrosonics, make this task easier with frequency coordination charts. In addition, RF coordination software is available to calculate usable frequencies between wireless systems from different manufacturers.

BLOCK 24

FREQ	SW SET	US TV CH
614.900	0,5	tv38
615.500	0,B	tv38
616.400	1,4	tv38
617.000	1,A	tv38
618.300	2,7	tv38
619.200	3,0	tv38
619.700	3,5	tv38
[illegible]0.500	3,D	tv39
[illegible].900	7,D	tv40
[illegible]100	9,3	tv40
[illegible]00	9,A	tv40
[illegible]	A,7	tv40
633.[illegible]	B,9	tv41
636.4[illegible]	C,2	tv41
638.700	D,C	tv41
[illegible]	F,3	tv42

BLOCK 25

FREQ	SW SET	US TV CH
640.500	0,5	tv42
641.100	0,B	tv42
642.000	1,4	tv42
642.600	1,A	tv42
643.900	2,7	tv42
644.800	3,0	tv43
645.300	3,5	tv43
646.100	3,D	tv43
652.500	7,D	tv44
654.700	9,3	tv44
655.400	9,A	tv44
656.700	A,7	tv45
658.500	B,9	tv45
659.400	C,2	tv45
662.000	D,C	tv45/46
664.300	F,3	tv46

Blocks 24 and 25 [illegible] the Lectrosonics Wireless Frequency Coordination Chart - Courtesy Of Lectro[illegible]nics, Inc. Used with permission.

These charts give blocks of frequencies along with compatible groups within those blocks. Having all your wireless systems within a specific block will help you avoid intermodulation interference. Keep in mind: while your wireless systems might use frequencies that are compatible, other systems near your location might use frequencies that cause interference.

Frequency agile wireless units allow you to tune the units to different frequencies. Some will even scan for available frequencies. Older wireless units were set to a fixed frequency, which meant if you wanted options in the field, you had to bring extra wireless units. Press conferences, sporting events, and other media-packed productions can quickly narrow your choices for usable frequencies. It's a wireless jungle out there! Scanners can make choosing an open frequency much easier. Today, wireless units are much more robust in both their audio quality and functionality.

When working on a set with a news crew or a behind-the-scenes production team, be sure to speak with the sound mixer to ask what wireless frequencies you can use without causing them grief. The same is true when working a concert or theatrical production. In any situation, remember that you are probably an unwelcome guest, so tread lightly. You are on someone else's turf and you should respect them. The goal is to find compatible frequencies so that you can both capture good audio.

Radio frequency interference (*RFI*) can be caused by sources outside of wireless systems. Electrical equipment, dimmers, motors, and light ballasts all create magnetic fields that can interfere with wireless systems. To make matters worse, radio-controlled camera systems that operate via remote control can also produce interference. This is where a frequency scanner comes in handy! Scan the location to find frequencies that are open.

The list of what causes RFI is long enough to suggest that it might be easier to explain what doesn't cause hits and dropouts! Here are just a few examples of things that can cause RFI:

- Metal Structures
- Engines
- Motors
- Cell Phones
- CB Radios
- Walkie-Talkies
- Fluorescent Lights
- Neon Lights
- Appliances
- Ballasts
- Airplanes
- Computers
- Hard Drives
- Speakers
- Garden Gnomes, Ouija Boards, and the phrase "I think this wireless is going to work out great!"

Don't be surprised if a frequency works in the morning, but then becomes unavailable after lunch. It only takes a short time using wireless systems before you will be convinced that there are unseen, dark forces working against you. If you have a lucky rabbit's foot, it wouldn't hurt to keep it on your sound cart at all times!

TRANSMITTERS

A *transmitter* is the device that sends the wireless signal to a receiver tuned to the same frequency. Most transmitters are connected to a lavalier and worn by the talent. These transmitters are called *body packs*.

The most common place to mount a body pack is in the small of the back of the talent. For some productions, seeing the body pack on camera is acceptable. However, for dramatic productions, you'll need to hide the body pack. Understanding the action of a scene will help you decide where to hide the transmitter. If a doctor will be taking off her lab coat, then you'll need to mount the transmitter under her shirt so that it remains hidden when the coat comes off.

Some body packs have a removable belt clip that allows them to fit in a transmitter pouch. These pouches have a Velcro strap that secures the transmitter in place and makes battery changes easy. When planning the location of a transmitter, consider the action of the scene.

You can place the body pack inside the wireless pouch and wrap the strap around the waist, underneath the shirt. You can also place the strap around a thigh or an ankle. The ankle is a tricky spot to place a wireless pouch, since the transmitter will rest against the bone. Slipping a small piece of foam inside the pouch will make this more comfortable for the actor. It's likely that the antenna will hang down past the hem of the pants and may be visible on camera. To correct this, you'll need to turn the pouch upside down. Strain relief for the mic cable is important, because the weight of the transmitter

Wireless pouch

may pull down on the cable. Be extra careful with the pouch's strap so that the transmitter doesn't fall out.

If the talent will be performing a stunt with a transmitter, be sure to protect him from hurting himself and damaging the transmitter. Transmitters might need to be secured if the talent will be overly active or very physical during the scene. Secure the straps around the actor (waist, leg, ankle, etc.) so that the straps are nice and snug. Make sure the talent is comfortable, but not too comfortable, because the weight of the transmitter will eventually start to pull on the strap, necessitating adjustments.

The body pack can also be placed in a pants pocket. With the wardrobe department's permission, you can cut a small hole inside the pocket to allow the wire to be passed through and up the shirt for placement. In any case, make sure the body pack is not visible. This includes bumps in the clothing where the body pack is hidden. Remove cell phones from actors wearing transmitters. Putting the cell on vibrate doesn't solve anything as it will still be receiving and sending a wireless signal that can seriously interfere with the transmitter.

Human beings are large sacks of water that can absorb some of the wireless signal. Avoid placing the transmitter directly against the skin as this may weaken its signal. Instead, try to provide a barrier between the transmitter and the skin, such as gaffer tape, clothing, or, in extreme cases (like a sweaty hockey player), you can wrap the transmitter in a condom or use a water-resistant transmitter like the Lectrosonics MM400C. And, for the record, a lubricated condom will not improve reception; it will only make things sticky!

For the best signal transmission, keep the antenna straight. You can achieve this by attaching one end of a rubber band to the end of the antenna, and the other to the clothes or costume. This will allow the actor to reach, bend over, or stand up freely. When deciding where to put the transmitter's excess microphone cable, remember the Ghostbusters' rule: Don't cross the streams! Of course, we're talking about crossing the microphone cable and the antenna. As Egon strongly warned: "That would be bad." While all life as you know it will not stop instantaneously with every molecule in your body exploding at the speed of light, the reality is that you will seriously decrease the range of your signal and introduce all sorts of ghostly problems. Don't cross the antenna and the microphone cable!

Transmitter antennas can get roughed up on a set and may need to be replaced. Some models have removable antennas that make this easy to do. Others have fixed antennas that will need to be sent to the manufacturer's authorized repair shop to be replaced. Attempting to replace a fixed antenna on your own may negate the manufacturer's warranty.

When setting a transmitter level, you can start by testing the mic with your own voice. Position the lav on your body in the same place where it will be worn on the actor. Speak in a loud voice to establish a parameter of when the mic will distort. In most cases a green LED will indicate when the transmitter is receiving a signal from the microphone while a red LED will indicate when that signal is overloading the transmitter. Adjust the transmitter's sensitivity so that the red LED does not illuminate. Next, place the lav on the actor and have him perform the same test. If the actor needs to raise his voice during the scene, have him speak at that level so that you can adjust the transmitter properly.

The purpose of testing the mic before wiring the actor is to ensure that both the lav and transmitter are working. Testing the actor's voice is necessary because his voice will be different than yours. Often, your test will have provided the same level as the actor's, so you won't need to make further adjustments. The less time you have to spend wiring up the actor, the happier the actor will be and the faster the production can move along.

Avoid telling the talent where the mute switch is located on the transmitter. If they are informed about this switch, they will be more likely to use it. This can cause a panic on the set if they mute their transmitters and forget to turn them back on. Newer wireless receivers have an LED to indicate if the transmitter is muted. This is a very useful tool for troubleshooting. Be respectful of private conversations, especially if the mics are being sent to the Comtek sets of other crewmembers. When an actor engages in a private, sensitive conversation, be sure to mute his channel. I've heard many interesting conversations over the years. And no, I'm not going to repeat any of them....

PLUG-ON TRANSMITTERS/CUBES

Another type of transmitter is the *plug-on transmitter*, sometimes called a *cube*. These transmitters can be used to make a handheld mic a wireless microphone. They can also be used on a boom mic, if the transmitter provides 48v phantom power. If the plug-on transmitter does not supply phantom power, you will need to use a boom mic that has an internal phantom power supply like the Rode NTG-2. In general, you should always hardwire a boom mic, but there are some cases that call for a wireless boom. Some sound mixers will use wireless booms for every shot, but run the risk of hits and dropouts. Do so at your own risk.

Sony Plug-On Transmitter

COMPANDING

Companding is the process of compressing and expanding an audio signal in a wireless system. The term is a combination of the words "compressing" and "expanding." The compression stage happens in the transmitter and the expansion stage happens in the receiver. The signal-to-noise ratio of an RF transmitter is about 60 – 65dB, whereas an acceptable signal-to-noise ratio for professional audio is nearly double that amount. A companding circuit squeezes the audio down to the 60dB range for transmission and the expanding circuit brings the signal back up to the original range. This allows the audio signal to be sent via RF by using the least amount of bandwidth and reduces any unwanted noise picked up in the process.

Over the years, the technology used in companding has improved so that it is not very noticeable in the final audio; however, no technology is perfect. When setting the levels of the transmitter, take care to not overdrive the companding process. Digital wireless systems operate in an absolute range with no deviation and therefore do not use companding. This gives digital wireless systems superior sound quality over analog systems.

RECEIVERS

Receivers will accept any transmission on the frequency that they are tuned to. Matching transmitters and receivers may not be tuned to the same frequency. Never assume this. Always check and verify that the transmitter and receiver are using the same frequency. When working with multiple wireless systems, it's a good idea to color-code matching transmitters and receivers with colored gaffer tape.

It is possible to send the signal from a single transmitter to multiple receivers tuned to the same frequency, but you cannot successfully receive signals from multiple transmitters on a single receiver. Sending a signal to multiple receivers can be a useful trick when shooting multicam, reality shows, and remote-routing configurations (monitoring stations, backup recorders, etc.).

Diversity receivers have dual antennas placed at a distance greater than a quarter of the wavelength. Inside the receiver is a circuit that monitors the reception of both antennas. The circuit actively selects the antenna with the strongest signal and instantly switches to that antenna to avoid dropouts. Because of the physical size of UHF wavelengths and the distance between the two antennas, it is highly unlikely that phase cancellation will occur at both antennas at the same moment. This makes diversity systems far better protected from dropouts than non-diversity systems. For this reason, nearly all professional and prosumer receivers are diversity systems.

A true diversity wireless system will have two antennas and two radio modules inside the receiver. When a signal from one of the modules drops below a predefined threshold, the unit automatically switches to the other module. The switch is so fast that the signal is not affected and goes unnoticed.

Some transmitters and receivers allow you to select the type of output signal (mic or line level). Be sure to match the signal level of both the receiver and the device to which it is connected. Mismatching levels will result in overdriven or weak signals. Do not send phantom power to the receiver. Some units don't see the phantom power and are unaffected by the voltage. Other units, like the Sennheiser Evolution Series, don't like phantom power as its presence generates hiss and noise.

Here are some examples of wireless systems:

- Lectrosonics 100 Series
- Lectrosonics 400 Series
- Sennheiser Evolution G3 100 Series
- Sony UWP-V Series
- Zaxcom TRX900 Series

WIRELESS ANTENNAS

Wireless systems work best with a clear line of sight. This will help prevent dropouts. Set walls, actors, props, and other objects may interfere with this line of sight. Elevating the antennas above these obstacles will help improve reception. Antenna adjustments can make a big difference in signal reception. Avoid a large crowd of crewmembers or on-lookers that gather in front of your sound cart. This mass of water and potential consumer electronics may cause serious interference with your wireless microphones.

There are antennas on both the transmitter and the receiver. The transmitter uses a *whip antenna*, which is cut to a specific length for a frequency range. The length is 1/4 of the frequency's wavelength and is called a *1/4 wave* or *quarter-wave antenna*. Given the fact that wireless systems use UHF frequencies between 470MHz – 698MHz, the whip antennas will range from 4.5" to 6". Remote Audio sells uncut antennas called "Miracle Whips" that include a cutting guide and color-coded caps.

Corresponding wireless antennas between the transmitter and receiver should always preserve angle polarity. That is to say that the antennas should be at the same angle. When the antenna hangs vertically from the transmitter, the receiver's antenna should also be positioned vertically. When the transmitter's antenna is positioned horizontally, the receiver's antenna should also be positioned horizontally. Variation in angle polarity will cause a reduction and possible loss of the signal.

Most wireless systems can work up to several hundred feet away. Higher-end wireless systems boast a range of 1000 feet; however, for optimal performance the transmitter and receiver should be as close as possible. After 100 feet or so, you should probably start to sweat or at least use a special antenna to boost reception.

Yagi and *log-periodic dipole antennas* (*LPDA*) will increase the range of the wireless signal. Yagi antennas look like the old-style television antennas that littered the rooftops of houses well into the 1980s. LPDAs are often called a "shark fin" or "bat wing" because of their shape. Log-period antennas are also directional, which means that they can be adjusted to optimally reduce interference and improve signal gain. PSC's log-periodic antenna (UHF Periodic Antenna) has a gain of 4.5dB, which triples the transmission power. Audio Technica's ATW-A49S has 6dB of gain, which quadruples the transmission power. An antenna like the Lectrosonics SNA600 dipole is omnidirectional and provides about 3dB of gain. This will double the transmission power and provide roughly 20% more range. Newer helical antennas like the Shure

HA-8089 feature a spiral antenna that provides 14dB of gain and greater bandwidth than traditional antennas. They are considered by many to be the best type of antenna available and are becoming more popular with sound mixers. Antennas can feed multiple receivers. Some sound carts are outfitted with a pair of antennas to assist with distribution.

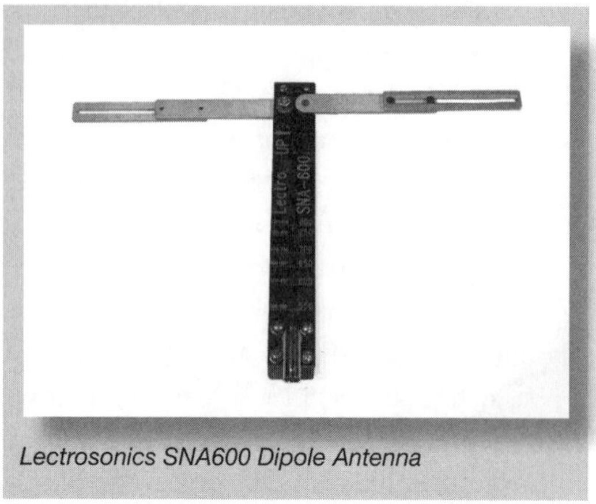
Lectrosonics SNA600 Dipole Antenna

The antenna is connected to the receiver with a coaxial cable like the RG58. Coax cable is heavily insulated and shielded, which effectively prevents interference. Shorter cable runs have less attenuation of the signal. A 100' coax cable at the top end of the UHF spectrum (700MHz) can attenuate your signal by as much as 17dBm. That reduction is nearly six times less than the original signal! At 100' low loss cable like RG8 will provide only one-third of the reduction of an RG58 cable at 100'. An increasingly popular choice is the PWS-S9046 cable, which outperforms RG58 in terms of less line loss.

In addition to loss of signal level, you also need to concern yourself with loss in higher frequencies. If you have to make an antenna cable run longer than 30', use a heavier cable like RG8 or consider moving the receiver closer to the transmitter. You will get better sound by running a longer microphone cable, rather than a long coax cable, to an antenna. Always try to keep the transmitter and receiver as close as possible. You can hide receivers on the set or just outside of a shot. Move the receivers during shots that allow you to get closer to the talent. Closer positioning will always give you an advantage. A utility person can carry the receiver during shots that require the actors to walk great distances. This puts the receiver closer to the action. In some cases, you can even mount the receiver to a camera dolly. Avoid using remote antennas that run long distances back to the sound cart. The distance will result in signal degradation.

ENG sound mixers really don't have much of a need for special antenna systems as all of their wireless systems are mounted inside of their sound bag.

In short, the wireless systems go where the sound mixer goes and the sound mixer is always close to the action. If you experience dropouts or interference, try repositioning yourself. Where you go, the antennas will go.

DIGITAL WIRELESS SYSTEMS

Digital wireless systems are far more reliable than analog systems. There is, however, a small issue of time delay. A digital wireless system has to convert an analog signal into a digital signal in order to transmit. Once the signal arrives at the receiver, it is converted from digital back to analog. It takes about 3.3 milliseconds to convert the signal from analog to digital and then back to analog. While this might seem like a big issue, it's hardly noticeable. However, when you mix a digital wireless signal with an analog signal, the timing difference may cause phasing issues or a noticeable delay. The workaround for this is to make sure that digital wireless signals are mixed or recorded to a separate track. This timing difference is similar to the effect of miking a source from two microphones at different distances (for example, using a lav on an actor along with an overhead boom mic at three feet away). Another solution is to put a 3-millisecond delay on analog sources, such as wired boom microphones and plant mics, via a digital mixer or recorder. This delay will realign the analog sources with the digital wireless systems effectively.

Lectrosonics Digital Hybrid Wireless System

Some of the newer digital wireless systems have backup digital recorders on the transmitters that can be used to salvage audio marred by dropouts or interference. If money is no object and you're looking for the best unit possible, you can't go wrong with a digital UHF diversity unit. Lectrosonics is considered to be one of the best manufacturers of wireless units and their products are found on nearly every film and television set around the world. ENG-grade wireless systems like the Sennheiser Evolution Series offer amazing sound at a third of the price.

BATTERIES

Batteries will affect the sound quality and radio signal of a wireless system. Always use fresh batteries in wireless units. When the battery level begins to decrease, so will the radio signal. Film productions have frequent breaks between shots that can allow for a quick battery change; however, live shots, interviews, and live events may not afford you the luxury of a battery change. If you need to use a wireless unit for a long period of time, replace the battery with a new one, even if it has 80% of life left.

If you are using a wireless system throughout the entire day, plan on changing the batteries around lunchtime. If the day goes long, you might need to change batteries again, but typically, you will go through two sets of batteries for each wireless unit in a given day. Extremely cold temperatures can quickly drain a battery's life. For long days in these temperatures, plan on bringing additional batteries.

Wireless systems will start to perform poorly when they begin to lose battery power. If your signal is getting weak, check the batteries immediately. Some wireless receivers will display an icon of the corresponding transmitter's battery power. This is very helpful when troubleshooting weak signals. If the battery level looks good, try moving the receiver closer to the transmitter or consider switching the frequency.

Lithium batteries can offer much longer life spans in a wireless unit. As a result they are more expensive, but offer less battery changes during production. On average, lithium batteries can last up to four times longer than standard batteries. The catch is that lithium batteries do not have a steady discharge curve. With other battery chemistries the signal discharges more evenly, allowing you to monitor the battery's life accurately. When a lithium battery reaches the end of its life, it dies fairly quickly. The battery level may show that it is fine and then die a half hour later. A lithium battery can be used over multiple days, making it difficult to track how much life it has left.

You can go broke using disposable batteries in wireless systems. Rechargeable batteries will save you money, but will still require constant changes. Some receivers can be powered externally. A battery distribution system will save you money and time on-set and can power all of your receivers and mixer from a single battery. Some cameras will have an auxiliary power jack that can be used to power receivers on the camera to save on battery changes, which will help keep down battery costs. Receivers and transmitters that do not have an externally-powered DC jack can be retrofitted with a dummy battery that converts to a DC cable.

WIRELESS HOPS

Audio can be sent to the camera via a wireless system called a *wireless hop*. The benefit of a wireless hop is that the shooter and sound mixer can work separately without a tether. The main drawback is that the signal is wireless and susceptible to common wireless problems like dropouts and hits. This is bad enough as it is, but to compound the problem further, there is no way for the sound mixer to monitor the signal reliably. Sure, you can mount a return wireless unit to the camera, provided that the shooter is willing to allow the extra weight and that the camera even has room. The main issue is that if you hear a hit or dropout, you won't know if it occurred going to the camera (primary signal) or coming from the camera (monitor signal).

Technically speaking, wireless hops are not a solid choice. Practically speaking, wireless hops are used every day and work fine. In some situations, the camera has to be free from a tether, but most of the time an ENG snake can be used. The decision should be left to you, the sound mixer; however, more often than not, the shooter will dictate whether or not to tether to sound.

To set up a wireless hop properly, first match the output of the mixer to the input of the transmitter for each channel. Some transmitters can receive mic or line level, but most transmitters need mic level. If no switch or menu option is available, then the unit is probably set to mic level. Check the transmitter's manual to verify this. Next, send tone from the mixer and adjust the transmitter so that it shows red on the indicator or meter, then back it down until the LED changes to green. Now, select the proper input for the camera's channel based on the output of the receiver. Always send line level when possible. Now, adjust the receiver's output making sure that the level is not distorted. Finally, adjust the input of the camera's channel so that it reads 0VU or -20dBFS. You'll need to do this setup for each channel being received.

Another problem with wireless hops is that they can eat into your battery budget fast! Plus, you'll have one more thing to remember to check throughout the day. If you're using a couple of wireless units for lavs as well as a wireless hop, you can easily run through thirty-two AA batteries each day! Think about it: You have two AA batteries in each transmitter and two AA batteries in each receiver. If you are using four wireless systems, sixteen batteries will need to be changed at least once in a full day.

USE WIRELESS SYSTEMS SPARINGLY

Modern wireless systems are far more reliable today than ever before. Unfortunately, wireless technology carries a host of problems. Systems that cost thousands of dollars can still experience interference and dropouts. While this might be few and far between, it only takes one hit to potentially ruin a take. Hardwire cables are more reliable and do not require batteries. Whenever possible, use hardwire cables over wireless systems. If a wireless system is used, it's a good idea to also use a hardwire boom mic for redundancy. With this redundancy, a boom mic can salvage a take if there is a hit or dropout on a wireless mic.

On the contrary, a wireless mic might make a perfect solution if you cannot track down an audio buzz or ground loop. These audio problems can arise with no logical explanation. The strangest audio problem I have ever faced was during a shoot with Eminem at the studio 54 Sound in Detroit. We were there to record a short but sweet "Thanks for this award/ sorry I couldn't be there" speech for some awards show. I showed up early, which is an understatement when working with Eminem. I had worked with him dozens of times and he never showed up on time. In fact, he was always at least four hours late! This was usually a blessing in disguise because shoots like this awards-show speech would only last about five or ten minutes, if that. My pay scale quickly turned from half-day rates to full-day rates because of his tardiness. Thanks, Eminem!

So, back at the studio, I showed up at noon and set up all the gear. A hardwire lav was tested and we toned up the camera. All was good. Then, we waited. We made good use of an arcade down the hall, caught up on business calls, and surfed the Internet. Around five o'clock, Eminem strolled into the studio and disappeared for about a half hour doing whatever multimillionaire rappers do. Finally, he walked in and sat down. I mounted the lav on him and put my headphones on.

For some reason, there was a horrible buzz in the audio. He sat only five feet from me and the mic cable was in the middle of the floor, far away from any power cables. I wasn't panicking at this point. I turned my attention to the camera to make sure that it was using battery power and disconnected the BNC cable leading to the video monitor. This didn't solve the problem. Next, I disconnected the mixer from the camera. The buzz was still there. I changed out the XLR cable and wired him with a different lav, but the buzz was still there.

Eminem began to grow impatient, despite the fact that all of this troubleshooting lasted less than two minutes. Now, I started panicking mildly. I plugged in my boom pole, appropriately named Old Faithful, and still heard the buzz! Finally, I switched to a wireless unit. Problem solved. Why? I have no clue. We speculated that someone in the building had turned on a nuclear generator of some sort, but we never knew for sure. When I got home I tested all of my gear and couldn't duplicate the buzz. I've done shoots in that same room since and the problem has never happened again. The point is, even when you follow all of the necessary steps with gear that works, things can still go wrong. In this case, the wireless mic provided better audio than the hardwire mic.

Wireless mics can be used for part of a scene, while the rest is covered with a boom mic. There will be a difference in audio (placement, perspective, consistency); however, it might be the only solution for a particular shot. Be sure to record ISO tracks of both the boom and lav, so that they can be mixed in post or if the sound designer chooses to use the lav for the entire shot. For example, if an actor delivers dialog in a car that pulls up to the camera, then gets out of the car and continues talking, you can start off with the talent on a wireless transmitter, then switch to a boom once the talent has exited the vehicle. As another example, if the talent walks into a restaurant, delivers dialog while walking and then sits down for the rest of the scene at a table, you can use a wireless for the walk-in and then switch to a hardwire for the table. Just because you need wireless units in part of the scene, doesn't mean you need to stay on wireless throughout. If the actors move or exit during part of the scene, try to use wireless for those shots and stick with hardwires for the rest. In short, only use wireless mics when they are necessary.

Wireless mics generally provide better results than ADR. Mic placement and the actor's movements along with clothing noise will be the deciding factors. In the ADR booth, you get superior sound in a controlled environment, but you rarely get the same level of intensity and performance that was delivered on set. ADR is always a compromise in quality. Wireless systems are an ace up the sleeve of the sound mixer, but before playing that ace, you should check the rest of the cards in your hand first. Always use a hardwire cable whenever possible.

CHAPTER EXERCISE You will need a wireless system for this exercise. Place a lav and wireless transmitter on a friend and have him walk around the room. Do you hear any hits or dropouts? Are you able to correct these? Next, have your friend leave the room and continue to walk around. Is there a difference in the wireless' performance? Now, find an open space like a football field or park. Have your friend stand next to you and talk. Finally, have him talk as he walks away from you. How far does he go before you start to notice dropouts? Do not attempt this exercise near the edge of a cliff.

CHAPTER 8

PLANT MIC TECHNIQUES

Plant mics aren't a type of microphone, but rather a type of microphone placement. Boom mics are mounted on a boom pole and lavaliers are mounted on the talent. A plant mic is any microphone planted in a location that is neither a boom pole nor the talent. In short, plant mics are alternative mic placements.

Plant mics can produce more natural sounding dialog than a lav mounted on the actor. Lavs have an artificial sound that is a forced perspective. An actor wearing a lav at thirty feet away from the camera will sound the same as an actor wearing a lav at five feet away from the camera. The very nature of a plant mic is that it is planted in one place; it is stationary. Like any type of microphone, plant mics can be hardwire or wireless. Hardwire is always preferred, but if a last-minute decision is made to use a plant mic between takes, a wireless plant will save time on the set. When hardwiring a plant mic, be sure to leave some slack near the microphone in case it needs to be repositioned. Keep this excess cable neat and hidden from the camera's view.

If the actor moves away from the plant mic, so will his audio. With a little ingenuity, you can mount plant mics on objects that move with the actor, such as a luggage cart. This allows the mic to move with the actor. Plant mics can also be useful for picking up sound effects on the set during a take.

You can place several plant mics throughout a set to pick up different lines of dialog as the actor moves around. The areas that the plant mics are placed are sometimes referred to as *zones*. For example, in a scene where the actor starts with a conversation at a desk, then walks over to the door and has a conversation with the deliveryman in the hall, and then walks over to an open window to shout to a neighbor, a plant mic can be placed in each of these zones to pick up the dialog. Multiple plant mics can create phasing issues in the mix, but if the plant mics are multitracked then the phase issues can be easily eliminated in postproduction by automating the mix to switch between the mics as needed. If you have to mix the mics onto a mix track or single track, be sure to use the 3:1 rule to avoid phasing problems.

Lavaliers are the most common type of microphone used as plant mics. Directional lavs are usually used in broadcast scenarios and not as effective as plant mics unless the talent is in a fixed position. The Countryman B6 is the world's smallest lavalier microphone and can be in plain sight of the camera without being seen. The head of the capsule is much smaller than the head of a matchstick. This mic was originally developed for theatrical stage productions, but, because of its size and natural sound, it was quickly adopted by the film and television industries. Boundary mics like the Sanken CUB-01 are great for covering larger areas than standard lavs. The Rode Pin Mic also provides a warm, natural-sounding solution.

Boom mics like cardioids and shotguns can be planted on a set to pick up stray lines of dialog that can't be picked up by the primary boom. Using the same model of microphone would help the post team match the primary mic used. This will offer the best consistency in the scene. If placement is a challenge or you have limited mics, you can use a lav or boundary mic, but keep in mind that the audio might need to be tweaked in post in order for the mics to match. An open-sounding lav will not easily match a tight-sounding shotgun. When possible, make the post team's job easier by matching mics on location.

Sit-down interviews can be boomed using plant mics. A boom pole can be mounted on a C-stand or light stand with a boom pole holder and positioned over the talent. This provides superior audio without your needing to hold a boom pole overhead for hours on end.

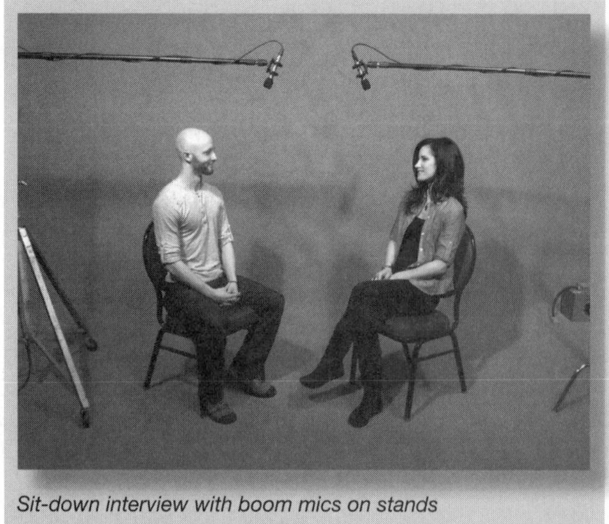

Sit-down interview with boom mics on stands

PLANT MIC LOCATIONS

Remember the inverse square law when using plant mics. Plant mics must be close to their source in order to be useful. If not, the audio you record will be too distant and will sound similar to using a mic on the camera — and that is never a good solution. Plant mics should always be hidden in front of the actors, not behind them. Position the mic so that it captures the dialog directly from the actors' mouths or the direction that they are facing.

Check the placement of plant mics on a monitor to ensure that the camera does not see them. The camera operator should be informed of the placement of the lavs. Camera operators can get grumpy if they notice a plant mic that they weren't informed about.

Plant mics can go anywhere. Every situation is different. Here are some common and not so common places to plant mics:

Tables

You can mike a group of people around a conference-room table or restaurant table by deploying plant mics hidden on or behind props on the table's surface. Multiple mics can be used to cover larger tables.

Flat Surfaces

You can plant a mic on a wall or flat surface to pick up dialog where the boom mic can't reach. This is useful for when the talent has to face surfaces such as a television, chalkboard, or whiteboard.

Using a vase to hide a plant mic

Plant mic hidden in a basket of tomatoes

Desktop

Scenes that have an actor standing in front of another actor seated at a desk can pose reach issues with the boom mic. The boom will enter the frame if it is lowered to pick up the dialog from the seated actor. A plant mic can be placed on the desk and hidden from the camera behind props.

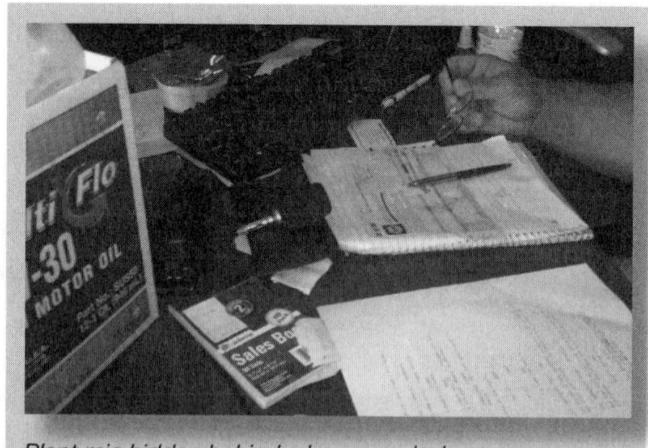

Plant mic hidden behind a box on a desk

Car Interiors

Vehicles can be mounted on a trailer bed with a camera and pulled by another vehicle. This is known as a *rig and tow* shot and gives the illusion that the actors are driving the vehicle. A rig and tow allows lights, camera, and sound equipment to be placed in and around the vehicle in a safe manner. *Poor man's process* is a shooting technique that photographs actors inside a stationary vehicle with the illusion of movement. This can be achieved with rear-screen projection or green screen. This saves the production company the added cost of a trailer rig and will provide a better solution for the soundtrack.

When the vehicle is in motion, the sound mixer will need to figure out where the recorder can be positioned. In some cases, the sound mixer can ride in the back seat, out of the camera's view. In extreme cases, sound mixers have been known to ride in the trunk of the vehicle. This is not recommended, as it is unsafe, dark, and downright uncomfortable! Sometimes a follow vehicle is used to shoot the picture car. Wireless systems can be used and the sound mixer can ride along in the follow vehicle.

When wiring the car for sound, cable breaks are important so that the car can pull away quickly if needed. Leave break points in the back seat to allow you to disconnect from the car. A quad cable or CAT-5 audio snake would make this easier for multiple microphones.

Sometimes it might be necessary to wire the vehicle for a wild drive, in which the car is rigged and the actors drive off without the crew. This is often the case when working with vehicles involved in races, such as NASCAR. An on-board recorder is strapped down and configured. When the vehicle is ready to take off, the sound mixer presses record and crosses his fingers. Obviously, this is a worst-case scenario, but usable audio can be achieved if it's the only option.

It may be important for the actors to hear the director's communication. A walkie-talkie is a simple solution, provided that the line stays clear during takes. A separate channel from the rest of the crew will ensure this. You can also use a speaker in the back seat. The Remote Audio Speakeasy v3a is a portable speaker that operates on a pair of 9-volt batteries and is perfect for the job. If you don't have a battery-powered speaker, you can use a power inverter plugged into a cigarette lighter to power an active speaker.

The talent can wear lavs for an interior car scene. Seatbelts can rub against the lav, so try to avoid placing the lav directly where the seatbelt strap will rest. A better choice would be planting mics on the sun visors or even on the dashboard. Sun visors are typically covered in padded fabric that offers protection from the vibrations of the vehicle. This will help retain some audio perspective for the shot. Cardioid mics can be used for this, although lavs might sound better.

A Sanken CUB-01 mounted on the ceiling is a favorite amongst many sound mixers. For multiple passengers, consider additional plant mics. A second CUB-01 can be mounted overhead of back-seat passengers as well. The backs of the front seats are the perfect height for placing plant mics to capture back-seat dialog.

Sun visor plant mic using a vampire clip

Rear seat plant mic

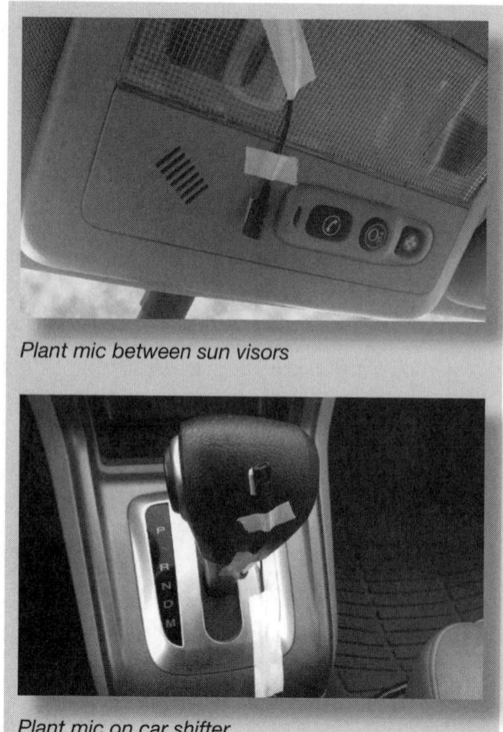
Plant mic between sun visors

Plant mic on car shifter

If the actors in the front seat are facing each other during the dialog, consider placing a mic between the two sun visors.

For shorter actors or children, you can mount a plant mic on the shifter between the seats.

If the actors deliver lines toward their windows or face opposite from the mic, try using another plant mic to pick up those lines of dialog. Phasing issues can occur when the mics are in such close proximity to each other as in the case of a car; however, multitracking ISO tracks may allow these mics to be mixed properly in post. Never bet the farm on the ISO tracks. Do your best to solve phasing issues on location. If you are mixing on the fly, try monitoring the audio in mono and pay close attention to the phase relationship of the mics.

Sometimes items from the vehicle that have been moved for the shot end up on the floor of the car. These items tend to produce unwanted sounds. Ask if they can be placed outside the vehicle at a staging area or at least wrapped in a blanket and placed in the trunk. Make sure that everything is "bolted down" in the car. Light fixtures, keys, loose change, and items in the glove box can create all kinds of sound problems. A simple fix for the keychain is to only use the key required for ignition. The other keys should be given to the prop department or the responsible party. Another solution would be to wrap the keys in gaffer tape to stop them from jingling or use a garbage tie to hold them together.

The air conditioning unit in the vehicle needs to be turned off. When the engine is on or the vehicle is being driven, the low rumble from the vehicle will be enough of a challenge as it is. The air conditioning can render the dialog useless. The actors can crank up the air between takes, but having the air running during a shot is unacceptable.

If the camera must shoot through the window, then the window will have to be rolled down. If these shots are combined with ones through the windshield when the windows were rolled up, then the production dialog will be inconsistent. But, this is the reality of production and some things are out of your control. For consistency, the post team will probably need to backfill the shots with the windows up with road and wind noise from those with the windows down.

Rolling the windows down will introduce a whole mess of problems from wind noise, car noise, and other traffic sounds. In this case, you can try to place lavs under the actors' clothes for better sound. This will help shield them from the extraneous noise. If you stick with plant mics on the sun visor, be sure to use wind protection. The dialog may need to be replaced with ADR, but it is your responsibility to try and get the best usable sound. If worst comes to worst, the audio can be used as a guide track.

Car Doors

Plant mics can be mounted on the sides of car doors to pick up dialog spoken by an actor standing outside the vehicle.

Plant mic mounted on the truck door to pick up dialog during a wide shot

Under the Hood of a Car

In scenes where dialog is delivered by an actor who is working under the hood of a car, a plant mic can be mounted in the engine compartment. Ideally, the mic under the hood should match the overhead boom for consistency when the actor moves from under the hood to continue the dialog. This should allow all of the lines to be captured with little or no EQ needed in post.

Plant mic placed inside the engine compartment of a car

Closets

An actor might poke her head inside of a cabinet or closet and deliver a line where a boom mic might not be able to reach, similar to an actor speaking from under a car hood. Plant mics can be hidden inside to grab these lines.

Plant mic hidden inside a kitchen cabinet

Doorways

In some cases, you might have the talent boomed overhead, but a third actor speaks through a doorway in the background. For this, you can cover the actor with a second boom operator, rig a second boom pole on a C-stand, or use a plant mic above the doorway.

Plant mic placed above a doorway

Windows

Scenes such as jail visits might have the actors on opposite sides of a window. This might not be practical to boom due to the actors' close proximity to the glass, preventing the boom from reaching in front of the actors. Plant mics can be positioned on both sides of the glass to pick up the conversation. Another solution could be to wire each phone with a lavalier, but this would require more prep time.

Plant mics placed on both sides of the glass in a jail visitation room

Courtrooms

News coverage of real-life court cases can be a challenge, especially if they are live broadcasts. truTV is a network that specializes in covering these types of broadcasts. Unlike a feature film, the event happens live. There are no second takes. If you miss the dialog, it's gone forever.

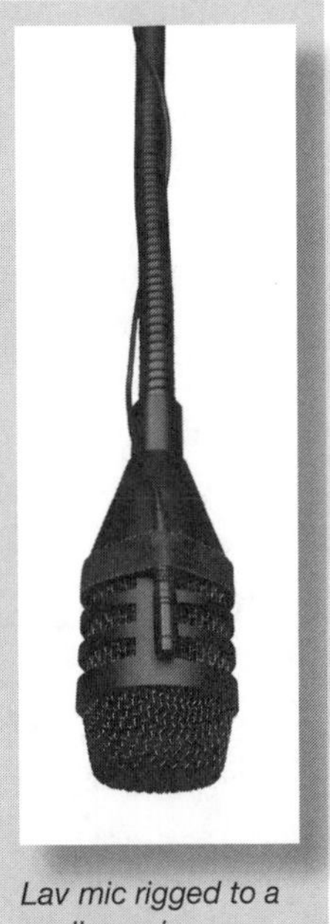

Lav mic rigged to a podium mic

Although the courtroom might have a P.A. system with mics positioned throughout, you should never tap into this system for the audio. The mics will be low-grade and the system will undoubtedly have a buzz. Plus, these systems are not actively mixed and the levels will be poor at best. You'll need a small arsenal of plant mics to cover the audio in the courtroom. Some of the key players will be miked with lavs, such as the attorneys and the judge. Sometimes, the judge will allow the broadcast, but will refuse to wear a lav. In this case, a lav can be planted on the end of the judge's podium mic or nearby on the bench.

Here is an example of common mic placements for a courtroom:

- Defense/Prosecuting Attorney — Wireless Lav
- Witness Stand — Hardwire Lav Plant on Podium Mic
- Jury Wall — Boundary Mic (**Note: not to pick up jurors*)
- Jury Banister/Ledge — Hardwire Lav Plant
- Judge — Wireless Lav or Hardwire Lav Plant on Podium Mic or Bench
- Attorney's Lectern — Hardwire Lav Plant on Podium Mic
- Attorney's Table — Hardwire Lav Plant on Desktop Mic
- A/V Equipment — Hardwire Lav Plant
- Room Mics — Boundary Mics on wall behind judge facing the audience

In some of the above locations, wireless mics may be necessary. Again, try to use hardwire plant mics before resorting to wireless systems. Keep a sharp eye on battery levels during courtroom breaks. The court session will not pause or allow you to approach the bench to change a battery!

Sporting Events

Covering sporting events is more than just gathering dialog. Plant mics can be used to heighten the action and make the event come alive to the audience. For example, hockey games are broadcast with a sound effects track provided by microphones planted along the board of the rink. The sound of a fan pounding his fists against the glass might be obnoxious, but that's all part of the experience. When you watch a hockey game at home, the broadcast is full of sounds including slap shots, the puck ringing off the goal post, and even player collisions. The game sounds more exciting on TV than actually being there.

I'll never forget going to my first hockey game back in 1997. This was an exciting season for the Detroit Red Wings, who went on to win the Stanley Cup. I was working for ESPN and we were covering the game's pre- and post-locker-room interviews. This basically means that we had nothing to do during the game but sit and watch, since another crew was covering the game itself. I sat in the stands with the shooter eating hot dogs and contemplating how cool my job was. It only took a few minutes of play before I realized that something was missing. The game was quiet, too quiet. Then, it dawned on me: this is what a hockey game really sounds like!

I had been spoiled by the up-close sound effects that were fed into the broadcasts I had watched for years. Sure, I could hear an occasional slap shot and the faint sounds of skates swooshing across the ice, but it was very subdued. I was disappointed. Why? Because the audience expects to hear the game! They want to hear the punches of a boxing match, the crack of the bat in a baseball game, the hard tackles of the Super Bowl. The audience can't hear these sounds unless mics are positioned to capture them.

While plant mics are typically used for hockey, other games like football will have several sound personnel standing on the sidelines with shotguns either handheld or placed in *parabolic reflectors* to capture the sounds of the action. A parabolic reflector is a dish that collects and reflects sound toward a mounted shotgun microphone. These are used as moving plant mics, but aren't considered plant mics in the literal sense. If you are in charge of the sound of the event, be sure to bring it to life with sound effects!

Here are some more creative miking positions for plant mics:

- Hidden in a floral arrangement (as a plant mic's name might suggest)
- Behind books on a desk
- Bed headboards
- Windows
- Mirrors
- Nearby props

- Props held by the talent (clipboards, books, etc.)
- Computer monitors that the talent is facing
- On traveling props or vehicles
- Shifters on cars
- Virtually anywhere!

PLANT MIC MOUNTING TECHNIQUES

Plant mics are essentially unconventional miking methods and therefore use unconventional mounting techniques. In a sense, the mounts are made up on the spot based on the surface where the mic needs to be planted. The main components for plant mounts are fasteners and shock mounts.

Fasteners

Gaffer tape is probably the most-used fastener on a film set. Everything gets taped down with gaffer tape at some point during the production. In general, gaffer tape works well on surfaces and doesn't leave a sticky residue like duct tape. However, gaffer tape can peel paint off some surfaces, remove varnish, and leave a sticky residue if the temperature is too warm. Other fasteners to use include paper tape, clothespins, spring clamps, and safety pins.

Shock Mounts

Professional shock mounts are designed to help isolate the microphone from the environment or boom pole. On paper, this makes them sound like the perfect solution for plant mics. In the real world, shock mounts are bulky and hard to hide on a set. Other methods of shock absorption are needed. Use foam or other soft material to help isolate the plant mic from the surface that it is mounted to. This helps when actors place or slam their hands on tables, set down or pick up props, etc. Pillows, a wad of tissue paper, and sponges can be used as shock absorbers for plant mics.

Gaffer tape rolled into a ball with the sticky side facing out can make a decent shock-absorbing mount for a plant mic. This serves as both a shock mount as well as a fastener. Simply stick the gaffer-tape ball anywhere you want to plant a mic.

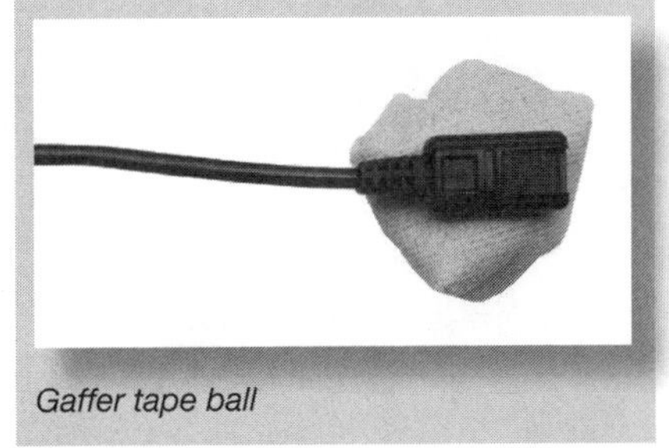

Gaffer tape ball

Gaffer tape can also be used to make micro-shock mounts for lavs. Create a double-sided loop and place one side on the lav and the other wherever the lav needs to be planted. The space between the loop will absorb minor surface vibrations for the lav.

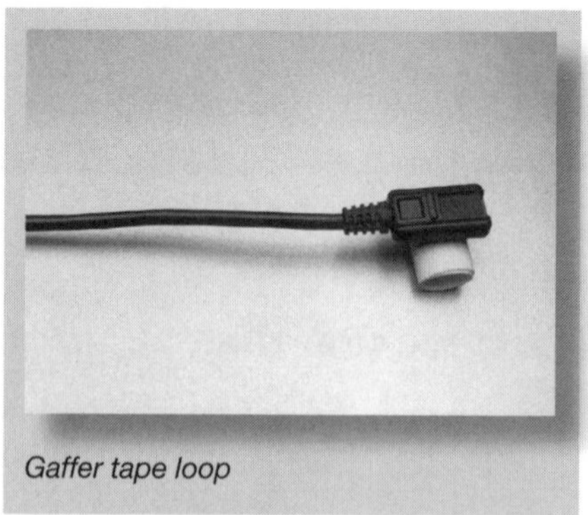

Gaffer tape loop

CHAPTER EXERCISE Look around the room that you are sitting in right now (coffeeshop, classroom, airplane, wherever). If you were shooting a scene in this location and didn't have access to a boom pole, where would you place plant mics? Try planting mics in unconventional locations. Record and listen to the results.

CHAPTER 9

MICROPHONE SELECTION

Choosing the right mic for the shot can make all the difference. There is no one-size-fits-all microphone. For a sound mixer, microphone selection usually comes down to three choices: boom mics, plants, and lavs. You should always use them in that order. This is your priority list for which mic will sound the best and which mic should be used as an alternative. Sound guru Fred Ginsburg refers to this list as the "Hierarchy of Microphone Techniques."

Essentially, the boom mic will always give you the best natural sound. Some locations, scenes, and camera angles will make the boom impractical to use. Examples of these would be wide shots, special effects scenes, and locations with excessive background noise. The plant mic would be the next choice. The last choice would be a lavalier. Your location will help you decide exactly which mic to reach for and the action of the scene will dictate whether you can use a plant mic or if you need lavs.

GENERAL GUIDELINES FOR CHOOSING MICS

Here are some general guidelines on which mics to use and how to use them. When in doubt, always remember: **B.P.L.** (Boom, Plant, Lav)!

Interior Locations

Boom	
▸ Cardioid/Hypercardioid Boom from overhead Boom from underneath (scoop)	▸ Shotgun Boom from overhead Boom from underneath (scoop)
Plant Mic	
▸ Omni/Lav	▸ Cardioid or Hypercardioid
▸ Boundary Mic	▸ Shotgun
Lav	
▸ Hardwire	▸ Wireless

Exterior Locations

Boom

- **Shotgun**
  - Boom from overhead
  - Boom from underneath (scoop)
- **Cardioid or Hypercardioid**
  - Boom from overhead
  - Boom from underneath (scoop)

Plant Mic

- **Shotgun**
- **Cardioid or Hypercardioid**
- **Omni/Lav**

Lav

- **Hardwire**
- **Wireless**

Once you've decided which microphone(s) to use for a setup, try to stick with it. It is more important to deliver consistent audio to the editor than to switch mics in the middle of a setup, even if you think one will sound better than another. Make your choice before shooting and then try to use that microphone to cover the setup. You don't have to use that microphone for the entire scene. Once you start a new setup, you can consider different options. Of course, this is a general guideline to follow. Some situations will require a mic change. The principle is to strive to maintain consistency in your tracks.

If the wide shot doesn't allow you to get the boom in close enough, do your best and rely on radio mics. In most cases, the editor will use the audio from the close-ups and the wide shot audio for reference.

Some microphones mix better together than others. Mixing different brands of microphones may sometimes cause a noticeable difference in sound quality. The sound of each microphone may be perfectly fine when used alone, but when combined, the characteristics of each mic can sound weird when mixed together or toggled back and forth. This can be especially noticeable in the background noise or room tone.

ENG productions don't allow for much microphone choices on location. Typically you'll have a single boom mic (usually a shotgun) and a set of lavs to use for just about everything you shoot. Microphone selection really comes down to the type of production work being done. On a film, the camera operator will use a matte box and filters. For ENG work, the camera operator will rarely put anything in front of the lens, for time's sake. This run-and-gun style of production can be frustrating for film crews that are used to taking the time to get the best quality image and sound. ENG work focuses more on speed as the productions will have more immediate deadlines and smaller budgets.

SOUND PERSPECTIVE

Matching sound perspective to camera perspective is a relatively simple concept, especially when you consider that the boom needs to be outside the edge of the frame line. In a wide shot, the boom will need to be further away from the talent to avoid being in the frame. This position will provide a perspective that matches the camera. Conversely, if the shot is close, then the boom can be closer to the talent. This will once again match the camera's perspective.

The balance between direct sound, indirect sound, and reverberation will shape the sound perspective. Microphone levels can be adjusted easily in post; however, perspective cannot. Plug-ins can be used to make a close perspective seem distant, by adding reflections and reverberation. But, plug-ins cannot make a distant perspective seem close by removing reflections and reverberations that exist on the track with the dialog.

Perspective is also shaped by the *dialog/background ratio*. This is the relationship between the level of the dialog and the level of the background noise or room tone. Wide shots call for a sound perspective that has the dialog more distant and the background noise more involved in the sound. A tight shot has the dialog as the focus with the background noise very subdued, if not almost absent. The levels of these recordings are not related to the perspective at all.

The perspective can be recorded at high or low levels, but still maintain the relationship between the dialog and the background respectively. In simple terms, if the dialog represents 80% of the sound and the background represents the other 20%, those percentages will stay the same whether the signal is recorded at -10dB or -40dB. The advantage to recording "hotter" levels is that it reduces the chance for system noise in post. This will come naturally once you've found your preamp's sweet spot. After that, it's just a matter of getting the mic in the right position. When you move the mic closer, the level will become louder naturally. In this case, it would be helpful to lower the level of the recorder to match the rest of the levels recorded for the scene. This keeps the levels consistent for the audio editor.

CAMERA ANGLE VERSUS CAMERA PERSPECTIVE

There is a difference between camera angle and camera perspective. Various camera angles might place the camera all around the subject: behind, above, below, beside. Camera framing might vary from medium, to close-up, or even an extreme close-up. In all of these cases, the audio perspective should remain consistent. The sound shouldn't change because the angle or composition has. However, a wide shot changes things. The sound's perspective will be different in that indirect sound will accompany the direct sound coming from the actors. If the camera is shooting a wide shot and the actors are far away it would be confusing to the audience's basic understanding of acoustics if the actors sound nearby.

If you move the microphone closer to the talent you are increasing the talent's level and decreasing the background level and the acoustical effects of the room. If you move the microphone away from the talent, you are increasing the background level and the acoustical effects of the room as well as decreasing the talent's level. Adjusting the microphone's gain is a technical practice, but mic placement and selection are where the job becomes more of an art form. If you're struggling to get the right sound or balance between actors, the background, and the acoustical effects of a room, the answer won't be found in any of the knobs on the mixer. Instead, experiment with mic placement. If that doesn't seem to work, try using a different microphone.

THE BOOM'S PERSPECTIVE

Booming a shot from an overhead position is the best way to maintain the perspective of the shot. Other mic techniques do not always easily match the perspective. Plant mics are usually stationary and lavs are mounted on the actors and always sound close. Using the boom and hugging the frame line allows the audience to hear the perspective that supports the camera's framing. Wide shots will sound distant and tight shots will sound close.

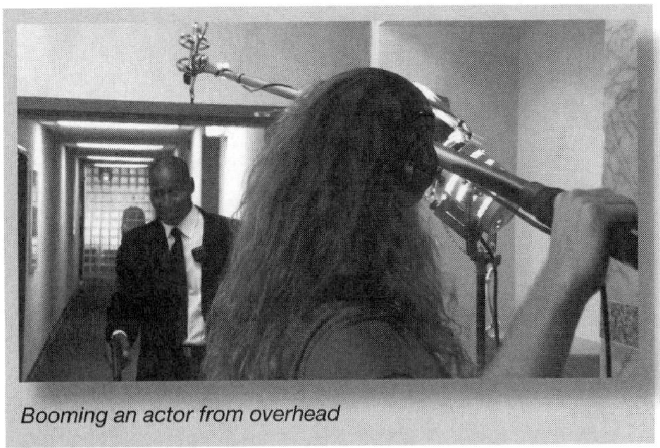
Booming an actor from overhead

In general, miking from directly beside or behind the camera should be avoided; however, in some cases it might be the best solution. For example, if the scene calls for the actors to hover over and look directly down at the camera (i.e., POV angle), the actors will be speaking at the lens. For this setup try placing the mic beside the lens pointing up at the actors. Be sure to address any noise that the camera might be making.

TRAVELING DIALOG

Movement will also affect sound perspective. If the talent is moving *away* from the camera, they shouldn't be moving *toward* the mic. This will make the actor *sound* like he is approaching, but *look* like he is leaving. The audience will feel slightly confused at the shot because their ears and eyes will not agree with each other. Conversely, if the talent is moving *toward* the camera, they shouldn't be moving *away* from the mic. In either case, the sound's perspective would mismatch the camera's perspective. Granted, the majority of the time the boom will follow the talent to gather an even perspective, but if the situation calls for unique mic placement or plant mics, make sure that the mix represents the action on screen.

Plant mics are usually impractical for *traveling dialog* (dialog that is delivered in motion). It would seem unnatural to have a plant mic in the middle of the actor's path so that the dialog floated in and out of perspective as the actor walked past the plant mic. This would sound especially weird if the plant mic was at the beginning of the actor's path, which would result in the dialog sounding more distant as the actor approached the camera. Plant mics are better used in stationary situations, to pick up lines from a particular actor or grab parts of a line that the boom can't capture. If a boom is not an option for traveling dialog, then a wireless lav might be the only solution.

MULTI-CAMERA PERSPECTIVE

Two-camera shoots can speed up production. However, if the angles from the two cameras are drastically different, this could pose serious problems for the sound department. For example, if A-Camera is in a medium shot while B-Camera is in a wide shot, then B-Camera will dictate the closest position the boom pole can be. The audio perspective will match B-Camera's perspective; however, A-Camera's shot will be mismatched with the sound perspective. In some cases, lavs may need to be used as the primary sound source for these types of shots.

The goal is to provide the audience with audio that matches the perspective of the shot. As humans, we expect things to sound distant when they are far away, and close when they are near. Altering the audio in a way that contradicts the audience's expectations will seem unnatural.

The key to great location sound is this: Get the right mic in the right place at the right time with the right level!

CHAPTER EXERCISE Experiment with mic placement to get a feel for direct sound versus indirect sound and dialog/background ratios. Place the microphone overhead about two feet away. Record and slate the take by stating what distance you are from the microphone. Say a couple of sentences, then step two feet back from the microphone. Announce your new distance and repeat the sentences. Step back a few more feet and repeat. Do this until you are about fifteen feet away. What has changed? Obviously the volume will be significantly lower at the greatest distance, but what else do you notice? Do you notice changes in direct sound and indirect sound? Do you notice changes in the dialog/background ratio? Try this experiment indoors and outdoors.

CHAPTER 10

SIGNAL FLOW

Signal flow can be defined as the path that audio takes from source to destination or, in simpler terms, from beginning to end. There are two components to signal flow: a logical path and the physical path that the signal needs to use to get there.

THE LOGICAL PATH

Understand the signal flow of your equipment. Where to connect everything to and from can be dizzying at first. There's a lot of stuff to consider. But, if you approach it logically, the battle is already won. Sources will always be connected to inputs, and outputs will always be connected to the inputs of the next device. My dad never understood this simple concept fully; to this day he calls me every time he gets a new piece of home theater equipment. When he asks me where to plug the output of a DVD or Blu-ray player, my answer is always "to the input of the device you want to send it to." Of course, I always end up saying this in a very impatient and condescending tone. Eventually, I end up at his house plugging in the device for him.

For complicated setups, you might want to draw a signal flow chart. Using a signal flow chart doesn't mean you don't know what you are doing. Many times it means that you *do* know what you are doing. Signal flow can be complicated and the urgency of production work will only add to your stress. Consider color-coding and labeling your gear. This will make tracking down problems much easier and faster. Many sound mixers will coordinate cable colors to specific channels that have matching color-coded faders. Wireless transmitters can be color-coordinated with matching receivers using colored gaffer or electrical tape. These techniques take only seconds to do and eliminate the hassle of having to figure out where everything goes. Cheat sheets and placards are also useful for setups, as well as operation and menu shortcuts.

Cheat sheet of shortcuts mounted on a Sound Devices 744T

What Exactly Is Signal Flow?

Signal flow is analogous to plumbing. In your house, water flows from one place to another, all in one direction. If you want water to come out of your sink, you simply open the spigot on the faucet. But, water needs to be flowing *to* the sink first. So, let's start at the very beginning. Where does the water come from? Let's assume that you live in a major city. Water is pumped from the city's water plant. This is your source. Water flowing from this point is pushed with the greatest amount of pressure. From here it will slowly decrease in pressure at each stage. The water might flow to a local junction point and then to your house. At your house, you have a main water valve that allows water into your house's pipes. Once the water enters your house's pipes it gets directed throughout your home to all of the sinks, toilets, showers, etc. You cannot increase pressure back to the water plant's original level without using a pump or special fittings. If you can understand this concept, you are ready to understand audio signal flow.

There are a couple of simple concepts to understand with the water illustration. First, no water will appear at the showerhead unless it has first been sent from the water plant and then allowed into your pipes from your house's main water valve. The same is true with your audio signal. Your microphone will not appear in the main mix if the microphone is not plugged in (i.e., the water plant is shut down).

Second, the amount of signal level from your microphone into the mixer is adjusted via the channel's gain control (i.e., main water valve). When a water valve is opened a little, only a little water flows through it. When opened fully, the greatest amount of water flows through. When you open the channel's gain a little, only a little signal flows through. When opened fully (to *unity*), the proper amount of signal flows through. However, the gain knob functions as a pump and not a valve. In other words, the gain knob controls an internal amplifier that increases the audio signal. When a channel's gain knob is completely faded, some amplification still occurs. Fading the gain knob completely will not stop the signal from entering the mixer, although in some cases the signal may be reduced to a low enough level where it is virtually absent.

Thirdly, the shower's spigot needs to be open. This is the channel's fader. While the analogy is simplified with the plumbing illustration, understand that audio signal flow is indeed simple; however, mixers can be outfitted with a significant amount of controls. That's a good thing.

More knobs and switches give you greater control over your signal: where it goes and how much is sent there. Regardless if your mixer has ten knobs and switches or hundreds, the idea is that each one of these controls either opens or closes a path for the signal to flow. If your audio isn't reaching the desired destination, simply retrace the signal flow's path and make sure that each valve is opened.

There is the issue of water pressure: the force or strength behind the water flow. This pressure is called "gain" in the audio signal. Take great care in deciding where and how much gain you apply to the audio signal. Too much gain will distort the signal or produce system hiss. Too little gain and your audio signal will be like the low water pressure in a shower at a cheap hotel. Enter the world of *gain staging*.

Gain Staging

It is critical to understand gain staging as it can make or break the quality of your audio signal. But don't worry; it's simple to understand.

The main principle behind gain staging is that the audio signal should always be the strongest at the beginning and maintain that same level or decrease from there. The audio signal should never increase to a point higher than the previous point. This is easy to understand if you realize that you would need to use amplifiers to increase the audio signal's level. These amplifiers can boost hiss and other system noise if pushed above their optimal setting, called *unity gain*.

Unity gain is designed to match signals between two devices so that they are both sending and receiving the same level of audio. This produces the best audio signal with the least amount of system noise. The unity setting is sometimes indicated on a gain/trim knob or a channel's fader with a "U" or a "0". Keep in mind: you may or may not keep the setting at unity.

For line level signals, unity is often the default setting on the channel's input gain control, but the channel fader (see page 190) might be higher or lower than unity depending on the amount of signal that you want to send to the main output. Raising the gain above the unity level for a line input can result in distortion.

A microphone signal is altogether different. First, you will need to boost the microphone level (about -60dB) to a line level (+4dB). If the microphone's signal is too hot due to a screaming actor, you will need to decrease the channel's gain knob to compensate for this. If this incoming signal is too hot, lowering the channel fader will reduce the signal to the main mix, but the signal will still be distorted. This is because the signal going to the channel fader was already distorted leaving the mic preamp (i.e., the channel's gain). Lowering the channel fader will only lower the amount of distorted audio, not the amount of distortion. Decreasing the channel's input gain in this case can eliminate the distortion. In some cases, the channel's gain will need to be attenuated even further via a pad. This will send clean audio downstream to the channel fader.

You cannot un-distort a signal once it has distortion. You can prevent distortion by observing proper gain structure, but once a signal is distorted, the distortion is permanent. It should be noted that some acoustic sources might overload the microphone causing distortion to happen in the microphone before it even appears at the channel's gain input. An inline pad or a pad on the microphone itself can correct this. If these don't help, then physically move the microphone further away from the source.

Gain staging is not just limited to working with more than one piece of equipment. Gain structure occurs within a single piece of gear, like a recorder or a mixer. The bottom line for gain staging or gain structure is that the level should either stay the same or decrease at each consecutive stage.

THE PHYSICAL PATH

Now let's talk about pipes. Pipes are the conduits in which the water flows. In audio signal flow these pipes are called *cables*. If the pipes aren't connected to one another, then water can't reach its final destination. It's humorous when it happens, but often signal-flow problems can be traced to a cable that wasn't plugged in. The unofficial industry term for this is "air gap." Internal plumbing, that is, the internal wiring of electronic devices and microphones, is rarely the problem. By rarely, I mean less than .001% of the time. If all the cables are connected to the right places and the signal is poor or absent then the first place to check is the pipes/cables. This is the physical path of the signal.

Once you know the logical path your signal needs to take, you'll need to start connecting your pipes together. This requires two key ingredients: *connectors* and *cables*.

Connectors

Male connectors always send the signal, while female connectors always receive the signal. Understanding this will help you avoid running a hundred feet of cable only to realize that you have the wrong end on the microphone's side. Since microphones send a signal, they will always have a male connector on the bottom. Therefore, you should always run a female connector to the microphone.

When connecting or disconnecting a cable, always use the connector. Never pull on a cable to remove it from the equipment. This can and will cause the wires inside of the cable to fray, which will result in intermittent shorts and potentially damage equipment. Be sure to listen for the click when plugging in most connectors. This indicates that the cable is securely connected to the device.

Types of Connectors and Adaptors

XLR

The *XLR* connector is found on the standard microphone cable, but they are also used for line level interconnectivity. The acronym evolved from a Canon connector. The female connector has a latch that keeps the male connector locked in place (insert marital joke here). Pressing the release latch on an equipment panel will disconnect male XLR connectors. Pressing the release latch on the plug can disconnect female XLR connectors from an equipment panel. The release latch prevents the cable from being unplugged accidentally.

- XLR Wiring Scheme:
  Pin 1 — Ground
  Pin 2 — Hot/Positive
  Pin 3 — Cold/Negative

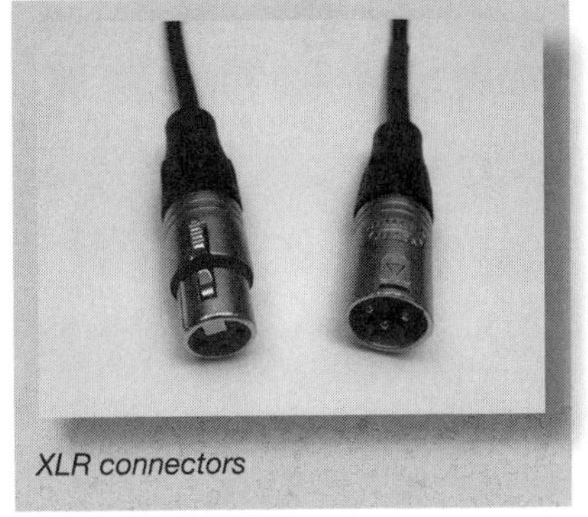

XLR connectors

As a word of caution, many years ago, there was a discrepancy between countries as to which pin carried the hot signal. As a result, some older equipment may have Pin 2 as cold. When in doubt, check the equipment's manual.

Phone Connector

This type of connector was originally invented for the telephone industry, hence the name. The phone connector comes in two sizes: 1/4" and 1/8". The 1/8" version is referred to as 3.5mm or sometimes "mini." When using non-locking connections like the phone plug, be sure that the connector is pushed in all the way. Failing to do this can result in no signal, poor signal, or a mono signal from a stereo source. Newer products on the market that use 1/8" mini-plugs include screw threads to ensure the plugs are inserted correctly and to prevent them from coming loose or unplugged. Both size phone plugs have two versions: TS and TRS.

- TS – Tip, Sleeve
  Wiring Scheme:
  Tip — Signal
  Sleeve — Ground
- TRS – Tip, Ring, Sleeve
  Wiring Scheme:
  Tip — Hot/Positive
  Ring — Cold/Negative
  Sleeve — Ground

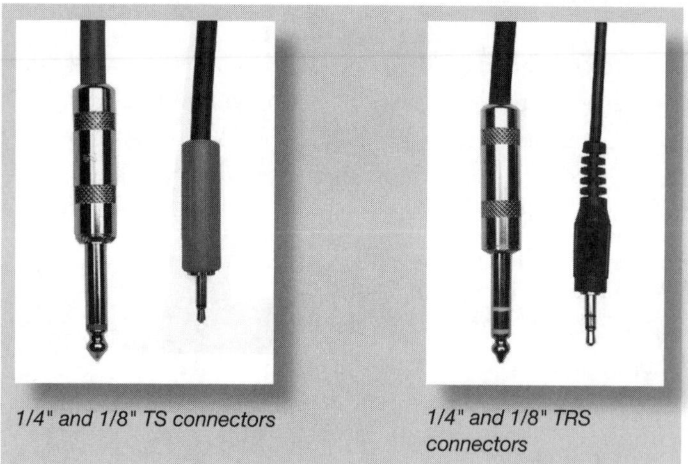

1/4" and 1/8" TS connectors

1/4" and 1/8" TRS connectors

RCA

The name *RCA* comes from Radio Corporation of America, the company that invented this connector. Also known as a phono plug or phono jack, this connector is most commonly found on consumer equipment, but is used on some professional equipment.

- RCA Wiring Scheme:
  Tip — Signal
  Sleeve — Ground

RCA connector

BNC

The *BNC* is a twist-to-lock connector used on video, RF, and timecode cables as well as some wireless antennas. BNC cables are never used for audio signals.

- BNC Wiring Scheme:
  Tip — Signal
  Sleeve — Ground

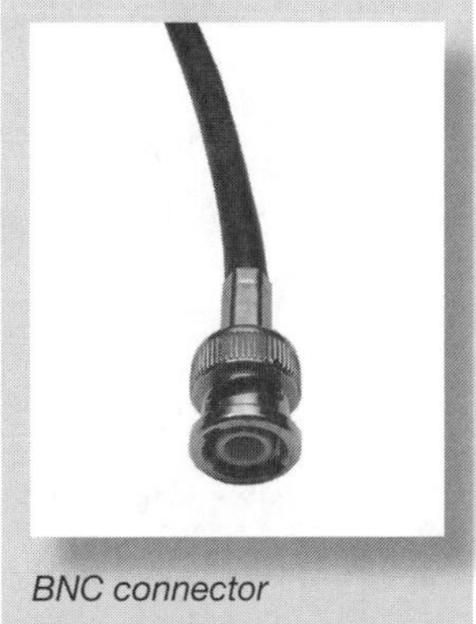

BNC connector

Adaptors

Adaptors change the connector's type from one to another. A variety of adaptors are a must-have for any sound mixer. They can allow a cable to connect to virtually any piece of audio equipment.

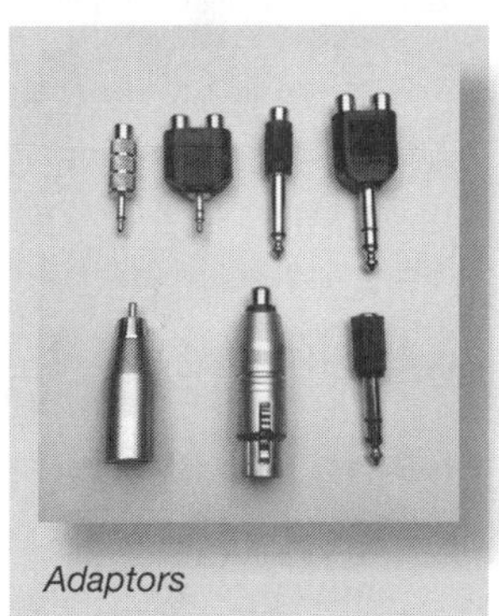

Adaptors

Barrels

A *barrel* is an adaptor that changes the sex of the connector. They are also called turn-arounds, sex changers, and gender benders.

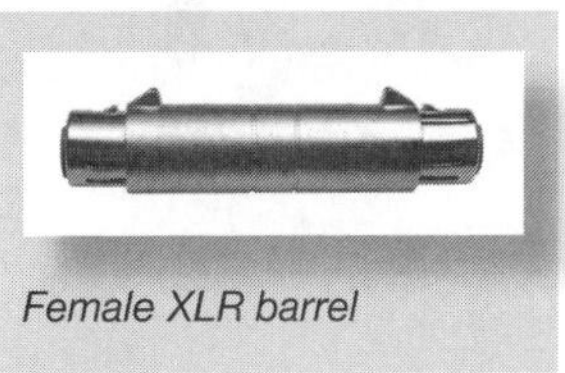

Female XLR barrel

Signal Degradation

Insertion loss is a loss of signal level every time a connector is added to the signal chain. The more connectors and adaptors that are used, the more signal is lost. When possible, use a cable that has the connector you need and only use an adaptor as a problem-solver. Try to avoid using multiple cables for a single cable run. Instead, use one cable that is the length you need.

At great distances, line loss can occur in a mic level signal sooner than a line level signal. This is because a line level signal is stronger than a mic level signal. There are formulas to help calculate this line loss. In the real world, mic signals are sent down hundreds of feet of cable every day with no noticeable loss in signal. For cable runs that approach 1,000 feet, a line level signal is the safest bet. These long cable runs are more common when working in television productions where there is a remote truck or satellite truck that needs to receive all of the signals for mixing and transmission. If you have to send mic level signals over extreme lengths, a distribution amplifier or line booster can prevent line loss.

Cables

A *cable* consists of wires that are insulated from each other and housed inside an outer case. Sometimes cables are referred to as a "hose." They are responsible for interfacing devices to one another. There are two types of cables: balanced and unbalanced cables.

Unbalanced cables consist of two conductors: signal and ground. These cables are generally used in consumer and prosumer equipment. They are acceptable for short runs (typically less than six feet) and are susceptible to interference and noise.

Balanced cables consist of three conductors: hot (or positive), cold (or negative) and ground. The hot and cold conductors are twisted around each other to prevent electromagnetic induction. Noise that is picked up along the cable will be picked up by both conductors. When the two conductors arrive at their destination, they are inverted, which effectively puts the noise out of phase. The phase cancellation of noise makes balanced cables the best choice for long cable runs

Star Quad cable

and other professional applications. Use balanced cables whenever possible! Star Quad cables use a twisted pair for each signal (positive and negative). This greatly reduces the chance for interference or induction. Professional microphone cables are balanced cables.

Always keep cable runs straight and separate from AC cables to avoid EMI (electromagnetic induction). If audio and AC cables need to run parallel, keep them as far apart as possible. Failure to do this can cause hum in the audio. If an audio cable needs to cross an AC cable, always do so at a 90-degree angle to reduce the chance of EMI.

While balanced cables offer the best defense against noise, these problems can still occur. Noises like buzzes and hums will spoil the audio. *Hum Eliminators* use an isolation transformer that breaks loop antennas, which effectively eliminates the noise. These can make fast work of buzz and hum issues that might otherwise take time to track down. Another popular choice is the Sescom IL-19.

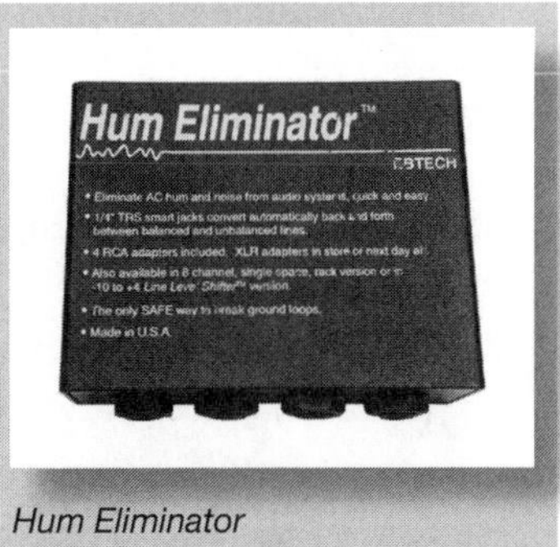

Hum Eliminator

Mismatched levels and impedances between consumer and professional equipment can also cause buzz and hum. Devices like the *Matchbox* will convert the signals so that they are equal.

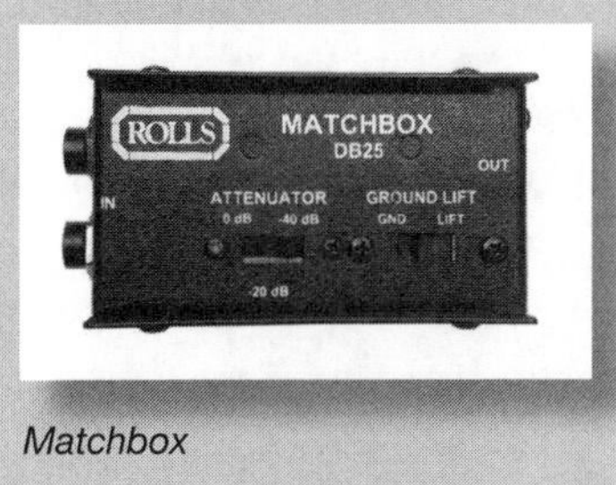

Matchbox

All pieces of equipment connected to sound should share the same circuit. If not, a potential ground loop can occur. This includes cameras, monitors, video-assist feeds, headphone DAs, etc. If a ground loop occurs, you can use an inline ground lift adaptor that removes Pin 1 from the signal path without the need to physically cut the wire to Pin 1. Remember: phantom power can only be sent down balanced cables. Using a ground lift will block phantom power.

Inline ground lift

Quality cables are a must for production work. True, cheaper cables can be used, but they will certainly not last more than a week on location. The gauge of microphone cables is between 20 AWG to 24 AWG. Cables almost always fail at or near the connector. Avoid using a cable with a molded connector as they are more easily damaged and cannot be repaired. Cables with standard metal connectors will last longer and can be soldered or repaired without difficulty. Never throw bad cables away! Keep the connectors and use them to solder and make new cables (even shorter cables). Cables that go bad should be clearly labeled for later repair. Mark these cables by putting a piece of gaffer tape over the connector so that it cannot be used or label the cable "NG" for "No Good."

Cable Management

Cable management is important in fieldwork. A single cable can quickly start to look like spaghetti. When you have several unkempt cables together, separating them in a hurry is a hopeless task. Work strategically with your cables and keep them tidy at all times.

Never wrap a cable around your elbows as you would a rope. This will damage the cable over time. Use the over/under method to wrap your cables. This method entails making alternating loops with your cables. The first loop is rolled clockwise; the next loop is rolled counterclockwise, and so on. By wrapping cables properly, you can "train" them to remain a certain way. However, by wrapping a cable improperly, you can train it the wrong way, and it can be very difficult to re-train. Properly trained cables can be spooled out easily. Be sure that the ends have not accidentally passed through the center of the loop before you unwrap the cable. If this happens, you will have a knot at each section of the loop. Upon noticing these knots, stop immediately, rethread the cable, and start over.

Strain relief protects the ends of the cable, whereas the over/under method protects the center of the cable. For cables that hang on the side of a sound bag, the loops should be between six and eight inches. Loops larger than eight inches can easily snag on objects as you move around the set. On a sound cart, cable loops can be as large as two feet since their lengths will be much longer than ENG cables.

Velcro cable loops on a sound bag

In ENG production, there are times when you have to throw the gear into the truck and dash to the next location. If you can, wrap the cables while in transit. At the very least, be sure to wrap the cables when you store your gear at the end of the day. Cables are run on the ground, through the grass, mud, sand, and all sorts of gross things like oil sludge on the floor of a mechanic's shop. Instead of rolling up the dirty cables and letting them sit with the rest of your expensive gear, bring a towel to wipe the cables down before you wrap them up. A nifty trick is to hold the towel in one hand and run each cable through the towel with the other. This allows you to wipe down the cable quickly. Another solution would be to keep the cables in a bin, separate from the rest of your gear. Bring hand sanitizer to clean your hands after wrapping cables that have been strewn all over the filthy floors.

When working in public, make sure you tape down your cable runs, for safety reasons. Doormats can be used in a pinch. If the cable needs to run through a doorway, be sure to prop the door open so that it doesn't close completely, which might damage the cables. Cable runs should be as far away from AC as possible and should be kept out of the path of the actors, the camera, the Steadicam operator, and the dolly track. Keep cable runs clean and neat to make troubleshooting easier.

TROUBLESHOOTING

Nothing can be more alarming on a set than when the signal flow is interrupted or nonexistent. While equipment can fail, operator error is usually the culprit. Don't panic. That will just make things worse. Work systematically to solve the problem.

In general, you should handle troubleshooting in the following order:

1. Power
2. Mixer/Recorder Settings
3. Cables
4. Microphones

Most of your audio problems can be traced to the gear failing to receive power. This could be because the power switch is off, an AC breaker was tripped, an extension cord came unplugged, or batteries need to be replaced. Next, check the settings on your mixer and/or recorder. Make sure the proper channel is up and that you are monitoring the correct channel in your headphones. Once that riddle is solved, check the cables to ensure they are connected properly at both ends. Any connection is a possible fail point. Cables are the weakest link in the chain of any audio setup. They take the most abuse of any equipment on a set. Failure to take care of your cables will result in intermittent or complete loss of signal, often at the most inopportune time. If signal flow checks out okay, then the microphone is probably the culprit. Check the microphone by either snapping your fingers or speaking into it. Never blow on a microphone! This produces higher-than-acceptable SPL on the diaphragm and can damage the mic. If you don't get a signal from the mic, swap it out for a new one. If this still doesn't work, retrace your steps and troubleshoot the problem again in this order. Pay close attention to the mixer/recorder as a single switch can cause all sorts of headaches! If a second pass at these steps doesn't reveal the problem, then you might have equipment failure.

Repairs that need to be done "under the hood" of your equipment will probably require a certified professional. Attempting these repairs on your own will usually void any warranty. Proceed with caution.

CHAPTER EXERCISE Practice by making your own cables. You can purchase a standard soldering iron at Radio Shack and most hardware stores. Make some short turnaround cables. At first, you'll need to get the hang of soldering. Once you can solder without burning your fingerprints off, try honing your newfound craft and make your solder points neat and clean. Heat-shrink tubing can be used to protect the loose wires at the end of the cable.

Here are some ideas of cables to make:

- XLRF — TRSM
- XLRM — TRSM
- RCA — TS

**Note: "F" and "M" denotes female and male, respectively.*

Once you've made a cable, be sure to use a cable tester to verify that the connections are correct. Never use a homemade cable for a production until it has been tested.

CHAPTER 11

RECORDERS

A *recorder* is a device that captures an audio signal and stores that signal for playback at a later time. The Nagra was the de facto standard location sound recorder for nearly half a century. Over the years, this 1/4" analog reel-to-reel recorder evolved from mono to stereo and eventually added timecode capability. In the 1990s, DAT (Digital Audio Tape) recorders were introduced and the analog dynasty began to crumble. The DAT recorder's reign was far shorter than Nagra's. Less than ten years after its introduction, DAT recorders began to be phased out by nonlinear hard disk recorders. Today, nonlinear hard disk recorders reign supreme and their empire is sure to last for a long time. The delivery medium, file formats, bit depth, and sample rates are sure to change, but the days of recording audio in any form other than digital are gone.

DIGITAL AUDIO

Unlike the metallic waveforms of analog tape-based audio, digital audio is stored as ones and zeros. This information is encoded and decoded through A/D and D/A converters. An A/D converter (Analog to Digital) scans the analog signal and stores the audio as information in a digital file. A D/A Converter (Digital to Analog) reads the file and converts the information back to an analog signal. The two elements that make up the sound wave's information in the digital audio file are the *sample rate* and *bit depth*.

Sample Rate

Sample rate is the number of times a sound wave is sampled within a period of one second. The process of audio sampling is similar to taking pictures of the waveform at specific intervals to be used to build a single, continuous waveform. For example, a sample rate of 48KHz means that the sound wave is photographed or sampled 48,000 times per second. Higher sample rates yield a higher frequency resolution.

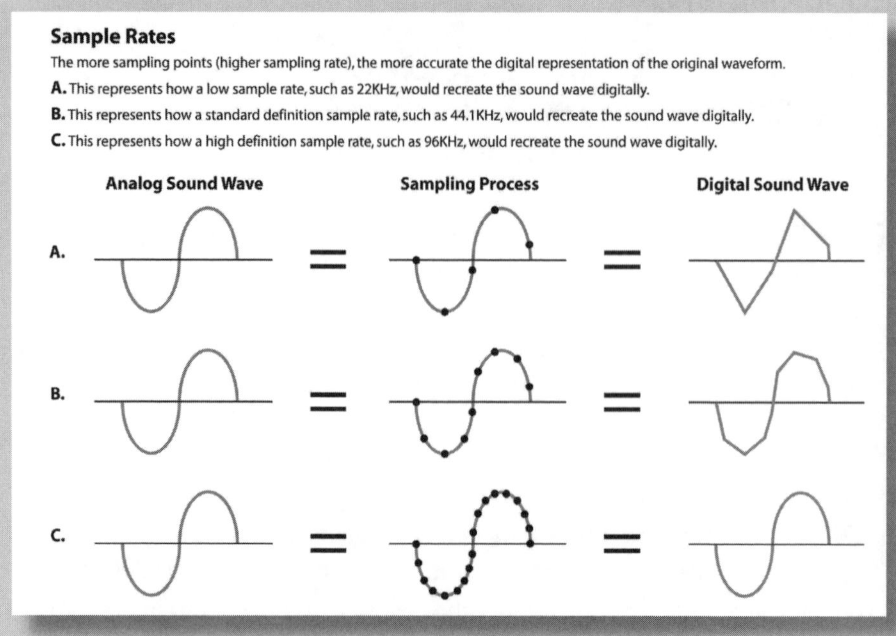

Sample Rates
The more sampling points (higher sampling rate), the more accurate the digital representation of the original waveform.
A. This represents how a low sample rate, such as 22KHz, would recreate the sound wave digitally.
B. This represents how a standard definition sample rate, such as 44.1KHz, would recreate the sound wave digitally.
C. This represents how a high definition sample rate, such as 96KHz, would recreate the sound wave digitally.
Analog Sound Wave
Sampling Process
Digital Sound Wave
A.
B.
C.

Sample rates are based on the Nyquist theorem, named after engineer Harry Nyquist. This theorem states that the sample rate must be twice as high as the highest desired frequency to be sampled. If the sample rate is less than the highest frequency, a phenomenon called *aliasing* can occur during the conversion process. Aliasing results in undesirable artifacts in the sound. In order to record frequencies up to 20KHz (the highest frequency heard by humans), the sound wave would need to be sampled 40,000 times per second. Sample rates were adjusted to record frequencies up to 22,050Hz to eliminate aliasing that occurred above 20KHz. This resulted in the standard CD audio sample rate of 44.1KHz. The standard sample rate for modern dialog recording is 48KHz.

Bit Depth

Also known as quantization, bit depth is the sampling of an audio signal's amplitude. On a graph, the sample rate is a horizontal measurement and the bit depth is a vertical measurement. A bit depth of 16 uses 65,536 steps to measure the amplitude. A bit depth of 24 uses 16,777,216 steps. This means that 24-bit audio has 256 times more resolution than 16-bit audio and gives a more accurate representation of the amplitude. This significantly reduces

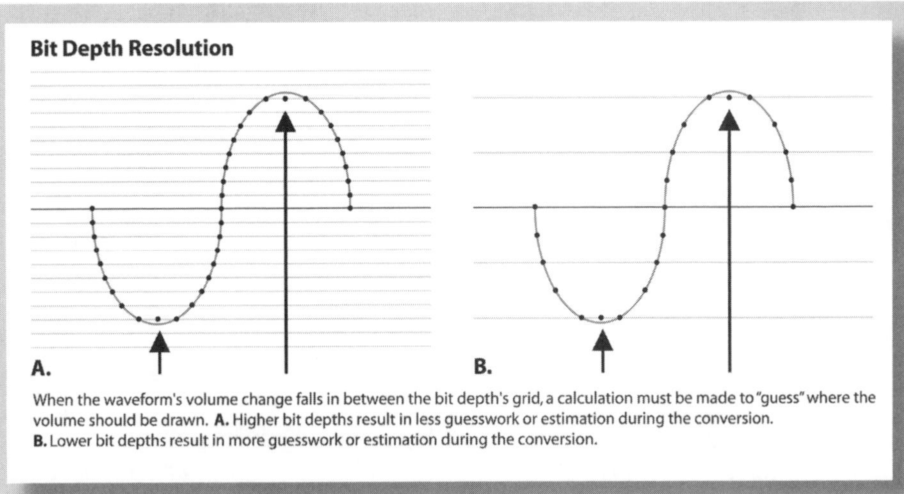

When the waveform's volume change falls in between the bit depth's grid, a calculation must be made to "guess" where the volume should be drawn. **A.** Higher bit depths result in less guesswork or estimation during the conversion. **B.** Lower bit depths result in more guesswork or estimation during the conversion.

noise in the recording. 24-bit audio is considered to be the standard bit depth for professional recording; however, most consumer and professional video cameras still use 16-bit audio.

Industry-standard film dialog is recorded at 24-bit/48KHz. ENG dialog is typically recorded at 48KHz, though the sample rate and bit depth is often based on the camera's recording capabilities. ENG audio may be recorded at 16-bit/44.1KHz, 16-bit/48KHz, 20-bit/48KHz, and 24-bit/48KHz.

Clipping

A digital file has an absolute ceiling, known as *digital zero*. If an audio signal exceeds that ceiling, the A/D converter simply maintains the last known sample point's position until the audio signal reenters the known sampling range. The result is the production of sound waves that are squared off. This produces a digital distortion of the audio signal that is unpleasant. Unlike analog signals that may appear warmer before complete distortion, *clipping* is a harsh, crunchy effect that should be avoided at all costs. In the past, clipping was a permanent issue. That is, there was no way of restoring the waveform back to its original state once clipping occurred. Modern plug-ins like those produced by iZotope can now interpolate the signal between the fixed holding points during clipping and almost perfectly restore the waveform back to its original form. Despite the safety net of modern plug-ins, great care should be taken so that a recording does not clip.

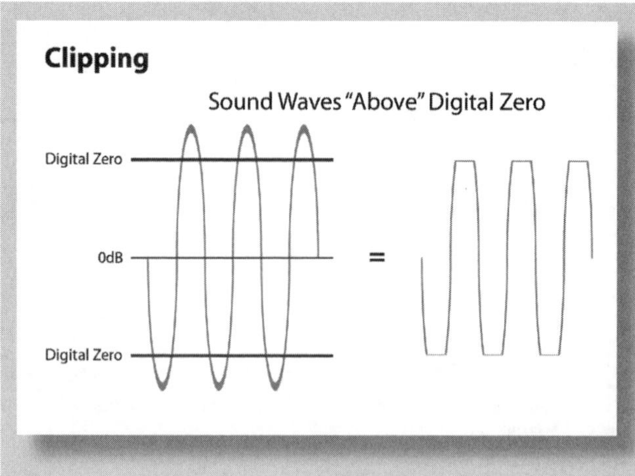

FILE FORMATS

Modern-day digital recorders use the *.WAV file format* developed by Microsoft. There are several versions of the .WAV file:

- Monophonic: a single file consisting of one channel of audio
- Stereophonic/Stereo: a single file consisting of two channels of audio
- Polyphonic: a single file consisting of multiple channels of audio

An advancement of the .WAV file is the .BWF file (*broadcast wave format*), sometimes referred to as *BWAV* (pronounced B-Wave). The .BWF allows the inclusion of metadata. A recorder can be configured to produce either monophonic or polyphonic .BWF files. For example, if you have eight tracks of audio, you can save them as a polyphonic .WAV file, which would be a single file consisting of eight channels. Using the above example, you also have the option of saving the eight tracks as monophonic .WAV files, which would create eight individual files.

Some recorders can record MP3 files, although this format is not used professionally. Generally, the only use for the MP3 file format in production work is for transcriptions. The MP3 file is a compressed format popular in consumer electronics such as the iPod. It allows the audio file to be compressed to a tenth of the original file size. This makes consumers happy because they can save valuable space on their devices and swear they can't hear the difference between an MP3 file and CD audio. The MP3 format makes audio professionals want to cram marbles in their ears and force Congress to pass a law that removes the letters "M" and "P" from the alphabet.

METADATA

Metadata is additional information (literally data about data) contained in a file. This allows searchable information to be embedded into a specific file such as timecode, file name, bit depth, sample rate, etc. With metadata, the postproduction process is much easier as the editor and post sound team can search through a bin of files and pull up specific scene takes. Syncing dailies can be set up in seconds. Other information to consider adding in the metadata would include the camera's reel number, tape number, hard drive or media card number, microphone information, character's name (not actor's name), date, scene number, take number, etc. It's virtually impossible to add too much information to the metadata.

Metadata is an extremely powerful tool, but it is rendered useless if the information it contains is not accurate. Therefore, it is critical to the workflow of postproduction that the metadata is precise. A simple step that would take seconds can quickly turn into hours of searching through hundreds of files if the metadata is incorrect. This information is expected to be correct, and compiling and entering it is now considered to be part of the sound mixer's job description.

Many recorders feature a port for connecting a third-party keyboard, which makes data entry much easier. Real estate is at a premium on the sound cart, so you'll want to look for a keyboard that has a small footprint. Recorders will have a crude data-entry function via a single knob or menu selection, but this makes it awkward to enter and edit data quickly. To save time, recorders can automatically generate successive file names based on a user-defined preset.

DIGITAL RECORDERS

Digital recorders are essentially computers designed to run on a proprietary OS that focuses on a specific task: file-based recording. Like most operating systems, the recorder can lock up, forcing the user to reboot the operating system. This is a rare occurrence, but it can happen. Digital field recorders now have extremely reliable and stable operating systems. Some digital recorders like the Zaxcom Deva offer fault-tolerant recording. This means that the recording will remain intact up until the moment of power loss.

Occasionally, software updates will be released to improve the recorder's operating system. Most savvy sound mixers will not update their operating system immediately, but will wait to see if the software update has any bugs or issues reported by disgruntled users. The last thing you want is for your livelihood to rest in the hands of software engineers. Check forums and blogs before updating your software. Don't be in a hurry. Remember, your recorder has worked fine thus far.

Digital gear is subject to digital gremlins. Unlike most analog gear, a fair amount of problems seem to magically go away after powering down and re-starting. If this doesn't work, try powering down, unplugging the power supply or battery, and powering up after ten seconds or so. Another troubleshooting technique is to review all of the menu settings and submenu selections.

Many recorders offer prerecord buffers that continually record audio. Once the unit is put into record mode, the file starts at the beginning of the buffered audio. For example, if the prerecord buffer is set to ten seconds, the recorded file will start from ten seconds *before* the record button is pressed. This time-travel function serves as a safety net for missed calls or on-the-fly recordings. The buffer can also help sync slaved machines together during the pre-roll before an edit point in postproduction. Buffer sizes vary between recorders and may be determined by the bit-depth/sample-rate settings (for example, higher bit depths/sample rates will lower the buffer size).

With the progression of solid-state technology, it is likely that laptop computers (or whatever the iPad evolves into) will become the recorders for future film production. Solid-state means that there are no moving parts. There will probably always be a need for stand-alone recorders, such as run-and-gun applications where laptops are impractical to carry. But, who knows? Maybe smartphones will become the recording choice of tomorrow. Only time will tell.

Today, laptop recorders are not recommended for location sound recording. The batteries don't last very long, making it necessary to use AC power. Special DC adaptors like those found on *www.mikegyver.com* can allow a laptop to be powered from an external 12-volt battery. Fan noise is another issue to consider. If you choose to use a laptop as your primary recorder, be sure to strip down the background applications and stay off Facebook and other unnecessary programs, to avoid crashes. Yes, I called Facebook unnecessary.

The recording medium should be an external hard drive. Never use your laptop's internal hard drive. The first reason is the operating system runs on the internal hard drive, which may cause the drive to be sluggish and result in glitches in your recordings. Secondly, you can easily lose data if your laptop crashes or there is a virus (insert Mac argument here). An external hard drive takes the workload off of the internal drive and is safe should anything happen to your operating system. Once all of these issues are resolved, you'll need a timecode source.

Boom Recorder by Vosgames and Metacorder by Gallery are software applications specifically designed for location sound recording on a laptop. They are used in combination with a third-party audio device connected to the laptop. Features include metadata entry and timecode can be fed into the software via an audio input channel.

Modern-day recorders offer functionality and audio quality that would seem like science fiction back in the golden days of the Nagra. The recorder has evolved from a single mono track to a stereo track and now offers multitrack recording. Let's take a closer look at the two types of recorders in use today: two-track recorders and multitrack recorders.

TWO-TRACK RECORDERS

Two-track recorders are often called "stereo recorders." Stereo is a word that is misleading in the production sound world. The true meaning of stereo refers to a relationship between the left and right channels. When combined, these two channels produce a single stereo image.

In production sound, stereo recorders are used to record two discrete tracks of audio that do not have a direct relationship between left and right. The terms "left" and "right" are used to indicate the path a signal takes to a specific track on a recorder. For example, the left channel refers to Channel 1 and the right channel refers to Channel 2. Therefore, panning a signal to the left sends the signal to Channel 1 and panning a signal to the right sends the signal to Channel 2. Beyond the correlation of left and right to the recorder's channels, the terms "stereo," "left," and "right" have no direct relationship to the actual soundtrack itself. More often than not, the dialog will be placed in the mono channel of the theatre and only panned to the other channels for effect.

Think logically when deciding which channel to assign a microphone on a two-track recorder. The goal is to provide editors with tracks that they can edit and mix later. Proper separation in your tracks will let them do this properly. Typically, on a two-track recorder, the primary microphone (usually the boom) is recorded on Channel 1 and secondary microphones (usually lavaliers) are mixed together on Channel 2. It should be noted that two-track recording often refers to Track 1 as Channel 1 and Track 2 as Channel 2.

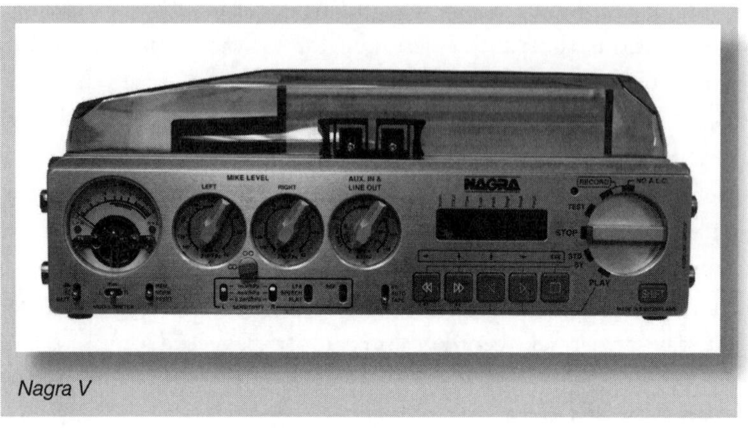

Nagra V

Here are some examples of two-track recorders:

- Fostex FR-2
- Nagra LB
- Nagra V
- Sound Devices 702T
- Tascam HD-P2

RECORDING TO THE CAMERA

In ENG production, the camera is basically a two-track recorder attached to a lens. The same channel assignments for a stand-alone two-track recorder apply to the camera: Channel 1 — primary mic, Channel 2 — a mix of secondary microphones. The challenge when using the camera as the recorder is that someone else operates the recorder for an entirely different purpose: capturing the image.

The audio controls on the camera are the sound mixer's responsibility. Most shooters are very picky about letting other people touch their gear. Establish your role with the shooter so that he is more comfortable with allowing you to make audio adjustments on his camera. If a B-roll shot is missing the audio from the camera mic, it is your responsibility. It's a good idea to check the audio settings on the camera during setup and wrap. This way, if the shooter steps out to grab B-roll and leaves you to wrap up the lights and other gear, the audio is ready for any shots he grabs.

I learned this lesson on one of my first episodes for *Dateline*. After we finished taping interviews in a local hotel room, which is a common location to shoot interviews for shows like these, the producer wanted to grab some B-roll of the subject walking down the sidewalk. It was a simple B-roll shot that didn't require a sound mixer, so I stayed back and started wrapping the gear. The shooter and the subject went outside to grab the shot along with some exteriors. A few days later, I received a call from a panicked producer. Apparently, there was no camera audio for the B-roll shot. I had assumed that the camera operator had switched the camera's audio inputs over to camera mic. In my defense, I'm pretty sure the shooter said he would change the inputs, but either way, the fault was mine for not verifying this.

The producer insisted that I travel back to the location to meet up with the subject and record her walking down the same sidewalk to provide footsteps and nat sound for the shot. Because the fault was mine, I did so at no charge. We recorded a few passes at different paces to make sure that we covered the audio and Fed Ex'd the tape off to New York. It was a four-hour ordeal once I added in drive time. That was the last time I assumed that the camera's audio inputs were changed on my behalf.

ENG snake with breakaway connector

The sound mixer will use an *ENG snake*, also called an *umbilical*, to connect the mixer to the camera. An ENG snake is a multiplex cable that usually consists of two XLRs (one for each channel) and a mini-plug used as a return feed from the camera's headphone jack. Some ENG snakes will have an extra mini-plug tap on the camera's end of the cable to allow the shooter to "tap" into the headphone jack as well. These cables can be a bit pricey, but are worth their weight in gold. They effectively consolidate the necessary signals that need to run from the mixer to the camera and the camera to the mixer inside one cable sheath.

Most ENG snakes will have a breakaway connection that allows the cable to quickly disconnect from the camera while still leaving the connected end of the snake attached to the camera. The breakaway connection will be a multi-pin XLR connector or a proprietary connector produced by the manufacturer. The XLR breakaway connectors are bigger, but are much easier to repair, while the proprietary connectors might have to be sent to a repair shop. A spare ENG snake can prove invaluable should your primary snake get damaged. If that should happen and there is no backup snake, you'll need to run separate cables for each channel. A cheap work-around is to bundle the cables using fasteners like gaffer tape, cable ties, or rope. There are significant drawbacks to these solutions. Gaffer tape gets sticky over time, cable ties get caught on things and can cut your fingers when you wrap the cable, and rope is messy and can slip along the cable. If you use two separate XLR cables, you'll need a method to distinguish between Channel 1 and Channel 2. Try using different colored cables or use gaffer tape on the end of one of the connectors to denote Channel 1 or simply label the cables.

When working with ENG snakes, strain relief on both ends of the cable is important. Hooks, clasps, or Velcro can be used to secure the cable to the sound mixer's bag to prevent the mixer from being damaged if the cable gets yanked. Cable ties, rope, or Velcro can be used to affix the snake to the handle on top of the camera. Velcro works best as it can be easily removed and placed back on during setups. Cable ties work in a pinch, but make sure you have a Leatherman or other means to cut the cable tie. Strain relief will protect the camera's connectors if the snake gets pulled or caught on something. A good trick is to pass the cable through the camera's handle one time before affixing the cable.

Once you're tethered to the camera, you will need to keep pace with the shooter. If he takes off and you're slow on the draw, he'll only get a few feet before the cable slack runs out. This will cause the cable to pull on

Cable strain relief on the handle of a camera

the camera and might smack the viewfinder up against his eye! When working with an ENG snake, try to use the least amount of slack between the camera and mixer as possible. This will make movement easier as you will have less slack to manage. Roll the snake up using the over/under method and keep the roll on the side of your bag with a Velcro strap. If you suddenly need extra length, you can pull on the Velcro strap like a ripcord and release more hose for the shooter. Once you catch up to the shooter, quickly wrap up the excess slack and place it on the side of your bag again. This technique can be very useful in run-and-gun scenarios when you're using the boom and don't have time for tidy cable management. Just pull the Velcro strap and the shooter is free to move further away while you continue to use the boom. Always leave at least one loop of the ENG snake in the Velcro strap on the sound bag to provide strain relief. This prevents the cable and mixer from getting damaged in the event someone trips over the cable. And yes, this does happen!

ENG Snakes typically come in 15' and 25' lengths. The best solution is a 25' snake. This will give you enough cable if you need it and can be easily shortened by rolling up the excess cable and hanging it from a strap on the sound bag. A 25' cable can easily become a 15' cable by rolling it up; however, a 15' cable cannot become a 25' cable if you need the extra length. Extension cables are available that will allow you to extend your cable beyond 25'.

Channel Redundancy

In situations where only one microphone is recorded, it is common practice to send the signal to both channels of the recorder. This is known as *channel redundancy*. This practice began in the days of tape-based media to prevent accidental overloads and protection from dropouts on the tape and has continued on in digital recordings. Since both channels will now contain the identical information, some sound mixers will lower the level of the second channel by -6dB for insurance against clipping.

CAMERAS WITH MULTIPLE CHANNELS

Some cameras have up to four tracks of audio that can be used. Be sure to always put the primary audio on the first two tracks. These will be the first tracks the editor reaches for during the edit. This was another lesson that I learned the hard way.

We shot an interview with Eminem for the behind the scenes of his movie *8 Mile.* I placed a lav on his shirt and had a boom mic overhead. The camera operator insisted that I put my audio on tracks 3 and 4 of the camera because he wanted to keep tracks 1 and 2 reserved for camera audio. I protested, gently, and asked if he would make an exception. He refused. I foresaw confusion happening in post and could already hear my phone ringing the next week with a call from the editor asking why the audio was so poor. So, I labeled the tape and the case, noting that the boom mic was on channel 3 and the lav was on channel 4. My phone never rang.

When the DVD was released, I skipped past the movie and went straight for the interview. To my chagrin, the editor used the audio from the camera mic. It was horrible. Despite my best efforts to notify the editor, they overlooked my notes or just didn't care enough about their work to even notice that the audio was crap. I take pride in my work. I didn't necessarily care if the client called complaining, because I knew my audio was solid. I cared more about the audio being the best it could be in the final product. I had covered my bases and the mistake was not my fault. I felt no shame; however, I was disappointed that my name went on such an awful-sounding piece. This lesson reinforces the concept behind placing the primary audio on the first channel of the recorder — be it the camera or a stand-alone recorder. When working with cameras that offer multiple channels, be sure to use the first two channels for your audio.

CONSUMER CAMERAS

Consumer cameras can be a big challenge for recording great audio. Even if you have top-of-the-line equipment gathering the sound, mixing the sources, and feeding the camcorder, you're still at the mercy of the camcorder's audio circuitry. To make this work, you need to run tests to ensure the audio works well for your production.

The first challenge you will face is that not all consumer cameras have an audio input jack. Unfortunately, this is a deal-breaker. You can never (ever, ever, ever) rely on a consumer camera's onboard microphone for the primary source of audio. In this case, you'll need to switch to a double system setup and record the audio on a separate recorder (more on this in Chapter 12). If you're using a consumer camera, it is probably because the project is very low-budget. That's fine. Low-budget projects need great audio, too! A Zoom recorder is a low-cost solution that can put usable audio in the reach of budget-conscious filmmakers.

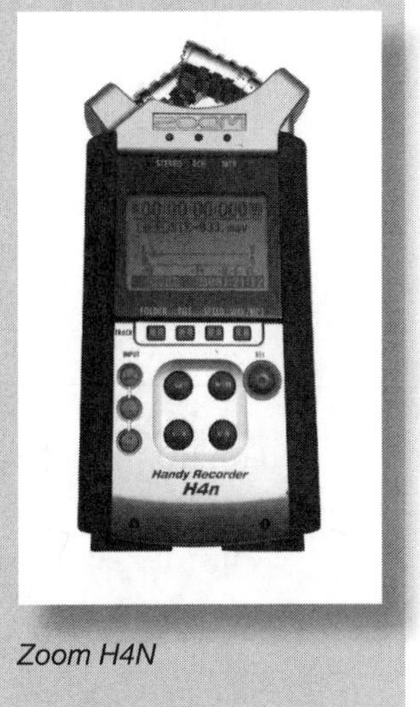

Zoom H4N

The second challenge with consumer cameras is the audio inputs are almost always at mic level. This means that the input uses a microphone preamplifier. The level you send to the camera's input must therefore be mic level, as a line level will certainly result in crunchy or distorted audio. Even high-end video cameras still have mediocre microphone preamps. Don't expect a consumer camcorder that only cost a few hundred bucks to feature stellar mic preamps. You'll need to determine how much noise is introduced into the final signal via those preamps. Typically, you will achieve better sound on the camera if the input gain controls are set at 50% or below.

The third challenge is monitoring the signal. Professional and most prosumer cameras allow you to monitor the audio via meters and headphones. Most consumer cameras don't have either capability. In effect, you're flying blind when sending audio to the camera. You won't know what you've recorded until you play it back on the set or, even worse, in the edit.

The fourth and final challenge is the connector. Consumer cameras feature a fragile mini-jack. Never use adaptors on the mini-jack as this will put unnecessary stress on the jack and can permanently damage the circuit board inside. If you need to use adaptors, do so at the output of the mixer via a short cable to protect the mixer's jack from unnecessary strain. If you're running a microphone directly into the camera that requires an adaptor, place the adaptor elsewhere. For example, you can attach the proper connector to the mini-jack via a cable that leads to the shooter's pocket where the adaptor is connected to the microphone's cable. A device like those offered from Beachtek will provide not only the connections that you need, but also mic/line switches and volume controls.

Once you've overcome these challenges, you'll need to figure out what levels to send to the camera. A good trick when setting your levels is to go to extremes in order to find a workable range. This can help save time when time is at a premium. Avoid baby-stepping your gain to find the perfect setting. Instead, crank the gain up to a significant amount, allowing it to dip into the red, and then back it down to a usable level. Understand how far the signal can go and make your decision based on that level.

To further complicate things, not all camera meters are precise. In fact, many camera meters aren't associated with numbers at all, but, rather, hash marks. This can be frustrating since there is no standard. So, one camera might show red on the meters, but that only indicates that you are in a "danger" zone and not actually experiencing distortion. With other cameras, red means "game over," i.e., the signal is distorting and will likely be unusable. Experiment with a new camera to find what the meters are really telling you. Don't believe everything you read in the manual. Listen to the signal with headphones.

Many cameras have a feature called ALC (Auto Level Control), also called AGC (Auto Gain Control). While this feature might be useful for one-man band operators, in general, sound mixers that feed audio to the camera should not use it. Unfortunately, some cameras will not allow this feature to be disabled. The results from ALC can be usable, but will not provide the same consistent quality that a sound mixer can deliver. ALC can be used as a way of determining optimal settings for audio level to the camera. The ALC circuit is designed to monitor and adjust the audio to deliver a level that is appropriate for the camera. While this level might be different from camera to camera, this could serve as useful information when trying to figure out a camera's metering system. You can engage ALC and feed dialog to the camera and watch to see where the meter's levels are adjusted. This will give you an idea of what your levels should look like on the camera's meter. Be sure to check playback to ensure that the audio is usable. Never trust a strange meter!

MULTITRACK RECORDER

Multitrack recording is a dialog editor's dream realized. For most of Hollywood's existence, dialog was shot as a mono track. It wasn't until the 1980s that stereo (technically two-track) recording became the standard. In the 2000s, digital multitrack recorders were becoming more and more popular with the advent of hard-disk recorders. Multitrack recording first began with four-track recorders, but quickly grew to eight tracks. Most productions are now using multitrack recorders as the standard, with as many as twelve or more channels on some shows. The idea behind multitrack recording is to record isolated (ISO) tracks for each mic used on set. This makes the dialog editor's job much easier.

Here are some examples of multitrack recorders:

- Edirol R-4 Pro
- Sound Device 744T
- Sound Device 788T
- Tascam HS-P82
- Zaxcom Deva IV

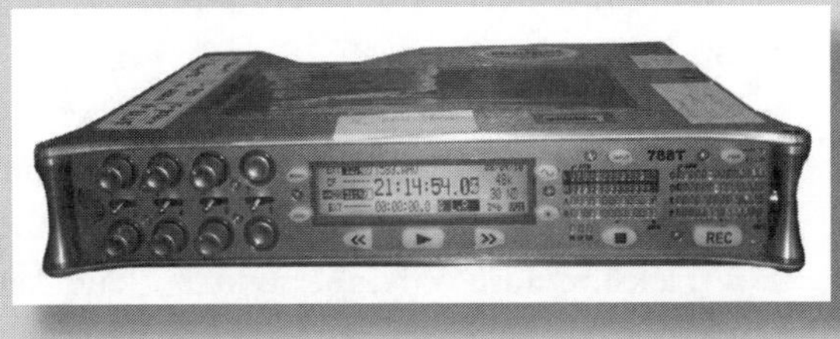

Sound Devices 788T

With more tracks to play with, the soundtrack was virtually reinvented with greater control and coverage of the dialog. However, the clouds quickly started to gather on our otherwise beautiful day. The new challenges were playback, dailies, and editing. With all of the unmixed tracks playing back at once, it was difficult to watch or cut the scenes. Producers began to complain that the soundtrack was horrible during daily screenings. So, despite this new step forward in technology, sound mixers found themselves taking one step back to mixing a mono track as they did in the early days of the Nagra monaural recorder. Today, standard multitrack practice uses Track 1 as a dedicated *mix track*. All of the tracks recorded on set are now mixed "on-the-fly" by the sound mixer and sent

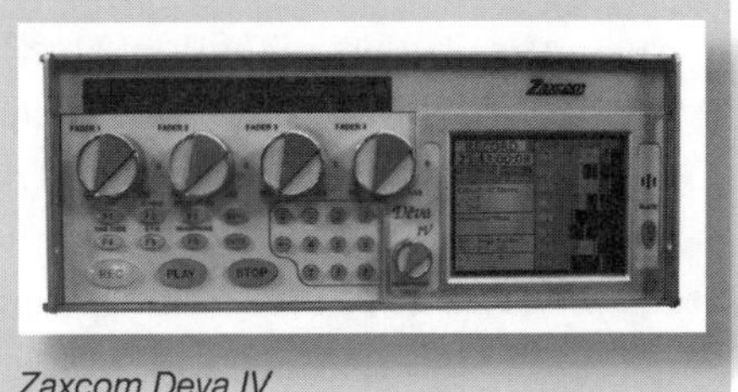

Zaxcom Deva IV

to Track 1 of the recorder. The remaining tracks on the recorder are then used as the ISO tracks.

ISO TRACKS

An *ISO track* (short for isolated) is a single recorded track with only one microphone, although ISO tracks can also be used for T.C. and music tracks. This allows each microphone to be isolated and treated in postproduction. A single ISO track may consist of multiple microphones, provided that the microphones are not heard at the same time. For example, an ISO track can have several lavaliers worn by different actors who speak at completely different times during a scene. This would still be considered an ISO track since the microphones are completely isolated from each other. Once microphones are mixed together on a single track, they cannot be separated or remixed. Therefore, it is imperative that ISO tracks have microphones that are separated.

Two-track recording often uses a combination of an ISO track and a mixed track. For example, the boom is recorded to Channel 1 and the lavaliers or other sources are mixed to Channel 2. Effectively, Channel 1 would be an ISO track and Channel 2 would be a mixed track. If only one lavalier was recorded to Channel 2, then both Channel 1 and Channel 2 would be ISO tracks because only one source of audio existed on each track.

THE MIX TRACK

The mix track can be either mono or stereo (two tracks). Mono track mixing is much easier since you are only focusing on one track. A mono track mix is perfectly acceptable in most situations as this provides audio for dailies and gives the editor a solid starting point. If other mics are preferred in post, the ISO channels can be used. Two-channel mix tracks are handled the same way as a stand-alone two-track recorder. The boom or booms will be mixed to Track 1 and the lavs will be mixed to Track 2 along with any plant mics. This can be more challenging since you have essentially two mixes happening at the same time.

Some multitrack recorders may offer an optional proprietary mix panel that can be added to control the recorder's mixing functionality. This mix panel can eliminate the need for an external mixer to create a mix track. It should be noted that on most units, analog signals do not pass through

Zaxcom Deva Mix-12

the external mixer. Instead, the mixer acts as a control surface allowing the sound mixer to put his hands on virtual functions. Because these mixers are control surfaces, the inputs and outputs are found on the recorder itself. Newer cart mixers have come to market offering a hybrid of this blend between analog controls and digital recording by integrating a digital recorder in the cart mixer itself. When choosing a mixing console, bussing and direct-out ports become more important features for multitrack recording.

TRACK ASSIGNMENT

When assigning mics to tracks on the recorder, put the mics in order based on priority. After the mix track, the first track should be the boom, then the next most important mic source and so on. One of the reasons that the mix track is placed on track 1 is because some telecine machines have the ability to automatically strip off track 1 from .BWF polyphonic files to be used for dailies. Try to stay consistent with track assignments for key actors' lavs. This will make the dialog editor's job much easier. Avoid randomly throwing mics on different tracks. Think of how the tracks will be used in post. Try to plan a system and stick to that plan when you can.

Here is an example of track assignments for a multitrack recorder:

- Track 1: Mix
- Track 2: Boom #1
- Track 3: Boom #2
- Track 4: Actor Lav
- Track 5: Actor Lav
- Track 6: Actor Lav
- Track 7: Actor Lav
- Track 8: Plant Mic

When mixing ISO tracks, it's important to realize that the ISO tracks' levels are determined by the gain setting, not the channel fader. The channel fader is used to balance the channels with each other. This holds true for dedicated mix panels and separate mixing consoles that use the direct outs for each individual channel. The beauty of using this technique is that any fader adjustments that are made will not affect the channel's ISO track. It's a real-world "undo" feature. If you make a mistake during the mix, you or the post team can default to the ISO track to remix. With most multitrack recorders, you can perform a remix on the set during a break to correct any mistakes that you might have made during the take.

Film and television productions each have a different view on the mix track. In film, the mix track is used for dailies, on-set playback, and editing. During sound post, the mix track is typically discarded and the ISO tracks are used as the primary sources of dialog. With most television productions, the pace of the post process is much faster in order to get the production to air. For this reason, the mix track is used as the primary source of dialog and the ISO tracks are used in case the mix track doesn't work for a scene. This is not to say that the mix track isn't as important for film mixers. Care should be taken to sculpt the best mix track possible in any production, even if it is only intended to use as a reference.

Some multitrack recorders feature ten tracks of recordable audio. The catch is, there are only eight inputs and therefore eight possible ISO tracks. The other two tracks are dedicated to mix tracks, meaning that their sources come from a user-defined combination or mix of the eight input tracks. This frees up all eight tracks to be used as ISO tracks; however, if you are using an external mixing console, you are limited to only eight recording tracks. These eight tracks will include a mono mix track, leaving you with seven ISO tracks, or a stereo mix track, leaving you with six ISO tracks. Other multitrack recorders like the Deva 16 provide sixteen channels of recordable audio by using a combination of eight analog inputs and eight digital inputs.

The benefit of an external mixing console is that you can configure the mix to meet your needs. For example, if you have ten mics in use, but only have seven available ISO tracks, you can sub-mix four channels to feed an aux output or subgroup (see page 198). Not every mic needs a dedicated ISO track, but it is important that every line of dialog have a dedicated space on an ISO track. In the example given, the additional four mics to be subgrouped might represent single non-overlapping lines given by characters at different times in the scene. Therefore, it's not important that these single lines have a dedicated ISO track.

In the case of reality TV, all bets are off on a decent mix. Reality TV is unscripted (at least, that's what we're led to believe...). So, it's impossible to mix dialog when you have no idea who is going to speak and when they will speak. This is where multitracking becomes invaluable. The sound mixer is essentially a technician who is multitracking everything possible. The editor will mix the tracks in postproduction. Reality TV is designed to capture the subjects' raw emotions. The expression of these raw emotions can range drastically from whispers and low-spoken gossip to full-on outrage and shouting matches. The mixer can be set for average levels of dialog, but it's the sound mixer's responsibility to follow the action and anticipate when levels will shift with the emotion of the moment. Don't get too comfortable with the fact that you aren't "mixing" the dialog. You need to have ninja-like reflexes and the foresight of a Jedi to predict and react in the heat of the moment.

MEDIA DELIVERY

In the days of Nagra and DAT, there were tape-based media that were delivered to the production at the end of each day. The current storage media for recorders are an internal hard drive, SD (Secure Digital Card), and CFC (Compact Flash Card). With hard-disk and card-based recording formats, there are a couple of options for media delivery. The first is to do a *drive swap*, meaning that several hard drives are used during the production. A sound mixer will record on one drive, deliver that drive for transferring, and continue the next day with a different drive. In effect, the hard drives are leapfrogged every other day so that production can continue while dailies are produced. The same workflow can be accomplished with compact flash cards and is often the case.

Optical drives (DVD-R or DVD-RAM) can be found on some recorders and are used to create a copy of the recordings to hand off to postproduction. Optical drives are still popular, but they take longer to write and are susceptible to environmental conditions (moisture, condensation, vibrations, etc.). Another solution is to use your laptop to burn a DVD. Once the preferred method of delivery, optical disks are quickly being replaced with flash cards as the delivery medium of choice. Flash cards are more stable and can be written faster. Unlike optical disks, flash cards can be reused over and over again.

Regardless of the delivery method that you choose, it is imperative that you keep a copy of the recorded material. If the delivered media is lost, damaged, or accidentally erased, the production company will ask you for a backup. They will assume and expect you to have one. These backups don't include a safety two-track recording of your mix that you may have made with a backup recorder. A true backup should consist of all the ISO tracks in the case of multitrack recordings.

Some digital recorders allow for real-time mirroring of recordings to separate media for backups and postproduction delivery. DVD-RAM is a popular media choice because of instant verification after it's written, whereas DVD+R, DVD-R, and DVD-RW can only be verified after the entire disc has been written. Without mirroring, it will be necessary to create a separate copy of the recordings at the end of the day. Digital ports, such as Firewire and USB, may be included to allow the unit to interface with a computer, external hard drive. or another recorder for mirroring and backups.

Calculate backups and burns into your wrap time. Begin your media backups before you start wrapping cables and putting away microphones. If you are using AC power from the grip department, let them know that you are still using power. It is common practice for them to give a "Power going cold" call so that any departments still using AC are informed of the impending loss of power. Unfortunately, this doesn't always happen. When in doubt, communicate this information to the gaffer. Be sure to eject media cards by using the recorder's menu or turn off the unit to prevent loss of data when ejecting media.

Label the media clearly. Include the date of production, sound roll, name of production, sample rate, bit depth, reference tone, timecode rate, etc. Don't just label the case! The media will eventually be removed from the case. Once this happens, it will be difficult to sort through the dozens of unlabeled media in order to find the right sound roll.

METERS

There are two types of meters: VU and peak. The difference between them is a matter of ballistics. *VU meters* are slower in response to the audio signal. A properly calibrated VU meter will take 300 milliseconds to reach "0" when sent a 1KHz tone. The fall time or release time is also 300 milliseconds. A *peak meter* is a blazing thirty times faster with a rise time of 10 milliseconds. However, the peak meter's fall time is extremely slow (usually about 1,700 milliseconds) to allow for the engineer to see the meter's response. The release time of peak meters is user-programmable on some equipment. Peak is also called PPM (Peak Program Meter).

The VU meter closely represents how the human ear perceives volume. It determines the overall average level of a program (film, television, radio, etc.). VU stands for "volume units", although most joke that it stands for "virtually useless." This might be true for location sound, given the nature of digital recording. Peak meters are not a luxury, but a necessity when recording to a digital recorder to avoid clipping.

Most of the analog mechanical meters (both VU and peak) have been replaced with LCD screen readouts and LED ladder-type meters. These are usually peak meters, but some LCD/LED meters can be set to VU, peak, or both. The scale of a VU meter typically reads between -20dB and +3dB. The scale of a peak meter typically reads between -40dBFS and 0dBFS. Using a VU meter with a digital recorder is a dangerous gamble. The VU meter might show that the signal is only at -3dB, however the digital recorder might be clipping. A peak meter will give you a true and accurate indication of the levels being recorded. If your levels clip during a shot, it's best to ask for another take for safety.

CALIBRATING EQUIPMENT

It is necessary to calibrate your equipment at the beginning of each setup to ensure that signal flow is working at the proper levels and to give the post team a reference level. In the days of videotape, it was standard practice to place thirty seconds of SMPTE color bars and a 1KHz tone at the beginning of each tape to give the editor both a picture and sound reference for aligning the signals with the post equipment. This was collectively referred to as *bars and tone*. Today, bars and tone are becoming more rare. Digital technology is not inclined to the wide-sweeping differences that were common in analog equipment. However, many production houses and networks still require bars and tone at the front of the media, even if the media is not tape-based. Regardless of the requirement to record bars and tone at the beginning of the media, it is necessary to send a 1KHz *reference tone* (also known as an *alignment tone*) to the camera or recorder to ensure that your equipment is aligned properly. This should be done often and at least once during every setup.

It is still common practice to record a reference tone on the recorder at the start of each day. The SMPTE standard reference level is -20dBFS. When your equipment is calibrated to -20dBFS, you effectively have 20dB of headroom before clipping. Incorrectly calibrating two devices that are using different meter types can be disastrous. It is imperative that the meters are communicating the same information. Using the 1KHz alignment tone, here is how the meters translate:

- Peak Full Scale = -20dBFS
- VU = 0dB
- Peak = -8dB

If the mixer doesn't have a tone generator, you can purchase a cable tester that provides a test-tone level or use a dedicated tone generator. If you don't have the means to generate tone, you can set up the mixer or recorder with some test dialog. Start by setting the levels on the mixer and then feed the mixer to the camera and set up the camera's levels to match the mixer's meters. When setting up levels without tone, it's a good idea to record a test and check the levels during playback. Many camera meters are improperly labeled or in many cases not labeled at all. When in doubt, run a test to figure out what the manufacturer means by these meters. If your signal is too low, you could introduce hiss from system noise. If your signal is too hot, you could cause distortion.

Cable tester

WHAT TO LOOK FOR IN A PROFESSIONAL RECORDER

Preamps are the single most important feature to look for in a field mixer and recorder. Professional preamps will have a dynamic range of 100dB or greater. Although the unit may have a zillion cutting-edge features, if the preamps are garbage, then the unit is garbage. Recorders should be able to handle vibrations, moisture, and condensation caused by extreme temperatures. Also consider the amount of tracks that the unit offers and the recording medium that it uses.

Once you've decided on a recorder, you'll need to give it a road test to figure out its limitations. Turn your recorder on and set your channel and master to unity (usually about 60% on most recorders). Record for about thirty seconds. Next, record with your favorite mic in the standard overhead position at two feet away. Record takes with the microphone channel's gain at different levels. Start with the gain at a low setting (20% open) and record a few sentences. Repeat this a few times and increase the gain by 20% each time. Play back your recordings in your headphones and listen for system noise. Next, play back your recordings in a studio through monitors and listen for system noise. What do you notice?

The purpose of this exercise is to allow you to understand the limitations of your gear better. This is a good test to run on any new microphones, mixers, or recorders that you purchase. It's better to find out your limitations in a controlled environment than to find out in the middle of a shoot on location!

BACKUP RECORDERS

Backup recorders are often used in parallel with the main recorder. This provides a safety net should the primary recorder fail or the recordings get lost or damaged. A backup recorder can be fed the output of the primary recorder or an output from the mixer. Some recorders will have AES/EBU or SPDIF outputs that can be used to send digital audio to a backup recorder and use a single cable that can carry two channels of uncompressed PCM audio.

Never underestimate the quality of a modest backup recorder like the Zoom H4n. These units can provide low-budget filmmakers with better sound quality than that of the camera's audio recorder. Correctly using the tools that you have available can provide usable audio, regardless of the price point.

Backup recorders can be a lifesaver when working with video cameras. I hosted a show called *Rode Rage* that featured interviews with over a dozen professionals from various industries (film, television, music, video games, etc.). My team and I flew from Detroit to LA for a couple of weeks and shot the two-camera interviews on a couple of Panasonic DVX100Bs. It was a standard ENG shoot and we were running all of the audio to the primary camera. We ran tests on the camera before we packed the gear. Despite the successful tests, we decided to bring along a backup recorder, just in case.

After all the fun in the sun, we flew back to Detroit and began editing over forty hours of footage. Sure enough, there was a buzz in the audio on the main camera — the camera that all of the audio was fed! After spending a couple of days in the hospital from a minor panic attack (slight exaggeration), we used the backup recordings. It was a snap to sync the audio, since the interviews were only a couple of takes each and we had slated the start of each take. Had we not used a backup recorder, we would have lost a significant amount of time and money. It cost us nothing but a few seconds of extra setup time to use a backup recorder that single-handedly saved the show. Do yourself a favor and consider using backup recorders. The time will come when it will be a show-saver for you.

CHAPTER EXERCISE Practice by recording at different levels on a recorder (extremely low and high levels as well as correct levels). Deliberately clip the signal. Listen to the results. What happens when you increase the low levels in an editing program? What happens when you decrease the high levels? Are you able to repair the clipped levels?

CHAPTER 12

SYNC

The miracle of film and television is a result of a perceptual phenomenon known as "persistence of vision." When pictures are flashed in front of the eyes at a certain rate, they appear to have motion. In reality, a movie is merely 24 pictures flashing on a screen each second. This frame rate convinces our minds that what we are seeing is actual motion. But there is no motion to the pictures; they're just a series of still images.

The illusion that persistence of vision creates is kicked into virtual reality when sound is incorporated. An actor on screen might appear to be stabbing another actor with a butcher's knife, but of course, he's probably using a fake knife and not coming remotely close to the other actor. When the sound of the inside of a watermelon being bludgeoned is played in sync with the stabbing images, the audience is thrust into a realism that will make them squirm in their seats or even look away from the screen. The illusion is now complete. They are convinced that what they hear is a result of what they see.

When the dialog of a scene is played in sync with the images on the screen, the audience associates the two forms of media, sound and picture, as being one source. They believe that what they hear is coming directly from the screen. Most movie patrons (including my dad) are unaware that there are speakers behind the screen. The moment the sound and picture appear out of sync, the audience is immediately taken out of the fantasy world of storytelling and realize they are being subjected to the technology. Older martial arts films are a classic case of out-of-sync dialog. The words move, but the dialog is delayed.

There are two methods of recording sound for picture: *single system* and *double system*.

SINGLE SYSTEM

A single system consists of a camera that records both sound and picture simultaneously. Sound sync is achieved as the image is recorded. Therefore, the camera serves as the audio recorder. The audio controls on the camera are impossible to manage during a shot, so with a single system setup, the sound mixer uses his equipment as a remote control of the camera's audio inputs. Once the mixer and camera are calibrated (i.e., inputs selections, channel levels, etc.), the sound mixer controls the sound recorded by the camera. It is common practice to place a piece of gaffer tape over audio controls on a camera that might get bumped or accidentally moved. Some newer camera manufacturers have solved this problem by adding plastic shields that allow you to see the controls without moving them. If the knobs are too dark to see in low lighting environments (often the case in production) you can place thin strips of glow-in-the-dark tape on them for orientation.

It is important to understand that the camera can be the audio recorder. While this isn't possible with film cameras (outside of Super 16mm), modern digital film cameras offer audio recording. Most ENG production is shot single system. A backup recorder can be used if the camera's audio is poorly recorded or the wireless hop experiences hits and drops.

Backup recorders are also used to record audio for transcribing. These transcription recorders do not need to provide superior audio, just a reference so that a transcription service can transcribe the interview or production content. Producers use these transcriptions during the editing process as a way of quickly finding sound bites for the piece. A handheld recorder, like the Zoom H4n, can be used for transcription recorders, but do not have timecode capability (see page 170). One solution is to record audio to channel 1 and timecode to channel 2.

DOUBLE SYSTEM

In a double system, the picture is captured with a camera and the sound is captured on an audio recorder. The audio recorder functions independently of the camera. With a single system, one button on the camera is used to record both sound and picture. In a double system, the recording process requires both the camera and recorder to be rolling. The picture and sound are synced together later during postproduction.

Modern-day digital film cameras, such as the Red One, are capable of recording audio, but are usually shot double system. The audio capabilities of these cameras are simply inferior to stand-alone recorders. However, you can send an audio signal to these cameras via a wireless hop, to be used for reference. Obviously, a hardwire cable will give the best results, but even a wireless signal, dropouts and all, can be useful for on-set playback and provide dailies that are already in sync. This can be a time-and-money saver for independent films. Be sure to have a harness or mount for the wireless receivers that are going to the camera to allow the camera crew to work freely without getting tangled up with your cables. Also, send reference tone during each camera setup to ensure the audio received by the wireless receiver is properly sent to the camera.

Avoid using the camera mic as a "reference" track in a double system. Instead, send a signal from the mixer or recorder to the camera. The distance from the talent to the boom mic will be different than the distance from the talent and the camera mic. This greater distance can cause a delay in the camera mic, which may create problems when syncing audio in post without timecode or a slate marker.

DOUBLE SYSTEM PROTOCOL

Double system setups require the use of a clapboard in order to sync the audio to picture efficiently. A standard protocol is followed for each take. This protocol provides information for both the camera and audio recorder.

At the beginning of each take, the following call will be made:

1st AD: "Roll Sound"

Sound Mixer: "Speed"

1st AD: "Roll Camera"

Camera Operator: "Rolling" or "Camera Speed"

1st AD: "Marker"

2nd AC: "Scene 1, Take 1, Marker"

The 2nd AC then closes the clapboard sticks to create an audible clap for a sync point.

Alternate terms might be used and different crewmembers might make these calls. The important thing to realize is the protocol. Sound will roll their media first and then audibly confirm their roll by saying "Speed" to let the crew know that their equipment is recording. Sound media is cheaper than film stock, so it makes sense to let sound roll first to save the cost of film. Camera will then roll film and confirm this roll audibly by saying "Rolling" or "Camera speed." Avoid hand signals such as "thumbs up" or simply nodding your head. Do not assume that someone is watching you or that they somehow realize that you are rolling. The production will wait for you to say "Speed" before continuing, so make sure that you say "Speed" nice and loud. If you say "Speed" and there is a long pause, you might confirm they heard you by saying "Sound Speed" a second time.

When the scene is marked, be sure to have the clapboard held close enough to the microphone so that the clapboard's sticks are heard when they close. In some cases, the clapboard might be held away from the talent for framing reasons. In this case, the boom operator should point the mic toward the clapboard to hear the sticks. If you are only using lavs or plant mics, try to have the clapboard as close as possible to those mics. This might include standing next to an actor wearing a hidden lav.

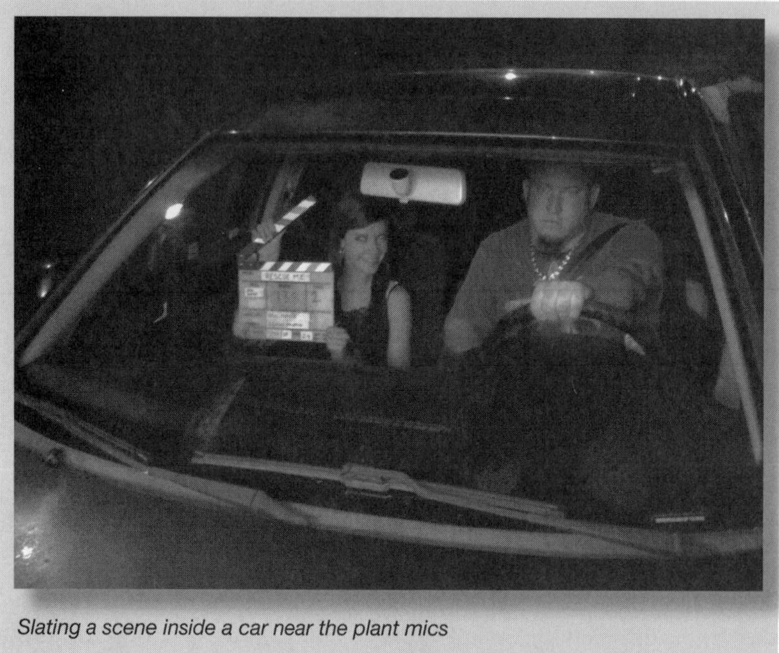

Slating a scene inside a car near the plant mics

It is imperative that the camera sees the information on the clapboard along with the sticks when they come together. This includes scene/take information and timecode (if using a timecode slate). In some situations, slating the shot might be difficult or impossible. For example, if the camera starts with an extreme close-up of an actor's eye and then slowly pulls out, the shot can be complicated to position and focus for a clapboard. If this is the case, you can "tail slate" the shot. This means that the slate happens at the end or "tail" of the shot. It is standard procedure to hold the clapboard upside down to indicate that the shot is being tail slated. Be prepared to preempt a "cut" call from the director so that the shot can be slated. Remind the director (who will probably begin the cut call with a paused "And… cut!") to tail slate by calling out "Tail Slate." If the shot is cut before a tail slate is called, be sure to note "No Slate" on the sound report.

Tail slate (hot chick not included)

In cases where it is difficult or impossible for front- or tail-slate sticks to be heard by the microphone, you can have the actors mark the take by saying the scene and take number and then clap their hands. This is a crude solution, but it works. Be sure to have the talent clap their hands so that both of their hands are seen coming together by the camera. There is a funny behind-the-scenes clip on the *Home Alone* DVD that shows actor Daniel Stern inside a van with fellow actor Joe Pesci. Since the clapboard was held outside of the van, Stern had to use handclaps to mark the scenes, often at the expense of Pesci's ears.

Second sticks refers to a shot that was slated, but the clap sticks were out of frame or not clearly seen by the camera. To avoid confusion in post, it is standard procedure to call "second sticks" before the clapboard is clapped for the second time. Always note "seconds sticks" on the sound report. If this is not noted, the editor might sync to the wrong marker.

Slating is a standard procedure in double system productions. If you are not able to slate each take, be it a lack of crew or lack of time, you can always manually sync up the takes using the waveforms. Keep in mind: this will cost you extra time in post.

SINGLE AND DOUBLE SYSTEMS: PROS AND CONS

Each system presents its own set of assets and liabilities. Here's a look at the most significant.

Single System Pros

The setup is much easier. One device records both sound and picture. Sync is achieved during the recording process, which saves time in postproduction.

Single System Cons

Cameras are manufactured to produce great images, not necessarily great sound. Nearly all cameras have substandard audio compared to low-priced, handheld recorders. The sound mixer must be tethered to the camera. If the tether is a wireless hop, the audio can suffer from hits and dropouts.

Double System Pros

A double system setup will always offer superior sound. The sound mixer operates independently of the camera, which gives the camera operator greater freedom. The audio can be properly monitored and adjusted from a single location.

Double System Cons

The setup is more complicated. Two separate systems are involved. Sound and picture will need to be synced together in postproduction.

EXAMPLES OF SINGLE SYSTEM SETUPS

- Mic to Camera
- Mic to Mixer to Camera
- Mic to Mixer to Camera and Backup/Transcription Recorder

- Mic to Mixer to Multiple Cameras
- Mic to Mixer to Multiple Cameras and Backup/Transcription Recorder
- Mic to Mixer to Satellite Truck with Return Feed for IFB and RTS/ Clearcom

EXAMPLES OF DOUBLE SYSTEM SETUPS

- Mic to Mixer to Recorder
- Mic to Mixer to Recorder and Camera (camera audio is used for reference)*
- Mic to Multitrack Recorder
- Mic to Multitrack Recorder and Camera (camera audio is used for reference)*

**Note: Sending audio to camera in a double system can provide a reference track for dailies or instant sync for quicker editing. The audio can be replaced with the recorder's audio in postproduction, but may need to be re-synced manually if the camera was not fed the same timecode from the recorder.*

SOUND REPORTS/SOUND LOGS

A *sound report* is a detailed log of every track recorded by the sound mixer. This is a crucial document for postproduction as all of the scenes, takes, and take information are kept on this log. The script supervisor gives scene numbers and takes. When in doubt, verify these numbers with her. This is especially crucial if there are any confusing situations such as tail slates that were forgotten or dead rolls. As a side note, it is common practice to skip over scene numbers with I's and O's as they are easily confused with ones and zeros.

Videographer Danny Stolker shooting double system with a Canon 5D

Additional information may include microphone types, sample rate, bit depth, reference tone, timecode rate, etc. Sound reports can contain several carbon copies that allow the same report to be distributed among the production and postproduction, as well as a copy for the sound mixer. Digital sound reports can even be generated as searchable .PDF files. BWF-Widget is a software application specifically designed to read and edit metadata contained in audio files. The software can also print sound reports and generate .PDF files. Handwritten logs should be printed legibly.

SOUND REPORT

DATE ________ PRODUCTION ________ ROLL ________

SAMPLE FREQ ________ DIRECTOR ________ MEDIA ________

BIT ________ MIXER ________ TIMECODE ________

SCENE	TAKE	SOUND FILE#	CAM FILE#	NOTES	CH 1	CH 2

PAGE # ________

Sound report - two channel

SOUND REPORT

PRODUCTION: MEDIA: ROLL: DATE:

DIRECTOR: SAMPLE FREQ: BIT:

MIXER: PHONE: EMAIL: TIMECODE:

SCENE	TAKE	SOUND FILE#	CAMERA FILE#	NOTES	CH 1	CH 2	CH 3	CH 4	CH 5	CH 6	CH 7	CH 8

PAGE #

Sound report - multichannel

ABBREVIATION	MEANING	DESCRIPTION
▸ TS	Tail Slate	The take was slated at the end of the scene.
▸ M.O.S.	Without Sound (Mit Out Sound)	The shot was filmed without sound.
▸ NG	No Good	The director said the shot was not good.
▸ PRINT	A Printed Take	The shot was approved and "printed" by the director. These takes should be circled on the sound report.

ABBREVIATION	MEANING	DESCRIPTION
▸ NGS or SNG	Not Good for Sound	There was a problem with the sound. The director may still use this shot, but the audio will need to be repaired or ADR'd.
▸ BIF	Boom in Frame	The boom mic entered the frame.
▸ WT	Wild Track	Sound recorded without camera.
▸ VO	Voiceover	A recorded narration or voiceover.
▸ PB	Playback	A take that used a playback track.
▸ RT	Room Tone	Ambient sound of the room (typically thirty seconds).
▸ SS	Second Sticks	The clapboard was clapped twice.
▸ FS	False Start	The take was aborted.
▸ FT	False Take	The take was aborted.

Always keep a copy of the sound report. This can be a lifesaver for the production, if the original sound report is lost, which will make you the hero. A copy of the report can also defend you from an accusation if a recording turns up missing or your techniques are in question. The sound report won't lie. If the director claims that you said the sound was fine, you can reference the shot on the sound report that states otherwise. Unfortunately, the postproduction stage of a film quickly turns into the blame game with everyone pointing fingers at each other trying to dodge responsibility for a botched shot. A sound report may be your only proof as to what actually transpired on the set. Many times this is the only reason the sound report is ever referenced. If you've done your job well, the editor can sail through the editing process without looking at the report at all. Metadata in the sound files will help guide the post sound team to the right file. Today, sound reports are mainly used as a backup to the metadata and for problem-solving take information from the camera's shot log.

PREPPING AUDIO FOR POST

Postproduction means different things for different projects. For some projects, there will be a team of a dozen or more audio professionals working on the audio tracks: sound effects, Foley, ADR, and the dialog tracks that you recorded on set. For other projects, it could be only one editor who might have very little audio experience, if any. You should fully understand how your tracks are going to be used before you arrive on the set. Clear communication should be established between you and the producer (in the case of video production) or you and the post supervisor (in the case of film production). For live television, all bets are off. There is no postproduction in live TV. Sure, the live event might be edited into other pieces at a later time, but for the most part — you are live! What leaves your mixer and heads out to the satellite truck or station feed is what the audience will hear, so you have to get it right the first time.

For features, speak with the post supervisor or directly with the picture editor to discuss all the technical specs for delivery. Subjects to cover might include timecode, delivery medium, sample rates, bit depth, and file formats. When multitracking on location, keep in mind that the picture editor will probably just need a mix track, whereas post sound will need all of the ISO tracks. Clear communication is key. All technical specs should be confirmed in an email or printed document so that everyone is on the same page.

If you do your job right, you should never hear from the other end of the chain. If your phone rings, then there is probably something wrong. Brian Kaurich, a former sound recordist at The Detroit Chop Shop, went on to become a very successful sound mixer for features and reality television shows. Recently, he received a letter from the sound editor of a film that he provided production sound for. The letter thanked Brian for his superb and consistent dialog. That never happens. But, if it does, savor the moment!

TIMECODE — BE PREPARED TO BE CONFUSED

Timecode is a counter for labeling each individual frame of a recording medium with a unique number. In the 1950s, the Society for Motion Picture and Television Engineers (SMPTE) developed the industry standard SMPTE timecode used in film and television production. SMPTE timecode gives each frame a specific number, much in the same way that each house has a unique address. This allows editors the ability to search and locate a specific frame in the program material for the purpose of editing and playback. These searches function in the same way that addresses allow a postal carrier to deliver the mail to a specific house. These assigned numbers are based on a twenty-four-hour clock and divided into four columns. Each column always contains two numbers: HH:MM:SS:FF (hours, minutes, seconds, frames).

Example: 01:02:03:04 = 1 hour, 2 minutes, 3 seconds, and 4 frames.

The first three columns stay consistent throughout different timecode formats. There will always be sixty seconds in a minute, sixty minutes in an hour, and twenty-four hours in a day. However, the last field is where things get a little fuzzy.

FRAME RATES

The *frame rate* for video was originally derived from the frequency of the electrical systems used to process video. In the United States, current alternates at 60Hz. So, 1Hz was used per field and there were two fields of video per frame, so 60Hz became 30fps (frames per second). This standard is used in NTSC (National Television Standards Committee) video. In Europe, current alternates at 50Hz, so 1Hz per field and two fields per frames became 25fps. This standard is used in PAL (Phase Alternating Lines) video.

In the beginning, NTSC video originally ran at thirty frames per second. So, the maximum timecode value would be thirty frames. The frame column's numbering system would start at 00 and end at 29. Given this parameter, the maximum number of timecode that could be recorded would be:

23:59:59:29 or 23 hours, 59 minutes, 59 seconds, 29 frames.

If we added one more frame to the number above, the total timecode number would exceed the twenty-four-hour time allotment and roll the numbers back to zero: 00:00:00:00. This is known as "crossing the midnight hour."

The midnight hour created all sorts of havoc with the old VTR decks. In the golden days of VTRs (videotape recorders), the motors and gears took a few seconds to spin at their proper speed. Without proper speed, the tape would start playback with glitches and slur in the video. During editing, it was necessary to pre-roll the videotape for a few seconds before an actual edit point to allow the machine to "get up to speed." In doing so, the video would play back properly at the edit point without any artifacts caused by the barbaric mechanics of the machine. Standard pre-roll time was set at five seconds. This time allowed the machine to reach and maintain proper playback speed.

During the editing process, VTRs would search for a given timecode by referencing the timecode at the tape's current position. Once the play or record button was pressed, the VTR would rewind the tape five seconds (pre-roll) and then begin playback or recording. The problem with the midnight hour is that if you had a tape with timecode that crossed the twenty-four-hour mark in the middle, the VTR would get confused and begin rewinding or fast-forwarding in a mad dash to find the correct edit point. In a sense, the VTR would become lost.

For example, let's assume that timecode was started at the beginning of the videotape at 23:45:00:00 and that we are fifteen minutes and two seconds into the tape. The timecode has crossed the midnight hour and the timecode now reads 00:00:02:00.

If the current tape position is 00:00:02:00 and the edit point is 00:00:03:00, a problem will occur because the VTR needs to rewind the tape five seconds prior to the starting point for proper pre-roll. Since the edit point is one second beyond the current position, the VTR needs to back up four more seconds in order to reach the five second pre-roll position. Once the VTR rewinds beyond two seconds, the timecode will read 23:59:59:29. When this happens, the VTR assumes that it has a full twenty-four hours of tape to rewind before it reaches the start point! This caused a serious predicament.

So, as with everything else in this industry, a workaround was devised to avoid crossing the dreaded midnight hour. Editors and camera operators would set the timecode at the start of each tape at one hour or 01:00:00:00. This would avoid confusing the VTRs during editing and life would once again be happy.

DROP-FRAME

The frame rate of 30fps worked great in the beginning days of television when shows were broadcast in black and white and the standard was, well, black and white. Then came color! The addition of color to the video signal screwed everything up. The television signal was altered to a different timing: 29.97 frames per second. This change caused a hiccup with the clocking system. SMPTE timecode was now running 3.6 seconds longer for each hour. The one constant standard in all of this mess was that TV networks were greedy bastards who coveted their advertising dollars and 3.6 seconds per hour meant they would lose two precious thirty-second commercials each day. So, something had to be done to adjust the frame rate. A bunch of geniuses in white coats got together and derived a system that would drop frame numbers throughout each hour to account for the overage. This new system was cleverly named *drop-frame*.

Drop-frame timecode drops the first two frames of each minute, except for each tenth minute (i.e., each minute that ends in zero: 00, 10, 20, 30, 40, and 50). It sounds crazy, but the math adds up. Here's how it looks:

Example of two frames dropped for each minute:

01:02:59;27
01:02:59;28
01:02:59;29
01:03:00;02
01:03:00;03
01:03:00;04

**Note that frames ;00 and ;01 were dropped from this sequence.*

Example of a minute ending in zero:

01:09:59;27
01:09:59;28
01:09:59;29
01:10:00;00
01:10:00;01
01:10:00;02

**Note that no frames were dropped.*

It can be a bit confusing when doing the math. I wouldn't be surprised if they further extended this rule to include that numbers ending in "7" gained two frames on every other Tuesday except during leap years! Nonetheless, this is the standard that we have to work with. I would hope that the standard would be reworked altogether to end up with a "true" numbering system called the "No Frame Left Behind" standard where every frame is accounted for and each frame is true to the frame rate of the format chosen (24fps, 25fps or 30fps). This would mean that each true frame is equally divisible by every second of a wall clock (e.g., 30fps would then mean each frame is truly 1/30 of a second). One can only dream.... In the meantime, most folks use NDF timecode because it assigns a number to each frame without skipping frame numbers. This is despite the fact that each hour will have an overage of 3.6 seconds.

It is very important to point out that the frames are not actually dropped at all. Instead the frame *numbers* are dropped. In short, drop-frame is simply a numbering system that skips numbers periodically. Also, drop-frame timecode should not be confused with *dropped frames*. Dropped frames are frames that are not properly digitized by your NLE or video-capture software when video footage is transferred in real time. The two names are completely unrelated.

A colon (":") before a column denotes standard non-drop timecode, whereas a semicolon (";") denotes the use of drop-frame timecode. These symbols usually appear before the frames column of the timecode:

01:02:03:04 = Non-Drop Frame Timecode (NDF)
01:02:03;04 = Drop-Frame Timecode (DF)

However, some readers will display drop-frame timecode with a semicolon (";") before each column:

01;02;03;04 = Drop-Frame Timecode

And of course, there is yet another variation where some readers will display a period (".") before the frames column:

01:02:03.04 = Drop-Frame Timecode

And what about the vogue 24fps that HD shoots at? You guessed it! It's not a true 24fps video signal. Instead, it's actually 23.976. Keep in mind: film is a true 24fps. This can cause problems when converting video back to film. In these cases, timecode can be used to record a true 24fps rate.

Frame rate (DF or NDF) tells us how the timecode will function. Now let's discuss *when* we want it to function. There are two options for when the timecode is recorded: free run or record run.

RECORD RUN

In *record-run* mode, the timecode starts and stops when the recorder starts and stops. If you record for exactly five minutes and the timecode starts at 01:00:00:00, when you press stop, the timecode will read: 01:05:00:00. The timecode will stay at this number until the next time you record. When the recorder starts recording again, the timecode will start recording from 01:05:00:00. This mode gives a measurable time of how much has been recorded on the medium. For example, if we started the timecode at 01:00:00:00 and the timecode now reads 01:24:00:00, we know that we have recorded twenty-four minutes worth of media.

For most ENG and video productions, each roll (tape, drive, or whatever new media is developed the day after this book is published) is started with the next hour of timecode. So, Roll 1 would have a timecode start of 01:00:00:00, Roll 2 would have a timecode start of 02:00:00:00, Roll 3 would have a timecode start of 03:00:00:00 and so on. The challenge with using the record-run mode in a double system is that the camera, recorder, and slate will all need to be connected (wireless or hardwire) in order to receive the correct timecode each time the recorder starts recording.

**Note: Cameras do not necessarily need timecode in a double system as the timecode can be referenced from a timecode slate. Providing timecode to the camera can assist with syncing in postproduction.*

FREE RUN

In *free-run* mode, the timecode behaves much like a wall clock. Once the timecode is engaged it will freely run forever (resetting back to zero once it crosses the midnight hour). Typically, free run timecode is set to the time of day (TOD). The time of day is based on military time. For example, if we start the day at 8 a.m. we would set the timecode to 08:00:00:00. However, if we start the day at 8 p.m. we would set the timecode to 20:00:00:00. Using the above example of recording for five minutes, let's say that we start recording for five minutes exactly at 8 p.m. Our starting timecode would be 20:00:00:00 and our ending timecode would be 20:05:00:00. If we take a ten-minute break before we record our next shot, our new starting timecode would be 20:15:00:00 instead of 20:05:00:00 as with record run. Being that 99.9% of all editing today is done digitally, there is no need to fret over the midnight hour if the shoot takes place in the middle of the night and timecode might cross the midnight hour in free-run mode.

A drawback of TOD timecode is that discrepancies between the recorder and slate are not easily detected. A good idea is to check the numbers on the slate against the numbers on the recorder periodically by having the boom operator read aloud the hour and minutes and then continuing with the seconds while the sound mixer checks that the seconds are in-sync by reading the timecode display on the recorder.

As a bonus, free run/TOD allows producers and other crewmembers to use their wristwatches as a general reference to timecode throughout the shoot. Of course, if there are large jumps in timecode, the timecode could indicate how much time was wasted during production. It is common practice for free-run timecode to be set to the time of day; however, the timecode can be set to start at any number. Once the number is entered and the timecode is engaged, those numbers will continually run until the user resets the timecode.

SETTING UP TIMECODE

Timecode can be produced on the recorder via an internal or external timecode generator. *Internal timecode* is the timecode generated by the recorder. *External timecode* is the timecode received by the recorder either wirelessly or through a hardwire cable. *Jam sync* is the process of telling an internal timecode generator to accept an external timecode source. Jam sync is almost exclusively used in free-run mode. With jam sync, the recorder receives the timecode once (this only takes a few seconds) and then the cable can be disconnected allowing the recorder to generate an ongoing timecode based on the timecode it received. This is commonly referred to as giving the recorder a "taste of timecode." In free-run mode, care should be taken to monitor the timecode periodically in case of drift or intermittent dropouts of timecode. To help prevent drift in timecode, it is common practice to re-jam timecode at least once each day. This is usually done after a meal break since drift can become an issue after eight hours or more.

Timecode is relatively simple to set up on your recorder once you've determined your frame rate (DF/NDF) and record mode (record run/free run). The industry standard for film timecode is 30NDF. However, if you are syncing audio to a video camera that shoots at 24fps, you will need to verify if the timecode is true 24fps or 23.976. If a 23.976 frame rate is not an option on the audio recorder, then stick with the standard 29.97NDF timecode for video. If your recorder needs to accept timecode from an external source such as another recorder or camera, then you will need to jam sync your recorder's timecode to accept the incoming timecode.

Use the following chart when determining which timecode rate is applicable for your production.

Timecode Compatibility

Video Frame Rate		Audio Frame Rate	
30 FPS	Old Black and White Television HD Progressive	30 FPS	Identical Frame Rates
29.97 FPS NDF	SD Color Television HD Progressive	29.97 FPS NDF	Identical Frame Rates
29.97 FPS DF	SD Color Television HD Progressive	29.97 FPS DF	Identical Frame Rates
25 FPS	PAL Television HD PAL	25 FPS	Identical Frame Rates
24.00 FPS	Film/HD Progressive	24.00 FPS 30.00 FPS	Identical Frame Rates Compatible Alternative
23.976 FPS	Film for Video/ HD Progressive	23.976 FPS 29.97 FPS	Identical Frame Rates Compatible Alternative
1080(59.94/60I)	HD Interlaced	29.97 FPS	Identical Frame Rate

Timecode Compatibility Chart, courtesy of Michael Orlowski

SLATES/CLAPBOARD

In the early days of film, audio was synced to picture in postproduction by referencing a *slate* or *clapboard* at the beginning of the shot. The clapboard was held in front of the camera, the take's information (scene number and take number) was read aloud, and then the clap sticks (simply called "sticks") were quickly closed. This created an audible clap (hence the name "clapboard"). The editor could see the frame when the sticks were completely closed and could then sync the audio's clap point to that exact frame. It was easy to identify this frame as it would be the first one where the sticks were no longer blurry or in motion. The information read aloud provided an audible cue of what take was being slated on the soundtrack. Without this information, the beginning of each audio take would have merely been a clap sound!

Clapboard

Today, audio is much easier to sync with timecode. Film slates without timecode can still be a very effective method of sync for the independent filmmaker. With modern day NLE systems, referencing the spike in the audio's waveform and lining it up to the camera's frame where the sticks are completely closed can easily sync non-timecode audio. Remember, Hollywood did it for half a century using flatbed editors back in a time when digits usually meant fingers and toes. Auto-sync software can also be used to automate this process.

TIMECODE SLATES

Recorded timecode gives editors a reference to work with, but their job is easier when they can see the timecode's starting point in the picture. To solve this problem, slates with a timecode reader display were invented. With timecode slates, the display holds the exact timecode when the sticks come together for a few extra seconds, making the editor's job much easier.

Video cameras can duplicate the same timecode as the recorder via jam sync (explained below), reducing the need to see the timecode on a slate for each take. If the video camera does not accept or produce timecode (such as some film cameras, DSLRs, or prosumer cameras), it's a good idea to use a timecode slate to display the audio recorder's timecode for the camera.

Timecode slates come in two flavors: *smart slates* and (wait for it...) *dumb slates*. A smart slate can read and generate timecode. A dumb slate can only display timecode that it receives. In other words, a dumb slate is simply a timecode reader that has no timecode-generating capability. The inability to think on its own is why it is known as a dumb slate. This should be a life-lesson for us all, but I digress...

Timecode slate

Dumb slates can be fed timecode via a cable, but film sets really don't need one more cable lying around the set and getting in the way. To solve this problem, a sound mixer named Mike Denecke invented the *sync box*. The sync box attaches to the back of the dumb slate and jam syncs timecode from an external source. Once the sync box has jam synced the timecode, it will continue to reproduce that timecode on its own. If a sync box is not available, then the dumb slate will need to accept incoming timecode from an external source continuously. Always make sure that the slate's settings match the timecode settings of your recorder (frame rate/DF or NDF). Timecode slates need to be set to receive (i.e., serve as a dumb slate) for music playback. This allows the playback's timecode to be displayed on the timecode slate for sync. Timecode can also be fed to a dumb slate via a wireless system. This can be sent via an IFB or Comtek box.

It is a good practice to compare timecode between the slate and recorder several times throughout the day. If you suspect any drift or dropouts may have occurred, report the error on your sound report. Any exposed buttons or switches on the slate should be taped down to prevent accidental pressing or switching. Inform the person using the slate (typically the 2nd

AC) not to turn the slate off to save batteries as this can create sync problems. If a camera is receiving TOD timecode, it will need to be re-jammed after powering back up from a battery change.

The bottom line with timecode is that all of this information boils down to one simple question: What frame rate is the production being shot at? This information is necessary so that the sound mixer can set the timecode rate for the recorder. The postproduction supervisor or editor should be contacted to verify this information. Be forewarned: phone conversations are easily forgotten or misinterpreted. Get the post team to sign off on the timecode in writing (email or whatever). Once shooting is wrapped, the blame-game begins. Protect yourself and your reputation. Get it in writing!

Timecode is seemingly black magic. It is important to discuss timecode in this book for two reasons. One, you need to have a basic understanding of how and why the timecode system works the way it does. Two, the topic is a bit wordy and my publisher is paying me by the final word count in this book. (Just kidding. They're actually paying me for the number of pictures I use in the book).*

**Note from the publisher: We've known Ric for years and think he's terrific.*

In truth, we pay him based solely on the quality and quantity of his soul patch.

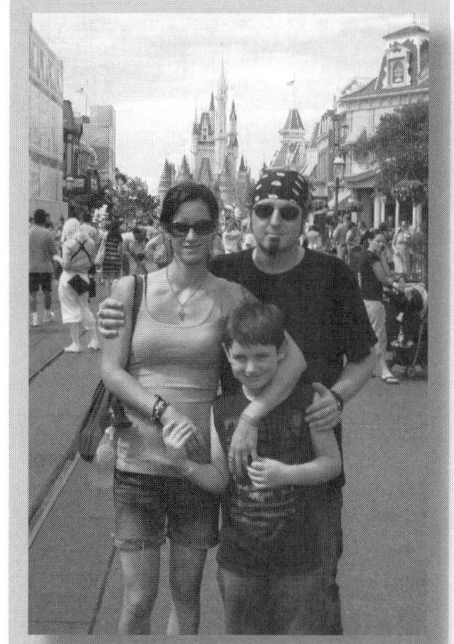
The author on vacation with his family at Disney World

WILD SOUND

Wild sound is any sound that is recorded without picture. The sound is not in sync with any picture and is therefore considered to be wild. Keep in mind: in a single system, the camera can be used to capture wild sound. In these cases it's helpful to the editor if the camera is focused on the sound source.

Types of wild sounds include room tone, wild tracks, sound effects, and voiceovers. It is important to record a voice slate at the front of each take. The audio files will probably end up in a bin somewhere and may be auditioned from software in rapid-fire succession. Try to start the voice slate within the first few seconds of the take so that the editor doesn't have to spend much time listening for it. The voice slate needs to be descriptive and should be accompanied by information on the written sound report.

Some sound mixers will run wild sound even when the camera is shooting an M.O.S. shot. This could be for an insert or an establishing shot where the camera department was in a hurry, didn't have time for sticks, or whatever reason. This can be helpful for gathering sound effects of an insert prop or general room tone of an event. Provide useful sound whenever possible.

ROOM TONE

Room tone is the sound of an environment in which dialog was recorded. It's used to provide a consistent background or as air fills to help smooth out a soundtrack and eliminate any holes in the background. As the name implies, room tone refers to the sound of an interior location. For exterior locations, you need to capture thirty seconds of nat sound, also called *area tone*. Some sound mixers use the term "ambience loop" as it can refer to either an interior or exterior location.

To record room tone or area tone, you should use the same mic, in the same place as it was during the shot. Reaching for a stellar sound stereo mic to bring out the environment will not help the editor cut the dialog. It might help the sound team build backgrounds for the shot, but the dialog editor needs a consistent bed that matches the dialog.

When room tone is being sent to the camera during ENG, it is common practice to point the camera at the microphone. Sometimes the producer will ask the shooter to roll on cutaways or B-roll during room tone to save time. This is usually not a good idea, as the editor might not realize that there is room tone associated with these shots. In addition, the camera or shooter may make noise that could spoil the room-tone track.

WILD TRACKS

Wild tracks are dialog that is recorded without the camera rolling. They are also known as *wild lines* and are typically recorded to cover dialog that was difficult or impossible to record during the take. For example, a fight sequence might include an important line of dialog that couldn't be picked up during all the scuffling, or maybe the actor was out of breath. After the take, you can have the actor deliver the line a few times so that the editor can choose the best one. These recordings give low-budget films additional tracks to play with if there is no budget for ADR. Other examples include an off-screen line, a script change after the take, or a misspoken word during an otherwise perfect take.

Wild lines are also useful if the actor delivered a line of dialog that distorted because it was much louder than the rest of the scene (for example, a sudden outburst or scream). In this case, it can be very difficult to bring the fader down fast enough to prevent the line from distorting and then back up again for the rest of the normal-level dialog. As with room tone, the purpose of a wild track is to record an element that can blend in with the rest of the elements gathered during the scene. Again, you should use the same mic in the same place as it was during the shot. If the set has been struck, or time is short and the crew needs to wrap, you may have to settle for recording the wild track off the set in a quiet location. Make sure the location matches the scene. Taking someone into a garage to record wild tracks from a scene that was shot in a bedroom won't help. In fact, they will probably have to ADR your wild tracks.

WILD SOUND EFFECTS

Wild sound effects are specific sound elements from a scene recorded separate from the camera. Production tracks that include wild sound effects can be very helpful for postproduction. This is especially true for independent films that will have to steal sounds from the production tracks because of budget constraints. You don't need to record every single sound from the scene, because the dialog microphone will generally pick up door slams and most prop handling. Elements, such as a specific prop, machine, or rare vehicle that is pivotal in a scene can be extremely useful. It's a good idea to keep a list of sound effects that need to be recorded. These sound effects can be gathered during M.O.S. setups or at the end of the day. If the budget allows and you get approval from the production manager, you can set up another day to gather key sounds for the production.

When recording sound effects, be sure to provide variations in your takes (loud/soft, short/long, etc.). There is a good book out there that deals specifically with recording sound effects, but for some reason, I can't remember the name of it....

VOICEOVERS

Voiceovers are usually recorded in postproduction at a recording studio. There are times when it will be necessary to record a voiceover on the set. You will need a quiet and acoustically dead place to record the voiceover. Often the quietest place on location is the interior of a car. Modern vehicles are designed with sound treatment to help reduce the sound of the engine and road noise. This works to a sound mixer's advantage. Plus, cars will always be available no matter where your location. I've recorded inside of cars numerous times and the tracks have always worked perfectly. Walk-in closets make perfect on-location recording booths as they are full of clothes, which helps treat the room acoustically. You'll get great tracks with little effort.

If these options don't work, create an environment to record in. A small, carpeted room is a good start. You'll need to treat the bounce from the walls without actually affixing things to them. Start by placing sound blankets on a C-stand in a "T" configuration. The more you have, the better treated the room will be. At minimum, use a pair of C-stands in a "V" shape so that the actor faces inward toward the point where the C-stands meet. This is where you'll place the microphone. Crewmembers working in an adjacent room should be asked to remain quiet during the take. Remember, they have work to do, so notify them just before you roll and once you cut to maximize the workflow on the set.

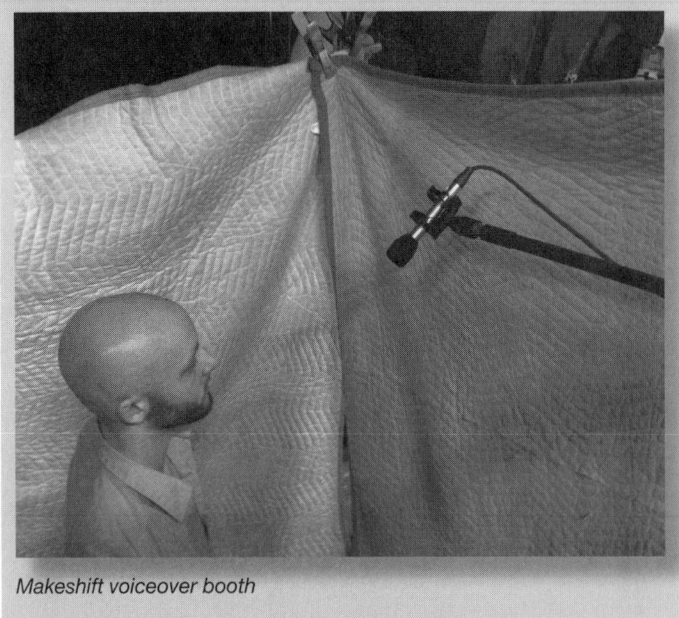

Makeshift voiceover booth

Another thing to consider when recording voiceovers is the positioning of the script. A voiceover booth will have a music stand on which to place the script. This allows the actor's head to be positioned facing the microphone as opposed to looking down at a piece of paper, and also eliminates handling noise from the script. As a bonus, pages that contain a continuing line of dialog can be placed side by side so the actor can finish the line without turning the page. On location, a music stand will be hard to find. You'll need to get a little creative. You can use gaffer tape to affix the script to a C-stand. In the car, you can tape the pages of the script to the dashboard.

The actor's mouth might produce weird clicks and moist smacking sounds that can be noticeable during the take. Granny Smith apples will help reduce this. Crackers can be used to calm grumbling stomachs. It's also a good idea to have a bottle of water on hand.

For newsgathering, a voiceover can be recorded as a separate element to be fed to the station or network to cut into a segment. If the segment includes man-on-the-street interviews using a stick mic, you could use that microphone for the voiceover, as it would match the audio from the rest of the piece. This type of mic will also help reduce background noise from the recording, but should only be used for news reporting. If your audio is going to camera, have the shooter point the camera at the person reading the script. If not, there will be no image and the editor might not realize that there is a voiceover there.

CHAPTER EXERCISE Try recording a scene using a double system. If you're using a video camera, be sure to turn the audio off. Slate the scene with a clapboard or simply clap your hands together. Try syncing the scene in an audio editor without using the sync point at the start of the take. Unless there are sound cues like doors closing or props being set down, the scene should take a few minutes to sync perfectly. Now, sync the sound and picture in the editing program by aligning the spike in the audio waveform with the frame of video that shows the hands together at the point of the clap. Notice the time that it takes to sync the audio with the sync point versus syncing without a sync point. Herein lies the logic of slating takes with a clapboard when timecode is not available.

CHAPTER 13

MIXERS

The mixer is the core hub of field mixing. All signal flows in and out of the mixer. Everything will connect to this device: mics, headphones, recorders, cameras, etc. This is mission control.

All mixers are different, but function in the same manner. A mixer is like a car — all cars have headlights and windshield wipers, but not all of the controls are found in the same place. I spent a week out in LA in a rental car that had the controls for the automatic windows in the center console. It took me an entire week to remember where they were because I was used to my car, which has the controls on the driver's door panel. Sure enough, when I got home, it took me a week to remember that the window controls on my car weren't in the center console. Mixers are the same way. Once you've used a mixer for a while, you get used to its sound and control layout. This can make it challenging when using a different mixer. When freelancing, it is helpful to become knowledgeable about different mixers that you might use.

TYPES OF MIXERS

The word "mixer" is a generic term, as there are several types. Names for mixers include field mixer, mixing board, mixing panel, mixing console, etc. Many industries use audio mixers for different applications: film production, television stations, radio stations, recording studios, nightclubs, stadiums, and even your local restaurant or bar. These mixers can range from large-format consoles with hundreds of inputs to a simple two-channel compact mixer. Their uses can range from Grammy-level music production, film scoring, and feature mixing to church P.A. systems, home-recording studios, and podcasting. In location sound, two main types of mixers are used: *field mixers* and *compact mixers*. The catch here is that the term "compact mixer" usually refers to the economy mixers offered by Behringer, Mackie, and others, with models starting as low as $30! However, in this category are more highly sophisticated and downright violent works of technical art that can run over

$10,000. So, to avoid confusion and to give the premium models their much-deserved recognition, we'll refer to economy mixers as *compact mixers* and the premium models as *cart mixers* (seeing as these mixers will always be used on a sound cart).

Compact Mixers

Compact mixers are extremely economical and can have features like aux sends, bussing, and direct outs. Despite their price, plenty of brands offer acceptable sound quality for many types of productions. The main drawback to these types of mixers is that they are A/C powered, which can be a problem for fieldwork. Also, these mixers have short throw faders (60mm) that are not as velvety smooth as the much more expensive cart mixers. Compact mixer prices range from $50 to $1,000.

Here are some examples of compact mixers:

- Allen & Heath XB-14
- Behringer XENYX 1204USB
- Behringer XENYX 1002B
- Mackie 1202-VLZ3
- Mackie 1402-VLZ3

Mackie 1202-VLZ Pro

Field Mixers

As their name suggests, field mixers are designed for location work. They are small, lightweight units that are rugged and operate on battery power. Professional field mixers will have a built-in tone generator and a host of routing and output options. The number of inputs varies between models. Typical ENG work uses three channel mixers, but reality shows require many more channels. Many field mixers can be linked to provide additional channels if needed. Because of their size and design layout, field mixers use *pot faders.* These small knobs can make smooth adjustments more difficult. Higher-end field mixers offer world-class preamps. Field mixer prices range from $200 to $4,000.

Here are some examples of field mixers:

- Fostex FM-3
- Fostex FM-4
- Sonosax SX-M32
- Sound Devices 302
- Sound Devices 552
- Wendt X5

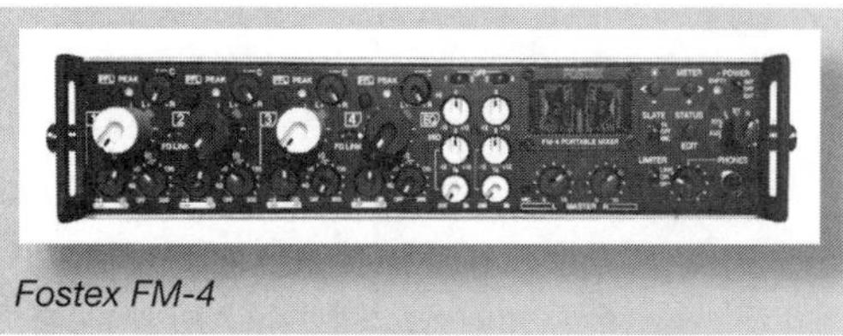
Fostex FM-4

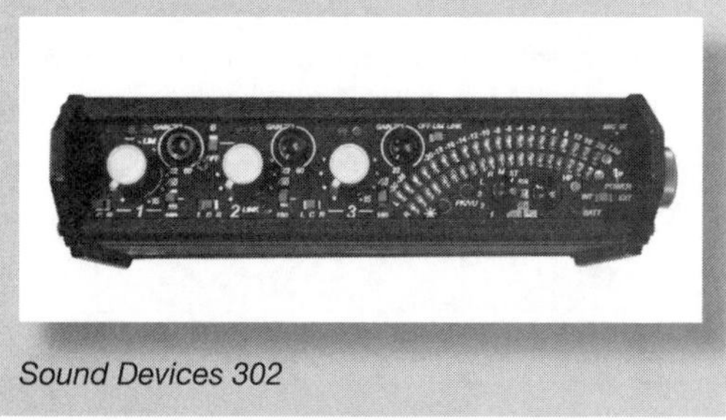
Sound Devices 302

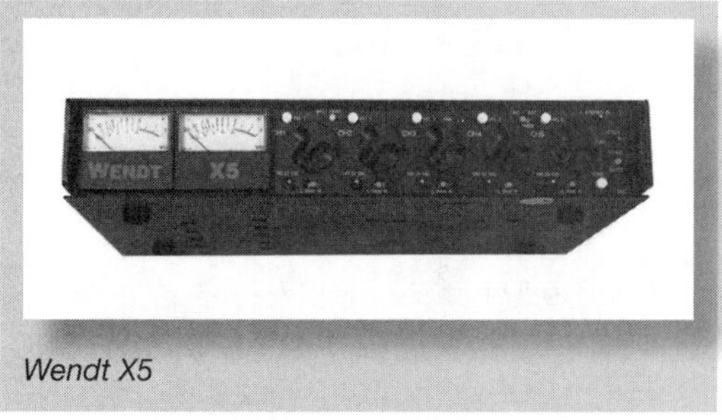
Wendt X5

Cart Mixers

With premium preamps and routing flexibility, cart mixers provide superior control and quality. These mixers have professional long throw faders (100mm), which make fades and adjustments more fluid. They include all of the standard features of field mixers and more. Some cart mixers even have buttons for bell and light systems, separate headphone mixes for boom operators, and recorder controls. Cart mixer prices range from $3,000 to $12,000+.

Some examples of cart mixers include:

- Audio Developments AD146
- Cooper CS 208D*
- PSC Solice
- Sonosax SX-ES64

**Note: Despite the fact that they have been discontinued, the legendary Cooper mixers are still in use today.*

Cooper CS 208D

The main difference between a field mixer and a cart mixer is portability. The field mixer's design allows it to be placed inside an ENG bag strapped over the sound mixer's shoulder. The mixer is positioned face-up so that the controls are easily accessible. A cart mixer is impractical for run-and-gun scenarios. Overall, the cart mixer is more refined with greater control of signal routing in addition to smooth, linear faders, but at the expense of being a stationary unit. Some sound mixers will bring a field mixer to a shoot in case there will be scenes that require them to be mobile, such as car rigs. The rest of the time, they will use a cart mixer.

Sonosax SX-ES64

MIXER BASICS

A mixer is comprised of three sections: *input section*, *output section*, and *monitoring section*. Here's an in-depth look at each section.

Input Section

The input section is where signals are introduced into the mixer. On a field mixer, the signal will always flow from left to right. For this reason, the microphone XLR inputs are located on the left side of the mixer and the outputs are located on the right. Cart mixers will have both the inputs and outputs located on the back panel.

Mic/Line Selection

An input selection switch will allow you to select either a mic or line level signal as the input source. The mic level selection will route the audio to the mixer mic preamps, whereas the line level selection will bypass the preamp and carry the signal to the channel's next stage.

Phantom Power

Mic inputs offer a choice between dynamic or phantom power. The dynamic setting is used for microphones that do not require phantom power or microphones that have a separate phantom power supply. Remember never to double-power a microphone. Some compact mixers offer a global phantom power switch that sends phantom power to all of the microphone inputs. Field and cart mixers use local phantom power switches that only send phantom power to a specific channel. Avoid turning on phantom power with a microphone connected to prevent a sudden spike in signal from damaging the microphone. Instead, turn phantom power on before connecting the microphone. For compact mixers that have multiple microphones connected, always power off the mixer before turning on global phantom power.

Gain Control

The channel's gain control is also referred to as the trim control. This control adjusts the mixer's amplification of the channel's incoming signal. The signal's level is monitored via an LED that will illuminate green to indicate signal presence and change to red when the signal is overloading. Some LEDs can be programmed to light red prior to overload to give the sound mixer time to react. There is no exact level to set the gain; however, you will find a sweet spot that works most of the time. To set the gain level, place the fader at unity and then adjust the gain knob. The goal is for the LED lights to show green with an occasional hint of red (think pink) on a few loud spikes.

Correctly setting the gain control can mean no further adjustments are necessary for average dialog. In other words, "set it and forget it"; however, loud sounds, such as screaming, will require the gain control to be adjusted. Some mixers have a variable gain knob that allows you to fine-tune the signal. These are sometimes designed as push pots to protect the knob from being bumped. Other gain controls may use a switch to select between different pre-defined gain settings such as -60dB, -40dB, -20dB. Variable gain gives more control over the signal and provides the best results.

With most field mixers, a gain level above 75% will result in system noise. If you have to raise the gain above 75%, try a different mic position, ask if the talent can speak louder, or try a different microphone.

Pads

A *pad* is an attenuator that reduces the signal level to prevent overload. They are useful when the source audio is too loud to be reduced by the gain control alone. Gunshots, jets, and other loud sources are examples of when a pad might be necessary. Some microphones have an on-board pad, but should only be used if the mixer or recorder doesn't have a pad. It is very easy to forget that a pad was used on a microphone, which can cause problems the next time the mic is used. Only use a pad if necessary. Using a pad when one isn't necessary will cause you to have to increase the gain of the microphone, which could introduce noise or hiss into the signal.

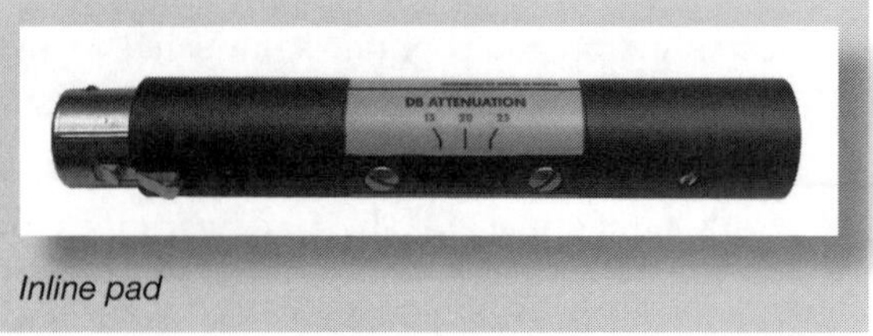

Inline pad

Polarity Switch

A *polarity switch* inverts the phase of the input signal. This helps to correct phasing issues between multiple microphone sources or improperly wired cables. When engaged, the polarity switch reverses the signal's phase 180 degrees by switching Pin 2 and Pin 3. Thus, it should be noted that this switch affects only balanced cables. Polarity switches are indicated with a special symbol.

Polarity symbol

Channel Faders

Channel faders are the primary controls used on a mixer. The channel fader controls the level of audio that is sent from the channel to the master output. When multiple channels are sent to the same track on the recorder, the faders are used to balance the relationship between the channels. This is the core concept of mixing: blending multiple sources. If no other channels are in use, then the channel's fader simply provides the sole source of audio to the mixer's output.

It is important to understand that faders are not gain controls and gain controls do not function as faders. These have separate functions altogether. I once worked on a project with an inexperienced engineer who was convinced he knew what he was doing. In setting up his mixer, he permanently placed all of the channel faders at unity and continued to mix the program by adjusting the trim pots on each channel. He argued that leaving the faders at unity allowed the maximum amount of signal to pass through the mixer. This is certainly laughable to anyone with any understanding of gain structure and perfectly illustrates the exact opposite use of these controls.

Gain controls make coarse adjustments and faders make fine ones. Use the gain control to provide the correct amount of signal into the channel and use the channel fader to control how much of that correct signal is used. If the channel's signal LED shows that the signal is overloaded, make the adjustment at the gain control. If the channel's signal LED shows that the signal is not overloading but the output of the channel is too high, then make the adjustment with the channel fader. You should always keep your fingers on the fader in case of a drastic fluctuation in level or the need to balance another microphone into the mix.

You may be using a traditional sliding fader like those found on cart mixers, or a knob like those found on field mixers. Sliding faders are linear and give the greatest level of control over the signal. Knob faders are used in an effort to save space on smaller units. A decent amount of "drag" in the fader knobs will help you make smooth fades, whereas loose knobs make subtle changes seem drastic. With sliding faders, several channels can be adjusted simultaneously whereas knob faders can only be controlled individually.

Most rotary faders will have unity gain somewhere between the twelve o'clock and two o'clock positions (somewhere between 50% to 70%). Each mixer is different and you should check the manual to see the optimal operating position. The need to increase beyond this range could indicate that the input gain was not set to the correct level.

Scribble strip

Despite the numbered indicators, channel strips and knobs can be dizzying, especially when they all look the same. Using scribble tape and color-coding is a good trick for staying organized and quickly identifying channels for fast changes. Some sound mixers will place a thumbnail pic on the channel that corresponds with the talent. This is particularly helpful when working with multiple actors or stars on a reality show.

EQ/Equalization

An *equalizer* is a filter that allows the attenuation or amplification of a specific band of frequencies. The common terms are "cut" for attenuation and "boost" for amplification. The frequency labeled on the control represents the center of the bandwidth that will be adjusted. The adjustments are typically between -15dB and 15dB of attenuation and amplification, respectively.

EQ section of a mixer

Parametric equalizers allow the user to define the center of the bandwidth to be adjusted, giving greater control over the affected frequencies. This type of EQ is typically centered on the mid-range frequencies and is sometimes referred to as "sweepable mids."

Parametric EQ

Equalization is a hot topic among sound mixers. While most agree that EQ should be left to the postproduction team, some believe that EQ is part of their responsibility. In general, you should leave EQ decisions for postproduction. They will have all of the elements in front of them and can listen objectively in a quiet, controlled environment. The sound mixer, however, can only monitor on location in a usually uncontrolled environment with headphones. True, the right amount of EQ can make the dialog sing in your headphones, but that doesn't mean it will sing in the professional monitors on the dub stage. Leave these calls to the post team, which will have a better listening environment and greater control over the signal.

Resist the urge to touch all the buttons on your gear. Just because you have the ability to use EQ, compression, and other goodies doesn't mean that you should! Focus your attention on what really matters: the things that cannot be adjusted in post, such as mic selection and placement. Some sound mixers will EQ the lavs to match the boom mic for the mix track. This is acceptable if the EQ is not sent to the ISO tracks. If the direct outs are post-EQ on the mixer, then the ISO tracks will be affected by the EQ. However, if the mixer's direct outs are pre-EQ, then only the mix track will be affected by the EQ. If you strongly feel that EQ is necessary, try adjusting the mic placement or use a different mic first. Broadcasting live on location is a situation where the audio cannot be adjusted after the fact. In these cases, it might be necessary to match multiple microphones with EQ.

High pass filters (HPF), also known as "low cuts," are a type of EQ that rolls off all frequencies below a predefined point. Some HPFs have a variable control that allows you to adjust the predefined point (the highest frequency affected by the cut). This range is typically between 80Hz and 140Hz. Other HPFs are simply a switch that can select between one or several frequencies preset by the manufacturer. Some microphones will have an HPF switch, but it is strongly recommended that you avoid using them. These switches are easy to forget about, which could result in them being left on. Instead, always use the HPF on the mixer.

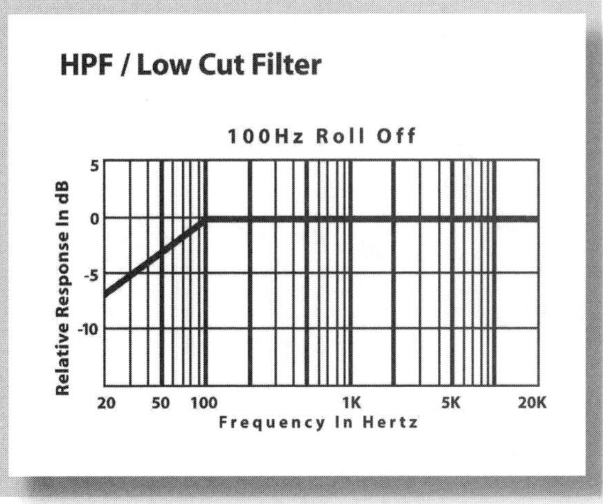

HPFs are the exception to the "don't touch that dial" rule of on-location EQ. Some guidelines should be followed when using low cuts. First, use HPF sparingly. The lower frequencies in the voice will be affected and can sound unnaturally thin.

Second, be sure to stay consistent with your settings at a specific location or set. Once you have made the decision to use or not use an HPF, stay with that choice for the location. Keep in mind this only refers to the interior or exterior of a location exclusively. If you were using an HPF for the exterior of a house, it would be acceptable to disable the HPF when you move to the interior of the house for the rest of the scene.

Third, avoid actively rolling the low frequencies during a take. For example, if a continuous shot starts exterior and moves to the interior, avoid activating or rolling the low frequencies during the transition. Unless there are extremely high winds that wreak havoc on your mic, it's best to leave these decisions for postproduction when the EQ can be precisely automated and adjusted. If you are in a live ENG situation, you might find that activating the HPF during the shot is your only solution. Try to do so without making it obvious or distracting to the audience. HPF switches are difficult to disguise, but variable HPF knobs can allow you to sneak in the roll-off without making it noticeable.

Finally, if you use an HPF for a location, be sure to note your settings in case you return to that location on another day. If the wind is heavy one day, but calm the next, the HPF might seem unnecessary. However, when the shots from both days are cut together into a seamless scene, the difference in filter settings will be noticeable and may create challenges for the post team.

In post, rolling off excessive low frequencies for wide shots can sometimes cheat perspective. The effect is that the talent doesn't sound like they're standing right next to the camera during a shot that shows them twenty feet away. You should leave this trick for post and avoid trying to EQ on set. This leaves options for the final mix, whereas location EQ can rarely be undone.

Pan

Panning is fundamental to the recording process. In location sound, hard panning is used for track assignment. The signal is assigned to one of three positions: left, center or right.

- Hard Pan Left: The signal is assigned to Track 1.
- Hard Pan Right: The signal is assigned to Track 2.
- Center: The signal is assigned equally to both Track 1 and Track 2.

Track assignment is necessary to keep different microphones separated. If all of the mics are mixed to one track during recording, the mics cannot be separated in post for further mixing. Once mixed, always mixed.

Upon connecting a microphone or other source to the mixer, you will need to determine the channel's assignment. Some mixers use a variable pan control called a *pan pot*. In postproduction and music, this allows the engineer to place the audio signal anywhere in the stereo field in relationship to left and right. Determining where a signal should be in the stereo field is never a call that should be made on location. For this reason, some manufacturers have replaced the pan pot with a switch that has three positions: L, C, R or left, center, right.

Location audio is recorded using mono microphones. If you are only using one microphone, it is common practice to pan the microphone to the center. If you pan a mono microphone (or any mono source) to the center you are essentially sending the signal to both the left and right output. However, this is not a true stereo signal. It is merely the same signal being duplicated on both tracks. Upon playback, the signal would be played equally through the left and right speakers and appear to be heard in the center. This effect is known as the *phantom center*. Further, if you have two lavs with one mic panned left and the other panned right you are still not producing a true stereo image.

A stereo microphone has two separate capsules in a fixed X/Y pattern that reproduce a stereo image. Stereo microphones might be used for B-roll or nat sound, but should never be used for dialog. If you use a stereo microphone, you will need to hard-pan the inputs of each channel accordingly. The left output of the stereo microphone will be hard-panned left and the right output will be hard-panned right. Some mixers will have a stereo-link switch that gangs two channels together. This allows one fader to control both channels.

Some sound mixers may choose to use MS (mid-side) microphones in special situations. The mid capsule functions as a standard shotgun microphone, while the side capsule uses a figure eight pattern that allows the stereo image to be adjusted in postproduction using a decoder. This type of recording can create unique soundtracks for exotic locations where the environment has character. It is highly recommended that only sound mixers with experience use MS microphones. An example of an MS microphone is the Sennheiser MKH 418S. The mid capsule in the MKH 418S is the same capsule as the MKH 416. Using only the mid capsule would cause the mic to function identically to an MKH 416 shotgun.

Output Section

The *output section* is where the signals leave the mixer. In some cases, your audio will need to be sent to multiple places. A complex setup might include sending feeds to the main recorder, a backup recorder, multiple cameras, a P.A. system, video assist, Comtek systems, and, of course the boom operator. That's a lot to keep track of! A field mixer can offer multiple outputs, but for complicated feeds like this, a cart mixer will offer more outputs and routing capabilities.

The outputs of a mixer are broken down into five sections: the main outputs, direct outputs, subgroup outputs, aux outputs, and tape outputs.

Main Outputs

The purpose of a mixer is to adjust and combine signals to be sent to a final source (e.g., camera, recorder, P.A. system, live feed, etc.). The main output section of a mixer is the last stage the signal passes through before the final destination. Often, the main outputs are connected to the mix track(s) on the recorder. This allows the signal to flow post-channel faders, meaning that channel fader adjustments will affect the main outputs' mix.

Compressor and Limiters

Prior to arriving at the main outputs, the signal may pass through a *limiter* or *compressor*. A compressor is a circuit that compresses the audio signal once it reaches a predefined threshold. How fast a compressor responds to a signal that exceeds this threshold is called the *attack time*. The *release time* is the amount of time it takes for the compressor to return the signal back to the threshold point once it has been compressed. In most plug-ins and outboard compressors, these parameters can be finely tuned and adjusted to provide different results. The compressors found on most field mixers and cart mixers have limited adjustments that can be made, but this does not stop them from being effective.

A limiter is essentially a compressor with a high compression ratio at a certain threshold. This helps prevent the signal from exceeding the threshold and safeguards against unpredictable spikes in the audio that can cause a digital recorder to clip. The limiter is not a brick wall. Digital recorders and cameras can still clip despite the use of limiters. It is okay to see the limiter kick on from time to time, but you should avoid having it remain active for long periods. If the limiter is constantly active, it's a safe bet that your signal level is set too high. Always use a limiter when working with digital recorders and cameras.

Many field mixers allow you to change your limiter's threshold. Only do this if the manufacturer's settings are causing serious issues with your audio. Although it can be fun to tinker and tweak, keep in mind that the manufacturer spent time and money on developers and engineers to decide what the defaults should be. When in doubt, don't tweak.

Here are some examples of default limiter settings:

- Shure FP33 factory threshold setting: +4dB
- Fostex FM-3 factory threshold setting: +12dB
- Sound Devices 302 factory threshold setting: +20dB

Dynamics can be the casualty of pushing the limiter too hard. In the broadcast world, the final mix will probably be squashed to death, but starting with audio that is already squashed and then squashing the squashed audio will only result in audio that sounds, well, squashed. The film world enjoys a good sense of balance and dynamics in the soundtrack. Recording squashed audio for film is unacceptable. Less is more, more or less.

On some mixers, the limiter can be independent for each channel's output (left and right) or the limiter can be linked (or ganged) to both channels. When the channels are linked, the limiter is activated if either channel exceeds the threshold. When the channels are independent, the limiter is only activated on the channel that exceeds the threshold. Typically, the limiter should not be linked. There is no reason to limit the right channel when the left channel exceeds the threshold.

Output Level Types

As with the input levels, the output levels can be set to either mic or line level. It is imperative that the output level of the mixer matches the input level of the recorder. Sending a mic level output to a line level input will result in a weak or barely audible signal. A line level output sent to a mic level input will result in distortion, as the signal is much hotter than the expected input level.

In general, the output level should be set to line level. Sending a mic level signal means that the mixer will attenuate the internal line level signal down to a mic level signal. Once the mic level signal reaches the recorder, it will be amplified back to a line level signal via the recorder's preamps. In effect, the signal is attenuated and then re-amplified, which can result in unnecessary hiss or noise. When using mic level as the output of the mixer, be sure that the recorder's phantom power is turned off!

Master Fader

The purpose of the *master fader* is to adjust the overall level of the audio signal before leaving the mixer's outputs. On some mixers, it might be necessary to set the master fader to zero when engaging the reference tone. This will send the tone to the mixer's outputs at the correct level. Once you've disengaged the tone (sometimes labeled as "1KHz"), you can keep the master fader at zero to start off with, but this doesn't mean you have to leave it at zero. If the output level starts to overload, simply turn the master down. Some internal tone generators bypass the master fader and send tone at 0VU or -20DbFS, regardless of the master fader's position. Check your field mixer's manual to verify this.

Direct Outputs

Some mixers provide a direct output for each channel. This allows each channel's signal to be sent directly to a multitrack recorder as an ISO track. The direct out signal is typically sent pre-fader, meaning that the signal is split before the channel fader. The signal continues to the channel fader and can still be mixed to the master output. The direct outputs are a line level signal, so be sure to set the input of the recorder to line level.

Subgroups

Also known as a *bus*, a subgroup allows the signals from multiple channels to be combined and controlled with a single fader. The output from the subgroup can be sent directly out of the mixer through a subgroup output or sent to the master fader. Subgroups are helpful when tracks are limited and you need to combine multiple channels to one track. In a sense, a subgroup serves as a master fader before the master fader.

A mixer can have two, four, or even eight subgroup channels. Mixers with subgroups will have a routing switch on each channel to determine the signal's destination (i.e., subgroup or master fader). A channel's subgroup button may be labeled "1/2", meaning that they can be routed to either subgroup 1 or subgroup 2. To route the signal to subgroup 1, pan the channel to the left. To route the signal to subgroup 2, pan the channel to the right. To route the signal to both subgroup 1 and 2, pan the signal to the center.

Aux Outputs

Found on compact mixers and cart mixers, an *aux (auxiliary) channel* is an additional output of the channel. A channel's signal can go to multiple aux channels at once. Some mixers will have a switch to determine if an aux channel is pre-fader or post-fader. In a pre-fader aux channel, the signal is outputted prior to the fader. Adjustments to the fader will not affect the level of signal sent to the aux channel. This allows for a sub mix to be created that is independent of the main mix and works well for separate broadcast mixes or monitor feeds. In a post-fader aux channel, the signal is outputted from the channel after the fader. Adjustments to the fader will affect the level of signal sent to the aux channel. Each aux channel will have a dedicated output jack. Some mixers will have a master fader for the aux channel.

Aux section of a mixer

Aux channels can be used to create customized mixes for monitoring. For example, let's say that you need to set up a headphone feed for the boom operator. You can select Aux 1 as the channel for this feed. On the boom microphone's channel, you would adjust the Aux 1 level so that the signal is routed to Aux 1's output. If this feed is sent pre-fader, then the boom operator would hear the boom microphone regardless of the channel fader's position. If this feed is sent post-fader, the boom operator will not hear the mic if the channel is faded. Additional channels can be added to this custom mix by simply adjusting the Aux 1 level on the appropriate channel. If the mixer includes a master fader for the aux channel, all of the Aux 1 signals will arrive at the Aux 1 master fader where the overall level can be adjusted before the output. This master aux fader can serve as the volume control for the boom operator. The catch is, aux outputs are usually a mono signal. This means that plugging the headphone extension cable into this jack will only provide audio to the left ear. In order to provide audio to both ears, you can use a mono to stereo adaptor. You can make a custom cable for this application by soldering a 1/4" TRS plug so that the ring is connected to the tip. The boom operator's feed is discussed further in Chapter 14.

Tape Output

A *tape output* is an alternate consumer line level (-10dB) feed from the mixer's master fader. The output can be used to feed a backup recorder or transcription recorder. Special attenuators can allow consumer recorders to accept this signal into their mic inputs.

You must use the correct output in order to achieve the best possible signal. Avoid splitting a primary audio signal with a "Y" cable. These cables can cause line loss. If you have to split a signal with a "Y" cable, try choosing a less critical signal path like the Comtek feed and the video assist feed. These feeds are for reference only and will not affect the final audio. If you need to route a signal from the mixer to both the camera and recorder, but only have one stereo output from the mixer, you should route the signal from the output of the mixer to the input of the recorder first. Then, route the output of the recorder to the input of the camera.

Slate Mic

A *slate mic* is a mixer's onboard microphone that allows the sound mixer to slate take information on the recording audibly. Some slate microphones will send a short 440Hz tone, known as a sub tone, prior to opening up the mic. In the days of Nagra, it was common practice to send a three-beep sub tone at the end of each recording so that the takes could be identified when fast-forwarding or rewinding the tape. With modern-day sound files and metadata, this is rarely done anymore. Most compact mixers do not have a slate mic. A workaround for this is to plug a microphone, such as a Shure SM58, into an open channel on the mixer and use it for slating the takes. Other mixers may have an input for an external slate or talkback mic.

Monitoring Section

The *monitoring section* consists of the master output's meter, headphone controls, and monitor selection. Adjustments made in this section do not affect the final audio; rather, they change how you monitor the final audio.

Meters

When properly calibrated with a recorder, the mixer's meters will read the same levels as the recorder. Newer LCD screen and LED ladder-type meters feature brightness levels to make the meters easier to read outdoors. Newer mixers offer the selection of VU, peak, or VU/peak metering.

Soloing

The *solo* function on a mixer allows you to select which channels will be heard in the headphones. If only one channel is soloed, the other channels won't be heard. If two channels are soloed, only those two will be heard. This is an extremely useful tool for problem-solving. The soloed signal can either be PFL (pre-fader listen) or AFL (after-fader listen).

Monitor Selection

Compact mixers have very limited monitor selections. This is usually limited to the aux, sub group, or main mix. Most field mixers and cart mixers provide more advanced monitor selections. Here are some common selections:

- Stereo Mix
  The left channel is heard in the left ear and the right channel is heard in the right ear.
- Left Channel
  Only the left channel (Track 1) is heard in both ears.
- Right Channel
  Only the right channel (Track 2) is heard in both ears.
- Mono
  Both the left and right channels are heard equally in both ears. This is helpful when listening for phasing issues.
- Monitor/Mix
  The signal is switched from the main mix to the *monitor return feed* from the recorder or camera.

Monitoring Return Feeds

In a single system, you'll probably rely on the mixer's monitoring to make critical decisions, since cameras give poor-quality return feeds. In a double system, you should always monitor directly from the recorder. This is the final link in the chain. The audio that arrives here is the audio that will be used in the production. On mixers with advanced monitoring selections (i.e., stereo, left, right, mono), these monitor selections will still function when listening to the return feed from the recorder.

The sound mixer should still monitor return audio from the camera periodically. Sure, the meters on the camera might be bouncing, but that might be audio from the wrong source like the camera's onboard microphone. Or even worse, it could be distorted audio from the mixer that is being sent at line level to the camera's mic level input. The only way to know for sure what is being recorded is to listen to the audio.

The problem with the return feed on most cameras is that it comes from the camera's headphone jack. The headphone amps on cameras are horrible at best, but can still give you an idea of what source is being recorded and whether or not it's cleanly recorded without distortion. Sound mixers should reference the return feed at regular intervals, usually at the start, middle, and end of a take. This reference might only be for a few seconds; just long enough to verify that everything is copasetic. The rest of the time, they'll switch back to monitor the mixer's output, which is more robust and true to what is being sent to the camera.

In ENG, it is imperative for the camera operator to monitor the camera's audio. A professional video camera operator should never shoot without wearing headphones or a single in-ear monitor (IEM) that allows the user to hear recorded audio as well as what's going on in real life. In-ear monitors are very helpful, since the camera's audio is a subjective audible view of the scene, but might not tip off the shooter to things that are happening off-screen that should be paid attention to and possibly shot.

Most shooters will have their own in-ear monitor, but it's a good idea to have a spare one in your kit just in case. Be prepared for some hesitation from the shooter. Although they should be monitoring the camera's audio, most of the time they feel that it's your job and they shouldn't be bothered with it. That's why they hired you!

Here's a quick guide to setting up the monitor return feed:

1. *Engage tone on the mixer and set the mixer's headphone volume.* There is no "technical" number to set your headphone level to. Typically, it should be annoyingly loud, but not painful. If the shooter is wearing headphones, warn him before you send tone. Usually, you'll make an announcement like "Watch your ears" or "I'm checking tone." Also, there is absolutely no reason to listen to tone through the headphones the entire time you are calibrating. Once you've verified the signal, take the headphones off. You will still be able to hear tone without fatiguing your ears.

2. *Connect the monitor return cable from the recorder/camera to the mixer.* Note: If the cable is unplugged or the recorder/camera is turned off, you will not receive a return signal.

3. *Engage the monitor switch on the mixer.*

4. *Adjust the headphone volume on the recorder/camera and toggle between monitor/mix on the mixer until both levels are equal.* This will allow you to switch between mix/monitor without volume changes. If the recorder/camera has headphone selections, choose stereo or L/R.

5. *Disengage tone and toggle between monitor/direct to see if there is any detectable noise.* The recorder/camera's headphone amp might be noisy. Familiarize yourself for what you expect to hear from the headphone return.

MIXER SETUP

The first step in setting up a mixer is to "zero out the board." This means that all of the controls are turned off or placed at their standard position. For example, the faders would be set to infinity, the pan knobs or switches would be placed in the center, the low cut filters would be turned off, etc. Zeroing out the board will reduce mistakes from overlooked settings used on a previous shoot.

The mixer should be set up and checked every time you arrive on location and after each new camera setup. Each channel's settings should be checked and tested every time you mic a new person. Never assume that because you set up your mixer at the start of the day that those settings will hold throughout the day. Knobs get bumped all the time. Be vigilant about your settings.

Here is a typical ENG setup for a three-channel field mixer using a boom and two lavs:

Channel 1
Boom Microphone
Mic Level
48v ON
HPF OFF
Hard pan left

Channel 2
Lav #1
Mic Level
Dynamic (48v OFF)
HPF OFF
Hard pan right

Channel 3
Lav #2
Mic Level
Dynamic (48v OFF)
HPF OFF
Hard pan right
**Note: Stereo Link should be OFF*

Master
Limiter ON
Set master fader to "0."
Set outputs to LINE LEVEL.
(Consumer cameras may require MIC LEVEL.)

Power
Turn mixer ON and check battery level

Headphones
Monitor Selection STEREO
Mix/Monitor to MIX
Monitor volume OFF

Bars and Tone
Connect mixer output to recorder/camera.
Set camera inputs to LINE LEVEL.
Turn Tone ON.
Mixer meters should read:
- 0dB for VU Meters
- -20dBFS for Peak Full Scale

Check headphones for signal in each ear at a low volume level.
Camera meters should read:
- 0dB for VU meters
- -20dBFS for peak

Turn the camera's SMPTE color bars ON.
Set timecode to 01:00:00:00 (or other specified timecode).
Record thirty seconds of bars and tone.
Turn SMPTE color bars OFF.
Turn Tone OFF.

Test Mics
Check microphones and set input gain on each channel.

If lavalier mics are the only mics being used, then Channel 2 should be hard-panned left and Channel 3 should remain hard-panned right to allow each lav to be recorded on its own channel for future mixing in post. If there are three or more lavs in use and you only have two channels on the recorder/camera, then choose one lav to hard pan left (e.g., host) and hard pan the other lavs right (e.g., guests). If all three lavs are for guests, determine the key talkers and separate them in the mix.

MIXING TECHNIQUES

Any production will have at least one other person handling your audio before it reaches the audience. Feature films can have a team of people working on your tracks. Your goal is to make the process as easy as possible for the editor, who shouldn't have to fight or struggle to achieve consistent levels from shot to shot. While extenuating circumstances may arise, if the editor must work extra hard to match the production sound's levels, it's generally a matter of sloppy work in the field.

The levels of each actor do not need to match perfectly, just consistently. If Actor 1 usually tracks at -12dB for the peaks, then try to keep that level for the entire scene. Whispers and shouts will obviously vary these levels. If Actor 2 is a bit softer spoken and tracks at -18dB, that's fine. There's no need to crank up the gain and raise the background level in the track in order to match the other actor's level. Instead, keep Actor 2's level at -18dB throughout the scene.

Remember, whenever you adjust a microphone's level you are also adjusting the background noise in the mix. If you change the relationship between the background level too much, then the scene may be difficult to cut together in post. Make the right decisions for the background level during setup and try to stick with them throughout the scene. Once several shots have been filmed, altering the game plan may affect the rest of the shots in the scene adversely. If the dialog level is too low, try a different mic placement before making big adjustments in the background level by increasing the fader's position.

Avoid "riding the faders" and making dozens of micro changes in the ISO track. Dynamics and volume differences between people as well as dynamic changes in a single voice naturally occur during conversation. For example, an actor might start a line quietly but then raise his voice. Unless there is a danger of overloading the track, leave the level where it was originally set. This will provide a consistent background for post. It is certainly necessary to adjust the faders to mix the track properly. The pre-fader ISO tracks will not be affected by these adjustments.

If you need to make a change in level during a take, try to make it quickly during a break in dialog. This will help the editor. Avoid slow or long fades. You might think that you're sneaking the level up, but you're just making the editor's job more difficult, especially if the shot is cut together with alternate dialog or other takes. Find the balance between quiet and loud actors. Raising the quiet actor's level may cause a noticeable shift in the background level.

In live ENG shots, the location sound mixer is the sole provider of the audio. As the location sound mixer you are in charge of everything. Granted, the audio will still be fed by a satellite truck and ultimately the network, but realize that other than minor-level changes, the audio will arrive to the audience the way it leaves your mixer. Try to avoid sudden boosts of volume during live shots with millions of people listening (no pressure, right?). This is when you'll want to try to be sneaky. If the audio is crunchy or if the talent starts screaming, drop the level as quickly as possible. Ideally, your changes won't be noticed, but live shots are unpredictable and you'll have to go with the flow. Be alert and ready for anything, because in field production, anything does happen.

Mixing is about being actively involved in the scene, not just watching meters and flashing lights. For this reason, many sound mixers will outfit their carts with a small video monitor (in some cases, more than one monitor) to watch the scene unfold. This helps clue them on which fader to bring up or down and lets them know if the sound's perspective matches that of the camera. Monitors are especially useful when the camera is using a zoom lens. This allows the sound mixer to see what the shot looks like.

These video monitors can be as small as five to seven inches and run on battery power (typically 12 volts). You can purchase all sorts of goodies and third-party gear for video monitors, including iPad apps and wireless video units. Try to get your video tap from video assist and not directly from the camera. Video assist provides playback for the director, actors, and necessary crewmembers to review a take or reference a previous take. The video assist's setup is known as *video village* and will need a sound feed from the mixer to record along with picture. In more complex setups at video village, digital signals are sent via Wi-Fi or other means that might produce a delay between the video and audio signals. In these cases, a digital delay can be employed to correct this so that both signals can be monitored in sync. The role of video assist is to provide video feeds, but you must provide your own video gear to use with the feed. On smaller productions without video assist, the camera department might be willing to let the sound mixer tap directly from the camera with a wireless video transmitter, but may be reluctant to be tethered with a cable. Keep in mind: video transmitters can cause interference with wireless microphones. Check the frequencies in use and make sure that there is no interference.

For the best soundtracks, try to leave the boom mic open. There is always a use for the boom mic. For example, if the talent is miked with lavs, a boom mic can help fill in the silence by capturing nat sound and prop handling. When mixing lavs and plant mics, only open up channels that are being used. This will reduce noise and unwanted sounds like movement, wireless hits, or breathing. This also helps eliminate phasing problems.

Loud sounds during dialog, like crashes, special effect devices, gunshots, and slamming doors, can cause a channel to overload. You have several options to handle these loud levels. The first is to adjust the fader. For loud sounds with long durations, like machine gun fire, you can reduce the level and bring it back up once the sound is finished. Some sounds might be so short that any attempt to adjust the fader will be painfully obvious.

The second option is to leave the fader alone and have the boom operator adjust the microphone placement. When the loud sound occurs the boom mic can be pulled back a few feet, aimed in a different direction, or a combination of the two. This technique is valuable for an ENG sound mixer who might not anticipate the sound or doesn't have a free hand to adjust the level.

The third option is to let the loud sound distort and rely on the post-production team to replace the loud sound with a different sound. It is much easier for them to replace a sound effect than for them to have to bring an actor in for ADR. This technique is useful for scenes where dialog immediately follows the loud sound and a fader adjustment isn't practical to capture both sounds correctly. Since dialog is the most important sound you are recording, you can let the loud sound bleed on the track and keep the dialog at a usable level.

The last option is to use a multitrack recorder and cover the sound effect with a different microphone set to a usable level. Of course, the loud sound will bleed on the boom mic, but the post team will have a clean version of the sound effect covered on a separate channel that they can blend into the mix.

CHAPTER EXERCISE Record a scene with a door slam in the middle of a take and experiment with the four options just discussed. Which option gives the best result? Is there another creative way to record the scene?

CHAPTER 14

MONITORING

A big part of the sound mixer's job is to assess the usability of the audio in real time. There is no point in mentioning bad audio after the talent has left the location and the truck is packed up to go. A seasoned director or producer will often ask the sound mixer if the shot was "good for sound" before wrapping a location or setup. However, if they don't, it is the sound mixer's job to inform them if the sound is marginal or unusable. For ENG work, it's a good idea to ask the producer how the final product will be used. There's no point in fretting over minor background shifts if the piece is going to have a constant music bed under everything.

During the recording process, there are two parts of the audio to monitor: *sound quality* and *sound level*. They are not the same thing. You can have great levels, but poor quality audio, and you can have great quality audio, but poor levels. In a sense, you are monitoring with your ears and your eyes. Sound quality is monitored with your ears: Does it sound right? Sound levels are monitored with your eyes: Are the meters at the right levels?

SOUND QUALITY

Monitor for clean audio without distortion or noise. Low levels can introduce hiss and levels that are too high can introduce distortion or clipping. You're looking for a Goldilocks balance: not too low, not too high, but just right. If you have to, choose noise over distortion. Sometimes, noise levels can be reduced in post, but you can never fix distortion. New technology has been introduced that can repair clipping (digital distortion), but don't count on it. Gather the right levels on location. In addition to the technical aspects of the signal, you're also listening for its quality. Are the mics in the right place? Does the sound perspective match the camera's perspective? Do you have a good dialog/background ratio?

SOUND LEVELS

There is no perfect answer for what dialog levels should read on a meter. There are, however, some good guidelines to follow. Real-world conversations have dynamics. People speak softly and loudly during a conversation. Allocate headroom when setting your levels to allow for spikes in dialog. A normal conversation, with proper mic placement, should read an average of -20dBFS. Peaks should read between -10dBFS and -6dBFS. Try to avoid going above -6dBFS with your peaks. This will give you a little bit of grace if an actor adlibs with loud dialog. Technically you can have peaks read up to 0dBFS, but then you run the risk of clipping and that is the unforgivable sin of digital recording. Find a good level and stick with it unless something extreme happens.

Freeing Up Headroom Using HPF

Low frequencies are much larger and stronger than higher frequencies. As a result, low frequencies can hog up your signal with audio that is either inaudible or inconsequential to the dialog. In these cases, you should use the HPF to reduce these frequencies. This will free up headroom and eliminate unnecessary low frequencies. In doing so, you will notice a reduction in the background's meter level.

General Meter Guidelines

Here are some general meter guidelines to consider. These examples are approximations. Different voices will have voice dynamics and active frequencies that will affect the average signal levels. Your main goal is to record the signal as hot as possible with no noise (hiss from levels set too low) or distortion (crunchy audio from levels set too high).

VU Meters

Whispers and soft dialog will read between -12dB and -9dB.
Average dialog will read between -9dB and -3dB.
Loud dialog will read between -3dB and 0dB.
Try to avoid levels that stay above 0dB for long periods of time.
**Note: VU meters do not "dance" as much as peak meters, but that little movement can equal big sound.*

Analog Peak Meters

Whispers and soft dialog will read between -20dB and -8dB.
Average dialog will read between -8dB and +4dB.
Loud dialog will read between +4dB and +8dB.
Try to avoid levels that stay above +8dB for long periods of time.

Digital Peak Meters

Whispers and soft dialog will read between -30dBFS and -20dBFS
Average dialog will read between -20dBFS and -12dBFS.
Loud dialog will read between -12dBFS and -6dBFS.
Digital peak meters should never reach 0dBFS.

After some practice, you'll find that your ears will act as an extension of your meters. In ENG work, you will spend more time watching the boom mic and less time focusing on the meters. This is especially true if you monitor at a consistent headphone volume. Your ears will tell you if something is too loud or soft (not to mention overloaded signals). If you monitor at loud levels, you will instinctively mix a track that is too low. Conversely, if you monitor at low levels, you will mix a track that is too high. Find the sweet spot and spend your career at that level. Your tracks will sound better and be more consistent, and your ears will thank you for it. In ENG work, always stand to the left of the camera to keep your eyes on the camera's meters.

Think of meters as guides rather than primary sources of information. When you drive down the road, painted lines let you know the parameters of your lane. If you cross these lines, you might get in to trouble. However, when we drive, we don't focus on the painted lines. We keep our eyes on the road and the traffic ahead. We see the lines in our peripheral vision, but we don't focus on them. Occasionally, we might sense that we are drifting. When this happens, we quickly shift our focus to the painted lines and then shift back to our driving. The same is true when monitoring a mix. Keep your eyes focused on the action for most of the time, while glancing at the meters to make sure you're in the right "lane" of audio parameters. This is a different concept than the "keep your eyes on your meters" advice that I gave in *The Sound Effects Bible*. The reason is that sound effects recording is usually more controlled and predictable than dialog recording. They are effectively different disciplines altogether.

Pay attention to the meters on the recorder more than those on the mixer. Distortion in the mixer will be heard with the headphones. The recorder's meters are more important as this is the end of the chain. Like the Hotel California, what arrives here, stays here.

Remember the primal instinct: Red equals bad. If your signal indicators or meters are blinking red lights, then you should react. This is your equipment's way of saying, "Danger, Will Robinson! Something bad has happened or is about to happen." Don't ignore these warnings.

Every camera's sound meters are different. Be sure to test the specific camera that you plan on using. Record dialog and test tone at different volumes to determine what the meters are actually telling you.

HEADPHONES

Sound mixing requires a subjective listening environment with the least amount of distractions. Working with headphones is unlike working with studio monitors. Every sound, every breath, even the high-pitch whistle of an actor's nose, will be crystal clear. Headphones give you a sense that the sound is coming from inside your head. Localization is completely distorted, especially when monitoring different channels in the left and right ears. With studio monitors you get a sense of space and separation from the source that is more natural sounding, whereas the headphones will sound much different than the final listening environment of the audience. That's okay. You want to be able to hear all of the sound elements up-close and personal. It's your job to be critical.

Headphones change your perspective. This can be a blessing and a curse. Understand how headphones work by playing back your recordings through speakers, a television, your computer, etc. Although it will take some time, you can train your ears how to listen through headphones eventually. Listen to the room with and without your headphones. What do you hear? How is it different? Headphones will not only amplify the volume, but also heighten your awareness to your environment. You'll feel like Superman. If there is a mouse in the room, you might hear it squeak with the naked ear. With headphones, however, you'll swear you can hear the mouse's thoughts!

Headphone Types

Headphones come in three flavors: *circumaural*, *supra-aural* and *in-ear*.

Circumaural headphones have cups that cover your entire ear and help reduce leakage both in and out of the ear cup. They allow you to focus on the mix without too much distraction from outside sound. The common term for circumaural is *closed-ear*.

Supra-aural headphones do not encompass your entire ear, but rather rest on top of the ear. They're often not very effective at reducing bleed and extraneous sounds. To compensate for this, most supra-aural headphone bands are designed to firmly squeeze the cups against the ear. This does not always make for the most comfortable fit. An example of professional supra-aural headphones would be the Sennheiser HD25.

Last, there are in-ear headphones. While there are professional types of in-ear headphones, the most common is the consumer "earbuds." Earbuds should never be used for professional mixing. They are, however, useful for the camera operator who can't wear standard headphones because his head rests against the camera's body. Always ask the shooter to monitor camera audio via an earpiece — even if you have a camera return to monitor. It is better to have an extra set of ears on the audio to help identify problems and background noise.

Hard hats are often required headwear for safety reasons at factories, construction sites, or other potentially hazardous locations. The challenge with hard hats is that you can't easily wear headphones. A couple of options are to keep your headphones on but move the headband to the rear of your neck. Some hard hats are large enough to allow you to adjust the inner headband of the hard hat so the headphones can be worn underneath. If these solutions don't work, you might have to use earbuds. But be warned, locations that require hard hats are usually noisy and the earbuds will be virtually useless.

Open-Back and Close-Back Headphone Designs

Professional headphones have a closed-back design, meaning that the ear cups are sealed. Open-back ear cups are designed for music listening and give a more open sound to the music. This is achieved through holes or grills that allow air movement into the headphones through the back of the ear cup. These holes allow extraneous sounds into the headphones and also allow the sound of the headphones to leak out. In addition to sound leakage, wind noise develops when wind enters through the holes. This wind noise may make it difficult to determine if the source is the headphones or actual wind noise from a microphone.

Headphone Features

Accuracy is critical when listening to your work. There are a few features that are must-haves with headphones. The first and arguably most important feature is a *flat frequency response.* Consumer grade headphones are designed to accentuate certain frequencies to make music sound "better" to the listener. They also take into consideration the average listening environments and curve frequency responses based on popular music. They are not accurate and the only use for these types of headphones is for the script supervisor, producer, or a director who doesn't care about audio. For the professional sound mixer, a flat response gives a true representation of the audio. This is a critical feature! The sound mixer needs to hear true audio, not artificially produced audio.

The second necessary feature is a *closed-ear design*. Closed-ear headphones have an ear cup that completely covers the outside of the ear. This helps isolate the ear from the environment and allows the listener to focus on the audio. Headphones with noise-canceling electronics are perfect if you are sitting on a plane next to a crying baby, but they are useless on a professional set. The noise-canceling technology will alter true audio into "more pleasing" audio. This falls under the consumer-grade category. It is possible that in the future some company will design accurate noise-canceling headphones, but as of now, they don't exist.

The closed-ear design not only keeps audio out, but will also prevent most leakage from leaving the headphones. Audio spill from headphones can be distracting to other crewmembers and in extreme cases, get picked up by microphones. Complete isolation is a plus, but most headphones do not offer this. Manufacturers like Remote Audio produce headphones similar to those used on airport runways and gun ranges that completely seal the ear from the rest of the world. They cost more, but deliver the best listening environment through extreme noise reduction intended for hearing protection.

The third, equally important feature is comfort. You will be wearing headphones for 60% of your career. That's a long time. Make sure to select headphones that don't cut off circulation to your skull, but are tight enough to allow the closed-ear design to function properly. In case you are wondering, the other 40% will be spent between scrambling for adaptors, troubleshooting gear, and hanging out at the craft service table. Consider wearing a hat when mixing. Headphone hair will probably never be in style!

Purchasing Headphones

Plan on spending at least $100 on a good pair of *cans* (industry slang for headphones). There are some places to skimp on price with your gear. A solid pair of headphones is not one of them. Million-dollar studios cost that much, not necessarily because of the equipment, but because of the cost of designing and constructing a true listening environment. Headphones are your million-dollar studio on the set.

Sony MDR-7506 is considered the industry standard for headphones and has been for decades (see note below). They are rugged enough to survive fieldwork, comfortable, and sound great. The headphones also fold to half their original size, which makes storage much easier as real estate is at a premium in a sound bag. Avoid using headphones with plastic headbands. Headphones take a lot of abuse on location. Choose headphones that can take a beating.

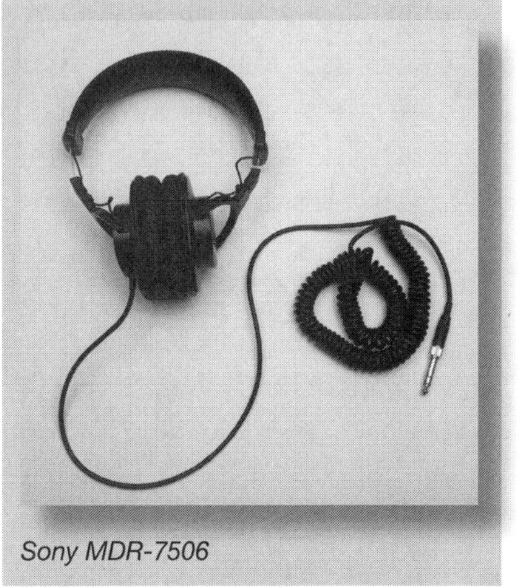
Sony MDR-7506

It should be noted that "industry standard" is a term that is used to describe a technique or piece of equipment that is widely used. This doesn't mean that the industry standard is the best. It simply means that this is what most people use. If you're starting out and you're not sure what to purchase, an industry standard is a good starting point. Once you get more familiar with the craft, it's not a bad idea to experiment with other brands and models. Try different techniques that you've heard of and borrow or rent a new piece of gear to hear how it sounds. You can test out microphones and recorders in stores, but that's not really the best way to get a sense of how something will sound in the real world. Take a new piece of gear out into the real world and stretch its legs. Listen to the results in a studio. Does it really have the sound and functionality that you're looking for?

One of the drawbacks to the Sony MDR-7506 is the special type of wire used inside of the cable. This wire is not easily repairable in the field and in most cases you'll need to replace the headphones altogether. The cost of the repair will run nearly as much as a brand new pair of headphones. The good news is the Sony MDR-7506s can last for an extremely long time. In fifteen years, I've only had one pair go bad. Of course, I've had a couple of pairs that have met with fatal misfortune.

The Sennheiser HD25 is another popular choice. There are premium-grade headphones that are more expensive and deliver premium quality audio, but beware: price does not always mean professional quality. Many consumer-grade headphones can run hundreds of dollars but should be avoided for professional use.

Impedance is usually not an issue when using professional headphones as they are designed for use with professional equipment. This impedance range is usually around 60 to 75 ohms. Lower impedance levels under 40 ohms can cause the audio to distort unnaturally, but is typically only found in consumer-grade headphones.

Coiled headphone cables are a plus with headphones. They keep the cable out of the way, which is especially important when working out of a sound bag. Care should be taken to not stretch out the coiled cable. Once you overstretch a coiled cable, it can lose its coil and turn into nothing more than a curvy straight cable that won't retract. One trick to prevent this is to run a small piece of rope down the center of the coiled cable and tie it off at both ends. This allows the cable to only stretch so far. Always pick up headphones by the head strap, not the cable. Even the most durable cable is vulnerable to strain.

Head-wrapped headphones (Don't try this at home!)

You should never head-wrap headphones. Head-wrapping means that the cable is wrapped around the headphones. This causes unnecessary strain on the cable, stretches out coiled cables, and will lead to future problems. If you do not have a coiled cable, loosely wrap the cable separately from the headphones and secure it with a hairball or other fastener. Never use tape (even gaffer tape) on cables. Gaffer tape doesn't leave a sticky residue when used for short durations, but over time, gaffer tape will start to decompose. This decomposition process is greatly increased in extreme heat and humidity. The tape might be firm in the morning, but turns into a slimy mess by the afternoon. I found this out the hard way.

Headphones are personal. You get used to the sound of your cans. They are familiar in both feel and sound. Once you've adjusted to a pair of headphones, it's a good idea to stick with them. You'll know what to expect and when to make critical decisions. Switching to a new pair of headphones should be done slowly. You'll need to spend time adjusting to the new sound. Every model of headphones sounds different, even if the same manufacturer makes them. You are hired for your critical listening decisions and your headphones are the single piece of gear that will allow you to make those decisions. You must choose, but choose wisely....

Setting Your Headphone Level

Unfortunately, most headphone volume knobs have a dial with no reference numbers at all. Some come with hash marks for a visual reference of where the knob is, but aren't a true indication of how loud the signal is going to the headphones. A tried-and-true method for properly setting a headphone level is to run a 1KHz tone and adjust the headphone level until the tone is irritating, but not painful. Once that level has been reached, note where the headphone control knob is and try to leave it there 99% of the time.

Normally with headphone levels, you should "set it and forget it." This will allow your ears to expect a certain level of sound from your gear. If an actor sounds quiet, you can focus on mic placement, channel faders, and other factors rather than worrying about if your headphones are loud enough. In general, you should only change your headphone volume if you are raising the level to investigate a potential background sound or lowering the level to compensate for loud dialog, explosions, vehicles, or other potentially harmful levels being recorded. Mixers and recorders that have push-pot headphone knobs are perfect for fieldwork, since the likelihood of the headphone knob getting bumped or moved increases a lot when running and gunning.

Don't be confused by the headphone volume control. The headphone level does not affect your main output level. Turning the headphone control up or down will only affect the volume sent to the headphones. If the audio level is too low, adjust the channel fader, not the headphone control.

Headphone Amplifiers

Some headphone amplifiers are noisier than the actual signal being recorded. This can be confusing when trying to figure out if the hiss you are hearing is coming from the mic preamp or the headphone amp itself. Know the sound of your headphone amp! Spend some time getting used to its sound.

Hiss can be worked around if it's coming from the headphone amp, which is post-master fader and doesn't appear in your audio. It is important that you determine where the hiss originates.

Nearly all camera headphone amps suck. Even if the audio signal is clean, the headphone amp might be so poor that the signal sounds faint or distorted. This is partially due to the weak signals that these headphone amps produce in a power-saving effort by the manufacturer. When corners are cut in camera development, sound is the first victim. So, you'll need to determine if the signal is truly poor. The only way to ensure that a clean signal has been received and recorded properly is to play back the recording on another device. This will help you understand what to expect from a specific camera's headphones.

Protect Your Ears!

You only get one pair of ears and when they're damaged the party is over along with your career in sound. Your ears will wear down as the day goes on. Different locations may require you to increase your headphone volume in order to monitor the dialog clearly, but be careful not to blast your ears to compensate for a noisy environment. Your ears should never hurt at the end of the day. They might be fatigued, but soreness is a sign that your levels were too loud. Also, if you have to drive to different locations throughout the day, don't crank up the radio in your car, as you'll just fatigue your ears unnecessarily.

Always turn the headphone knob to the "off" position before putting on your headphones. Start with the knob in the "off" position and slowly raise it to the normal setting position to protect your ears from excessive volume sources you might not be aware of. Failing to do this can seriously damage your hearing temporarily or permanently.

Gunshots, pyrotechnics, and other loud percussive sounds should never be monitored with headphones. Keep the headphones on to help shield your ears from these loud sounds, but disconnect them or turn the headphone amp off. Sometimes, you'll need to wear earplugs underneath the headphones for added protection. Carrying extra earplugs for other crewmembers will make you a local hero.

MONITORING A MULTITRACK RECORDER

Multitrack recorders allow you to select individual tracks and some give you the ability to set up monitoring matrixes. When multitracking, monitor the

ISO channels individually while setting the levels, but during the scene, you should monitor the mix track's signal. You can set most multitrack recorders to monitor some or all of the channels. In any case, you should know how to solo a specific mic or channel should you need to monitor only that source critically. This will make troubleshooting much easier.

If you are not mixing a mix track, you should monitor the boom channel. When using multiple lavs in addition to a boom mic, you have a couple of monitoring options:

1. You can listen in stereo (e.g., If the boom is hard-panned left and the lavs are hard-panned right, you will hear the boom in your left ear and the lavs in your right ear).

2. You can "set and forget" your lavs and only monitor the boom channel (e.g., If the boom is hard-panned left, you would select the "Left Channel" option and concentrate only on that mic). The reason for this is that the lav positioning is not as critical since they are fixed to the talent. The boom pole, however, is in motion and needs to be monitored for positioning and level purposes.

Use the second option only if the lavs are being used as a backup. If the lavs are a primary source of audio, then use the first option. If you are sending the director a headphone feed, send the boom channel. This will allow the director to focus on the scene without having to worry about any phasing issues, clothing rustle, or wireless dropouts.

CONFIDENCE MONITORING

Like their analog predecessors, some digital recorders offer *confidence monitoring*. In this mode, the recorder will allow the sound mixer to listen to the recording directly off of the media instead of monitoring the signal that is being sent to the media. This gives the sound mixer confidence in the recording as the audio file is recorded and played back in real time.

There is a delay with confidence monitoring. In analog recorders, this delay was the time it took for the tape position to pass from the record head to the playback head, which was about a half second or so. The delay in digital recorders is the time it takes to convert the analog signal to a digital file, then access the digital file and convert the audio back to an analog signal. This delay can range from near real time to several seconds. Another perk to confidence monitoring is that the delay is an indicator that the recorder is recording. When monitoring the signal that is sent to the recorder, if you fail to press record and verify the counter you might not realize the error until after the take. With confidence monitoring, the delay is another indicator that you are rolling.

THE BOOM OPERATOR'S FEED

The boom operator should always wear headphones. Always. Without headphones he is flying blind, effectively. The headphone feed will be sent from either the mixer or directly from the recorder. The sound mixer may control the feed's level or the boom operator may have a headphone amp to adjust the volume level independently.

JK Audio Remote Amp

A duplex cable is used to send the microphone signal from the boom operator to the sound mixer, and the return headphone feed from the sound mixer to the boom operator, using a single cable. The duplex cable is connected to a duplex box worn by the boom operator. This box will have input and output connections for the microphone, an output for the headphones, and sometimes features a headphone volume control. A carabiner can be clipped to the boom operator's belt or pants to help hold excess cable.

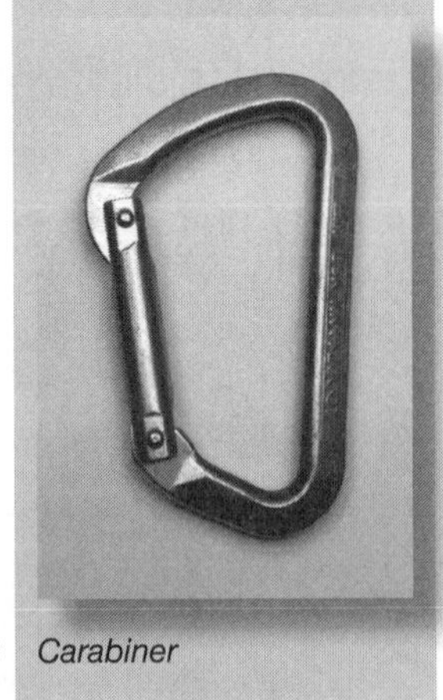
Carabiner

Now, let's discuss where the boom operator's feed comes from. There are two schools of thought. The first method is to send the boom operator the same mix that the sound mixer is listening to: the mix track. This mix is a selective and subjective combination of microphones that are being mixed by the sound mixer. The idea is to allow the boom operator to hear and understand what is being mixed and how their boom microphone fits into that mix. This can be helpful in avoiding overlaps between multiple microphones that are covering the same sound, phasing, and missed audio cues. This type of feed will also allow the boom operator to hear problems that need to be addressed, such as clothing issues with the lavs, wireless hits, etc.

The second method is to provide the boom operator with only the audio from the boom microphone. This allows the boom operator to focus on his mic placement and positioning. The logic behind this method is that the boom operator should only focus on his microphone. Providing him with the audio from other microphones could be confusing and distract him from the task at hand. Phasing or double coverage is not the boom operator's problem, but the sound mixer's.

Sound mixers who agree with this philosophy would argue that giving the boom operator a feed that includes other mics is equivalent to providing every Super Bowl camera operator with a separate video monitor for each camera in use during the broadcast. How in the world can the camera operator focus on her shot if she's busy wondering what everyone else is shooting? In the case of the Super Bowl, it is the responsibility of the technical director to give the camera operators direction on what to shoot. In many multicam situations, camera operators are given specific shots to focus on. For example, A-Camera might shoot close-ups. B-Camera might shoot a wide shot. C-Camera might be responsible for crowd reactions. From these general directions, the technical director can then give further instructions. For example, C-Camera can be directed to grab a close-up, while A-Camera makes an adjustment, etc. The same is true with boom operators. They should be directed to follow the dialog in the scene and let the sound mixer, the technical director as it were, decide which microphone to focus on in the mix track.

Personally, I think that monitoring audio from other microphones can impair the boom operator's judgment. This can confuse him as to what microphone he is hearing and where his microphone is positioned. It's best to let him focus on only his job. When in doubt, start with the second method and experiment with the first. See what fits the type of production you are working on. Ultimately, this should be the boom operator's decision as he needs a headphone feed he is comfortable with and allows him to perform optimally.

COMMUNICATING WITH THE BOOM OPERATOR

Two-way communication with the boom operator is called a *private line.* Without a direct, private line of communication the boom operator will have to use the boom mic to communicate with the sound mixer. This is not ideal since the boom pole will need to be retracted every time the boom operator needs to communicate (not always an easy task). A private line can be achieved by using headphones with a microphone like the Sennheiser HMD280-Pro. Remote Audio offers a retrofitted Sony MDR-7506 with an adjustable microphone called the BCSHSDBC. These units will provide a direct line of communication between the sound mixer and the boom operator.

The boom operator is usually the mouthpiece of the sound department because the sound mixer is off set or in another room. Often, the boom operator has to filter the sound mixer's angry rants to the crew/director and turn them into pleasant and heartfelt requests. This is always done in a calm and soothing tone. If the boom mic is being sent to the mix track that feeds the rest of the crew's headphones, the communication is not a private conversation. It's easy to forget that there are other ears listening in on what is being communicated. Usually by the time this is realized, too much has already been said.

HEADPHONE DISTRIBUTION

Apart from yourself and the boom operator, you may need to supply headphones to other crewmembers. This usually will include the director and script supervisor, but may also include a 1st AD who needs to cue extras, a special effects technician who is waiting for a cue to trigger an effect, etc. Clients will probably want a headphone feed. Most of the time, they will wear them around their necks to feel important. That's fine. But, make sure you have enough headphones to hand out on shoots with multiple executives on the set.

It is an unforgivable sin to deny an executive or person of importance a pair of headphones on a set. Most of the time, the headphones are kind of like having their name on the back of a chair. It makes them feel powerful. These headphones can be used to help a client make important decisions on verbiage used in a script, specifically when working on commercials where the communication of a message needs to be precise. Be sure to carry extra headphones for these situations.

I worked on a car commercial that had a panicked production manager calling me the night before the shoot. She told me to expect at least a dozen executives on the set and to have a pair of headphones for each one, in addition to a couple for the director and script supervisor. At that point, it was too late in the evening to call a rental house. I dashed out the door to Guitar Center and bought a Behringer HA4700 headphone amp to support that many feeds along with a few buy-four-get-one-free consumer-grade headphones and a dozen headphone extension cables. I shelled out a few hundred bucks, and of course charged the production a hefty rental fee since it was a last-minute request/demand. Of course, not a single pair of headphones was used on the set. That's how it goes sometimes.

There's a bit of a speech that you need to rehearse for handing out headphones to a newcomer who isn't part of the crew. It goes something like this: "Here you go. I've turned the volume all the way down to protect your ears. The volume control is here. Please, remember to bring them back to me when you're finished." Failure to give this rehearsed speech will result in that person bothering you at the most inopportune time to tell you that his headphones are broken because he couldn't figure out the volume control.

The Sony MDR-V150 is an inexpensive headphone solution for clients. You can usually find them on sale as a package of 5 for $99. They sound good and don't have much leakage for super-aural headphones, considering the price. Some sound mixers will have a small pair of speakers on their sound cart so that bystanders can listen to playback. Keep tape-based stock away from monitors. The magnets in the speakers can cause problems on the tapes.

An economy line level mixer can be used at video village to allow the director to selectively choose what he is listening to. It is rare that a director will want to do this, but if the request is made, solutions can be found for only $100. You will also need additional cables to supply feeds from multiple channels to the director's mixer. These can be sent from aux channels, direct outs from the mixer, or aux outputs from the recorder.

Alcohol wipes can be used to clean sweat from community headphone cups. This sanitary action will benefit both you and the user. Remember, you'll be handling the headphones, too! I never let anyone use my personal headphones. I carry plenty of spares to hand out, but I keep my headphones with me at all times. This cuts down on the abuse they take and the only germs on the ear cups are my own. Plus, people with large skulls tend to stretch out the headbands if they wear them for long periods of time.

IFB

IFB (Interruptible Feed Back or *Interruptible Fold Back)* is a return program feed sent back to the broadcast position. This allows the talent and crewmembers to monitor the program. In broadcast news, the IFB mix is typically done by the network or local station. In the event that you need to supply the IFB mix from the broadcast location, always remember to send a *mix-minus feed* to the talent. A mix-minus feed is the program material minus anything that is unnecessary for the talent to hear. The most important thing to minus is the talent's mic. It can be very distracting for the talent to hear her voice. This is much more of a problem when the IFB is being sent back to your location from a satellite or wireless feed, which will cause a delay. The delay makes it very difficult for the talent to talk while hearing her voice a second or two later.

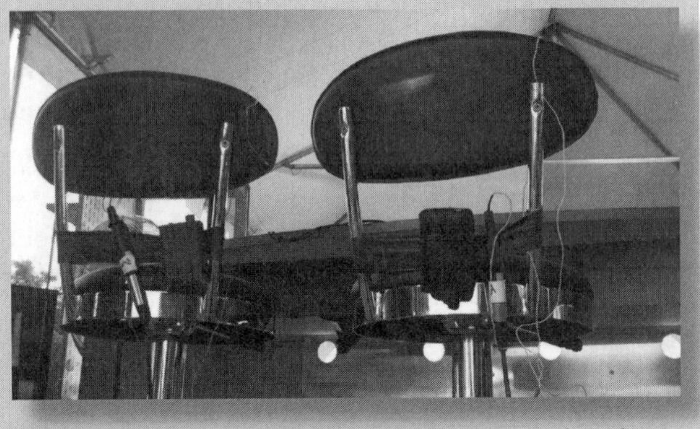
IFB receivers attached to anchor chairs for a remote broadcast

It is strongly recommended that the sound mixer monitors the IFB signal sent to the talent. On live remotes the sound mixer is the only crewmember on location who can fix or solve any IFB issues. Without wearing an IFB, the sound mixer may be completely unaware of any problems.

Many years ago, I worked on the Jenny Jones trial for Court TV. The coverage lasted a couple of months and was the longest single project I've ever worked on. It actually started to feel like a "real" job. There was a predictable routine to the day. We would show up to the courthouse at 7 a.m. and set up the broadcast tent where all of the live shots were fed. A satellite truck was parked nearby that provided IFB and Clear-Com feeds as well as received video and audio feeds from the broadcast tent. Inside the tent were several chairs for the correspondents and guests, cameras, lights and audio.

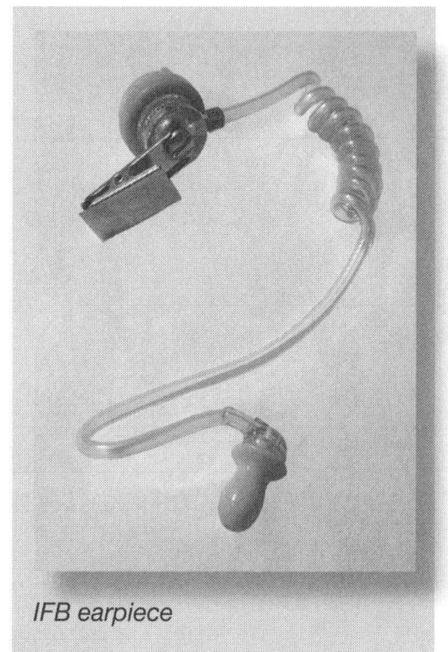
IFB earpiece

The audio setup included a mixer that fed the satellite truck a mix of lavs, an IFB feed that was daisy-chained to each chair via XLR. The end of the chain was an IFB box at the mixer so that I could monitor the IFB signal. By being at the end of the chain, I could be confident that the other IFB boxes also received the signal I received. Finally, the producers requested that I also wear a Clear-Com headset so that I could take directions from the network. Since I had three devices to monitor (mixer, IFB, and Clear-Com) and only two ears, I had to get a little creative. My solution was to wear an IFB earpiece in my right ear with the right headphone cup on top. The Clear-Com headphone cup was worn over my left ear. I looked like a villain from a cheesy science fiction B-movie, but it worked. I was able to take direction while mixing the audio and monitoring the IFB feed.

Once the tent was set up, the day was a snap. At 8:30 a.m., we shot a live broadcast that recapped the previous day's hearings and an overview of what was planned for the day. At 9 a.m., the hearings began and we were on a break until the hearing broke for lunch, at which time

The live-shot crew of the Jenny Jones trial for Court TV

we would do another live shot to recap the morning's events. A separate crew, located inside the courtroom, fed the hearings live. This gave the broadcast tent crew several hours to do absolutely nothing. But, we had to be ready to rock the moment anything happened. After the live shot at lunch, we were again free to sit around and do absolutely nothing. Occasionally, there was a mid-afternoon break and we would broadcast any exciting developments on the case. If not, we waited until 5 p.m. for a final live shot to broadcast the day's events.

The predictability of the schedule and setup made it easy to get lulled into a false sense of security. After all, it was a routine. What could go wrong? Well, of course, there were plenty of things that went wrong. This was a good learning experience for me. Despite the same setup with the same gear at the same location interviewing the same people on the same case for months, something always seemed to happen. The IFB feeds were often the problem. Several times, the mixer at the network would forget to minus the talent's mics so we would get a delay that would trip up the talent. Monitoring the IFB channel made it easy for me to quickly identify and report the problem through my Clear-Com channel.

On one occasion, during the middle of a live shot to discuss an earth-shattering development in the case, the plaintiff's attorney began to mess with his IFB earpiece. He was struggling to hear the network's correspondent. Finally, his IFB signal died. He glanced over at me and the director began shouting in my ear, "Do something!" Being at the end of the IFB chain made it easy for me to quickly realize it was the attorney's IFB box that had crapped out, since I was receiving audio in my IFB box. I jumped out of my chair and grabbed my IFB box. I glanced at the shooter's monitor to get a sense of the frame line and then slid on the ground underneath the high-back chair where the attorney sat. A quick swap between his dead IFB box and mine and we were back in business. I raced back to my mixer to hear what appeared to be thunderous applause in my Clear-Com from the satellite truck for my quick response to the crisis. Had I not been monitoring the IFB, the broadcast would have been forced to go to a commercial until we figured out the issue. If that had happened, the thunderous applause would have undoubtedly been replaced with grumbling and condescending remarks directed at me. It was my forethought to monitor the IFB signal at the end of the chain and my ninja-like response time that had saved the day.

If you find yourself in a live breaking-news event and the IFB system completely fails, the reporter can use her cell phone as a last-ditch effort to communicate with the studio. As barbaric and clunky as this may look, it might be the only way to establish a two-way conversation during a live shot. Hopefully you'll never have this problem, but if all else fails, use your iPhone!

To supply the IFB mix locally, you can send the signal via a pre-fader aux channel on the mixer. IFB boxes can be hardwire or wireless. In the event that a wireless IFB box is needed, but unavailable, you can use a standard wireless system with a headphone jack on the receiver. The talent will wear the receiver and use the receiver's headphone jack to listen to the IFB signal sent by the transmitter. Aux channels operate at line level. If the transmitter you are using requires a mic level input, you'll need to use a pad or adjust the aux channel to send an appropriate signal. This will reduce any distortion caused by the level difference.

Wireless IFB systems can suffer from the same dropout and interference problems that wireless mic systems have. However, these issues are not mission-critical. A line dropping out in the middle of a take in an IFB feed is annoying, but won't affect the take. That same dropout on a wireless mic can require a retake.

IFB earpieces come in many shapes and sizes to fit just about any ear. Be sure to have a good selection to choose from. A small earpiece will easily fall out of a large ear canal and a large earpiece won't fit into a small ear canal. Personal, custom-fitted earpieces are popular with professional on-air talent. These are used for both comfort and sanitation reasons. Alcohol swabs are a must for IFB earpieces. They will protect both the talent and sound crew from germs. Earwax can be gross. I've seen earpieces come out of ears that had huge hunks of… well you get the idea.

COMTEK

Comtek is a brand of wireless receivers that are fed from a single transmitter base. This allows for wireless headphone distribution to crewmembers and keeps the set floor clear of excess cables. Because of their prominent use in the industry, the brand name Comtek is synonymous with wireless headphones. Comtek feeds are sent to everyone with a receiver. This is important to realize. Private communication should never be sent over the Comtek channel. All ears are listening! IFB systems are better for communication between the boom operator and the sound mixer. While considerably more expensive than Comtek systems, wireless IFB systems can be used in place of a Comtek box for crewmembers.

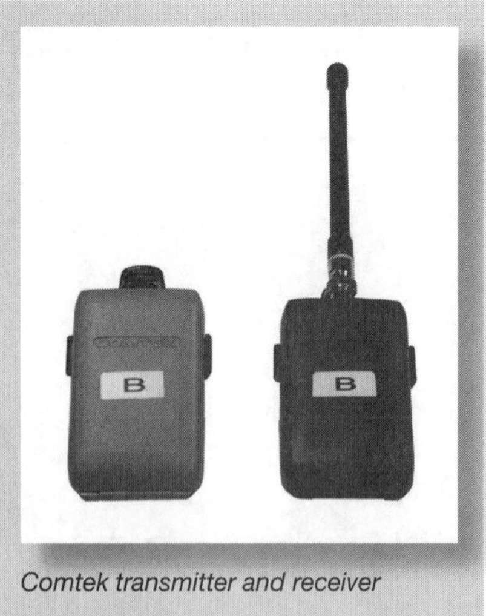

Comtek transmitter and receiver

WIRELESS HEADPHONES

Consumer wireless headphones don't have much use on a professional set; however, they can be an economical solution for independent film crews that don't have the budget for the higher priced Comtek systems. As with any wireless system, be sure to verify that the wireless headphone's frequency does not interfere with wireless systems used for production.

CHAPTER EXERCISE Talking with a delay in an IFB earpiece is harder than it sounds. Try calling your cell phone from another cell phone. Place your cell phone up against your ear and speak into the other cell phone. Notice how you start to slow down your words as your brain is trying to process both the incoming and outgoing information. This exercise is more fun when you start by saying "Citizens of the Earth, I come in peace."

CHAPTER 15

POWER

The enemy of a clean audio signal is dirty AC power. 60Hz hums and much higher-pitched buzzes can not only spoil the audio, but can also be very problematic in tracking down. It's a good idea to power your equipment with batteries. This eliminates the hums and buzzes and keeps you self-contained. Heavy-duty battery systems can power several pieces of equipment.

Field mixers have to use portable power. Standard batteries like AA and 9-volts won't last a full day if left on all the time. Other more robust batteries like NP-1s can last a full day on a single charge. In either case, it's a good idea to power down the mixer when it's not in use. It is important to check your battery life often. The last thing you want to happen is for the mixer to die right in the middle of an important interview. If you are doing a live shot or covering an event that will last a while, change out batteries for a fresh pair. Putting a piece of gaffer tape over the top of a used battery is a good way of indicating which batteries still have some life left so that you aren't needlessly wasting them. For 9-volts and NP-1 batteries, this tape also helps cover the contacts that could touch metal objects in your sound bag and cause the battery to short out. Not only can this cause the battery to leak, but it could potentially start a fire.

There are three powering options for equipment:

- Internal DC power
- External DC power
- External AC power

**Note: Many devices will offer all three options via a switch.*

INTERNAL DC POWER

Internal power refers to a battery inside the unit. This battery might be a fixed battery that has to be charged (like an iPhone) or it can be a battery compartment that allows you to swap out batteries. These compartments can use all sorts of batteries: AA, 9-volt, NP-1, proprietary batteries, and even camera batteries like the NPF. A portable field mixer might include an AC adaptor, but it is imperative that they have DC power. Without DC power, the field mixer ceases to be portable! Often, in the field, AC power may not be available and if it is, it might not be clean AC.

NP-1 battery

EXTERNAL DC POWER

External DC power comes in the form of a DC jack, 4 Pin XLR, Hirose, or proprietary connector that allows the use of an external battery. This connection also allows you to supply power to the device via an external DC power source, such as an AC to DC power adaptor (aka a "wall wart"). Some equipment will automatically switch from the internal battery system to an external source when one is detected so that you don't have to remove internal batteries when using an external source. External batteries intended for ENG work are relatively lightweight and will fit inside the sound bag. Larger sound-cart batteries can handle all of your equipment's power needs for the entire day. They are heavy, but that's not an issue since they're mounted on the sound cart.

EXTERNAL AC POWER

External AC power is a standard power cable. This might be a common computer cable socket (IEC C14) or an attached cable that runs directly into the unit. Use power filters to clean up any dirty AC power and keep your audio free of hums and buzzes.

Cart mixers are designed specifically for production work and will be DC powered, but may have AC capability. Some compact mixers intended for other industries (Allen & Heath, Mackie, etc.) can be used in field production work with professional results. However, the drawback is that they are AC powered. Every electronic device operates with DC voltage, even though they might have an AC power cable. Inside these devices is a rectifier that converts AC voltage to DC voltage. A savvy engineer can retrofit these devices to bypass this rectifier and accept DC power directly. Be forewarned: converting your unit will negate the manufacturer's warranty. If you are not qualified to do this, it's best to find another mixer or hire a professional. Incorrectly wiring your device can fry the circuits.

Never use AC power on a film set without clearing it with the gaffer first. You don't know how much power is available on a given circuit or what other equipment is intended for that circuit. Usually, gaffers are more than happy to run a stinger (filmspeak for a heavy-duty extension cord) for you. Beware of using dimmer packs with lighting equipment. Sure, it will make the picture look sexy, but it can create all sorts of buzzes in the audio signal. If dimmers are in use, make sure that all AC-powered equipment stays separate from devices connected to the audio. If your audio is sent to a camera that is battery powered, but plugged into a monitor that is powered by AC, you can end up with a nasty buzz in your audio. Isolation transformers can reduce buzzes and hums. Ground lifts can also eliminate these problems.

ONLY USE FRESH BATTERIES!

Always replace partially used batteries with fresh batteries at the start of the day. You can keep the used batteries for non-production-related use. I keep a bin of "not-dead-yet" batteries for flashlights, remote controls, and even toys (my son's toys, of course, because my toys get fresh batteries!). Rechargeable batteries can be difficult to keep track of without a system. Color-coding or numbering rechargeable batteries can make this easier. Using this type of system with multiple pieces of any gear (blimps, lavs, wireless, etc.) helps with troubleshooting in time-crunches as well. Never procrastinate with rechargeable batteries. Get into a routine of placing batteries on the charger as soon as you get home or back to the shop.

Test your batteries, even if you just pulled them out of a brand-new package! This seems like a weird statement, but it's true. Of course, I have a war story to share about brand-new batteries that were dead. I was on an MSNBC crew that followed Vice President Al Gore for a weeklong tour during the 2000 Presidential campaign. The election would become the most contested election in U.S. history.

The trip started in La Crosse, Wisconsin, and followed the Mississippi River down to Hannibal, Missouri. The Vice President traveled on a riverboat while camera operator Wes

Gore Tour press pass

Heath and I traveled in Wes' trusty old red van. We would race ahead of the riverboat to arrive at the next stop and set up the gear to capture the Vice President's arrival, speech, baby shaking, and hand kissing. Once that was all over, we would hop back in the van and race off to the next stop. There was a lot of pressure on us as we had only one chance to capture each event.

Before the trip, we coordinated on what gear we needed and packed extra mics, boom poles, mixers, and two of anything else that was mission-critical. I stocked up on cases of 9-volt batteries to power my mixer and wireless units. I also packed my DAT recorder for recreational sound effects recording, but that's another story.

After a few cities, we quickly got the hang of the routine. We would show up to the town with our press credentials, check in with the Secret Service, find a good spot for the camera, set up the gear, check sound/picture, and then wait for the Vice President to show up. The song "Let the Day Begin" by The Call would start blaring over the P.A. speakers. The crowd would start cheering and begin to sway to the music. Finally, Al Gore would take the stage and deliver his motivational sermon of hope. It went like clockwork. Despite the long hours, it was an easy gig.

A few days into the trip, we arrived at a town, ready for another day of the same setup, the same song, and the same speech. By this point, the Secret Service knew us by name. We offered them jokes and they gave us blank stares for a moment before finally cracking smiles. Once we were past the security checkpoint, we set up the camera on the press riser. I toned up the camera. I noticed that my batteries were running low, so I powered down the mixer and replaced the 9-volt batteries with a fresh pair from a new case of batteries. All was good. There was nothing to do

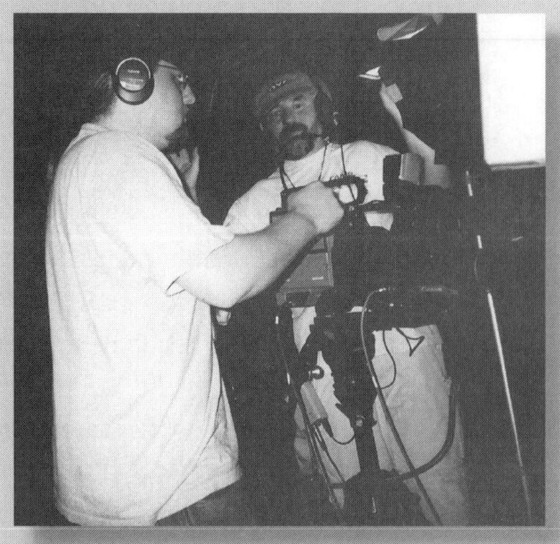

Ric Viers and Wes Heath on the 2000 campaign trail

but sit and wait for The Call's driving bass line. About twenty minutes later, the music started. It was show time.

Wes and I powered up our gear. Much to my surprise, the mixer was dead. I was shocked. I shook my head in disbelief, reminding myself that I had just replaced the batteries. I only had about a minute to fix the problem before Al Gore would appear. I kept my cool and quickly swapped out the batteries for another pair of fresh ones from the case. I flipped the switch. Nothing! I instantly felt like Han Solo on board the Millennium Falcon, wondering why the hyper drive wasn't working. The guitar and piano continued to hit the three-chord riff and the crowd swelled with excitement. I, on the other hand, was swelling with panic.

I grabbed yet another pair of batteries. Still no power! It then dawned on me that the entire case of batteries was dead. There was another case of batteries in the van, but that was several hundred feet away. It might as well have been ten miles away, because the singer started singing the lyrics to the song and it was now a matter of seconds before Gore took the stage. I, along with my batteries, was dead in the water. Suddenly, a hand appeared in front of my face holding two 9-volt batteries. I looked up, half-expecting to find an angel standing beside me. Instead, I found a fellow sound mixer who had taken sympathy on my plight, offering me a pair of his batteries. I gave a sigh of relief and nodded with a smile. Two and a half seconds later, the batteries were loaded. I fired up the mixer. The green power LED kicked on to the tune of Handel's "Messiah." This song quickly cross faded into "Let the Day Begin" as I looked up to see Gore take the stage in his trademark blue jean shirt. He waved his hands at the crowd. The shot was saved. Even though I had been prepared with brand-new batteries, I should have checked the batteries' levels. That was a mistake I would never make again. To this day, that song makes my heart skip a beat. It is burned in my mind forever as an anthem of panic. It's a reminder to double-check my battery levels, even if they're brand new.

RECHARGEABLE BATTERIES

In general, rechargeable consumer batteries can save you money, but can cost you in the long run as they are notorious for shorter life spans and sudden drops in power. More heavy-duty professional and prosumer batteries will cost more, but offer a longer life span and can last for more than a day of production. Professional and prosumer batteries like camcorder batteries, NP-1 batteries (sometimes called "Hershey bars"), and Anton Bauer batteries (sometimes called "bricks") are the most common. These batteries can be used in battery distribution systems that can power multiple devices in a sound bag. Battery distribution systems will save money on disposable batteries and allow for faster battery changes, because only one battery is changed, instead of a dozen or more.

BATTERY TYPES

There are a few types of battery choices out there: NiCad (nickel cadmium), NiMh (nickel metal hydride), and Li-Ion (lithium ion). There are pros and cons to each type. Here's a breakdown:

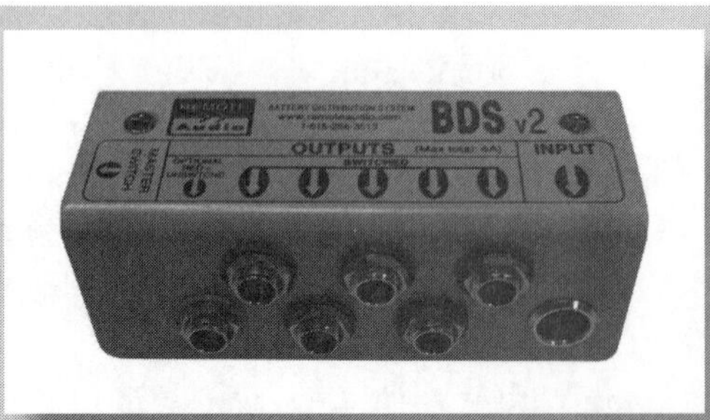

Remote Audio's Battery Distribution System

NiCad Battery

- Heavy
- Memory effect
- Durable
- Steady discharge
- Performs well in cold temperatures
- Long life when properly charged

NiMh Battery

- Some are lighter than NiCad, but roughly the same weight
- Higher capacity than NiCad
- Shorter life span than NiCad
- No memory effect
- Faster discharge rate
- Loses charge over time when not in use
- Loses charge faster in extreme heat and cold temperatures

Li-Ion Battery

- Light
- No memory effect

- Performs well in cold temperatures
- Longest life span
- Faster recharge time

Some people swear by one type of battery over the others. Li-Ion batteries are the most popular amongst sound mixers. Whichever type you choose, you should have at least two so that one can be used while the other recharges. For this reason, you might consider buying a dual charger that can charge both batteries overnight.

CHAPTER EXERCISE Determine how long your battery will run your equipment. Turn on your equipment and leave it on until the battery finally dies. Try this with different types of batteries. Note that devices that provide phantom power will not last as long when phantom power is on. This is a good test to perform with new equipment and batteries. The results will give you an idea of what to expect when you are on location.

CHAPTER 16

BUILDING A SOUND PACKAGE

Great gear can sound bad if you use it wrong. Okay gear can sound great if you use it right. Bad gear will always sound bad.

PURCHASING GEAR

Gear doesn't make great sound; the sound mixer makes great sound. Gear can help, but the quality of the sound rests in the hands of the sound mixer. Mediocre gear can be made to sound fantastic and fantastic gear can be made to sound mediocre. To believe otherwise would be to fall into the trap of clever marketing ads.

When you start the process of purchasing your field package, stay focused on what is important. There will always be more gear to buy. Don't get caught up in the shiny lights and contoured knobs. It's easy to get lost in all the options. Know what you need and start there. If not, you'll go broke chasing rainbows.

While different productions might require a few unique pieces of gear, the majority of the time you will need a core package that consists of the following:

- Microphone
- Cables
- Recorder
- Headphones

Of course, there are dozens, if not hundreds, of items that you can add to this list. However, you will always need a microphone to capture the sound. You will always need a cable to connect the microphone to the recorder (which might be the camera). And finally, you will always need headphones to monitor the signal. Everything else that you purchase will serve and support the needs of this core package.

There are certain features to look for in the core-package items. Microphones should have a good *signal-to-noise ratio* (SNR or S/N) and be able to handle high SPL. Signal-to-noise ratio refers to the amount of desired or usable signal in relation to the amount of system noise. The recorder needs to have high-quality mic preamps and timecode capability for double-system work. Headphones must have a flat frequency response, closed-ear design, and should be comfortable. If you plan on using a mixer, look for a unit that has high-quality mic preamps, the appropriate number of inputs for your productions, and flexible routing and output options.

When considering which gear you want to rent or purchase, use the following mantra: ***Trust your ears, not the manufacturer's specs***. Equipment manufacturers are famous for touting certain specs, while masking others. Just because the specs look great on paper, doesn't mean that the gear will sound great on location.

Here's an example of mic specs vs. cost:

	Microphone Manufacturer "A"	**Microphone Manufacturer "B"**
▸ **Transducer**	Condenser	Condenser
▸ **Polar Pattern**	Supercardioid	Supercardioid
▸ **Frequency Response**	50Hz – 20KHz	20Hz – 20KHz
▸ **Dynamic Range**	102dB	116dB
▸ **Signal to Noise Ratio**	72dB	71dB
▸ **Street Price**	$160	$1,699

Overall, these specs are pretty close. Manufacturer "A" has 1dB more of S/N (which in the real world is unnoticeable), while Manufacturer "B" has a deeper frequency response and 14 dB more dynamic range. The most measurable difference between these two microphones is the price. The price of the microphone from Manufacturer "A" is $160 and the price of the microphone from Manufacturer "B" is $1,699! That's more than a $1,000 difference. Now, keep in mind, this is listening to the microphone with our eyes (i.e., the specs) and not with our ears. I have personally listened to these two microphones and there is definitely a $1,000 difference in the sound.

Conversely, I've listened to a $700 microphone and a $1,300 microphone with roughly the same specs and found the $700 microphone sounded better. In this case, we learn the higher price does not always mean higher quality. So, be savvy to the marketing mumbo jumbo. Listen to the products with your own ears, don't just read the specs on the side of the box or automatically reach for the higher price tag. Audio manufacturers are in business to make better profits, not necessarily better sound.

Unless you are independently wealthy, you will have to make some compromises when purchasing your first package. In short, you will probably not be able to afford the best of everything. So, something's got to give. You'll need to sacrifice in gear selection without giving up audio quality. Don't worry. As you progress in your career and build up your client base, you'll be able to afford better gear. The real question is: Where can you compromise?

The audio chain is only as strong as its weakest link. High-quality mixers, microphones, and recorders are expensive. In the past, there were only a handful of quality choices and the prices weren't too friendly. Today's mid-priced gear offers better quality than some of the high-end gear of twenty years ago. There is hope! The bottom line is don't add a link to your chain that will cause your overall sound quality to suffer. Instead of a high-quality $2,000 microphone and okay-quality $500 mixer, consider a good $1,000 microphone and a good $1,500 mixer.

Try to purchase the best of some of the lower-priced items like headphones, production bags, cases, etc. Sure, you can save $20 here and there, but that's not really going to give you enough leftover cash to purchase a $3,000 shotgun over a $1,000 shotgun.

Brand names can offer an artificial sense of quality for some mics. In most cases, mics that have great sound quality are dismissed as cheap because of a low price point. Choose the mic that's best for your wallet with your ears and not with your eyes. The producers and audience members won't know (or care) which mic you used. They will, however, notice poor sound quality.

In addition to the ability to produce quality sound, other important aspects of field equipment include reliability and durability. Gear must stand up to the hard, fast-paced, guitar-player-in-a-hotel-room kind of abuse. If the gear you're interested in can't meet these challenges, then choose a different piece of gear. Sure, you might save a few bucks on your purchase, but it might cost you gigs and clients if the gear craps out because it can't handle the rigors of the field. Always choose reliability over price.

It's a good idea to have "expendable" microphones for adverse recording conditions. I have several microphones that I use specifically for dangerous sound effects recording like mic placements near down range when recording guns. These mics sound great, but are not nearly as expensive as others. If a stray bullet were to hit one, it wouldn't be an expensive mistake. I keep the more expensive microphones out of harm's way. Cheaper, but quality microphones like electret shotguns, can be used in the rain, on boats, or for other shots that take place near adverse conditions like dust and debris. It's better to lose a $300 shotgun than to lose a $3,000 shotgun!

Also, try to be savvy about where you purchase your gear. A multimillionaire once told me that he "never paid full price for anything." That struck me as odd because he of all people should be able to afford to pay full price for everything! I suspect that this mindset was one of the reasons he was a multimillionaire. To this day, I have never paid full price for any of my gear. I either wait until an item goes on sale or I try to work with a salesperson who can cut me a deal. You'd be surprised what you can get when you simply ask. I've even had managers at retail stores like Best Buy cut me deals on large purchases. It also helps if you purchase the majority of your gear at one time, from one store. This gives you bargaining power. Sure, you might be able to buy a single item for twenty dollars cheaper elsewhere, but you might be able to shave hundreds of dollars on your entire purchase by dealing with one store. Before you buy, shop around, ask questions, and try to make deals.

WORKING IN THE FIELD

When you're on location, you will only have what you bring with you! Sound gear is not available at your local hardware store, so most locations might as well be deep in the jungle. Apart from your core package, make sure your sound package has plenty of support gear and problem solvers to help you deal with whatever's thrown at you. Here's a list of things to consider bringing with you in the field:

Sound Package Contents

- Microphones (Boom Mics and Lavs)
- Microphone Support (Boom Poles, Blimps, Wind Protection, etc.)
- Mounting Accessories for Lavs and Plant Mics
- Mixer
- Recorder
- Backup Recorder
- Backup Media
- Wireless Systems
- Headphones
- Comtek
- IFB
- Sound Reports
- Battery Distribution Systems
- Cart Power
- Disposable Batteries
- Rechargeable Batteries
- Power Invertors
- Extension Cords
- Cell Phone Charger
- Laptop
- Adaptors
- Cable Testers
- Cables
- Ground Lifts
- Inline Pads
- Phase Invertors
- Cases
- Cable Ties/Zip Ties
- Gaffer Tape — black 2" roll
- Gaffer Tape — white 1" roll
- Garbage Bags
- Hairballs
- Rubber Bands
- Bongo Ties
- Bungee Cords
- Rope
- Allen Wrenches
- Voltage Meter
- Leatherman
- Maglite
- Sharpies
- Soldering Iron/Solder
- WD-40
- Air Duster
- Goo Gone
- Poncho
- Sound Blankets
- Chair*
- Pop-Up Tents
- Towels
- Umbrellas
- Bull Horn
- Walkie-Talkies
- First Aid Kit
- Aspirin
- Bug Spray
- Hand Sanitizer
- Sunscreen
- Power Bars/Snacks
- This Book! ;)=

**Note: Production sound mixing is perhaps the only job in the world where you need to bring a chair to work!*

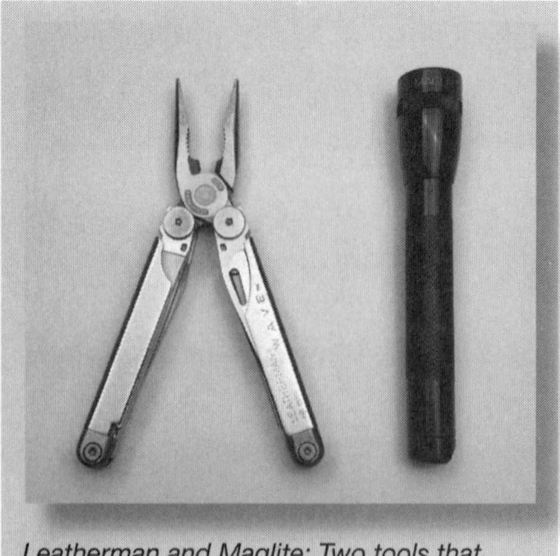
Leatherman and Maglite: Two tools that every sound mixer should carry!

Any item that is discarded after use is considered an *expendable*. For audio accessories, this includes media that will not be reused, disposable batteries, tape and other adhesives such as Moleskin, Hush Heels, and Band-Aids. Gaffer tape does not work well when left in cold temperatures (for example, leaving a roll in a car overnight). If this happens, you will need to let the tape warm up a bit before it can be used. The Leatherman/Maglite combo pouch is a handy tool set to carry. It can be very useful for gear repairs and working in low lighting conditions to trace cable runs, patch cables, etc. Sound blankets serve many functions, such as reducing reflections in a reverberant room, reducing noise coming from under a door or window, and protecting your gear during transport.

PORTABILITY

The very nature of location sound is mobility. The catch is sound mixers need a fair amount of equipment in order to perform their job. In ENG work, the sound mixer carries all of the necessary equipment in the sound bag. Feature film work involves much more equipment that would be impossible to lug around over the shoulder, so the equipment is placed on a sound cart. Your field package should allow you to be portable.

No two sound bags or sound carts look the same. There really is no standard. As a sound mixer, you will intuitively configure your bag or cart to fit your needs and style of mixing. Gearheads and techies can spend hours and even long weekends reconfiguring their equipment, even if it's not necessary. The main goal behind the configuration of your rig is to be able to operate like an ambulance driver – have what you need and know where it is!

SOUND BAGS

The sound bag quickly becomes overcrowded with all sorts of gear. The blinking lights, knobs, and switches can be overwhelming at first, but quickly become familiar tools and problems solvers. Soon, you'll only look at them when you have to. The rest of the time, you'll be watching the action and paying attention to mic placement. It's similar to playing a guitar. When you first start out, it feels like there are too many strings and a countless number of frets. Once you've got the hang of it, you'll be able to rock the crowd without looking down to see what your fingers are doing. Rock legends like Steve Vai even have guitars with extra strings on them because there weren't enough strings to play with. In time, you'll know the gear like the back of your hand and start looking for even more complicated gear to add to the bag.

Here are some examples of sound bags:

- camRade AMATEII audioMate
- Kata Koala-3
- Petrol PS607 Deca Mixer Bag
- Porta Brace AO-1X

ENG sound package

Sound Bag Setup

The hub of your sound bag is the mixer. Most manufacturers have designed sound bags to allow for this workflow. There are special pouches for wireless systems, strategically placed holes to pass through cables from separate compartments, places for headphones, cables, and just about anything else you can think of. The catch with these bags is that the majority of them use Velcro as the fastening system for pouches and compartments. Velcro is extremely noisy. There's no quiet way of using Velcro during a shot, so any adjustments need to be made prior to shooting.

The boom cable should be routed to the right side of the mixer bag. This is where the end of the boom pole will live most of the time. If you leave the boom cable on the left side of the bag, then the cable will cross in front of you when you boom (not to mention it will get tangled up in your headphones' cable). Since most field mixers have their inputs on the left side of the mixer, you may want to permanently place an 18" XLR cable in the bag to extend the boom cable to the right side of the bag. This short XLR cable is sometimes called a *shortie*. If you are left-handed, disregard everything you just read.

The ENG Snake/Breakaway cable should also stay on the right side of the bag where the outputs of the mixer are located. This position will also keep the ENG snake out of your way when you are standing on the left side of the camera. Typically, you should have a pair of 20' XLR cables on the left side of the bag for hardwiring lavs.

Headphones can be stored in a pouch located on the outside of most sound bags. Keep excess headphone cable stored in here when booming so that the cable doesn't get in your way or tangled with other cables. Try to avoid hanging the headphones outside of the bag. This can damage the headphones and cause them to get tangled up with other gear and cables.

Sound bags get heavy! Some might be as light as five pounds, but most can weigh well over ten pounds once you add wireless systems and batteries. Try to travel as light as possible. This will allow you to be more agile and make it easier to run and gun. If you don't need it, leave it in the truck! Adaptors and other loose items may rattle around and make noise when you're running. A good trick is to place these items in a bag with foam inside to prevent them from rattling.

Most sound bags come with a single shoulder strap. Do not rest the strap on your shoulder. The bag will just slip off. Trust me, I know. Instead, drape the strap over your left shoulder and across your chest to your right hip. This will keep the mixer on your right side allowing you to face the camera's left side while holding a boom pole.

Sound bag with shoulder strap

For the best results, invest in a good shoulder harness that will protect your back. This will make operation much easier and will save you the money you would have spent on a chiropractor after years of wear and tear on your left shoulder. The harness distributes the weight evenly and helps secure the bag

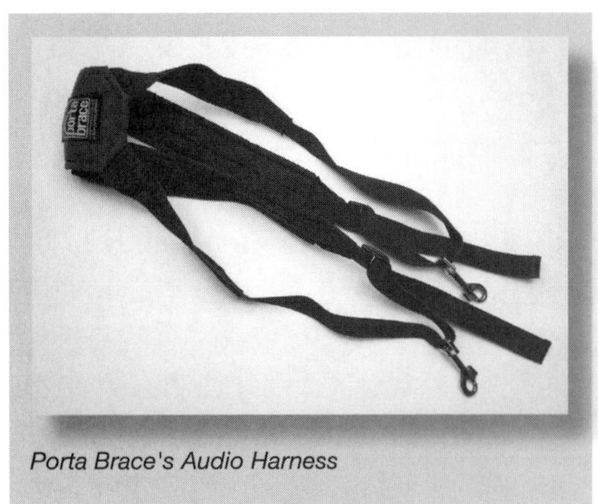
Porta Brace's Audio Harness

from bouncing around. The shoulder harness costs about $75, but will be one of the best investments you'll make.

Regardless if you use a shoulder harness or strap, you should keep the bag positioned so the mixer's controls are just below your sternum. This makes the controls easier to reach and allows you to move without spilling gear everywhere or sounding like a junk truck when you take off running. Go for an Eric Clapton guitar placement versus the Slash guitar placement. You might not look as cool as Slash, but the mixer will be easier to operate.

Sound bag with Audio Harness

Sound Cart

The most important features of a sound cart are the size and portability. The sound cart will not only need to fit in your vehicle for transportation, but must also be able to fit through doorways and navigate tight corners on location. Larger wheels will allow the cart to travel over rougher terrain like grass and gravel. There are a handful of premade sound carts on the market that are made out of lightweight aluminum and some that can collapse for easier storage.

Here are some examples of sound carts:

- Chinda Cart
- Filmtools Thin Profile Junior Sound Mixing Cart
- Kortwich "Tonkarre" Sound Cart
- PSC SC-4
- RastOrder MB Cart
- RastOrder Foldup Cart

Battle-worn PSC sound cart

The downside to these carts is their price point. A good, sturdy sound cart can cost well over $1,000. In a league of its own, the Chinda cart lists for (wait for it…) $7,500! Rest assured, the Chinda cart comes complete with shock absorbers and features precision design, although I'm not sure if they provide roadside assistance. Personally, if I had the coin to drop on a Chinda cart, I would reconsider spending the money on a better recorder or microphones. But, that's just my opinion.

Makeshift sound cart using an A/V cart

Homemade sound carts can be a fun project and cost half as much as most premade carts. If you decide to build your own cart, be sure to have plenty of shelves and storage options such as a place for a cart battery, boom pole holders, and hooks for cables and headphones. Carpeted shelves will protect your gear and make for a quieter work surface. Everything should be virtually bolted down on the sound cart. This will prevent things from falling off when wheeling the cart around. Your sound cart needs to be lightweight, but sturdy. You might have to carry it up and down stairs and across football fields, and even roll across a sandy beach.

Jeffrey Pendergrass' homemade sound cart under construction

The sound cart is a portable workstation and should remain self-contained whenever possible.

Keep everything on the cart at all times. This is basically your office. A follow cart can be used to carry additional cases and can serve as a workspace for building plant mic rigs, etc. Liquid and electronics are not good bedfellows. Try to use bottled drinks that have a cap on them to avoid spilling liquid on the gear. If you have a can or cup with no lid, try placing it inside a roll of gaffer tape to prevent it from getting knocked over.

Jeffrey Pendergrass' finished sound cart on location

CASES/PROTECTING GEAR

Always use cases to protect your gear. Transport your gear in sturdy cases that have foam inside to serve as shock absorbers should the gear get dropped or knocked around. Cases might be expensive, but they're a lot cheaper than replacing the gear inside! While on set, try to keep gear in their cases when not in use. This will keep your area of the set clutter-free and prevent any tripping hazards or accidents from happening. Your cable runs are always going to be a tripping hazard, so be sure that they are out of the way as much as possible. When a cable is not in use, keep it rolled up and stored neatly. A useful trick is to place several pieces of gaffer tape on the outside of your cases. This might be a lifesaver if you forget to bring a roll of gaffer tape and only need a small piece to secure a lav.

Scott Clements' sound cart

Working in the field presents all sorts of hazards for your gear. Dirt, dust, and moisture can shorten its life span. Keep gear away from these hazards. Cover equipment that's exposed to dust and other debris. Use a can of air to remove dust from the crevices of your gear.

Avoid leaving equipment in extreme temperatures for long periods of time. This includes leaving gear in a vehicle overnight. Condensation and extreme temperatures can damage microphones and other electronics. Theft is another issue to consider. When working on the road, it might be impractical to bring all of your gear into the hotel room. Keep gear out of plain sight by covering it with a blanket or placing it in the trunk. Be sure to bring batteries and a charger inside to recharge them overnight. Don't forget to bring the charger with you when you leave to go back to the location. You never know when you might need to charge a battery on the set. A power inverter can be used to charge batteries at a location without AC power.

Film sets are not safe places. Gear can grow legs and walk off a set. Sometimes this is malicious theft, other times it's a case of mistaken identity when dealing with other departments that might have similar gear or cases. Clearly label your gear to avoid this and keep all of your equipment near the sound cart or stored in your vehicle. Keep your vehicle locked at all times!

TRAVELING WITH GEAR

Pack light when you travel. Buy disposable batteries when you get to your final destination to save on baggage overages that can be far greater than the cost of the batteries. If you are going to hit the ground running when you land, pack enough batteries to last until you can find a store. When traveling to foreign countries, you should check to see if the batteries you'll need will be available and, most importantly, purchasable near your location. Be sure to have the proper AC adaptors for your battery chargers when traveling to other countries.

Pelican cases are somewhat of an industry standard for transporting gear and travel. The 1600 and 1650 models are the most common. The 1650 is larger and comes with an extendable handle and wheels, which make it easier to navigate through an airport.

Whenever possible, bring your sound bag on the plane with you as a carry-on. You'll get strange looks at the security checkpoint and probably get "randomly" selected for a private screening, but it will be worth it. I have never checked my sound bag for air travel. It never leaves my side. It goes where I go. I'd rather have my luggage

Pelican cases - 1600 (top) and 1650 (bottom)

lost than have my sound bag turn up missing or lost in transit. When you land, you'll at least have gear to work with, which is why you traveled in the first place! If you check cases of gear, make sure they don't have "Sound Department" or "Audio Gear" stickers all over them. These are basically broadcasting the fact that the case's contents are worth being stolen. A large sticker that says "Dirty Diapers" is probably a safe bet for deterring thieves.

Always arrive to the airport at least two hours before a flight. This gives you plenty of time to check your baggage (other than your sound bag!) and get to the gate. Checking in at the last minute could mean that your baggage won't make the flight. Traveling can be exhausting. The last thing you want to do is overlook a case in a hurry to get to the hotel. A common practice for traveling with multiple cases is to number them. Most crews will label each case with a number (for example, "1 of 6," "2 of 6" and so forth). This is usually done with camera tape or bright colored gaffer tape. The numbers will remind you how many bags you checked in and how many made it to your destination. I've had baggage get delayed by as long as a week. Thankfully, this was on the flight home during a week that I wasn't booked, so I wasn't completely screwed.

GEAR MAINTENANCE

While it is very helpful, it is not vital for a sound mixer to fully understand audio circuitry and the science of audio technology. In fact, very few sound mixers are qualified to service the equipment they work with. What is vital is that the sound mixer fully understands how sound works and how the equipment is used. *Techniques will always trump technology*. A racecar driver might win the Indy 500 without a complete understanding of how to service every component under the hood, whereas a certified mechanic may not even qualify to enter the race. Both have their place and are equally necessary, but that doesn't mean that they are equally intertwined. Of course, having an advanced understanding of both technique and technology will quickly put you at the top of your game!

Knowing *why* to do something is more important than knowing *how* to do something. The *how* might change from situation to situation, but the *why* will never change. This is the key principle to understanding location sound. The *why* will always be to deliver clean, consistent, and intelligible dialog. The mechanic knows *how* the car runs in the race, but the driver knows *why* the car needs to maneuver a certain way on the racetrack. Most of the maintenance that you will do will be superficial anyway.

Gear can break down or get damaged for many reasons. Sometimes the gear just "goes bad." Actors or other crewmembers might knock something over. These problems are usually beyond your control. It would be a shame if you were the cause of equipment failure from misuse or lack of maintenance. Remember, no one will take care of your gear better than you. After all, you rented or paid for it. It's your responsibility!

Crackles or distorted noise can be the result of a bad cable. If you have a cable or piece of gear that is damaged or experiencing intermittent problems, mark it with a piece of tape. It's easy to fool yourself into thinking that you'll remember to check the gear later. Because tape can leave a sticky residue on the cable, it's a good idea to place the tape on the sleeve of the connector. It only takes a moment to mark the gear and this can save you a big headache later on. Plan a regular maintenance day to solder poor connections, test intermittent gear issues, and clean out your sound bag or cart. The spare change you find alone will be worth the effort!

Internal batteries in some equipment like lavs, shotgun mics, and digital devices will eventually need to be replaced. Test these batteries periodically — say, once a year. Include replacement batteries in your package in case they die without warning on a set in the middle of nowhere. Also, check the shock mount inside the blimp to make sure that the screws are tight and the rubber bands are securely fastened. This will prevent the shock mount from rattling or bumping against the inside of the blimp.

Moisture buildup in equipment, especially microphone diaphragms, can affect performance. Silica gel packets, like those that come with electronics and other products that are adversely affected by moisture, should be kept in your cases. This will absorb moisture and protect your gear. A good supplier of silica gel is *www.silicagelpackets.com.*

Remember, preventative maintenance will avoid costly maintenance! Take care of your gear and your gear will take care of you.

OWNING GEAR VERSUS RENTING GEAR

At face value, you will save more money in the long run if you own your gear. If you are starting out and aren't sure if location sound is the right career path for you, consider renting gear until you're confident in your choice. If you are an independent filmmaker who makes films on the cheap, purchasing a sound package can save you money after only a few projects. There are pros and cons to owning your gear.

Pros to Owning Your Gear

- You can make money on the rental package!
- Having your own gear can bring in more work.
- You are the only one who uses the gear, so you know how well the gear has been treated.
- You can accept last-minute gigs.
- You don't have to spend non-billable time picking up and returning rented gear.
- Gear might not be available to rent if there are a lot of productions going on in your city. If you have enough time before the shoot, you can rent gear out of town and have it shipped to you. However, you will incur the cost of shipping and take the risk of the gear not arriving before the shoot.
- Audio equipment is a relatively safe investment, since audio technology stands the test of time (or at least lasts far longer than camera technology).
- Gear is cool and will help you attract members of the opposite sex.... (Not really, but I couldn't resist).

Cons to Owning Your Gear

- A basic sound package can be a costly investment. A modest package can run at least $10,000.
- Maintenance problems are your problems. Not only will you have the headache of dealing with a repair shop, but you'll also have to pay for the repairs.
- You will need to pay for insurance to cover equipment damages and theft.

Many sound mixers will only accept jobs that include their rental package. Others will work the job, but will only use their own equipment, even if the production doesn't pay for the rental.

Rentals

Renting gear is part of the business. Even if you own your gear, there will still be jobs that require the rental of additional gear. Some producers will send you a list of required equipment to work on a show. In general, this will consist of:

- Field Mixer with at least three channels
- Boom Pole with Shotgun and wind protection
- Two Lavalier Mics with Wireless Systems
- Headphones
- Necessary Cables and Batteries

Other times, the producer might send you a list with special requirements. If these items are not included in a standard package, they might be billable as an additional rental, such as extra radio mics. If the production company sends you a list of required gear, do not assume that the list is a standard gear package. Read the list thoroughly to make sure that you have all the gear that they require. If you need to rent equipment to satisfy the list, call your local rental house or beg fellow sound mixers to make sure that you can provide the gear for the shoot. It's a good idea to line up additional rentals as soon as possible. It's amazing how fast gear can fly off the shelves at rental houses. The last thing you want to do is wait until the last minute to book rental gear only to find out that everyone in town is working and the gear is not available. Knowing if the gear is unavailable in advance might give you the extra time you need to rent and have it shipped from out of town. In some cases you can charge for prep days to pick up and return needed rental gear or the production might have a PA handle this for you.

If you rent a piece of gear that is not used by the production, you are still owed the rental fee. The producer might argue that the gear was never taken out of the case, but you need to remind him that the gear was ordered even if it was requested for insurance purposes. The rental company will bill you regardless if the gear was used or not. Stand firm and invoice for the gear.

When renting equipment, always check the gear before leaving the rental house. All too often, gear rentals are picked up at the last minute, late at night or on the way home from a long shoot day. Don't be in too much of a rush. The extra five minutes that you take to double-check the gear can save you a headache on set or production time lost when you have to send a runner back to the rental house to get that missing cable.

Checklist for Renting/Borrowing Gear

- Is the gear in perfect working order?
- Do you know how to operate the gear?
- Is there any special documentation?
- Do you have all the right cables?
- Are the connectors on the cables compatible with the gear that you will be using?
- If battery operated, is there an AC cable/power supply for emergencies?
- Are the batteries fully charged?
- Is there a battery charger?
- Is special media needed?
- Is a special tool needed to service or operate the gear?
- Do the wireless units have mics, mounts, matching transmitters/receivers, spare antennas, etc.?
- Are the wireless frequencies legal where the gear will be used?
- When does the gear need to be returned?
- Is the gear scheduled for another shoot? This is an important question to ask in case your shoot gets extended to additional days. Will the gear be available if this happens?

Never take rented equipment on a set without testing it first. Always turn the gear on before leaving the rental house! Although I can't prove it, I'm pretty sure that "assumption" is the Latin word for "*expecting to fail.*" If a PA is sent to pick up gear on your behalf, provide him with the above list of questions.

Gear Insurance

Most rental companies require production insurance before you can rent their equipment. If the production company has insurance, the rental house can be added to the rider. This is discussed further in Chapter 20.

CHAPTER EXERCISE Sometimes we need to reevaluate what is really important when making decisions. Imagine that you have $20,000 to spend on a sound package. Create a list of what gear you would purchase with that money. Once the list is complete, imagine that half of the money was unavailable. Now, how would you spend $10,000? What about $5,000? The items that you eliminate in this exercise will help reveal which pieces of equipment are really necessary and which pieces are just "cool toys" to have. Be frugal when you purchase your gear.

CHAPTER 17

THE TEN LOCATION SOUND COMMANDMENTS

Location sound is 20% operation and 80% problem-solving. The reality of filmmaking is that it's a creative process that uses technology and not a technological process that needs creativity. It's an art form. And as with all art forms, there are no rules. Instead, and much like the Pirate's Code, there are guidelines. However, there are ten rules of location sound that you should always follow. These rules are infallible. They have been tested and proven to be true. They are the Ten Location Sound Commandments. To break them, would be a sin....

1. Thou Shalt Provide Clean, Consistent and Intelligible Audio
2. Thou Shalt Check Thy Equipment Before Going Into the Field
3. Thou Shalt Know Thy Gear and Keep It Maintained and Organized
4. Thou Shalt Tone Up Thy Camera or Recorder
5. Thou Shalt Eliminate Background Noise
6. Thou Shalt Critically Listen to Thy Audio
7. Thou Shalt Discourage M.O.S.
8. Thou Shalt Play an Active Role in the Production
9. Thou Shalt Gather Room Tone
10. Thou Shalt Be Prepared for Anything

COMMANDMENT 1
THOU SHALT PROVIDE CLEAN, CONSISTENT, AND INTELLIGIBLE AUDIO

The dialog that you capture should be as pure as possible, easy to work with and easy to understand. This can be achieved by following the key to great location sound: *Get the right mic in the right place at the right time with the right level!*

Clean

The audio should be free of excessive background noise, overlaps of dialog, prop handling, crew noise, and incidental noises. These sounds are not only distracting, but can also make the dialog difficult to understand and even harder for the editor to cut.

Overlaps occur when actors step on each other's lines. This might be fine if both actors are on camera and the exchange can be seen. For ENG sit-down interviews, it is common practice for the producer or interviewer to ask a question and wait for the response. The idea is to not step on the response with the question. This makes editing the piece much easier as the question may not be heard in the final piece. However, during an exchange or heated debate between the interviewer and the interviewee, an overlap is acceptable as it is part of the conversation.

The same is true with feature work. Overlaps happen all the time on screen. It's part of the storytelling process. If an overlap happens during a master or two-shot, be sure that both actors are covered with a microphone(s). However, if a shot is a reversal of one of the actors, try to eliminate the overlapping lines from the off-screen dialog so that the on-screen actors' dialog can be recorded cleanly. If the audience doesn't see the off-screen actor's lips, they don't need to hear that actor in that particular shot. When actors step on each other's lines, the dialog is extremely difficult to edit. Scenes with fast-paced, back-and-forth dialog can be easier to cut in post with non-overlapping dialog tracks.

Some actors prefer to have a real exchange with the off-screen actor to help them with their performance. In this case, try to have off-screen actors hold back on the overlapping parts of the dialog to help with the soundtrack. Reversal shots might see an actor's mouth moving from behind, but the overlapping dialog can be pantomimed so that the on-screen actor's dialog can be recorded cleanly. Ultimately, this will be the director's call. The director may want to capture the heat of the moment. When this is the case, make sure that both actors can be clearly heard on the track. If you only have one boom and must make a choice between on-camera or off-camera dialog, always go with the on-camera dialog. It's much easier to replace off-camera dialog in post, provided that there were no overlaps.

Clean audio also means that the sound is recorded at the proper levels. Levels that are too low may introduce hiss into the track. Levels that are too high may cause distortion. In either case, these are ugly blemishes on what should be a beautiful soundtrack. Observing proper gain staging and maintaining good signal levels will ensure that the sound is recorded correctly. With critical listening, you will quickly spot any flaws in the audio.

Techniques for dealing with background noise are covered in great length under Commandment 5.

Consistent

Consistency is more important from shot to shot rather than from scene to scene. An overall consistency in the tracks that you deliver for the entire production will certainly be appreciated in postproduction. Strive to maintain the same dialog/background ratio; that is, the same amount of separation between the actors and their environment. This means that there shouldn't be a noticeable shift in background level over the dialog for different camera angles within a scene.

Change in microphone placement and equipment settings will affect the consistency of your dialog. Keep mic selection and placement along with gain and filter settings consistent from shot to shot within a location. For example, using a high pass filter halfway through a day's shots could cause problems if the shot is cut together with a shot from earlier in the day when the HPF was off. Make the right decisions during setup and stick with them. The editor will thank you for it (probably not, but it's the thought that counts).

Extreme changes in sound appear as acoustic jump cuts or continuity problems. Imagine a scene in a living room that has a lamp in the corner. If the lamp is off in one shot and on in another, the audience will be alerted to the change. This event will take them out of the story. The same is true with the scene's audio. If an actor is talking in the same living room with no sound in the background in one shot, but in another shot we hear through the window the sound of a truck driving down the street, the audience will be drawn to the irregularity and, again, taken out of the story. Acoustic jump cuts and continuity issues are some of the most common problems in location sound.

You will need to change perspectives when switching from a wide shot to a tight shot. This is a natural acoustic change. An actor three feet from the camera shouldn't sound the same as an actor thirty feet from the camera. You shouldn't change the position of the mic from different shots of the same perspective. This will cause the sound to be inconsistent.

Intelligible

The audience should understand every line of dialog easily. This is where microphone selection and placement make the biggest difference. The intelligibility of dialog is greatly affected by the balance of direct sound and reverb. If the microphone is placed too far away from the actor, the dialog can be washed out with reverb. This can make the actor's lines difficult to understand. Having more reverb than direct sound is the equivalent of shooting a picture that is out of focus. The microphone needs to be positioned so that the voice is picked up without obstructions or great distances that would affect intelligibility.

An example of poor mic selection and placement would be a home video camera. These cameras do not use directional microphones; in fact they are usually substandard stereo microphones, which just makes things worse. The mic is in a fixed position on the front of the camera. For older, tape-based cameras, this meant the microphone was placed less than an inch from gears and motors that moved during the recording, creating audible mechanical noise. To top this off, the audio was subject to the camera's angle. If the camera turned 180 degrees during a shot, the audio would all but disappear. In shots where the camera panned back and forth between two people having a conversation, the audio would shift back and forth based on whomever the camera was pointing at. When all of these problems were combined, the dialog would be washed in a sea of reverberant room noise or wind noise and nobody could understand half of what was said.

Another example would be an actor driving in a car with the camera shooting through the windshield. The microphone should be placed inside the car to pick up the dialog so that the audience can understand the words. There's a fair amount of cheating that is done in the storytelling world in order to capture performances. Just because the camera is shooting through the window doesn't mean that's where the microphone needs to be positioned. Doing this would result in audio that is unintelligible.

If the sound mixer is concentrating on the dialog and can't understand what is being said, then the audience will have no chance of comprehending the dialog. Do whatever it takes to make every single word discernible.

COMMANDMENT 2
THOU SHALT CHECK THY EQUIPMENT BEFORE GOING INTO THE FIELD

Prepping your package before a shoot is like getting ready to go camping. Hardcore campers will air out all of their camping gear and line it up along their driveway to make sure that everything is accounted for. They'll check batteries for the flashlights, make sure there is enough propane for the stove, and plenty of marshmallows for the s'mores. When they head out into the wilderness they know that they have everything and that it is all in working condition. Once they are alone with Mother Nature, they will only have the supplies they packed. Fieldwork is like camping. In the field, you only have what you brought with you.

Make a checklist of important items and laminate it. This is similar to a pre-flight checklist that pilots use before every flight. When you prep for a job, go through the list and make sure that you have everything. It can be very frustrating to drive all the way out to a location only to find that you forgot a 6" cable that you need to connect your wireless receiver to your mixer.

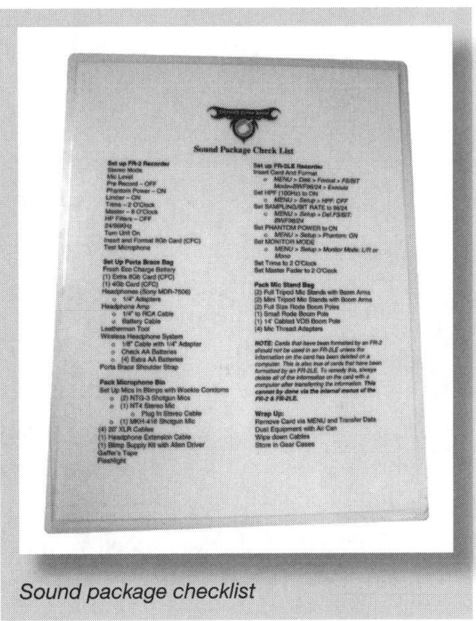

Sound package checklist

Turn on and test every piece of gear to make sure that they work and have a full battery charge. Load media into your recorder, format the drive or card, and record a test take to make sure it works. Verify that the wireless systems are tuned to the proper matching frequencies. If you change mics from the blimps often, check to make sure that the right microphone is in the blimp. I've taken empty blimps into the field before. Test your microphones by wearing headphones. This will ensure that your headphones work and will let you hear the quality of the mic signal. Meters lighting up doesn't mean that the mic signal is clean.

COMMANDMENT 3
THOU SHALT KNOW THY GEAR AND KEEP IT MAINTAINED AND ORGANIZED

Don't be fooled. Owning the gear does not mean you know how to use it! Just like owning a guitar doesn't make you Eddie Van Halen. You need to know your equipment the same way that a soldier knows how to disassemble and reassemble his weapon blindfolded. Understand every knob, switch, and menu option. Know what to do when something stops working. Certain models of mixers and recorders can offer unique options that might not be found on other makes and models. Don't expect your new recorder to offer the same functions as other recorders and certainly don't expect the same functions to be found in the same place!

Unfortunately, there is a lack of standards between equipment manufacters in the audio industry. No two devices are built the same way or have all the same features. Some field mixers have master faders, while others don't. Some recorders use XLR jacks for their outputs while some use a combination of different connectors. And don't get me started on the lack of standardization with knob indicators!

If you like a specific manufacturer's quality, you'll have to get used to their way of thinking. While this might seem inconvenient for a beginner, once you understand the basics of the technology, signal flow, and how all the gear connects, it's just a matter of figuring out where the manufacturer has hidden your favorite feature. This feature might be hidden in a submenu somewhere, but once you've located it, you'll remember where it is the next time. The same is true with cars.

I used to scoff at people who would get into a new car for the first time and take a moment to familiarize themselves with all of the controls, adjust the mirrors, and make note of the gauges. It made more sense for me to just jump in the car and jam my foot on the accelerator! My thinking changed one night while I was traveling out of town.

It was a dark and stormy night. I just picked up a rental car from the airport. Five minutes later, I found myself sixty miles away, barreling down the highway. It should be noted that I only drive at one speed: faster. It started to rain. In fact, it was a downpour. I scrambled to turn on the windshield wipers. I reached for the control that engages the wiper blades on the rental car. The result: the right turn signal started to blink. Oops! I tried another control. Nothing happened.

Frustrated, I reached for the dome lights so I could see what I was doing. Unfortunately, the dome light switch wasn't in the same place as my car's switch. The rain began to seriously impair my driving. Because I didn't familiarize myself with this particular vehicle's controls, I had to pull the car over to safety and regroup. I hate detours and delays. After saying nasty things about the car's engineers and their families, I found all of the controls I needed to traverse through the storm safely. I even adjusted the side mirrors, which were obviously positioned for an NBA basketball player. Off I went, this time with all the information I needed in order to safely operate the vehicle.

The same is true with equipment. You should always take a test drive with a new piece of gear before recklessly throwing yourself into a storm on location. While it might not make sense to you immediately why a feature isn't where you expect it to be, more than likely, the manufacturer's engineers spent a great deal of time in making that decision. Of course, my stubborn self still insists that I could design better gear. Then again, I should also mention that a few days into my trip I spent a solid ten minutes trying to locate the lever to open the fuel door. As it turns out, I had to push the fuel door in for it to open. Today, I stop, open the glove box, and read the manual before I waste time cursing engineers who I haven't met.

Only use gear that you are familiar with. Read the manual, watch tutorials, and play with all the menus. Know the gear inside and out. If you don't know what a specific function is for, find out. Bring the manuals with you on location for important pieces of equipment. Smart phones are a great way of downloading equipment manuals, but don't always rely on this technology to bail you out of a jam on a set. Nothing beats a hard-copy manual, especially if you find yourself out in the middle of nowhere without a cell signal!

Equipment can be confusing sometimes without the stress and pressure that productions bring. When gear is unorganized and not maintained properly, this only adds to that stress and pressure. Spend time maintaining and organizing your equipment so that you can work more efficiently in the field.

On location, it is necessary to keep your equipment organized. Cables should be free of spaghetti-like tangles. You don't want to hold up a shot because you have to stop and unravel a mic cable. Adaptors should be located in one place so they don't clutter up the sound bag. Media and other important items should be stored safely. When you need these items, you'll know where to find them fast and they're less likely to get damaged in transit.

At the end of a long shoot day, it's tempting to throw all the gear in the truck and go home. Resist the urge and wrap your gear properly. This will help you account for missing gear before it's too late. Plus, you'll have to spend less time prepping the gear for the next job.

COMMANDMENT 4
THOU SHALT TONE UP THY CAMERA OR RECORDER

Check tone when setting up the gear, after every camera setup and after every break. Tone verifies signal flow and proper levels. This simple test takes only a few seconds and can save you precious moments on location. If something isn't plugged in correctly, the tone signal will let you know instantly. By looking at the meters and indicators on all of the equipment in the chain, you'll quickly discover the knobs and faders that may have been bumped. Before you engage the tone switch, alert other crewmembers who might be wearing headphones.

Early in my career I learned a good lesson about checking tone to the camera. During a long day shooting interviews for *Good Morning America*, the producer decided to break in the middle of an interview to allow the guest to catch some fresh air. In truth, we all needed a break. During our downtime, the producer asked the shooter to grab some exterior shots. He disconnected his camera, switched the audio channels to camera mic, and headed out the door. I waited inside. Upon his return, he reconnected the camera and we continued with the interview.

Thirty minutes later, it was time for a tape change. I sent tone to the camera, but alas, the camera was not receiving any tone. Puzzled, we checked the connections. Everything was right. The camera's meters were bouncing during the interview, so I was positive that sound was being recorded. After another minute of investigation, we realized that the camera's audio was set to camera mic. We sheepishly told the producer that the last thirty minutes of the interview needed to be re-shot. Needless to say, the producer was steamed. Although the shooter changed the switches and reconnected the cable, it was 100% my fault for not double-checking the audio settings with tone when he came back. To this day, I've never made that mistake again. Always check tone when the camera is moved or connections are changed.

COMMANDMENT 5
THOU SHALT ELIMINATE BACKGROUND NOISE

The camera lens and the microphone do not work the same way. A camera operator can easily frame a shot to exclude certain elements by panning, zooming, flagging, or even placing props and set pieces to hide objects from the lens. Sound, however, is omnidirectional. It bounces, penetrates, resonates, and reverberates. Using the above framing techniques will not work with a microphone. While the camera can pan left to avoid seeing passing cars in the background during a shot of an ancient Greek battle scene, the microphone will still hear the traffic under the actor screaming, "This is Sparta!" The point is, you can't simply add a set wall and eliminate the noise that originates from that area. Panning a microphone will reduce some of the direct sound, but not all of it and certainly not reflections or reverberation. Sound is not only noisy, but it's messy. It comes from everywhere and spreads out in every direction. Care should be taken when selecting a location to shoot. Failing to do so will result in either poor sound or a need to ADR the scene.

Anyone can record good audio in the studio, but it takes skill and experience to record good audio in the field. Studios are quiet; locations are not. Choosing the right location to shoot can solve most sound problems. Unfortunately, most production companies fail to involve the sound mixer on this decision. This puts the sound mixer at a severe disadvantage. More often than not, the sound mixer is placed into a situation that requires heavy problem-solving just to make the soundtrack sound "okay." Including the sound mixer in the location scout will greatly improve the quality of the soundtrack.

When you arrive on set, pay attention to what you hear. This is easy for a two-person ENG crew, but can be difficult on large productions with a symphony of activity that includes drills and motors. Once the camera is set up and you know the position for the talent, stand where they will stand and listen to how it sounds. This is where the microphone will be placed. If you can hear problems with the naked ear, you will certainly hear them through the headphones. You may even want to throw up a couple of mics and put your headphones on for a more accurate reading on the background level. For a sit-down interview, you can hang the lavs over the side of the chairs facing the same direction they will be facing when they are on the talent. If you need to, ask the crew to remain silent for a moment while you track down the problem. Don't be shy. You'll need time to fix the problem and the time to do it is during setup, not when everyone is ready to shoot. This will just hold up the production.

Understand that you will have some level of background noise. The question is: how much background noise is too much background noise? There is no real answer. Ideally, you would record in a vacuum, but that's not realistic. The trick is to balance the background noise and the dialog so that the dialog is clean and easily understood. Unfortunately, the world is a noisy place. Even the countryside is littered with the sounds of insects and birds. Do your best to separate the dialog from the background. In the end, that's all you can do. A healthy understanding of the postproduction process will help ease any anxiety you may have about background noise. The sound gathered on location might not always be used along with the images they are shot with. Sound bites and voiceovers are cases where the audio must be crystal clear. Excessive background noise can make sound clips more difficult to cut and paste over B-roll.

There are three types of sounds to reduce in the background: *acoustics*, *ambience*, and *incidental*. The acoustical properties of a room are unique to each location; no two rooms sound the same. Ambient background sounds are environmental. They can be constant or intermittent. Incidental sounds are usually momentary and accidental. First, let's look at how to treat unwanted acoustical sounds.

Acoustics

Background ambience is always a challenge when working outdoors. Indoors, there is usually less background noise to deal with; however, acoustics now become the main challenge you will have to face. Sound waves will reflect and produce reverberation based on the size and shape of the room and the type of walls used in its construction. Sometimes this reverb is a short slap back and other times it will have a long decay.

Locations will color your sound. This is a fact. A racquetball court will sound like a racquetball court and a garage will sound like a garage. Once the sound is colored by the location, the acoustic signatures and reverb can't be removed. Some post magic can be attempted, but don't count on it. If the dialog has reverb on location, it will have reverb in post. Reverb isn't necessarily a bad thing. A racquetball court *should* sound like a racquetball court and a garage *should* sound like a garage. But, if you are using a warehouse as a soundstage with sets built for a small house, then you're going to have problems.

It is common for ENG crews to use hotel rooms for interviews. When framed properly, the shots look very warm and intimate. However, hotel rooms are long rectangles with hard surfaces that can make a warm intimate shot sound very cold and echoey. In these cases, you need to treat the room. You can start by hanging the bed covers from C-stands to kill some of the bounce. Standing the mattresses up against the walls will make the room look like a rock star stayed there the night before, but it will help soak up the echoes. As long as the objects aren't in the frame, it's fair game.

For Monty Python's climactic musical finale in *The Life of Brian*, Eric Idle recorded the song in a hotel room by making a vocal booth out of the mattresses. This famous tune shows no signs of being recorded in such a simple place. If it worked for the Pythons, it could work for you. Never underestimate what simple tricks can achieve and… "Always look on the bright side of life!"

Your best defense against a crappy location is to participate in the location scouts. Unfortunately, location scouts on big-budget films don't always include the sound mixer. Experienced low-budget filmmakers are more likely to include the sound mixer to help avoid excessive problems in post, not to mention ADR costs and scheduling.

ENG and film work approach sound differently. While the techniques are similar, the use of background noise in each type of production is unique. ENG productions often incorporate the location as part of the story. If you're shooting an interview with an NBA player on a basketball court, it should sound like he's on a basketball court.

Working on soundstages isn't all it's cracked up to be. It's not sound nirvana and your work isn't always cut out for you. The idea of a soundstage, as the name suggests, is that it has been treated acoustically and soundproofed from the outside world. This includes the walls, the floor, the doors, and even the ceiling. But, not all soundstages are created equal. Even professional soundstages can still offer a host of issues to deal with.

First off, don't take "soundproofed" for granted. Nearby noises such as those produced by factories, train tracks, and airports can still leak onto the soundstage. There is one specific soundstage in Detroit that is located next to a stamping plant. This is a multimillion-dollar building used by many of the major automotive companies for commercial work. The massive stage was professionally designed and treated; however, a few years after the soundstage's construction, a stamping company bought a building fifty feet away. Now, there is a low frequency thumping noise that appears in the production sound if the sound mixer forgets to use a roll-off filter.

Once inside the "cone of silence," you'll still find all sorts of sound issues. Most will come from inside this cone of silence, like equipment, crewmembers, and the sets themselves. Sets are typically built out of *flats*. Flats are basically wood frames skinned with thin sheets of plywood. They might have additional sheets of Styrofoam or other material to look like stone or brick. The problem is they will still sound like wood flats. It's helpful to discuss set construction in preproduction to determine what can be done to reduce acoustical problems you might face during shooting. Hollow wood platforms and stairs might be deadened with insulation or foam to make footsteps softer and less bassy. Carpeting certainly helps, but the hollow structure makes the wood more resonant.

Many independent films will use warehouses instead of soundstages because they are cheaper to rent or purchase. Warehouses look like soundstages, but do not *sound* like soundstages. Painting the walls and floor black and putting some foam on the walls will not make the building a suitable soundstage. These buildings offer the crew all of the shooting advantages of a soundstage without any of the sound perks. Given the nature of warehouses, these buildings are often located near a railway, highway, or an industrial complex with heavy traffic such as semi trucks.

If you have to shoot in a warehouse, let the production manager know that rainy days may cause serious sound issues since the roof has probably not been properly treated. You might have to consider shooting at night when traffic will be lighter, if the surrounding traffic or highway is too noisy. The acoustics will be poor even before you start building sets. In short, warehouses are great for still photography, but awful for motion pictures. But, that's the nature of the beast. The *Lord of the Rings* trilogy was shot on soundstages next door to an airport. This blockbusting, high-budget film production wasn't extremely interested in choosing the best sound location to work in. Don't be surprised if your production isn't either.

Rooms are hard to tame with even large budgets. Special architectural firms are contracted to build acoustically dead studios. This takes a lot of time and money. On location, you will have neither. If a room is too crazy with reverb, suggest a different room. If this isn't possible, then you'll have to look at ways to tame the room. It should be noted that you cannot "soundproof" a location. To correctly soundproof a room, you need to treat the inside of the walls, ceiling, and even the foundation under the floor. Instead, you can only treat the room.

The position of the talent in the room or camera location might help reduce some of the effects of the reverberation. The center of the room will have the most amount of reverb build-up. Sound blankets can be hung to help knock down some of the bounce. Closing doors that lead to hallways or echoey rooms will also lessen excessive reverb. Drawn curtains and throw rugs can make a big difference.

Ambient Noise

Now that we've dealt with the acoustic challenges, let's look at ambient problems.

Traffic

Traffic is by far the most common type of background noise. Cars are everywhere! For interior locations, the first step in dealing with distant traffic is to close all windows and doors. You might need to coordinate with G&E (Grip and Electric Department) in case AC power is brought in through windows or doors that will prevent them from being closed. If the traffic is still heard, try positioning the talent and camera away from the windows. You can't close a door or window when working outdoors. This makes exterior locations much more challenging. On a film set, you have ITC (Intermittent Traffic Control) with local police controlling the flow of traffic in between shots. This not only prevents unwanted objects in the background, but can also provide a quieter environment for sound.

Furnaces/Air Conditioners

Thermostats or other controls for these units should be located and tested to find out how they work. Some air conditioners take a few minutes to shut off. Once the air conditioning is turned off, listen again. This will help you discover sounds that might have been masked by the A/C. Once you're satisfied with your background level, you may want to leave the air conditioning on until the last minute to keep the room cool. The talent will get hot under the lights, so every bit of coolant can help. And don't forget, exterior shots may be located near an air conditioning unit that might need to be disabled as well.

HVAC (Heating, Ventilation, and Air Conditioning)

Office buildings often have A/C unit controllers that affect an entire floor or section of the office. In some cases, you will not be allowed to turn off the A/C. If this is the case, try baffling the air duct. For vents on the floor, this can be done with a coat or an equipment case. For overhead vents, you'll need to be a little more creative. You can try using a C-stand with a flag to help redirect or even stop airflow. If the vent cover can be removed, try stuffing the vent with a coat.

Once you've turned off the air conditioning, the room can heat up fast. The body heat from crewmembers, lack of airflow, and a couple thousand watts of light can cause the talent to sweat and the crew to get sleepy. It's a good idea to leave the air conditioning on until you're ready to roll to help keep the room as cool as possible. Also, be sure to crank up the air conditioning during long breaks or if the room becomes so hot that the talent starts to melt.

I'll never forget the heat in the room of the longest interview I've ever worked on. We were shooting an episode for Court TV (the network has since been renamed truTV). The producer was green and as a result she overshot the entire piece. New television producers are often anxious to impress their bosses and have no clue how the editing process works. They're afraid of not getting enough coverage, so they ask the same question five different ways.

The final runtime for this interview was about five minutes, including B-roll and cutaway footage of the event they were recalling. Normally, an interview like this would last an hour, maybe two if the topic was hot and the guest was gushing. We shot for more than five hours! Finally, we ran out of tape stock. The shooter had to go to the van and use the *airplane crash tape*. This is a tape that is stashed away in the van for emergency purposes only, a common practice among news crews (e.g., If the crew is driving down a road and a plane crashes in front of them, they will have a tape to shoot the event). This was the only time I'd ever seen someone use this tape.

The room was small and the lights were slowly baking us like a holiday turkey. As a sound mixer, I was wearing headphones that acted like earmuffs making me twice as hot as everyone else. The air-conditioning was turned off and I was seated behind the lights in the dark. It was only a matter of time before I fell asleep. In fact, it was some of the best sleep I've ever been paid for!

I must have dozed off at least three or four times. I didn't feel so bad because every time I woke up, I saw the shooter sleeping too! He had the camera locked off on the tripod and drifted off to the dulling sound of the producer constantly asking, "And then what happened?" The interview was so long that the shooter demanded a break a few hours in. He went into the break room of the office complex where we were and actually reheated a day-old pot of coffee in the microwave and slammed it like a frat-boy at a spring break kegger!

Finally, the producer left with an entire case of tapes along with a handful of Hallmark cards we'd given her for her two birthdays we celebrated during the painfully long interview. I would've paid to have seen the editor's reaction when she dropped off the footage. Hopefully they were able to edit the epic saga that she produced in an air-conditioned editing suite.

Refrigerators

You can disable a refrigerator by simply unplugging the unit from the wall. If you can't reach the plug because the refrigerator is too awkward to move, you can turn off the breaker to that plug or adjust the thermostat to prevent the unit from kicking on. The trick is to remember to turn it back on! One of my favorite techniques to remember to turn a refrigerator back on is to put my car keys inside the refrigerator. This way, I am unable to leave the location unless I retrieve my keys.

A few years back, I had an intern who read this tip in my book. While working at my house, he decided to record sound effects of my garage door. Inside the garage I have a refrigerator that we use to stock food for parties. Remembering my tip, he left his keys in the refrigerator when he unplugged it. When he was finished, he retrieved his keys and went home. The only problem is, he forgot to plug the refrigerator back in! We didn't notice this until a couple of weeks later when my wife found $300 worth of spoiled meat! So, if you use this tip, remember to turn the unit back on when you get your keys out!

Computers

If a computer screen is not seen by the camera or will be replaced by CGI, turn the computer off. The fan inside the computer generates noise. If the screen is in the shot, you could try to cover the tower with a sound blanket. When doing this, leave a hole in the back for the fan, so the computer doesn't overheat and cause damage to the CPU. If the screen and tower is an integral part of the scene and has to be seen on camera, try to place the tower in another room and run a long cable to the monitor. A separate, unplugged tower can be used as a silent double in the shot.

Monitors and Television Sets

Some LCD and plasma monitors have fans that can be disabled. If not, you may have to move them or cover them with a blanket. Older CRT monitors and television sets may produce an annoying 15KHz high-pitch sound. Placing a blanket over the top and back of the unit can help reduce this. If this doesn't work, ask if the monitor can be turned off or moved further away from the mic. If the audio is plugged directly into the camera and the camera is plugged into a video monitor, there might be an audio buzz that you will have to deal with. Sometimes you can eliminate this buzz by running the monitor on batteries.

Fans

Obviously fans should be disabled; however, if there is a practical fan on the set, you'll have to live with the consequences. In this case, ask if the fan can be positioned so that the airflow does not intersect with the mic placement. If it must be positioned toward the mic placement, you will need to use a blimp and a windsock. Keep in mind: some fans can operate at a lower speed so the fan blades are seen rotating on camera without producing gale-force winds.

Music (Radios, Stereos, P.A.s, etc.)

When working in public locations, such as malls and restaurants, speak with the manager to disable a P.A. system playing music. This shouldn't be a problem for closed sets where permission or permits were acquired to shoot at the location. Music is an issue for two reasons. First, it interferes with the dialog. Second, there are copyright issues. Without a rather expensive licensing fee, a production can't use music in a work that will be sold. If you're shooting a film, you cannot allow the music on the soundtrack without proper clearance (not to mention the fact that the dialog track will be littered with music, especially if there is any editing done at all). ENG work such as field reporting is a different animal altogether. There is grace when it comes to reporting news events where music is playing in the background. This is considered to be under fair use, but even still, you should try at all costs to minimize or eliminate background music.

Clocks

Ticking clocks are easy to miss at first. Their lulling drone is often buried among the movement of the crew and general ambient sounds when setting up. Once the set is quiet and the camera is rolling, their soft metronome-clicks become like pounding drums. Removing the batteries will silence these little drummer boys. This will also help with scene continuity, as the script supervisor will want the time on the clock to stay consistent within the scene. Cuckoo clocks should be dismantled and buried in shallow, unmarked graves outside.

Light Ballasts

Fluorescent lights tend to have noisy ballasts. The older the bulb, the louder the buzz becomes. When a production is shooting in locations like gymnasiums or ice rinks, the fluorescent lights may become necessary in order to evenly light such a large space. In these cases, the DP may want to leave the lights on. While this is not the ideal situation, it won't be as much of a problem since the buzz will be consistent throughout the scene, provided that the buzz is not overpowering. However, if there is one ballast that is inconsistent or much louder, you can ask if that bulb can be replaced or if the shot can live without that one bulb. As always, be sure to gather room tone.

Rain

Rainy days may force the production to shoot in an alternative location called a *cover set*. This will keep the rain out of the shot visually, but can cause all sorts of problems for the soundtrack if the rain continues to beat down on the roof. Heaps of hog's hair or other material can help treat roofs so that the rain falls silently. A cheaper solution would be to cover the roof with hay or pine needles.

Noisy Neighbors

Nothing seems to entice neighbors into mowing their lawn like watching a video crew shooting an interview in their neighbor's backyard. Part of the enticement might be that they need an excuse to stand outside and watch the production. But, what they fail to realize is that their lawn mower is a showstopper. Most of the time, a friendly request to hold off on the lawn work will suffice. Other times, you might need to give them a "Jackson Handshake" (i.e., slip them $20).

In general, people aren't aware of how much noise they make. Everyday activity is noisier than you realize, until you need to be quiet. Then, everything seems super-loud. For example, packing a lunch seems harmless enough, but trying to pack a lunch early in the morning when everyone else is sleeping will make even the gentlest folding of a brown paper bag seem like a roaring fire! It's easy to get used to all the sounds we make on an everyday basis.

The Public

It's amazing how offended some people get when you ask them to lower their voices or to be quiet for a couple of minutes. When working in places like office buildings, post signs that read: "Quiet Please, Filming In Progress." A PA can serve as a doorman to keep doors from slamming and to alert the public of the filming in progress. Keep in mind: if you are in a public place, people have the right to make noise, regardless if it affects your production. Dirty looks will only make them want to be louder.

When working on an ENG shoot in a public place, a good trick is to avoid eye contact with bystanders. The shooter is busy looking in the viewfinder with one eye and the other eye closed. The reporter is busy looking at the camera's lens. Because they are focused on their tasks, people don't try to engage in conversation with them. The sound mixer appears to not be doing anything (big surprise). If you

Shhh!

keep your eyes focused on your meters or your boom, people are less likely to ask, "What television station are you with?" or the less intelligent "What movie are you making?" My default answers are *Die Hard 5* or *Jaws 5*. The latter is funnier if you are shooting nowhere near the ocean (think Nebraska).

Crewmembers

Cast and crewmembers who are seasoned professionals understand the need for absolute silence when shooting. However, there are times when they get caught up in a conversation or other noise-making activity, like trying to wrap equipment. Resist the urge to scold them! Sound mixers have a reputation of yelling at crewmembers making noise.

Care and tact should be used when dealing with crewmembers. Your best bet is to relay the situation to the director or AD and let them deal with it. Simple eye contact is usually enough. You don't want to burn a bridge with a crewmember whom you might need to ask a favor from later. Remember, it's a small world and you will probably end up working with that crewmember again on another project.

During shots, non-working crewmembers tend to gravitate to the craft service table where all manner of treats await them. Needless to say, if craft service is located near the set, whispering conversations, coffee makers percolating, and candy wrappers will quickly appear in the soundtrack. For a sound mixer, crew noise is like walking in front of the camera operator's lens during a shot.

Generators

The generator, fondly referred to as the "genny," should be placed as far away from the set as possible to avoid littering the soundtrack with engine noise. Experienced gaffers will do this automatically, but you might have to ask some to cooperate. Be prepared for complaints about long power cable runs. In the end, having a generator too close to the set is like the sound department using a 2k Fresnel as a work light for the sound cart. In the same way that light would spill from the work light onto the set and affect all the hard work that the gaffer put into lighting the set, the noise from the generator would also spill onto the set affecting all the hard work that the sound crew put into miking the set. As always, be nice when asking. That whole "spoonful of sugar" thing works! If you run into a hard-nosed, doesn't-play-well-with-others gaffer who refuses, simply relay the information to the 1st AD.

Planes, Trains, and Automobiles

Despite what the DP might believe, there is no "Airplane Filter" on the mixer. Sometimes, producers and directors need to be aware of this. If there is a plane in the background, give the producer or director a hand signal. Don't yell, "Cut!" That's not your call to make. If you find yourself in a location that is plagued with air traffic, advise the director that the scene will work better for sound if it's broken up into shorter takes. These shorter takes between plane pass-bys will give clean audio that can be cut together.

Certain extraneous sounds that are short (car horns, dog barks, etc.) are easy for the editor to cut out, provided that room tone is gathered on location and that the sounds don't occur during dialog. But sounds that are not short, such as plane, train, and automobile pass-bys can be nearly impossible to cut around. This is due in part to the *Doppler effect*. Named after its discoverer, Austrian physicist Christian Doppler, the Doppler effect is a shift from high to low frequencies as an object passes by. A good example of this effect is a police car siren driving by. Essentially, there is a discernable change in pitch from the start of the sound to the end. Therefore, cutting or fading around the sound can be very challenging. If the dialog is critical (for example, a guest breaks down and cries while discussing a sensitive subject during an interview), you might want to have everyone hold still while the camera continues to roll and capture the tail end of the event. This will give the editor something to play with if they decide to use the take with the extraneous sound. If not, there will be a jump cut in the audio.

When waiting for intermittent background noise (e.g., plane bys, traffic, etc.), it's not necessary to wait until the sound is completely gone before you start rolling. In fact, it's a good idea to start rolling before you achieve relative silence. This allows the camera and sound to reach speed and slate the next shot so when the background noise is quiet, the director can call action. If not, you can waste precious moments of silence waiting for sound and camera speed.

Extras

When a scene takes place in a crowded environment like a bar or party, the background actors will pretend to speak, but actually remain silent during the take. This allows for only the dialog to be recorded and the background walla (unintelligible crowd noise) can be added in post. Unfortunately, most actors will speak at normal levels instinctively. This will sound fine during the take, but in post their performances will seem unnatural because in the real world they would have to shout over the background noise. Suggest that the actors speak at higher levels to give a sense of the environment that the scene calls for. If you are shooting for ENG work and the background is uncontrollably loud, ask the talent to speak up in order to be heard above the background.

Pets

Animals are difficult to silence from the background, especially dogs. There are a couple of options to deal with noisy canines. First, ask the owner to take the dog indoors. Second, try feeding the dog. Nothing will shut up a Doberman pinscher faster than a good steak or peanut butter cookies. Third (and only as a last result), try shooting the dog. No, I don't mean shoot the animal with the camera. I mean actually taking a gun and firing it at the animal. Of course, you should never kill an animal for the sake of a production. Instead, try wounding the dog by shooting one of its legs. Care should be taken that no members of PETA are involved in the production.

Special Effects

Let's face it. Special effects are cool. In my early days, I did special effects on several projects and was also a licensed pyrotechnician. I got to work with bands like Kid Rock, Rammstein, and Limp Bizkit; light guys on fire and even blow up cars! Today, I still have all my fingers, which in the special effects world means that I was pretty good at my job.

While special effects add the wow factor to a shot, they also add a fair amount of noise. Wind machines, smoke machines, flame forks, pyrotechnics, and all the rest of the magical devices may be necessary for a shot and often cannot be controlled for sound. In these cases, be sure the director is aware that the scene will probably need ADR work. Even though the production sound may not end up in the final product, be sure to record the best sound possible to provide the actors with a usable ADR guide track. If a special effect is operating, but the effect is not seen on camera, ask if the device can be disabled.

Camera Noise

Sometimes the noise on the set comes from the camera itself. This is not only true of film cameras, but also video cameras using tape stock and hard drives. You can use a *barney*, which is a sound-dampening fabric cover specifically made for cameras. In a pinch, you can use a sound blanket or even a crewmember's coat to reduce the sound of noisy cameras. Never touch a camera without the camera operator's permission! This is like grabbing a cop's gun. Always ask first, but don't be surprised if the camera operator gets a little grumpy when you ask to place things on top of his camera.

Video cameras aren't always quiet, either. Cameras that still use tape have motorized gears that turn the tape, which can produce unwanted noise. Digital cameras that record to hard drives aren't quiet, either. The hard drives have a fan that can produce noise as well. Camera hard drives can overheat easily. If you have to cover the hard drive for a take, remember to remove the barney between breaks to prevent overheating. And don't even get me started on the much-coveted Red One cameras!

As of this writing, Red One cameras give insanely gorgeous pictures at the price of noise in the form of a tiny blow dryer all over your soundtrack! There is a software update with a setting that will disable the fan when the camera rolls, but some DPs are reluctant to use this setting because the camera is notorious for overheating, which forces the camera to shut down. I worked on a film for five weeks in Florida with a Red One camera that overheated at least a dozen times. It became such an issue that the production rented a second camera to use whenever the primary camera overheated. For this reason, the DP was reluctant to turn off the fan. I would plead. He would concede. The camera would shut down. Eventually, we just had to live with it. Disable the fan whenever possible.

Incidental Noise

Now that we've discussed background noise, let's look at how to prevent or correct incidental noises.

Cell Phones

Cell phones should be turned off during shooting. Period. Putting a cell phone on vibrate can still interrupt a shot when the cell phone vibrates, especially if the phone is sitting on a surface. In addition, cell phones may interfere with audio signals — both hardwire and wireless. iPhones seem to be the worst offenders when interfering with audio signals.

Telephones

Make sure that the telephone's ringer is off. If you can't figure out how to disable the ringer, unplug the cord from the wall. This keeps the cord attached to the phone for the shot and kills the ringer. Keep in mind: there may be other telephones at the location that may still ring.

Chairs

Creaky chairs should be replaced with ones that do not creak as much. Swivel chairs should be avoided during interviews for two reasons. The first is that the actor will move back and forth during the shot, which is not good for picture. Secondly, the chair may make a squeak when it moves, which is not good for sound.

Elevators

When working near an elevator, ask if a PA can take the elevator to another floor and keep the door open. This will stop the elevator from opening or its bell ringing during a take. If possible, use a walkie-talkie to let the PA know when the shot is done so that other members of the building can use the elevator.

Creaky Dolly/Dolly Track

Most professional dollies are dead silent. This is one of the reasons why they cost so much. When using the dolly, the crewmembers pushing it are often the noisy culprits. Some surfaces might creak when the dolly rides overtop of it. Sound blankets underneath the track may help. For squeaks, some people use baby powder or talcum powder on the track. However, you should relay this information to the grip department and let them handle the noise. Dance floors can be useful underneath a dolly track that has to be placed on a creaky floor.

Cheaper dollies can be noisy. The low-cost, but very effective, doorway dolly is made of plywood and can be particularly creaky when the sideboards are added with crewmembers standing on them. Work with the grip and camera departments to help quiet them.

Lighting Equipment

Scrims, gels, and diffusion can make noise during the slightest gust of wind. Ask the gaffer if they can use clothespins or other means to secure them.

Jewelry

Noisy costume-jewelry issues should be discussed with the wardrobe department. If you are shooting interviews, ask the subject to remove any jewelry that might rub against their lav or bracelets that might jingle when they talk with their hands.

Factory P.A. Systems

Speak with the plant supervisor to minimize or temporarily suspend P.A. announcements. Some actors will hold their lines during the announcement and then continue afterwards to speed things along. This is fine if the reverberation from the announcement has completely faded.

Noisemaking Props, Set Pieces, and Vehicles

Functioning set pieces, props, and machines should be pantomimed or left silent during dialog. If an actor starts a scene by turning off a car and getting out, the car doesn't actually have to be running at the beginning of the scene. Remember, it's the magic of movie making and the engine sound can be replaced later. However, if the sound of the car engine running is recorded with the dialog, it cannot be removed. Other working props should be turned off whenever possible. For example, if an actor is delivering lines while washing her hands, but the camera doesn't see the faucet, she can simply fake the action of washing without spoiling the dialog track. After all, she's an actor!

Props

Props are especially intrusive to the soundtrack when handled by actors during dialog. Take the necessary steps to quiet them. Padding can be placed under tablecloths to stop dishware from clanging and you can place a piece of felt under a teacup that will be set down on a saucer. Squeaky props can be oiled. Check with the grip department to see if they have a can of WD-40 on the grip truck.

Some noisemakers are practical. They are in the shot for a reason, so it's okay to hear them. If they're particularly loud, try to dampen the sound they make. For example, ice cubes might be practical, but can clink overtop of the dialog. Ask the prop department if they can use fake ice cubes instead. These can be found at prop houses and most novelty stores. Avoid the ones with fake flies in them in case they show up on camera.

Paper bags can be incredibly noisy when handled during a scene. Ask the prop department if they can spray the bags with water to reduce their sound.

Some sound mixers will have misting spray bottles to solve this problem. Plastic bags are the worst. They continue to make noise even after they've been set down. The best defense is to replace them with another type of bag. If this is not an option, then try to fill the bags with newspaper or other items so that there isn't much settling room for the bag to collapse on itself.

Sets

Constructed sets can be noisier than actual locations. The materials they use are often lightweight and intended to look real without costing much to build. As a result, the doors are often misaligned and can make awkward sounds when they open and close. Try to have the doors aligned to reduce this. If an actor has to slam a door, put a piece of foam in the doorjamb to stop the noise. Stairs on sets are often hollow and resonate a lot of low frequencies. Sound blankets can be stuffed underneath to help deaden the sound.

Props, flooring, and other set pieces may be painted to look like one surface, but sound like another. Papier-mâché rocks will sound like thin cardboard when dropped. Spaceship doors made of plywood will sound like plywood. Wood floors painted to look like concrete will sound like a wood floor. Each of these examples will require different techniques to salvage the dialog track.

For set pieces and props, the best solution is to avoid overlaps with the dialog. If this is not possible, try to reduce the sound they make. For flooring issues, it's nearly impossible to avoid overlaps from the footsteps in the dialog when using a boom microphone. Footsteps are not as noticeable on lav mics, but are obnoxiously loud when a boom mic is positioned above the actors pointing down at the floor. It's natural to walk and talk. You can't really cheat that on camera as you might with closing a door before delivering the dialog. The only option you have is to eliminate the sound from the footsteps.

Covering the floor with carpet, sound blankets, floor mats, or other deadening materials can be a quick and easy fix. If the floor does not appear on camera, simply cover the area where the actors will walk. If the feet aren't seen on camera, ask if the actors can remove their shoes. In wide shots and shots that allow the camera to see the floor the only option you'll have left is to deaden the shoes. This can be done with Hush Heels or pieces of felt taped to the bottom of the shoes. Background extras can pull their steps so they're not so intrusive to the dialog. If this doesn't work, the background extras' shoes will need to be treated as well. Anticipate this problem ahead of time. You don't want to halt production after the first take to put Hush Heels on fifty extras. That will take a significant amount of time. Instead, determine what needs to be done when the scene is blocked and start fixing the problem while the lights are being set up. The wardrobe department might be willing to lend a hand. It never hurts to ask.

Cheating

Shots can be cheated to include or exclude props or set pieces in the frame. Actors might stand on apple boxes and props might be slightly adjusted so that they aren't growing out of the actor's head in the shot. The audience is none the wiser. These cheats are easy to get away with. Cheating can also be done to improve the sound. Moving the camera location or the actors during reversals or cutaways can help cheat excessive background sounds. Use these cheats whenever possible to help improve the soundtrack.

If you have a scene that requires sound effects to be associated with an image during dialog (e.g., police car sirens, car alarms, microwave beeps, etc.), try to shoot the scene clean and leave the sound effects for the post team. You can turn on the police car lights without the siren running; a car alarm can be simulated by using a remote key to lock/unlock the car doors, which will make the lights flash on and off. This will give the post team visual cues to add sounds to later while giving you a clean background to record the dialog.

It's easy to add sound effects to a scene, but it's difficult to remove them from the dialog track. Have faith in the Foley team and sound editors. Grab what nat sound you can, but don't sweat every on-screen movement. If a prop is too noisy, see if the actors can fake their interactions with the prop or at least minimize the sound it creates. If an actor tosses a beer bottle into a garbage can during a line of dialog, place a blanket inside the garbage can to muffle the impact of the beer bottle landing inside. If this is not an option, ask if the actor can time his dialog so that the beer

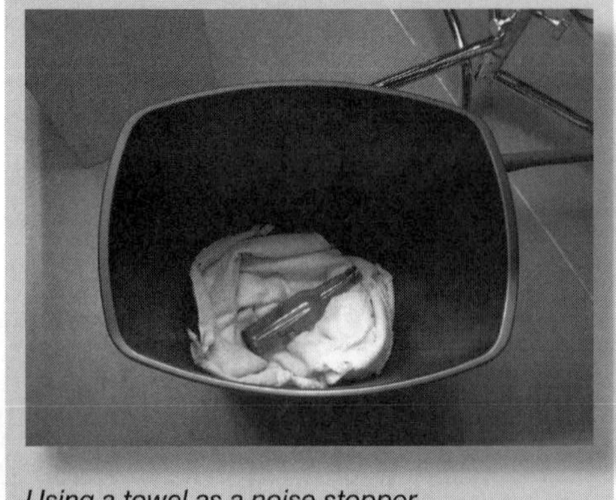

Using a towel as a noise stopper

bottle lands in between sentences or during a natural break in the lines. Other tricks, like taping foam underneath props, can help quiet their movements.

With ENG work there is very little, if any, sound treatment that will happen in postproduction. Levels might be balanced and mixed with a music bed along with an occasional voiceover, but the reality is the production sound will be the sound used in the final piece. So, it makes sense to have the talent use the sink — faucet and all — for the B-roll shot, even if the faucet isn't seen.

Camouflaging Background Frequencies

Backgrounds containing frequencies that compete with the dialog frequencies need to be addressed on location. These frequencies can mask or camouflage dialog, making words difficult to understand. Once recorded, the frequencies cannot be equalized in post. Unfortunately, you can't EQ the problem on set, either. If the frequencies are the same, then the adjustment will affect both the dialog and the background. When this is the case, you need to consider mic selection and placement, or, in extreme situations, ask the director if the talent can be repositioned to help reduce the background noise. If the background frequencies are below the speech range, you might have a fighting chance. High-pitched frequencies in the background will distract the audience from the dialog more easily. In general, if your mic is open and the background is reading -30dB or higher on your meters, you're going to be fighting for intelligible dialog. Background noise below -70dB is a gift. Take the gift and be happy about it.

Good Background Noise?

If you see the source of the sound on camera, it's okay to hear it as long as it doesn't overpower the dialog. This is especially true for ENG work. If you see traffic in the background, it's okay to hear the traffic. However, the audience shouldn't have to strain to hear the dialog above the traffic.

ENG shoots are shot in real locations. This will include real-world background sounds that would normally need to be rebuilt in post for a film. Background sounds are part of the story and should be included, but the dialog should never compete with the background to be heard. However, if the shots are all medium to close-ups, then the audience might not understand the source of these background sounds. Wide shots can help establish the source of these sounds. A simple two-second shot of factory machines in the background will help the audience realize where these sounds are coming from when the shot cuts to the interior office of the plant manager.

There will always be noise in the background. Your goal is to diminish the background sound as much as possible and then find a way to keep that background consistent. If you don't hear something, then you've either damaged your ears or you are in location sound nirvana — so, leave a breadcrumb trail for other sound mixers to find it.

COMMANDMENT 6
THOU SHALT CRITICALLY LISTEN TO THY AUDIO

It goes without saying that a sound mixer should always wear headphones. Mixing without headphones is like taking pictures with your eyes closed. But, there is a difference between hearing and listening.

Hearing is an involuntary process. Unlike your eyelids, your ears never close. You can never stop hearing sound. Listening is a conscious choice. You choose to actively focus on a specific sound and filter out the surrounding noise. The noise is still there and your ears are not hearing any less of it, but your mind is filtering out those sounds to allow you to focus on a specific one. For example, you could be in a crowded restaurant having a conversation with someone across the table. If a person at the next table mentions someone you know, you might direct your aural attention to his conversation. Your eyes might still be looking directly at the person across the table, but your ears are listening to another source altogether. Then, after a minute or two, you redirect your attention to the person across the table who is now staring at you, waiting for you to answer a question that you didn't even hear her ask!

When mixing, don't be overwhelmed by everything you hear. Focus on the voice first. Can you distinguish what is being said? Is it clearly separated from the background? Just because you can understand what the actors are saying doesn't mean it sounds good. You can understand most of what is said in a home movie and they sound terrible!

Next, focus on the background. Is the background level consistent? Is it overpowering? If you are shooting at a factory with heavy machinery, then the background will probably be loud, but that's consistent with the image. In this case, you can't fix the background level, so you'll need to focus on reducing the background level with microphone selection and placement. For example, try different shotgun positions or a lav. Finally, listen for inconsistencies in the background (e.g., intermittent traffic that will get louder as the intersection light changes vs. consistent highway traffic; office phones ringing; nearby businesses with machinery, air conditioning units that turn on periodically, etc.). How frequent are these inconsistencies? Are they predictable? How will this affect the shoot? Inconsistent sounds are easily overlooked. Listen carefully.

Once you've determined your dialog levels, managed background levels, and corrected possible inconsistencies, try to focus on only the dialog. If you do this, changes in background level will be noticed easily. It's like noticing movement out of the corner of your eye when staring forward. Sudden changes in the background will catch your attention if you're focusing on the quality of the dialog.

The time will come when the words blur into sound shapes. You won't hear what the talent is saying because you're too busy concentrating on how it sounds. To mix metaphors, you can't hear the forest for the trees. Many times a producer would ask me what the guest said during an interview and I would tell them I wasn't paying attention. Instinctively, they assumed I wasn't doing my job. It makes sense for them to think this. After all, I was the only crewmember in the room wearing headphones. It stands to reason that I would be listening to the interview. Instead, I was using critical listening. I wasn't focused on what was said, just how it sounded.

Listen to the final product to get a better understanding of how your audio was used. Your work will sound much different on headphones than over a TV set or in a movie theatre. Having an understanding of how it will translate over these media will help you in your decision-making on the set. When I would do live shots, I would set my VHS player to record the live shot (this was way before DVRs). When I got home, I would sit down and listen to what went out over the air. This helped me understand what the shot sounded like to the audience.

There is an ENG saying: "Editors make the best shooters." What this means is that by having a working knowledge of the post process, the camera operator will have a better understanding of what to shoot and how much will be needed in order to provide the best footage for the editor. The same is true with production sound. If you can spend some time with a post team or work on a project of your own, you'll gain a better understanding for how production sound is used and what you can get away with on location.

As a sound mixer, you need to learn to use critical listening. With time and practice you will be able to filter out all sorts of background noise and focus on the tiniest details in the soundtrack. You'll also learn to redirect your attention to the slightest creak of a door in the next room that is affecting the dialog track. Often you'll seem like a wizard as other crewmembers ask, "How the heck did you hear that?" This ability can also serve as a curse. The softest sound of someone snacking on popcorn during a movie immediately makes my skin crawl. Distant noises at night make it hard for me to sleep. I wake up every time the furnace kicks on. It can be a heavy burden to bear, but this ability allows me to make better soundtracks. In time, you'll discover this ability for yourself. You were warned.

COMMANDMENT 7
THOU SHALT DISCOURAGE M.O.S.

The acronym *M.O.S.* stands for "without sound." In other words, there is no sound being recorded with the picture. This can apply to both video and film productions. If this term is new to you, then you're probably asking yourself why it is spelled M.O.S. instead of W.O.S. Good question! Legend has it that during a shot being filmed without sync sound, a German filmmaker instructed his crew that they were shooting "mit out sound." Whether this was a matter of broken English or a mashup of two languages is unknown. Either way, the term has been used for decades. There are other interpretations as to its meaning, but "mit out sound" is the most widely accepted story.

Here are some common possible definitions:

- Without Sound
- Motor Only Shot
- Minus Optical Stripe
- Minus Optical Sound
- Missing Optical Sound

Noting an M.O.S. take on a clapboard

It is standard practice to note an M.O.S. shot on the slate, shot log, and sound report. If no indication is made, the editor may assume that sound is missing due to a technical error and phones will start ringing in a mad dash to locate the sound.

There is no reason to shoot video M.O.S. Even if the shot is B-roll, you should at least use the camera's onboard mic. You never know what the editor is going to need, so pack the soundtrack full of options. Most independent films can't afford Foley work, so they need to take advantage of any free sounds they can steal from the production track. On these productions, you should push to grab nat sound for just about every shot.

It should be pointed out that in ENG work, the acronym M.O.S. stands for "man-on-the-street." This is the name for interviews with random people in a public place, typically on the side of the street or sidewalk. This acronym is usually written on a worksheet. If the acronym is spoken, it usually refers to a shot without sound.

COMMANDMENT 8
THOU SHALT PLAY AN ACTIVE ROLE IN THE PRODUCTION

Don't sit back and relax. Be a part of decision-making whenever possible. If you can, ask to attend the location scout. This can help save the production time on the set and money in postproduction. The look of the location will almost always trump the sound of the location. It's very rare that a director will change a location "just for sound." If the director does, it's because the project is on a tight budget or the location's acoustics or environmental sounds are pretty extreme.

Location scouts mainly help you understand what challenges you will be facing during shooting. The more information you can gather during the scout, the better prepared you'll be when prepping for the shoot. Always visit the location at the same time of day that you will be shooting. Background sounds change throughout the day. A location might sound great at 11 a.m., but have excessive traffic between 4 p.m. and 7 p.m. If your shoot is scheduled to take place during these hours, you could be in for a rough time. Insects and birds are more vocal in the morning and evening hours. Keep this in mind when you scout a rural exterior location.

Here are some things to consider during the location scout:

Trains, Planes, and Automobiles

- Is the location near a railroad? If so, is there a train schedule for the location?
- Are there flight paths over the location?
- Are there nearby factories or other noisy buildings? If so, what time is the shift change for the factory? Shift changes will produce a significant amount of traffic noise for about an hour. This might be a prime time for the production to break for lunch until the traffic dies down.

- If shooting near a busy street, can an ITC permit be pulled?
- Are there schools nearby? If so, what are the bus schedules? When are the recess times? Kids are extremely loud at recess. Some schools might alternate recess times for different grade levels. This might mean that recess times can last for a couple of hours.

Building Issues

- Are there any acoustical issues with the location? A quick trick that will help you understand the reverb of a room is to stand in the middle of the room and clap your hands once. Listen closely to the amount of reverb that is produced and how long it takes for it to fade.
- What is the sound of the room like? Walk around larger rooms and determine if there is an optimal area for sound. Different parts of a room may have better acoustics than others.
- Are there any plumbing issues, such as noisy pipes or water flow that will interrupt takes? If so, are they predictable or intermittent?
- Where are the climate controls? Can they be disabled easily?
- Are there appliances or machines that will need to be disabled or removed?
- Where can production generators be located?

Neighborhoods

- What is the neighborhood like? Are there dogs nearby? Is there a playground that might become active after school hours?
- Is there a football field or baseball diamond that might have games scheduled during the production?

These are just some general questions to consider. Every location is different. Always suggest that filming on location takes place during off-peak times. For example, it might be nice for the production to get permission to shoot in the back room of a bar, but if the production takes place during business hours, the customers in the adjoining room will create unwanted background noise that will be inconsistent and impossible to control. Business owners who are willing to allow you into their establishment get grumpy when you start approaching their customers.

If you can't attend the location scout, be sure to attend the preproduction meeting. This is a chance to meet the other department heads and get a sense of the crew you will be working with. A production meeting will help you understand the director's perspective on the importance of sound. But, don't get too excited about a director's commitment to great sound. The director might start off the production with a passion for sound, but quickly warm up to the idea of ADR once the project is behind schedule and over budget. ADR should be especially discouraged for genres like comedies. Comedies are all about timing and delivery of the dialog. Recreating this timing and delivery in ADR can be more challenging than in other types of film. The director needs to understand this.

Important Questions to Ask During a Production Meeting

- Can I get a copy of the script to help me prepare?
- Where is the location of the scene?
- Does the sound of the shooting location match that of the script's location?
- How many actors will be speaking during the scene?
- Will the actors be mobile or stationary?
- Will any of the shots require more than one boom operator?

Be proactive during the production, not reactive. Sounds don't just go away. Pretending you don't hear something doesn't mean it's not there! Report problems immediately. Don't wait to listen for sound problems until after the crew has spent an hour setting up the shot. By then, it's too late. Stay alert to your surroundings. Anticipate problems; don't wait for them to happen.

The sound department is usually the last one to be ready because they have to wait for lights, camera, and everyone else to get out of the way. Therefore, sound is always perceived as holding up the set. Don't give the production any extra reason for this perception. The sound department often waits for hours and then only has seconds to do their job. Although this is completely out of your hands, all eyes will be on the sound crew that appears as if it has been sitting around all day neglecting its duties. Don't let the crew wait any longer than it has to. Anticipate problems that might arise by watching the crew as it works. Ask the AD questions about concerns you may have based on changes being made. Have the talent's lavs standing by. Check the mics before you move them into position. Be ready when the time comes.

During ENG projects, report sound issues to the producer immediately. If you report it to the shooter, he might not care and discard your problem because it might cause him more work or the solution might not be optimal for camera. Some shooters will have a team attitude and want the best for the client. Others are day players who simply want to shoot and go home. The quality of the sound is the sound mixer's responsibility. Take charge of sound issues, regardless if it costs a little extra time to do it right. Never settle for *okay* sound. Always try to get *great* sound. Sometimes you'll win and sometimes you'll lose, but always push to get the best sound possible.

COMMANDMENT 9
THOU SHALT GATHER ROOM TONE

Don't ask for room tone; call for room tone. Nine times out of ten, there won't be time for room tone. You need to be firm. It is your responsibility to provide postproduction with room tone. This is just as much a part of your job as delivering clean audio.

Once the shots are finished for a specific location, say, "Please, hold for room tone." For ENG work, the camera will be used as the recorder. Have the shooter point the camera at the microphone. Confirm that the camera is rolling and note the time on your watch or keep an eye on the camera's timecode. When working with actors or guests who are unfamiliar with the process of gathering room tone, you will need to let them know to hold still or settle prior to rolling. If not, the first ten seconds of room tone will consist of you asking them to settle.

A useful trick is to gather room tone before the first take. This will give the crew and actors a moment of Zen to prepare for the whirlwind of challenges that the rest of the day will bring. Plus, if the room tone changes throughout the day, you'll have a sample for the beginning takes. If the room tone changes, be sure to gather a second sample of room tone after the last shot. Room tone should be gathered for different areas of the same location. A kitchen's room tone will sound different than the living room or bedroom of the same house.

Be sure to gather nat sound/area tone at exterior locations. Fountains, birds, traffic, insects, and other background sounds might be needed in post to build a BG track (background track) to help fill holes in the dialog. It is your responsibility to provide these tracks to post.

What may take an entire day to produce on set might be cut down to a scene that only lasts a minute or two. The difference in background tone will be huge if a shot from the morning is played right after a shot from the late afternoon with different background sounds. For example, morning traffic might be heavy, but light in the afternoon. When the shots are cut together, there will be jumps in the background. While post sound will have sound libraries they can reach for to help hide the jumps, the best sound will come from the sources the sound mixer provides from the set. In the case of different traffic levels, it might be a good idea to grab BGs before breaks and at the start and end of the day.

When gathering room tone, keep the same mixer settings and mic placement as during the shot. Things like buzzing lights that were heard during the shot should be left on in order to match the dialog during the scene. If the talent was wearing lavs, make sure to keep the lavs on and have them positioned where they were during the shot. Also, if the talent was seated in chairs, have them stay seated. These steps will help the room tone stay consistent with the dialog from the scene. A useful trick is to also provide an on-axis recording of a specific background noisemaker to give the post team a clean recording to help notch out the sound in the track. This recording can also be used as a source for noise reduction.

COMMANDMENT 10
THOU SHALT BE PREPARED FOR ANYTHING

If there is one constant in location sound it is that everything will change constantly! Anything that can happen can and will happen. Part of your job is to be prepared for whatever happens. Think like a Boy Scout.

The idea behind this commandment is to have enough ammo to fight any battle you encounter. Most of the time, these battles can be won before they even start. Think of it as preventative maintenance of the unknown. It is better to have it and not need it than to need it and not have it.

Backups and replacement parts for mission-critical gear are a must for fieldwork. You don't have to have the exact make and model as your go-to recorder or microphone, but you need to have something. Gear gets stolen (or as the saying goes "gear can grow legs…"), coffee gets spilled on gear, and gear stops working for no reason. Inexpensive equipment can save the day. It's amazing how useful a "sub-standard" piece of gear can be when it's your only option. You should always bring backup recorders, mixers, and mics with you to the set. You never know when you might need them.

The "Oh @#$%!" Kit

A tackle box full of connectors, adaptors, tools, and other problem-solvers can be a lifesaver on location. You might not have a cable for every situation, but with the right adaptor you can turn any cable into the right cable.

I always bring my "Oh @#$%!" kit with me on location. While I might not be able to carry it with me for ENG work, I can still keep it in my car nearby. This kit gets its name because if I'm ever in a situation where I say "Oh @#$%!," I know what kit to reach for! I built this kit over ten years ago and I've yet to be in a jam where this little lifesaver couldn't get me out.

Don't let the production company dictate your equipment needs to you. This is a pitfall do be avoided. If you're told that you are only shooting an interior two-person sit-down interview, still bring your full kit (extra lavs, boom mics, pole, etc.). If the producer decides to do a stand-up, he will expect you to whip out a stick mic (you know, the one that the assignment desk told you that you wouldn't need). ENG work often falls prey to the blame game. The assignment desk will quickly forget that they told you to only bring a pair of lavs and the fault will rest on your shoulders. Always bring all of your gear!

The "Oh @#$%!" Kit

Being prepared for anything is more than just bringing gear. Arguably, there isn't a van big enough to schlep every possible piece of equipment with you on location. You'll need to make sure you have your wits with you. Your mind is your most important piece of equipment. Not every problem can be solved with gear. You'll need to learn to channel the spirit of MacGyver and use whatever you have available.

CHAPTER EXERCISE Make a list of things you forgot to bring or need to purchase when you're on a shoot. Don't be fooled by thinking that you'll remember an item for next time. Your brain will be scrambled eggs by the end of the day and you'll probably forget what you forgot, which means that you'll probably forget it again! Evernote (*www.evernote.com*) is a good app to download that allows you to create and access your notes (including pics and audio recordings) from any computer or smart phone. Of course, you could go old school and just shoot yourself an email as a reminder.

CHAPTER 18

APPLICATIONS

The principles of microphone placement, dealing with background noise, signal flow, and recording are the same for ENG work and film production. There are many similarities in workflow, but they are two very different animals. The following is a general overview of different applications for location sound.

ONE-MAN BAND PRODUCTIONS

A *one-man band* is a production in which the camera operator is the only crewmember. Essentially, he is both the camera and sound department. This type of production can deliver good audio, if the proper steps are taken. Granted, they probably won't deliver great audio and certainly not the best possible audio, but good audio can be achieved.

It's impossible to run a camera and hold a boom pole at the same time; so one-man band productions will require a reporter's handheld mic or lav mics. Since there won't be a sound mixer to run the microphones through a mixer, these microphones will be connected directly to the camera. The camera's mic will probably come into play at some point. Other than physically moving closer to the subject, there's not much adjustment that can be made with the camera's onboard microphone. But, setting and monitoring the levels of a handheld mic or a lav can provide newsworthy footage. This is certainly not recommended for other types of productions, but at the end of the day, you'll have to play the cards you're dealt.

If you find yourself in a one-man band situation, don't panic. Take a few minutes to set up the audio properly and test the levels. If you wait until a few seconds before the shot, you're probably going to forget something or rush through the necessary steps. News crews have delivered perfectly fine roadside reports for decades using a one-man band. You'll do fine if you take the time to check your levels. If you are a shooter who plans on doing a fair amount of one-man band shoots, you should invest in a high-quality shotgun mic for the camera.

ENG

The sound mixer on an ENG crew represents the entire sound department. That person is responsible for all audio tasks such as booming, mixing, and miking the talent. The sound mixer also doubles as a pack mule for the shooter by carrying extra camera batteries, tapes or media, etc. During B-roll shots, the sound mixer will help the shooter by carrying the tripod (sometimes called "sticks") or packing gear while they're shooting.

In small-budget video productions and even on some local news crews, the sound is not considered very important. So, the sound mixer is viewed more as an assistant who also happens to have the responsibility of running microphone cables and wearing headphones to make sure that nothing is distorted. If you find yourself starting off your career in this scenario, keep your head up! Even though you're "just the assistant," you can still hone your skills to become a great sound mixer. Everyone has to start somewhere. Dig in and milk the experience for all that it's worth!

The key to ENG work is to be ready to hit the ground running when you arrive on location. This means that the gear should be set up, the camera should be toned up, and the bag is ready to go. When tethered to the shooter with an ENG snake, it is important to mirror the moves of the shooter. You go where the shooter goes or you both won't be able to go! You also need to help guide the shooter when walking backward and help alert him to actions that might be happening outside of his viewfinder. There's a lot to juggle between watching the talent, the boom pole, the levels on the mixer, and predicting the shooter's next steps. You have to be fully alert to your equipment and surroundings or you won't cut it as an ENG sound mixer.

The very nature of ENG production is improvisation. Rarely are the days completely planned out. It is the polar opposite of film production. You have to be ready to think on your feet and make lemonade out of lemon tree seeds. The shoot days for ENG can go long and sometimes the producer doesn't provide a break for lunch. To avoid going hungry, always bring snacks and drinks with you.

Ambushes are a type of interview situation where the interviewee is not aware that he's going to be interviewed until the camera is shoved in his face. These interviews are usually news stories intended to expose something or someone. Here, the job can be similar to that of the paparazzi, but with a little more taste, given the subject matter. Other times, ambushes are used to cover high-profile people caught in the middle of a scandal or important event. Whatever the case, you need to be ready to capture the audio with your boom, since the subject is unlikely to stop and let you put a lav on him. It's a good idea to run the boom mic to Channel 1 and the camera mic on Channel 2 in case you get separated or your boom isn't in the right spot at the right time. In this case, the camera mic can be a safety net.

Be ready to run the gauntlet when following the subject of a news story who doesn't want to speak to the press. It's a madhouse sometimes. Crews are running backward, bumping into each other and the subjects, who swear they have nothing to say, will always end up chiming some off-handed comments or protests to the cameras. All the while, you're running alongside the camera operator with fifteen pounds of gear strapped to you trying to navigate a pole overhead without lancing an innocent bystander or fellow sound mixer with the other end.

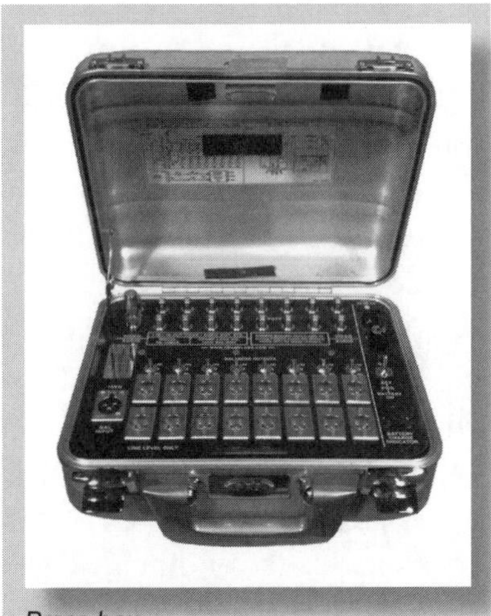
Press box

Events like press conferences may use a *press box* that splits a microphone feed into dozens of XLR jacks for news crews to tap into. The press box will often have a mic/line switch for each individual output. Press boxes are notorious for ground hum, so be sure to bring a ground lift. If a press box is not available, it becomes a case of "every news crew for itself." Each crew will need to use a stick mic or shotgun on a stand to capture the audio. If space is limited, use a mount like a Pig-E-Bak clamp, which allows a microphone to be planted on another microphone. In addition to the press feed, have a shotgun mic ready to pick up room tone and questions from the reporters.

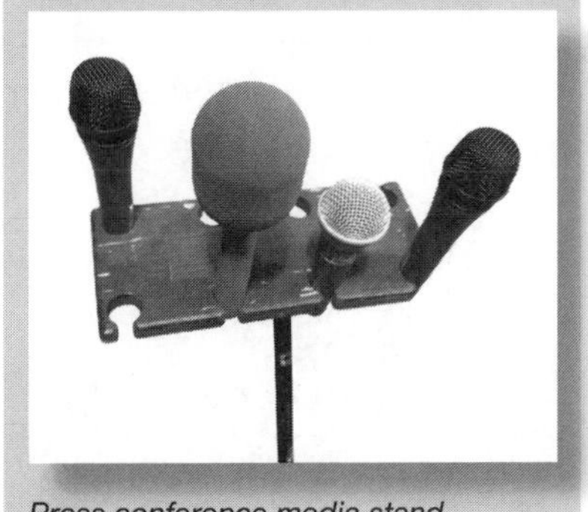
Press conference media stand

Sit-down interviews are a staple of ENG production. When the subject arrives, put the lav on her as soon as possible. This will allow you to get a sense for the sound of the room and the level that the subject will be speaking at. Waiting until the shooter is ready to roll to check for sound problems will cost the production time (and time is money). Instead, be proactive and start tackling sound issues during setup. This might be a bit challenging, as crewmembers can be noisy when setting up the equipment. Don't be afraid to ask the crew to hold for a sound check. Be sure to have all of your gear in place before asking the crew to hold their work. They're not going to be happy watching you work as they stand in silence. Instead, have your mixer set up and a mic in the proper position before testing. Once the crew has settled, listen closely to the sound of the room, background noise, and any other issues. Be quick about your work. Realistically, you should only take about ten to fifteen seconds to do this. For a two-camera sit-down interview, you may be asked to send audio to both cameras. If not, send audio to the primary camera.

A *speaker phone interview* is an interview shot on location with the subject, but the producer asks the questions from a remote location via a speaker phone. The questions are usually discarded from the location audio and reshot for the piece with the producer. This gives the illusion that the producer was on set. And you thought everything you saw on television was real? In other cases, audio from the telephone may be necessary to record. Telephone audio can be recorded using a special device that taps into the phone line or cell phone and converts the signal to a line level.

Live shots are the epitome of "what you see (hear) is what you get." A live shot is broadcast in real time. There is zero room for error. Mistakes cannot be fixed, because you are live! The success of a live shot hinges on your preparation.

Here's a list of things to do when setting up a live shot:

- Set up audio gear
- Check battery level
- Test microphones
- Send a line level tone to satellite truck
- Set up/test Clear-Com
- Set up/test IFB
- Help shooter with lights and camera
- Be a stand-in if necessary

Live shots are set up at least an hour or more before the actual broadcast. This leaves a fair amount of downtime until the shot. Ten to fifteen minutes before the live shot, you should double-check everything again. This will give you plenty of time to troubleshoot or fix anything that might not be working.

The ENG sound mixer is in the heat of battle, sometimes literally. There are all sorts of situations that an ENG sound mixer will face. Many of these situations are real-world versions of what a production sound mixer would capture as a theatrical performance. From battlefields, to terrorist attacks and race riots, to documenting real-life gang bangers, an ENG sound mixer has to be in the middle of it all to bring the news to the world. It takes a special kind of person to tackle this type of job. Personally, I'm not too crazy about risking life and limb for a piece that might only air for a few minutes on CNN.

One of the most dangerous jobs I worked was for Animal Planet's show *Animal Cops: Detroit.* The reality show was based on the Michigan Humane Society's team of investigators that dealt with deadly animals, illegal dogfights, and animal cruelty. There was never really a fun day. The days were either really dangerous or really sad. Regardless of what was planned for the day, we always started out by putting on bulletproof vests, a sobering experience.

The nature of working around wild pit bulls that could attack at a moment's notice was scary enough, but we were also faced with dog owners who were known to shoot at the investigators confiscating the dogs used in illegal dogfights. It was a lose-lose situation. Now that I'm older and have a son, I would never work a job like that again. It's just not worth it. However, this might be the adventure that you're after in your career. That's up to you. But, don't forget to wear your bulletproof vest!

It never ceases to amaze me that ENG sound mixers are considered the "grunts" of location sound. Sure, they have to help carry camera batteries, set up lights, and unload gear from the truck, but their skills are finely tuned to grab a usable sound bite at a moment's notice — even when the person giving the sound bite doesn't want to be heard.

Some feature-film sound mixers turn their noses up at ENG sound mixers. This is because they don't fully understand or appreciate what it takes to deliver great sound for ENG work. There is no such thing as ADR in ENG work. An ENG sound mixer often has only one take to get it right. True, the final product isn't shown on a forty-foot screen, but there are other forms of production that need great sound, too!

ENG is not a glamorous field by any stretch of the imagination. There's no chair to sit in, no craft service to provide a nice hot cup of coffee, and certainly no one to hold the boom pole for you. Unfortunately, ENG sound mixers make about half of what a feature film sound mixer makes. But, that's the biz. Regardless if you're shooting a feature film that might be up for an Academy Award or if you're shooting a simple standup for the evening news, you should take your job seriously and do the absolute best that you can.

EFP

Often, EFP will use a satellite truck to broadcast live events. Large-scale productions, like sports, will have a production truck on location to handle camera switching, graphics, and sound mixing. Sports events can have several ENG crews gathering locker-room interviews, interviews on the playing field, and press conferences that are handed off to the production truck. There may be several broadcast positions, such as sideline reporters and announcers. Both positions will need IFB feeds and microphones. Given the nature of sporting events, the sideline reporter will probably use a stick mic. Announcers will use either a stick mic on a desktop stand or a headset mic. *Cough Drops* are a special device with a momentary push button that temporarily mutes a microphone in case the announcer needs to speak off-air or cough (hence, the name).

Concerts can be a lot of fun to cover. To start off, you'll probably get to meet the band. Second, you get paid to listen to music. It's a win-win! Oh yeah, you'll probably have some work to do as well. Concerts can be recorded with stereo mics, camera mics, or shotguns, but the best sound will come directly from the house console. You can get a feed from the FOH (front of house) mixer and send it directly to a recorder to be synced later or you can send a wireless feed from your mixer to the camera. The FOH mix is not intended for broadcast and can drastically fluctuate, so you'll need to keep an eye on the levels. In addition to the FOH mix, you'll need to grab ambience of the screaming fans.

The coolest concert experience I had was when I worked with KISS. We were shooting for the VH1 show *Fanatic*. The episode centered on a Gene Simmons fan. We followed her experience as she got to meet her hero. During the concert, the producer wanted footage of the band performing, but wasn't concerned about the audio because they were taking an audio feed from the house. This meant that I had nothing to do during the show. Since I was sending crowd ambience to the roaming camera via a wireless hop, I asked if I could hang out at the front of the stage and watch the show. Surprisingly, they agreed.

The concert was amazing. The heat from the pyrotechnics was intense and the music was deafening, despite my earplugs. I stood stage-left so I could soak up the magical licks of lead guitarist Ace Frehley. Although I did not know it at the time, this would become the last performance the original members of the group would play together in Detroit. Known for their guitar-pick-flinging skills, the band sniped the fans with guitar picks throughout the evening. I caught Ace's eyes and he nailed me in the chest with a guitar pick. The pick bounced off of my chest and landed on the ground. After picking it up, I glanced to my left to see a young girl with puppy-dog eyes who obviously was envious of my prize. I looked up at Ace, who was only four feet away, and looked back to the girl. With an understanding smile, I lowered my head and handed the fan Ace's guitar pick. Ace seemed a bit surprised at my surrender of the pick. He nodded, shot me a smile, and then reached over and flung another pick into my sound bag. These magical moments make the long, hard days worth enduring.

A once-in-a-lifetime souvenir!

FEATURE FILM PRODUCTION

Feature films heavily emphasize picture over sound during production. This is an unfortunate fact. What is more unfortunate is that many filmmakers are under the delusion that sound can always be fixed in post. Yes, it's true, things can be fixed in post. But, that's not always the best solution.

Production managers have only one goal: deliver the film on time and under budget. They are concerned with the production budget, not the post-production budget, so it's easy for them to say "fix it in post." This is because it will speed things up on the set, thus saving them time and money from the production budget that they're responsible for. Many independent filmmakers need to realize that they cannot afford to "fix it in post."

Sound mixers should perform their work as if there is no such thing as post. In feature films and episodic television, there is an entire department devoted to treating and replacing the location sound. For the rest of productions, it's pretty much minor level adjustments and straight cuts of your audio. So, always deliver the best audio you can.

What You Can and Can't Fix in Post

While there are no absolutes in this world (which in itself, is an absolute statement…), there are some things that can and can't be fixed in post. It's important to understand when things can be *fixed* and when they have to be *replaced*. Here are some good rules to follow:

Levels

You can fix mismatched levels between tracks, but you can't fix mismatched dialog levels if there was only one mic source and the actors' lines overlap.

EQ

You can fix the sound quality between two mics by equalizing them in post, but you can't remove equalization from mics that were equalized on location.

Noise

You can fix low levels or noise to a degree, but you can't fix overmodulated or distorted levels.

Acoustics

You can fix the acoustic properties of a relatively dry audio signal (e.g., adding reverb to make a soundstage sound like a cave), but you can't remove excessive reverb in a track to make a cave sound like a soundstage.

Background

You can fix a scene that needs airplanes flying overhead by adding the sound effect of an airplane in post, but you can't remove airplanes flying overhead from an actor's lines.

Perspective

You can fix the perspective of close-miked dialog to make it sound more distant, but you can't make distant-miked dialog sound closer.

ADR

You can fix poor dialog by performing ADR, but you can't perform ADR unless there is a guide track for the actors to follow.

Music

You can fix a bar or club scene by adding music to the background under the dialog but you can't remove music from under a dialog track.

WHEN THE SOUND MIXER IS THE SOUND DESIGNER

There is a growing trend in the indie film community where the sound mixer also serves as the film's sound designer. Digital technology has made quality soundtracks a reality for low-budget films during both production and postproduction. Having one person in charge of the entire soundtrack can lead to better prices for filmmakers who use a single source for all of their sound needs. The process makes sense.

Judgment calls by the sound mixer/sound designer are more likely to be listened to by the director who might otherwise dismiss the sound mixer's plight by arguing that the post sound team will deal with a given issue. In these cases, the sound mixer is the post sound team and will know what he has to work with before the film is even edited. I've done dozens of short films this way and it can be a lot of fun. When the film is finished the soundtrack is your work from start to finish, although a composer may be hired to compose the score.

THE SOUND CREW

Filmmaking is the process of creating a cohesive story through organized chaos. When a crew takes over a location, it's like the circus has come to town. Film work is like living the life of a carnie, without the cabbage smell. There's a gaggle of crewmembers working together and gear sprawled out over the set like a swarm of hungry locusts invading a fresh crop. For this reason, a hierarchy of departments is used to maintain control and functionality in an otherwise cluttered process.

The sound department on a feature film consists of a sound mixer and a boom operator. On larger productions, a third crewmember can be added called the utility person or second boom. Each of these positions has a different set of responsibilities.

The *sound mixer* is the head of the sound department. Here's a list of their main responsibilities:

- Booking sound crew
- Determining equipment needs and rentals

- Mixing
- Recording
- Signal routing for monitoring and playback
- Generating sound report
- Providing media deliverables
- Coordinating with postproduction

The *boom operator* is responsible for positioning the boom mic during the shot. Of course, there are many more duties for the boom operator to perform.

Here's a list of some of these other responsibilities:

- Miking the talent
- Communicating between the sound mixer and the set
- Paying attention to and participating in blocking and rehearsals
- Memorizing lines or key words in dialog for cueing
- Practicing boom movement
- Listening for noisemakers (footsteps, props, etc.) and correcting these issues
- Presenting potential issues that can't be solved to the sound mixer

The primary role of the *utility/second boom* is to be an assistant to the boom operator and sound mixer. The utility/second boom allows the sound mixer and boom operator to focus on their tasks, which speeds up the production and causes fewer errors. Below is a list of the utility's responsibilities. If the production cannot afford a utility, these responsibilities would fall to the boom operator.

- Acting as second boom operator when necessary
- Preparing and labeling recording media
- Checking battery levels/charge batteries
- Prepping and distributing Comtek/clip Comtek receivers to chairs
- Providing feeds to and from video village
- Prep timecode slate/jam sync
- Running cable to boom operator
- Pulling cable for boom operator
- Helping wire talent
- Setting up plant mics
- Cleaning dirty cables at wrap

- Replacing batteries
- Retrieving lavs from actors
- Operating playback device
- Running induction loops
- Setting up bell and light system
- Helping manage wireless antennas
- Prepping and distributing IFB
- Coordinating with G&E to provide AC to sound cart
- Distributing Hush Heels to actors
- Handling noisy props or environmental challenges
- Helping move carts
- Distributing and collecting walkie-talkies
- Handling paperwork (time sheets, sides, etc.)
- Restocking expendables (media, batteries, etc.)
- Performing minor repairs
- Setting-up/tearing down tents
- Bringing coffee, water, snacks to sound mixer and boom operator

Utility can be a good entry-level position into film sound. The seemingly menial tasks will help acclimate the utility person to all of the aspects of production as well as participate firsthand in many roles of the sound crew.

Quiet on the Set!

The sound mixer may have to ask for quiet on the set before rolling. Be sure to ask the cast and crew to turn cell phones completely off (not just on vibrate). *Bell and light systems* are used to inform crewmembers that shooting is in progress. A single bell means that shooting is starting. Two bells mean that shooting has cut. Never walk on to a soundstage when the red light is on! Not all soundstages have a bell and light system. Some sound mixers will have one in their kit. If no bell and light system is available, ask if a PA can stand guard at the door to inform crewmembers and visitors when shots are taking place.

Safety Takes

A *safety take* is an additional take shot for the purpose of providing more coverage in case the primary take had problems with either the sound or picture. If you are not 100% sure that the audio was clean, ask for a safety take. In some cases, playback can be reviewed to verify that a safety take is necessary. Other times, it might be faster to simply shoot another take. Don't feel pressured into moving on. Your job is to record clean audio. A camera operator wouldn't accept a take if there is a smudge on the lens; you shouldn't accept a take that has errors either. When in doubt, ask for a safety take.

Where Do You Park the Sound Cart?

The short answer is: anywhere you can! Some sound mixers prefer to keep their sound cart close to the set, whereas other mixers like to be isolated from the set. Being close to the set allows you quick access to the set for troubleshooting, hand signals, etc., but being in another room or outside allows you to focus only on the sound coming through your headphones without hearing or feeling the physical acoustics of the room. Many sound mixers will stay close to video assist. This will be where the script supervisor usually lives and will make note-comparing easier. This position means shorter cable runs and keeps the sound gear out of the way of set traffic.

Dolly Shots

For some shots, the boom operator may be able to ride on the dolly along with the camera operator. This will make it easier to keep the mic out of frame and at the same distance from the talent during walk-and-talks or other moving shots. A good trick is to run the duplex cable the entire length of the dolly track to avoid tension on the cable that could pull on your boom pole. Ask your utility person (if you have one) to manage the cable during the shot. If the talent is stationary, but the camera dollies toward or away from the talent, choose a stationary position off the dolly.

On-Set ADR

Digital filmmaking is making on-set ADR a reality. Shots that are impossible to record properly can be ADR'd immediately following the shot to give maximum performance in the recordings. It makes sense. The actors are still in character and the performance, cadence, and energy are still fresh in their minds. Plus, there are no additional costs to bringing the actors back and renting a stage to record. As a bonus, the ADR is recorded in the proper environment, which will sound more natural. It's a win-win for everyone!

Sound Playback

A playback track usually consists of music, although sometimes sound effects or prerecorded dialog tracks are used (sometimes referred to as *blended audio*). The talent will need a way of hearing the playback. If there is no dialog recorded during the scene, as in the case of a music video or dance number, the audio can be played over speakers. If the scene has dialog in the middle of a playback track, the music may be faded down (off) during the dialog section to allow for a clean recording. Once the dialog is finished, the playback track can be faded up to allow the actors to continue dancing to the beat. The use of a second slate might be necessary for playback sync when dialog is also being recorded. The first slate will be for the dialog sync and a second slate will be used for playback sync.

A playback track is given to the sound mixer who is responsible for noting where the track should start and cueing up the track after each take. Another member of the sound crew, such as the utility, can also do this. The playback track will usually have timecode. The music is played when the AD or director calls "playback." Music can be placed on Channel 1 and a click track on Channel 2 of the playback track. The studio can provide a click track from the session files or you can create a click track by using a metronome, provided that the song doesn't change BPM (beats per minute).

A standard CD can be used for playback, which is common for smaller-budget independent films. Be aware that drift becomes more noticeable the longer the CD plays. This could be a problem if the scene is a single shot from one camera, but if there will be cuts, the editor can simply sync the track back up. For higher-budget productions, the playback track will have timecode that can be seen on camera via a timecode slate, allowing the editor to easily sync the track in post without any drift issues. When in doubt, shoot some tests to ensure that proper sync can be achieved with your playback audio.

Clubs and other venues may have a P.A. system that is available for the production to use. However, they might not allow you to make any changes to their system, which would make the availability of the system pointless. Other times, they might try to charge the production to have their own sound engineer manage the system on your behalf. In either situation, it will save the production company money by renting a P.A. system. Always bring a P.A. system with more power than you think you'll need. Although playback is intended for reference and not entertainment, it is vital that all of the performers hear it. Larger venues like concert halls will need a system that can push more power than a small nightclub.

For long dialog sections that require the actors to keep in step with the beat from the playback track, you might need to use a thump track or in-ear monitors. A *thump track* is simply the beat of the music. The beat is equalized so that only extremely low frequencies are heard on the set (typically 50Hz or less). These low frequencies can be removed from the dialog track in post since that part of the frequency spectrum rarely contains frequencies used by the human voice. Keep in mind: you will need a large speaker or subwoofer that can handle the low frequencies. Also, listen for things on the set that might rattle or vibrate when the thump track is played back as this will intrude on the dialog.

Playback can be fed discretely to the talent via an induction loop. A room loop can be used to provide an induction loop around a large area, such as the dance floor of a club. An induction cable that connects to the speaker post of an amplifier is placed on the floor. Stranded cable allows the signal to travel as several loops around the cable. When inside the loop, induction occurs that allows the earpiece to receive the signal. Phonak makes inductive hearing systems that can be used inside of a room loop or via an induction loop worn around the actor's neck. Today, many sound mixers stick with in-ear monitors over induction loops.

During a scene where the talent uses a hand held mic (P.A. systems, singing, etc.), the audio from the performance mic can be recorded to a separate audio track; however, this should not be considered as the primary source of dialog for that scene. Instead, you should still boom and/or lav the actor to record clean dialog. Performance mics don't translate as well on screen as they do in a live setting. On playback, the audio from the handheld mic will sound dull and flat. Handling noise produced by holding the microphone is also a concern since the mic is not shock-mounted. Any major hand movements or gestures from the talent and the audio will go off-mic quickly. This is also true of lectern mics or other "prop" microphones that the actor uses on camera.

CHAPTER EXERCISE Practice being a one-man band! Shoot an interview with someone and try to operate the camera while maintaining good audio levels. Don't just use the camera mic. Practice by setting levels for a handheld, a hardwire lav, and a wireless lav. Record the scene several times, using a different mic each time. Listen to the results. How did you do?

CHAPTER 19

SET ETIQUETTE

There are no written rules of etiquette for production, but many unwritten rules are followed on film sets, television shows, and other types of productions. Most of these rules are common sense, but many are passed down from generation to generation. Breaking these unwritten rules can get you kicked off a set or stop your phone from ringing. So, in the interest of keeping you gainfully employed, let's go over the code of conduct for a sound mixer.

UNDERSTAND THE ROLE OF THE SOUND MIXER

The core components of any production are sound and picture. The two crewmembers responsible for these components are the camera operator and the sound mixer. All of the other crew positions are helpful, but not primary. Unfortunately, this sentiment has been lost in Hollywood over the years and now the sound mixer falls into the ranks as another tech required for operating equipment. The craft is just as important now as it was then, but its importance has seemingly decreased.

Sound is half of the process. The other half is picture. What's funny is that you can have a crew of forty people on a set and only two or three are dedicated to sound. The rest are all there for the picture (except craft service — they're on everybody's side!). This greatly exaggerates the mindset of "sound crew vs. the rest of the crew." The job seems less significant than others because only a tiny portion of the crew works on sound and, to make things worse, nobody can see the fruits of your labor. So, it looks like you're just sitting around all day! Of course, this is far from the truth.

Directors may not care for or even notice your techniques and hard work, but rest assured, they will notice them in postproduction. That is to say, they won't notice when you did a good job; they'll only notice if you did a bad job! At the end of the day, the sound problems are only your problem for that day or a specific shot; however, sound problems will haunt the director in post. Some experienced directors, especially independent directors who are hypersensitive to their budgets, are more willing to give the sound crew adequate time to do their job correctly, but don't be dismayed if the majority of your jobs have a director who is insensitive to sound.

Understand that nobody compliments the sound in a production when it is good. They only complain about the sound when it is bad. Get used to it. It's a thankless job. On the set, only you and your boom operator will know how good of a job you're doing until the postproduction phase. This can be frustrating. When a DP is finished lighting a shot, everyone crowds around a monitor and gives the usual "oohs" and "aahs." The DP's work is instantly recognized and appreciated. You'll never find a group of people gathering around a sound cart with headphones saying "ooh" and "aah" to your sound. When you do a good job, you'll just have to settle for visualizing the dialog editor smiling at the great work you've done. If you're a fragile soul who needs to be complimented on your work every five minutes, then become an actor. Getting another gig from the production company is the only pat on the back a sound mixer needs.

As the saying goes: "They might not like you on the set, but they'll love you in post." You have to work with this mindset. It's almost as if you are a messenger from the future. You know what they have; they just haven't realized it yet. That day will come soon enough.

You are the only one responsible for the production's audio. Don't be intimidated by other crewmembers who try to muscle you into making decisions that you don't agree with. It's funny how fast producers will change their minds on a decision they made once they are in post and realize they should've given you another take. Of course, they won't admit to this and you'll probably take the blame. Shooters might try to sway your decision on which mics you use or whether or not a safety take is needed. Stand firm when you must, especially if the sound was unacceptable during a take.

Avoid asking producers and shooters for advice or to collaborate on audio issues. They're not the audio professional; you are. Asking audio questions will almost always get you incorrect information and shows a lack of confidence in your own work. This will lead to their lack of confidence in your work. Make the right decisions on your own and stand by those decisions. This is what the production is paying you for.

ATTITUDE

Attitude will make or break your career. I've met sound mixers who were audio geniuses, but had "know-it-all" attitudes. As a result, they didn't get much work. On the other hand, I've met sound mixers who had no idea what professional line level was, but they were easy to get along with. As a result, they got tons of work. Many production companies will hire sound mixers based on their ability to play well with others and deliver good audio. They would rather hire a decent sound mixer with a great attitude over a stellar sound mixer who delivered premium audio, but had a bad attitude. The lesson here is to be the best you can be, but make sure that your attitude is better than your skills.

Know your place as the sound mixer. You are not in charge of the production. You are in charge of the sound gathered during the production. You do not have the final say in the matter. Having a bad attitude when someone overrides your decision will not help matters. In most cases, it will only make matters worse and people will notice. Accept the decisions made by the producer or director and move on. Some calls will be made for you, despite your input. Not every shot will be good for sound. Get over it.

Often, the sound mixer's only communication with the director is negative. The only time you talk to the director is to report that there was an airplane in the background, clothing rustle, a wireless hit, or a crewmember talking on the set. It's no wonder why sound mixers are often stereotyped as complainers. Let me explain why by using an old parable:

A monk joined a very strict monastery and took a vow of silence. The exception to this vow was that he was allowed to say just two words every ten years. After a decade of service, the head monk asked the newcomer what two words he would like to say. "Bed… hard," said the monk. The head monk simply nodded. Another decade passed and the head monk again approached the monk to ask what two words he would like to say. "Food… cold," said the monk. The head monk nodded. Another decade passed and the head monk again approached the monk to ask what two words he would like to say. "I quit!" said the monk. The head monk smiled and said, "That's no surprise. All you ever did was complain!"

The moral of the story is that your words add up. Other than the traditional "good morning" and "good night," the majority of the time all the crew hears from the sound mixer is a firm "Quiet!" "That's no good," or "For the love of God, will someone please shoot that dog next door!" While these words are few and far between, when added up over time the overtone is generally negative. Sound mixers are known as the "fun-wreckers" and the "killjoys." Such is the burden of the job. It's important not to come off as the grumpy ogre behind the mountain of cables and gear. Service with a smile gets more tips. Sound mixers with a pleasant attitude will get more jobs.

No matter how frustrated you get, never walk off a set. You will certainly be excommunicated from the business. The only situation that would warrant this is if your life is being put in serious danger. Other than that, if you choose to leave a set, you should plan on driving straight to the unemployment office. No matter how heated an argument gets or how much disrespect the director has for you, never walk off a set. If you quit a job, you could very well be quitting the business.

BE PUNCTUAL

I have a rule for call times: If I show up on time, I'm fifteen minutes late! Always arrive to the location early. This gives you ample time if you run into traffic, get lost, or have a difficult time finding a parking space. Never be the reason why the production gets off to a late start. The last thing you want to do is start the day frazzled and stressed as you scramble to get your gear ready for the first shot. This will only lead to mistakes.

When working multiple days, confirm the next day's call time and location before leaving the set. If the producer says they will contact you, check your email/voicemail to confirm. If you don't receive a call time before you go to bed, follow up with them to confirm that their message didn't get lost in cyberspace.

ADAPT, IMPROVISE, AND OVERCOME

The mantras of fieldwork are "Whatever it takes," and "By any means necessary." Filmmakers are problem-solvers. That works out well, since there are lots of problems to solve in filmmaking! The one constant in production is that everything will change at the last moment. You need to be ready to switch things up at the drop of a hat. Scenes will get reworked or even cut. Props and vehicles can stop working. Environments can quickly become problematic — especially exterior locations that are subject to weather. Get used to change. Don't complain about the change. Stay positive and roll with the punches. If you're looking for consistency in your work, get a job in an air-conditioned studio or in post. When you're in the field, you're in the Wild West where only the toughest cowboys survive.

You may hear the term *D.F.I.* on a film set. The original definition is "director's further instructions," meaning that the director changed his mind (again). Today, it refers to "different flipping idea" or other less family-friendly definitions. This term is usually called out to stop a crewmember who has been sent off to retrieve a certain piece of equipment that is no longer necessary. While it is easy to blame a director for not thinking things through before arriving on set, realize that different, sometimes better, ideas arise in the middle of the process. Other times, changes are made as a workaround for problems. In order to succeed in production, you need to adopt the Marine Corps mantra, "Adapt, Improvise, and Overcome." If you have a solid understanding of your craft and the filmmaking process, these changes are made easily, albeit sometimes with angst.

BE PREPARED

Many days are filled with a "hurry-up-and-wait" routine. There is a sudden flurry of activity and then all is quiet for a while. This is very common in ENG work where the subject matter is uncontrollable. Crews will race to get everything ready and then sit for hours waiting for something to happen. Film sets have plenty of "hurry-up-and-wait" days as well. Production crews are like emergency personnel. They know the drill. When the bell rings, everyone springs into action, performing their duties with surgical precision. At times, the hardest part is staying awake. Although there might be nothing to do, you can't take a nap. You need to be ready at the drop of hat. When the 1st AD makes the call, you need to be ready to roll. Use your down time wisely. Check your gear, fill out reports, read equipment manuals, talk shop with other crewmembers who are also waiting and, of course, network with people to find what jobs are crewing up.

The day will always start slow and end fast. There is a natural momentum to a production day. This is not always a good thing. Often, this is because the day got off to a late start. Production is a machine with lots of moving parts that takes time to get up to an operating speed. By the time this happens, the day is usually half-over, so everyone is forced to pick up the pace for the last half of the day to make sure that the production stays on schedule. Time seems to bend and stretch on the set. Before lunch, the production seems like a train getting ready to leave the station. Passengers are boarding, luggage is being loaded, and the engineers are putting coal into the furnace. The pace is steady, but slow. The whistle blows and the train begins to chug. Slowly and steadily the train inches away from the station. Cut to the set after lunch when the production manager realizes that you'll never get all the day's shots done and then the train ends up barreling down the track at breakneck speeds! This happens on every set in every city on every day of the year. All aboard!

BE A TEAM PLAYER

In a recording studio, sound is the only focus. In filmmaking, sound is only part of the focus. The picture is very important. This book focuses on the importance of sound, but it is only part of the filmmaking process. Keep this in mind when you are tempted to go to blows with a DP who keeps insisting on shooting everything as a wide shot. It's true, tighter shots will yield better sound, but a picture is worth a thousand words and when you add sound to those pictures, you've multiplied those thousand words a thousand times more! Those wide shots might help sell the emotion or scope of the scene. Be prepared to work as a team. Hopefully, the DP will do the same.

When packing your equipment for the day, be sure to leave your ego at home. It won't be welcomed on the set. Team spirit is critical to the success of the film. If every department demands that they have their way, the film would never get made. Voice your concerns and needs and be willing to make compromises. Disunity on a film set makes for uncomfortably longer days.

A film crew is a community. It's like a small village. As with all villages, ultimately borrowing and lending will start taking place. Favors will be exchanged. This is general human behavior. While you might think you are a rogue member of the crew, the time will come when you need help.

If you've spent your time ignoring other people's plights or opportunities to help, karma will be your enemy. Filmmaking is a team effort. Be courteous and helpful to other crewmembers, provided that this does not impair your ability to handle your own responsibilities. If you go the extra mile, it will be noticed and remembered. If you are stubborn and difficult to work with, it will also be noticed and remembered. Be a helpful and pleasant crewmember and karma will be your friend.

In ENG work, the sound mixer takes on the role of assistant to the shooter. This means carrying camera gear, setting up lights, and using your sound bag as the shooter's personal backpack. It's all part of the job. The more you know about lights and cameras, the more useful you'll be to the shooter. This will bring you more work.

In your career, you will work with crewmembers who are nice and some who are jerks. This is nothing specific to the film biz, that's just life. You cannot control how a person acts, but you can control how you react to that person. Try to avoid blowups on the set with other crewmembers. It just brings negative energy to an already stressful situation. Sound is half the experience of any production, whether the director or DP realizes it or not. You don't have to defend your role. Instead, focus on your job and avoid conflict at all costs. Honey is sweeter than vinegar. You'll be surprised how helpful people can be if you are nice to them.

Never burn bridges with other crewmembers! The industry is very small. Bad news will travel fast. You will run into those crewmembers again and you will be forced to spend long, uncomfortable days with them. Keep your tongue firmly gripped by your teeth.

While working a film with a longtime friend of mine, I reminded him of an old production truth: "You're not here to make friends. You're here to make a movie." Friendships can be a byproduct of the filmmaking process, but they're not the goal. You need to work together without incident, but you don't need to sacrifice the quality of your sound in order to make friends.

BE SAFE

Sets are not the safest workplaces. Nothing is permanent and rarely is anything locked or bolted down. Crewmembers do their best to keep everything out of the way and to mark hazards clearly, but that can only help so much.

The floors are littered with cables and gear. Do your part to keep the set safe and be sure to tape down cable runs that cross doorways or high-traffic areas.

Learn to have "set feet." You have to pay attention when walking around a set. If not, you could hurt yourself, someone else, or the equipment. Set feet give you the ability to navigate around cables and lights without tripping or knocking something over. It is a cautious method of treading lightly and watching where you are going. And don't forget to look up! There are plenty of overhead hazards as well.

DRESS CODE

The dress code for production work depends on the type of production. Film sets are usually very casual. Sometimes the crew looks like a mix between rock and roll roadies, SoHo artists, and English professors. Personal style and flair are the norm and no one is judged, at least not verbally. As lighting is hard to control, darker clothes are preferred so the crew doesn't reflect light. The same is true of stage work and live events. In these cases, the crew needs to blend in or not be seen at all. ENG productions usually follow this dress code. Television stations and networks might have a specific dress code that they want employees to follow. Special productions may ask you to dress in business casual, a suit and tie, or even a tuxedo if you're interviewing someone of importance like the President at a formal event. Be sure to stick to the dress code. If no dress code is specified, then dress casually. If you tend to sweat, it's best to wear a hat. Water is the enemy of electronics and a sweaty forehead can inadvertently shower a mixer's controls with sweat when you look down to manage the knobs.

Wear the right clothes for the job. Never wear flip-flops to an ENG shoot. This will impair your ability to run and gun! On a film set, you should wear shoes or boots that completely cover your feet. A film set is like working in a factory or shop. A lot of heavy equipment (lights, stands, etc.) is carted around and feet often become the victims of slips and accidents. Also, avoid wearing jewelry that will make noise when you work.

Dress appropriately for the weather. Believe it or not, weather forecasters are sometimes wrong in their predictions for the day! I was a slow learner on this one. I spent many freezing days standing outside in a T-shirt and a spring jacket. I finally started keeping a jacket and gloves in the trunk of my car after a few fingers fell off from frostbite (okay, so I'm being a little overdramatic…). You never know what the day will bring. It's better to be prepared for the worst. Dressing in layers is always a good idea. If you get warm, you can shed a layer and keep working.

Here's a list of things to consider having with you at all times:

- Poncho
- Coat
- Gloves
- Sunglasses
- Extra Socks
- Umbrella
- Sweater/Sweatshirt
- Hat
- Boots or Spare Shoes

Always dress comfortably, not fashionably. It's easy to get distracted by discomfort. This will affect your performance in the field. If you forgot to bring a coat or poncho, don't be "that guy" that complains all day. Nobody likes a whiner! Suck it up and make sure you dress appropriately for the next shoot.

The "But honestly, I'm with the band…" line never works! Don't lose your backstage passes! A backstage pass is part of your attire when working on location. It is your responsibility to keep track of your credentials. Losing your pass will slow down production while you get new credentials. Carrying a sound bag and wearing headphones won't get you past security without a badge.

Yes, I'm with the band!

FILM SETS

Set etiquette on a film set is quite simple. Do your job without getting in the way or holding up anyone else. There are, of course, numerous other things to consider.

There is a hierarchy on a film set. You must respect the chain of command. Department heads should speak with the director about their departments' concerns or needs. A boom operator should never approach the director on the sound mixer's behalf without being asked to do so.

Communicate your needs to the right person. Don't bother the director if you need a wardrobe adjustment for a wireless mic. Instead, discuss that need with the wardrobe key. There are some things that you need to communicate to the director: a bad take/request for another take, volume adjustments from the actors, etc. It is the sound mixer's responsibility to communicate takes that are no-good to the director. Do not assume the director heard a noise in the background during a take. If the director signs off on a bad take, that is his decision. Push for another take, but realize it's not your call to make. If the director decides to "fix it in post," then be sure to write that in your notes on the sound report. This will release you from responsibility and finger-pointing later. Don't complain or come off as a tattletale in your comments either (e.g., "director refused to listen to me..."). Instead, simply note, "director signed off on take" or "director wants to ADR this."

Being a great sound engineer in a studio doesn't mean you will be a great location sound mixer. While some of the technology is shared, they are two different worlds. Recording studio techniques are like tapping your foot in beat to the music, whereas location sound is more like choreographed dancing. In the studio, the engineer is a king who sits behind a throne of knobs and faders decreeing his will over the talkback system. In the field, the sound mixer is far from royalty. He's not as lowly as a commoner, but perhaps more akin to a knight who takes orders from a director who serves as a king who understands battle, but has no idea how to hold a sword.

Understand the politics of a film set. First off, filmmaking is not a democracy. If it were, then the first film ever made would still be in production today. Nope. Filmmaking is a monarchy and the director is the king. The king gets what the king wants. If you disrespect the king, you will be cast from his kingdom, er, set. A good handle on set politics is often as important as knowing your craft. Choose your battles with other departments. Not every situation needs to blow up into a drawn-out fight. Concede when necessary and move on. There will be plenty more concessions to make and you won't win them all. Remain calm. No matter how good you are at your craft, you are not in charge. It's not your film. The calls are not yours to make. True, the sound mixer is the head of the sound department, but don't get too cocky. Your department only consists of two or three people. While you are not on the bottom rung, you are nowhere near the top. Keep your ego in check and your meters bouncing and life will be swell.

Don't cast your pearls before the swine. If a director is obviously not interested in sound or accommodating the sound department, then do the best you can with what you have. There's certainly no use in arguing or pushing the issue. If the director is not interested, it's your job to make up for the slack. Don't have a bad attitude and think, "If they don't care, then I don't care." This might be justified in your mind, but when the project reaches post, you'll look like the bad guy. The last thing you'll want is for your reputation to be tarnished because you lost your cool on the set. Take it with a grain of salt and work through it.

Always communicate issues with the director between takes. Never interrupt a shot verbally. It is not the sound mixer's role to call for a cut. Instead, use hand signals so that the director can decide whether to cut or continue the shot. Every director and producer is different. Some will care about sound and others won't care at all. If you constantly slow down production with minor sound problems, you'll not only cost the production money, but you'll hurt your reputation. There is a fine balance between what is acceptable and unacceptable. Experience will be the final teacher of this lesson.

Conversations with the director should be short, sweet, and to the point. Directors are under a tremendous amount of stress and don't have time for chummy chitchat. Approaching producers or executive producers about your own projects is a no-no. If a conversation leads to an exchange of contact information, contact them after the production is wrapped. Avoid over-socializing on a set. You certainly don't want to distract other crewmembers who have jobs to do. Be friendly and polite, but remember, time is money and you are there to work.

Cell phone conversations should be kept to an absolute minimum. If you have to use your cell phone, be sure to walk off the set so that you aren't bothering anyone. That said, never leave the set without notifying someone. I left the set once to use the bathroom. I was certain that I had plenty of time as the director was still discussing blocking issues and lights were being repositioned. A few moments later I heard an outburst of laughter. Upon my return, after I washed my hands of course, I found out the director had called for a roll and everyone waited in silence for me to call "speed." The director called for a roll a second time and again they waited in silence. Finally, they realized that I wasn't at my cart. It was a small indie film, so I wasn't crucified for my absence. On a bigger-budget set, that would've been a different story.

Walkie-talkies or radios are used on larger sets for crew communication. If you need to leave your post, be sure to monitor your radio in case you are called back to the set. This can be difficult to remember since the sound crew usually turns their radios off so they can work.

Never invite friends or family members to the set. In fact, don't even ask. It's unprofessional and can slow down the flow of the set. If someone you know wants to break into the business, you might be able to convince the production manager to let you use that person as an unpaid assistant. Keep in mind: you will be responsible for that person's actions, so be sure to have them read this chapter first. Underage assistants aren't a good idea, as they may need to sign contracts such as NDAs and release forms in order to walk on the set.

KNOW WHEN TO CUT

Sometimes a director will forget to call "cut." In these cases, you might need to gently remind the director that you're "still rolling." It is imperative that the sound mixer continues to roll until told to cut. This is not an executive decision that you can make. Cutting before the director tells you to cut can result in a spoiled take that will be entirely your fault. Never cut until the director tells you to. When in doubt, ask if you should cut (usually by asking "Cut?") or simply state, "still rolling." Avoid prematurely rolling or over-rolling on takes. This can eat away at your available medium and gives the post team unnecessary file sizes to load, transfer, and manage.

WORKING WITH THE TALENT

Dialog is the focus of location sound. The people who deliver the dialog have different titles. Here are some definitions of on-screen people you will work with:

- *Talent*: Talent is a general term that can refer to Hollywood stars or local actors. Talent can also refer to a professional reporter or spokesperson.
- *Actor*: An actor is a person who portrays a character from a script. An actor's lines are written for him.
- *Star*: A star is an actor with clout. Usually, the success of the show hinges on the star's performance and involvement. The star is the audience's draw to the theatre.
- *Reporter*: Typically found in ENG production, this person delivers news reports and interviews people.
- *Announcer*: This person is a voiceover artist, sportscaster, or any other role that does not necessarily require him to appear on-screen.
- *Guest*: The guest is the focus of an interview or story, also called an interviewee.
- *Host*: The host is the center of a show. A host can be an interviewer, announcer, or star who engages the audiences.
- *Subject*: A subject is the person who is the focus of a story or particular shot.

It is common practice to treat the talent like royalty. This is not because they are of royal descent and certainly not because they are better than the crew. They do, however, have power and weight to throw around. And, they have been known to throw their weight around.

Everyone has heard horror stories about actors and actresses who berate the crew, make absurd demands, storm off the set, and make the general work environment miserable. This is not the norm, but it does happen from time to time. When you come across people like this, learn to nod and smile. There's really nothing you can do to improve the situation, but saying or doing the wrong thing can easily make the situation worse.

One news correspondent actually demanded that I use gaffer tape to make her blouse appear as if she were skinnier. She was adamant about it and known to make calls to the news agency to complain about her crews. Unfortunately, there wasn't enough gaffer tape in the state of Michigan to solve her problem. Instead, I kept putting more gaffer tape on her blouse until she felt more attractive. Talent can be downright rude and belittling, but you still have to work with a smile and do your job.

The director is in charge of the actors. Although you might have a legitimate direction that you need to communicate to the actors, make sure that any major decisions, including having the actors deliver their lines louder or softer, are cleared with the director first.

Respect the actors' privacy. They have performances to prepare for along with blocking and lines to rehearse. They need to focus on their job, just like you need to focus on your job. Keep the mood on the set neutral during intense dramatic scenes. Knock-knock jokes and humorous haikus should be avoided when an actor is getting ready for his award-winning death scene. And yes, I've been scolded on this issue multiple times.

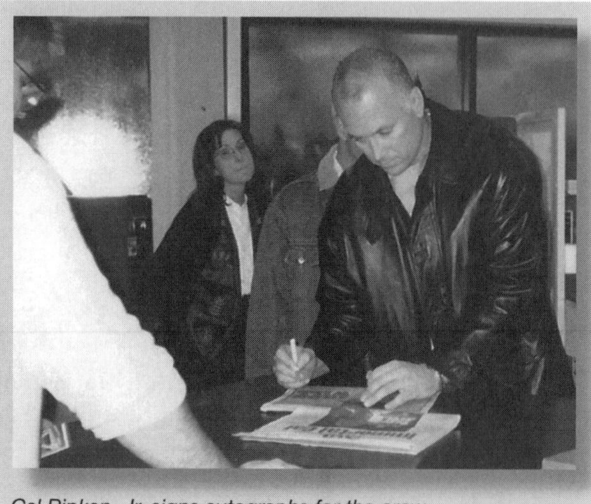

Cal Ripken, Jr. signs autographs for the crew.

Avoid asking for autographs. It's generally frowned upon. In all my years, I've only asked for maybe one or two autographs. This was in the beginning of my career. Nowadays, the producer's signature on a check will suffice. Pictures should also be asked for delicately. Sometimes, the actors will warm up to members of the crew and do a picture session at the end of a shoot. That's the time to ask for a picture. Never take a picture without permission. Set paparazzi usually won't get hired for another project, especially if the picture is posted online with ill-received results.

I once worked for three days with baseball legend Cal Ripken, Jr. The funny thing is I am not a sports fan and I had no idea who he was. The production was an internal corporate video for a Detroit automotive company. I assumed he was just some random spokesperson. When the shoot wrapped, Cal began to sign autographs for the crew. I quietly leaned over to the gaffer and asked why everyone wanted the spokesperson's autograph. The gaffer simply shook his head. I had the same experience with Bret Favre the year that Green Bay won the Super Bowl, but that's another story. The point is that the talent might have clout, but at the end of the day, he's just another person on the set doing his job. Respect his privacy.

NDAS

NDA stands for "non-disclosure agreement." It is a legal contract that you may be required to sign in order to work on a project. Essentially, a typical NDA states that you agree to keep any information about the production private. This includes on-set rants by actors and directors, cell phone pics, videos, and important story plots or twists. Breaching this contract will not only cost you big money, but may also damage your career permanently. Tweets and Facebook posts can be career-enders even if you didn't sign an NDA. What happens on the set should stay on the set.

CHAPTER EXERCISE Make a list of people whom you have a hard time working with. Next, list their character traits that rub you the wrong way. Now, make a list of character traits that you have that could rub others the wrong way. Be honest. If you're afraid of what others will think of your list, use invisible ink. Finally, ask yourself how you can improve on your weaknesses to make yourself more fun to work with. Remember, more often than not, a crew is hired for their ability to play well with others, not just their ability to operate equipment.

CHAPTER 20

THE BUSINESS OF SHOW BIZ

They call it "show biz" because it is a business. Business is about making money. Period. While filmmakers are out to make their dreams come true, show biz is about turning those dreams into dollars. Overhead cuts into the production company's profit. As a crewmember, you are part of that overhead and productions will do their best to make sure that they pay you as little as possible. Welcome to the world of show biz!

Artistic industries like music, film, and television are different than any other industries in the world. People have a passion for these industries. They will do anything to be a part of these industries, including working for free to get their feet in the door. In time, this passion will wear off. Don't get me wrong, it will still be a lot of fun, but the thrill and excitement will soon settle down to simple enjoyment.

The evolution of your career will probably go something like this:

1. It's a Hobby

You'll start off star-struck with the industry. This phase includes a fascination for movies and television shows. Soon, you will start visiting consumer and professional electronic stores to find inexpensive equipment to play with. Your nights and weekends will be filled with amateur filmmaking. After a short time, you will work yourself up into such frenzy that you'll realize that you have to do this for a living. Now, you'll look for ways to get your foot in the door. This might lead you to film school.

2. Getting Your Foot in the Door

Once you've educated yourself, either through film school or the school of experience, you'll look for any chance to work on a real set. You'll call all of the professional sound mixers in your area to see if you can help out for free. Of course, the pros will tell you that they're not impressed with your film degree and that you need more experience on a set. Next, they'll tell you to be patient and to start slow and work your way into the business. You might be a little taken aback by this seemingly cold advice. This will make you more determined to prove them wrong. Now, you'll start trying harder. Your efforts will pay off and you'll eventually find yourself interning or working as a PA on a set.

3. Low-Paying Jobs

Eventually, you'll catch a break and start getting paid. The pay won't be great and you could never make a living off the money, but family get-togethers will find you bragging about your first major step into the film business. The honeymoon won't last very long, though. At best, you'll last a year or two before you'll start looking for real money. Then, you'll move on to the modest-pay phase.

4. Intermediate Professional

Once you've reached this phase, the fantasy has turned into reality and you'll be less impressed by the phone conversations you have with the Hollywood elite. Your apartment walls will start closing in and you'll need a respectable income in order to start looking for a home. Prior to this phase, your significant other has already started to refer to your career as "just a hobby." Now, you'll feel the need to prove that this is a real job. You'll start purchasing your own equipment and will slowly begin to raise your rates.

5. Professional

Finally, you'll move into the last phase. You're now a professional. You'll turn your nose up at low-paying gigs and give a tongue-lashing to anyone who posts a "low/no pay" gig on Craigslist. You'll be more confident on the set and last-minute disasters will have you smirking and rolling your eyes as opposed to the sheer panic that would have overwhelmed you a decade earlier. Now, your phone will start ringing with youngsters who are dying to get their feet in the door. You'll tell them that you're not impressed with their film degrees and that they need more experience on a set. Next, you'll tell them to be patient and to start slow and work their way into the business. This is the circle of life in the production world.

FREELANCING

The majority of sound mixers are freelancers. The life of a freelancer can be very challenging, but very rewarding. For starters, you get to be your own boss. Not really, but it's fun to think of it that way. You will always have to answer to the client.

With freelance work, it's either feast or famine. You can crush some months and other months you get crushed. I always recommend the ant's approach to work: *Work when there is work to be done, because winter will come soon enough*. This approach has served me well. I never understood why some freelancers weren't very business-oriented with work. They would never answer their phones or return pages. They didn't seem interested in getting work. They were like the grasshoppers that played throughout the summer and starved during the winter. Myself, I never refused work unless it was a holiday. I was quick to answer calls and pages. I worked any chance I could, because I knew that lean times were always right around the corner.

I had many clients who would put me at the top of their call list, simply because they knew I would answer the call or return their page as soon as I could. I was surprised to hear them tell me this. I assumed that everyone was hungry for work. Apparently, I was wrong. Simply being accessible will help bring in work.

If the phone doesn't ring, pick up the phone and call someone! I was so proactive at getting work that I would call clients and let them know my upcoming schedule for the week so they knew what days I would be available. If you want to win at freelancing, you have to play the game. Sitting around waiting for the phone to ring won't pay the bills.

As a freelancer, your greatest form of advertising is word of mouth. Networking is the key to survival. The best investment I ever made in my career was a $45 box of business cards. They looked slick, too! I carried them with me everywhere I went. I stashed some in my wallet, the glove box of my car, my sound bag, and all of my cases. I always had a business card on me. To this day, I still find stray business cards that I had printed fifteen years ago!

Attend networking parties, freelancers' balls, and other local events to meet people and share information. Join Facebook groups for your area and stay in touch with what's happening around town. Be courteous and respectful to everyone, regardless of their current status. Lowly PAs can become powerful producers overnight!

There are many online resources that will help production companies find you. Here are some starting points:

- *www.Mandy.com*
- *www.ProductionHub.com*
- *www.RealityStaff.com*
- *www.Globalproducer.com*
- *www.iCrewz.com*

Most freelancers will help each other out by referring one another to clients. This works in both parties' favor. The referral gets work, while the referrer gets to help out a client — an act that doesn't go unnoticed by producers. It's a small, tight industry. Helping others out is part of the game. But be sure to never steal someone's client. If you substitute for someone, don't give the client your business card. This is considered unethical. The client technically belongs to your colleague. Instead, tell the client to contact you through the person who got you the gig if they want to hire you again. If a referred client tries to re-book you, let your referral know first. It's good business. Some freelancers can be snakes and steal clients. They will eventually burn enough bridges that no one will refer them anymore. Instant karma will get you! Be ethical in your business.

GETTING HIRED

There are three ways to get hired for a job as a freelancer. The first is to be hired directly by the production company. When this happens, you'll need to sign a *deal memo* (see page 325) or contract. A payroll company may require you to fill out a time sheet or you may have to submit an invoice for payment.

The second is to be hired by a *crewing agency*. A crewing agency works as the middleman between the production and freelancer. They will want a cut of your day rate in exchange for their service. There are pros and cons to working with a crewing agency. You may get more work through them, but at the expense of paying them a percentage of each job.

The third is to be hired by a shooter. This is very common in ENG production. Shooters may be hired directly by the production company or through a crewing agency. They usually charge a flat rate for the gear rental, themselves, and the sound mixer. When the production is finished, the shooter will submit an invoice to the client and you will submit an invoice to the shooter. The client will pay the shooter, who will in turn pay you. This slows the payment process and kills more trees. The shooter will charge a flat rate for you. For example, he may charge $450 for the sound mixer and the package. If you used the shooter's sound package, then you would submit an invoice for only your day rate. This can be quite profitable for the shooter if your rate is only $200. He is able to pocket $250 for the sound package that would normally be billed at $150. Whenever possible, I use my own gear whether or not I am getting a rental fee. Using someone else's gear in stressful run-and-gun situations can cause mistakes to be made. I know my gear and would rather use something that I trust. Over the years, I've had good experiences with shooters who were willing to let me use my own gear and charge them a rental fee as well. They didn't have to do that, but they remembered how hard it was to get started. I used the rental fees to help build my package with better equipment. If you are fortunate enough to have such luck, be sure to pay it forward as you progress in your career. Karma has the memory of an elephant.

DEAL MEMOS

Production work should always be accompanied by paperwork before the job begins. This paperwork is known as a deal memo and is quite literally a contract between the sound mixer and the production company. ENG productions rarely use deal memos as the work is usually only contracted for one day. The deal memo will detail all the points of the agreement such as day rates, overtime rates, gear rental, production insurance, travel costs, per diems, invoice pay terms, etc. If the sound mixer is in charge of booking his crew (boom operator and utility), the sound mixer can sign the deal memo on the crew's behalf. Once you've worked with a client for a while, you might be comfortable forgoing the deal memo for each job. However, if the production company is a start-up company, first-time filmmaker, or someone whom you've never worked with before, you should always sign a deal memo so that there are no misunderstandings about your fees.

RATES

When you finally make the decision to start charging for your services, you won't have enough time or experience under your belt to command top dollar. You'll need to work your way up. On the other hand, if your rates are too low, people won't take you seriously or realize that you are a professional. A good place to start is the lower half of the middle-of-the-road day rates.

Now let's discuss business. Sound mixers usually charge a *day rate* for their services. A day rate is a flat rate for a predetermined amount of hours. Overtime starts once you've passed the predefined work hours. Most production day rates are based on a ten-hour day. Some films will ask for a twelve-hour day rate.

Day rates vary from region to region and depend on the type of production work. Here are some ballpark rates to consider:

	Average Day Rates	Independent/ Low-Budget Day Rates
▸ Sound Mixer	\$250 – \$500	\$50 – \$250
▸ Boom Operator	\$200 – \$350	\$50 – \$200
▸ Utility Person	\$200 – \$350	\$50 – \$150*
▸ Gear Rental	\$100 – \$750	\$50 – \$200

**Note: If you see a utility person on an independent feature, make a wish because it's your lucky day....*

Your rate should be firm. You may be told the production just doesn't have the budget to pay your rate. Sometimes this is true; other times the producer will tell you this to see if they can get you for a lower rate. This is the dance of rate negotiations. Your job is to record great sound. The producer's job is to produce a great production while saving as much money as possible (i.e., getting a great crew for pennies on the dollar).

Your job is to make money! The production's job is to save money.

If you have a reputation for selling out on your rate, word will travel fast and you'll find yourself constantly negotiating your rate. Asking for you to knock $50 or $75 off your rate is simply a cost-saving tactic. Those dollars won't really affect the bottom line of the production. The producer might plead poverty, but the reality is production costs have been around for years and they already know what to expect from crew rates. I know some guys who have never lowered their rates for a job and they seem to have plenty of work year-round. I know other guys who are constantly lowering their rates to get jobs. At the end of the year, the guys who stuck to their guns were happier and made more money.

Every couple of years or so, you can increase your rate by 5 to 10%, but be ready for clients to start complaining. Once they've paid you a certain rate, they'll feel slighted when you start asking for more. Some clients will understand, but others might threaten to stop hiring you. It's a sticky situation. One thing that will help your case when you raise your rates is your skill level. Do everything within your power to increase your skill. Practice, read books, read blogs, and ask tons of questions. Clients are often willing to pay more for an experienced crew than to save money on an inexperienced crew.

Raising your rates is inevitable. Realize that you will cross this bridge one day! Starting off with extremely low rates will make it much harder for you to eventually work your way up to even a modest salary. Present-You might not understand this now. It might seem like lower rates will provide you with more work. This could be true, but Future-You is going to be very grumpy when meeting Present-You down the road. The two of you will engage in an intense conversation over why you were so quick to sell yourself out. Future-You will tell Present-You about the mortgage that needs to be paid. And about the small business loan for equipment Future-You is still paying off. And those kids that Present-You swore you'd never have are now asking to go to Disney World! Such is life. It will happen. When it does, you'll remember what I'm telling Present-You now. Present-You might disagree, but Future-You thinks I'm a genius!

OVERTIME

Overtime accounts for any time worked above the agreed day rate hours. If you're on a ten-hour day rate and you work for eleven hours, you should bill for one hour of overtime. Overtime is typically 1.5 times your hourly rate. So, if you charge $300 for a ten-hour day, your hourly rate is $30. One hour of overtime would be 1.5 times $30, so you would charge $345 for the entire day ($300 for the day and $45 for the additional hour of overtime). This rate is called "time and a half," since it's 1.5 times the calculated hourly rate. Some crewmembers will charge time and a half for the first two hours of overtime and then increase the hourly rate to double time, which is twice the calculated hourly rate. Production days can be very long with some days lasting as long as sixteen hours! Remember to address overtime charges before production begins. This information should always be included in your deal memo.

TURNAROUND TIME

Production companies are responsible for giving the crew an adequate turnaround time. This turnaround time may vary, but is usually between eight to ten hours. In the case of ten hours, this would mean if the show wraps at 10 p.m., the next call time would be no earlier than 8 a.m. the next day. Unions have strict guidelines for turnaround times. Unfortunately, many independent films do not follow this rule. There are times when you have to bite the bullet and special situations might require you to bend these rules. Be safe. Remember that your safety is far more important than the production.

I worked on a breaking-news story for NBC that required my crew (namely me and my good friend Wes Heath, who was the shooter) to camp out near an airport to await the arrival of several POWs who had been released from overseas. Going into the day, we knew this would probably become an overnighter, so we brought some books, a portable television, and tons of snacks. We ended up sitting in Wes' van for nearly twenty-three hours! Of course, Wes and I took turns sleeping, so we weren't in any real danger as we were both well rested. Finally, word spread that the POWs had landed. We raced to get some footage, but unfortunately, the POWs were whisked away before anyone even knew what happened. We made a ton of money from NBC that day. As NABET union employees, we were entitled to all sorts of penalties, including excessive overtime and meal penalties. As a sound mixer it was the most money I ever made in a single day. Most of the time, news agencies will send a replacement crew to relieve a crew approaching overtime hours. It all depends on the crew and the situation. Personally, I looked forward to overtime because I wanted to make as much money as I could. Now that I'm older, I'd be happy to hand the overtime over to a younger crew.

Independent films seem to have a life of their own with production days lasting far longer than sixteen hours. This is very dangerous. It's easy for crewmembers to get exhausted, which is a serious issue when they have to drive home at the end of the day. Such was the case with Brent Hershman, a second camera assistant on the film *Pleasantville*, who died while driving home after a nineteen-hour workday. This tragedy infuriated crewmembers and unions, who felt that production companies were ignoring safety issues on set. Today, unions carry hefty penalties for productions that exceed recommended workdays and do not provide adequate turnaround times.

HALF-DAY RATES

Most of the time, day rates are charged. It is rare for a sound mixer to charge an hourly rate for freelance work. Union jobs can be based on hourly rates and some have a minimum amount of hours per day. For shorter days, a *half-day rate* can be charged for freelance work. A half-day rate is defined as being shorter than five hours. Once the clock passes the five-hour mark, the rate switches to a full day rate. So, six or more hours would be billed as a ten-hour day. Although the day is half the amount of time, it is common for sound mixers to charge 75% of their day rate as a half-day rate. For example, if your day rate is $300, then you would charge $225 for a half-day.

I know some sound mixers who refuse to lower their rates even for half-days and their clients are willing to pay the full day rate even for a few hours of work. The reason behind this is that the sound mixer is blocking that day for the production and usually cannot make any more money that day. The exception to this would be *double-dipping*. Double-dipping means that you are working more than one job on a single day. This can be quite lucrative. If you charge both productions a half-day rate of $225 you'll end up making $450 for ten hours worth of work that would normally be billed at $300 (using the above example).

Care should be taken when double-dipping. You need to make sure that the first job has a hard wrap time. If the first job runs over, then you'll be late to the second job. For example, I used to do a fair amount of live shots for *Good Morning America*. The show ran from 7 a.m. to 9 a.m. If we were shooting a live shot at 7:15 a.m. that only lasted for five minutes, I knew that I'd be wrapped and on my way home by 8 a.m. If another production needed me on location at 9 a.m., I knew that I could finish the first job and arrive on time for the second job. This was a fail-safe way to double-dip.

On one occasion, when I was much younger and more foolish than I am now, I decided to stack four jobs back to back. The first job ran from 7 a.m. to 5 p.m. The second job was an overnighter that ran from 7 p.m. to 5 a.m. The third job ran from 7 a.m. to 5 p.m. The fourth job was actually the second night of the second job, which again ran from 7 p.m. to 5 a.m. The jobs kind of snowballed on me. I first agreed to the two-day gig that involved the overnighters. Then, I got a call for the first day's shoot, followed by another gig the next day. I was just starting out and the four jobs combined would net $1,000 in forty-eight hours. Back then, that amount of money would pay for my rent and utilities in two days! How could I resist?

The first twenty-four hours were cake. I bounced around the set and felt great. By the second morning, there wasn't enough coffee on earth to keep me awake. It was hysterical. The third job saw me falling asleep during horribly long and boring interviews. Fortunately, the shooter was a super-cool guy who took sympathy on my young greediness. I still remember glancing up from my catnaps to see him smiling as he shook his head. Refreshed, but a little embarrassed, I finished out the fourth job. I woke up sick several days later and like somebody suffering from a bad hangover, I swore I would never do that again. Pace yourself. Double-dipping is nice, but it can get you into trouble if you're not careful.

TRAVEL

Half-day rates are normally charged for *travel days*. In addition to your day rate and travel days, it is standard practice to charge a *per diem* (the Latin term which means "for each day"). A per diem covers miscellaneous expenses that you incur while traveling, such as meals. The per diem does not cover your travel expenses (taxi fares, luggage check-in fees, and parking). The receipts for these charges are submitted along with the invoice. So, keep your receipts! Production companies usually will not reimburse charges that cannot be accounted for via receipts. Some production companies will give you cash or a check for the per diem before travel, while others will agree to a per diem but include it with the invoice payment. The production company should book and pay all of the travel costs for you. At no time should you use your own money to pay for any travel costs for a production. If a production company asks you to do this for them, the answer should always be no. The question alone should raise a red flag.

WORKING FOR "CREDIT"

There are two promises that seem to be the most common among indie filmmakers. The first is that they promise to give you credit in the film. Big deal! Of course your name should go in the credits — you worked on the film! The second promise is that they'll remember you on the next film. This is often referred to as "the big one." Don't get persuaded into participating on a film just because it might lead to "the big one." It seems that every filmmaker makes this promise. "Help me out on this and I'll remember you when I get the big film." I honestly don't think I've ever worked with an independent filmmaker who hasn't said this to me. I'm sure in their hearts they truly mean it, but that doesn't matter. If they do get the "big" film, they will probably be forced to hire an A-list union crew. If you happen to be on that crew, that's nice, but it's just another gig. The "big one's" days will be billed as your normal day rate. Still, the image of working on "the big one" — the one that's really going to take you someplace — can be very alluring. Don't plan your career around magic beans. Know that a career is built on hard work.

It's important to get some work under your belt so that people will recognize your skills. Credit on a reputable project can do this for you. It's a double-edged sword because working for free gives you experience, but lowers the value of professionals who are trying to make a living. However, the reality is that no one will hire you to work on a professional shoot unless you have worked on other projects. It's the same catch-22 that teenagers find themselves in when trying to get a job to make enough money so they can purchase a car. They need the car to drive to work, but can't afford the car until they make money at work.

Independent filmmakers will say anything to get you to work on their films. They are desperate. They have hearts full of passion, but their wallets are filled with blank IOUs. I don't mean to slam independent films. I love independent films and help them out any chance I get. I do my fair share of freebies and gear rentals at little or no cost at all. They have the best of intentions, but haven't had enough real-world experience to know that they need to have all of their funding before they start production. To start a film with the hope that the rest of the money will come in is not only artistic suicide, but also an injustice to the hard-working crew. The point is to know what you are getting into. Hopefully some of my experiences will help you understand the business of independent films. It's a shaky business, but there are a lot of cool films that you can be part of. Apart from the business side of independent films, there are the relationships and connections made on the set. These can be far more valuable than the rate you'll receive for working on the film itself.

RENTAL RATES

Gear rental is usually not included in your day rate. Some sound mixers are hired to operate equipment that is provided by the production company or shooter. Other times, sound mixers are expected to have their own equipment or rent a package from a rental company for the shoot. Rental rates, also known as *kit rentals*, typically range from $75 to $150 per day for a basic ENG package that consists of a mixer, boom mic/pole, a pair of wireless lavs, headphones, and the necessary cables and adaptors. Film sound packages range from $200 for low-budget films to $600+ per day for higher-budget productions that require a wide variety of equipment. On some jobs, you can make more money from the rental fee than from your day rate! If the production company requests additional equipment that is not included in your standard rental package (typically, extra wireless units), they will need to pay an additional rental fee for these items. Most rental houses offer weekly rental rates that are three times the daily rental rate.

Different cities and countries have standard ranges for rental package rates. When starting out, check around to find the acceptable price range for rental packages in your area. Don't try to undercut the competition. Even though they are your competitors, you're all in the same business. Being the cheapest around will hurt you and the rest of the community. It's common courtesy to yourself and others to maintain consistent prices.

Rental houses require insurance to rent their equipment. The production company will need to provide the rental house with a *certificate of insurance*. Avoid using your own insurance on behalf of the production company. They may indeed cover your deductible, but they will not cover the annual increase in your insurance premiums! The production company's certificate of insurance will need to list the rental house as the additionally insured party. This certificate should also list you as additionally insured if your equipment package is being rented. All this might seem like a bunch of hoops to jump through, but this is an important part of the business. Equipment will get damaged or stolen. If this hasn't happened to you yet, be prepared. It will. When it does, the only promises that count will be the ones that were written and signed.

There are crooks out there. People will take advantage of your charity. It's okay to throw in a free rental here and there, but once a client realizes that you're willing to provide something for nothing, they'll expect that the next time around. Remember, this is "show business," not "show charity."

CANCELLATIONS

"The show must go on" is more than a catchy phrase to encourage performers. It's a way of life for film crews. Other industries can survive when employees take sick days. When a fry cook at a fast-food restaurant calls in with the flu, the stress is passed on to another cook who has to pull double duty. But, when a sound mixer calls off for a shoot the same day, all hell breaks loose. Crewmembers have specific duties and, unlike fry cooks, there aren't many of them around. Calling in sick for a shoot is virtually unheard of in the film industry. In all my years of doing location sound, I've only cancelled a few gigs. When I did have to cancel, I called reliable and quality sound mixers to make sure they could fill in for me before I called the client. Calling a client and telling them that you can't make a shoot without already having a replacement is an unforgivable sin.

I'll never forget calling one of my clients to tell them that I had a medical emergency and couldn't work the next day. The client was irate, even though I already had a replacement for them. They told me that I was hired for my skill level and that they didn't know if my replacement would be as good. Even though I had worked with that client on at least a dozen shoots, they never called me again. That was nearly ten years ago and I haven't spoken to them since. Don't be surprised if you call the production manager to tell him that you're in the hospital with a broken arm and his response is "So, you're going to be a little late today?" When you're hired for a gig, you are married to the gig. Being faithful to your clients will bring more work and will improve your reputation. Calling off gigs will cause you to lose work and harm your reputation.

The cancellation policy goes both ways. There is an unwritten rule that if a client cancels a shoot less than twenty-four hours before the gig, they are responsible to pay your full rate. For this reason, a client may call you and place you on a "hold." This means they intend to work that day, but if another production calls to hire you, the client has the right of first refusal. If the job gets cancelled, they will call and "release" you. This is done so they can avoid a cancellation fee. Other times, a client will give you a "firm" booking. This means that they are committing to hiring you for a specific day and that you should refuse any other work for that date. In all my years, I only had one client that didn't pay a cancellation fee. It could have been because they were from out of town, but they never paid the invoice. All of my clients have always paid cancellation fees, even if there wasn't any paperwork to prove their commitment. I certainly wouldn't suggest arguing with a good client over a cancellation fee, but if they constantly cancel jobs, you could be losing money from other paying clients.

BILLING

The standard invoice pay term is thirty days. This means that the invoice should be paid in full within thirty days of the work date. Some production companies like to play the invoicing game where they only pay an invoice thirty days from when the invoice was received and not from when the work was performed. Some film companies will pay via a payroll company. Others may pay via a check at the end of each week. If you are working on a long-term project (longer than a week), an invoice should be submitted at the end of each week. Some sound mixers have different policies when working with new clients outside of their state. It is not uncommon to request that a new, out-of-state company sends payment in advance of a work date to ensure that payment is received.

You have two types of billing options with a client. You can bill "portal to portal," meaning that your paid time starts when you leave the shop. When working with a crewing agency or company that requires you to show up at their building to collect or prep gear for the shoot, it is customary to start your paid time when you arrive at their building. Your paid time would end after you return the gear to their building at the end of the day. The other option is to start your paid time when you arrive on set. This means that you are on the clock when you get to the location and are off the clock when you leave the location. If your day involves multiple locations, you remain on the clock until you leave the last location. Travel time and fuel charges are usually applicable for locations that require you to travel more than fifty miles. Whatever billing option you decide on, you should make the client aware of this before the shoot. It's always best to get this in writing (emails or texts will suffice). This will give you necessary proof of the arrangement should a billing issue arise after the shoot.

Some clients may ask if you are willing to work for a few hours at the beginning of the day and a few hours at the end of the day but only bill for a standard day. Sometimes these requests are reasonable and other times the downtime between shots should be considered part of your working hours. This is a call that you'll have to make based on the type of production and your relationship with the client.

Receipts for excessive mileage, parking fees, and other incidentals should be submitted with the invoice. Keep a photocopy of these receipts in case the originals get lost in the mail. That said, most invoices are now submitted via email as .PDF files. Avoid sending editable documents through email as they can be altered. Using .PDF files will ensure that the document cannot be changed.

COLLECTIONS

One of the joys of production work is chasing down invoices. Some clients are quick to hire, but slow to pay. It's sad, but true. You want to keep a good relationship with your clients at all costs. Sometimes this means waiting on unpaid invoices. The standard is thirty days, but this often drifts into the forty-five-day range. Clients get a little agitated if you call them on Day 31 asking for payment. It's a good idea to cut them some slack. Unfortunately, your landlord will have no problem banging on your door at the first of the month asking for rent. That's how it goes.

Independent filmmakers are notorious for running out of money. This could be due to careless accounting, unforeseen costs, or nervous investors who back out. In any case, it's the crewmembers who end up shorthanded.

Friends of mine directed some of the films I worked on. They had every intention of paying me, but somehow the money just wasn't there. It wasn't always their fault, but that didn't really matter. There was no paycheck at the end of the week. To save friendships and keep business relationships, I began charging independent films up front before I would agree to work the show. Anytime I broke my policy, I ended up having to fight for the money. This has translated to my post work. I will not work on an independent film without payment up front. If they can only afford 50%, I'll work on the film, but I won't release the final mix until payment is made in full. Producers will promise you that the money will be there. They will sweet-talk you and even try aggressive tactics like acting offended that you're asking them to sign a deal memo. The bottom line is that talk is talk and money is money. You're not working for talk; you're working for money. No money, no sound.

Fortunately, in all of my years, I've never been completely stiffed on a payment, although I've had to fight hard sometimes to get paid. It's frustrating to show up to the set on time and work to the best of your ability only to have the production company make you wait months for payment. The most extreme late payment I ever received was on an independent film that shall remain unnamed because it did fairly well at Blockbuster and had a limited theatrical release. Plus, a friend of mine wrote the screenplay, but enough with the hints....

The producer seemed like a nice guy. I had worked with him twice before. Both times he paid late. For the third film (I know, I'm a sucker for punishment), we agreed that payment would be made at the end of each week. He also agreed that the DAT tapes would not be released until after payment was made. By payment, I meant cash, because a few of his checks had bounced on previous films. He convinced me that this film would be different and that investors with deep pockets had agreed to back it. I cautiously proceeded to work on the film.

Sure enough, a few weeks into the show, rumors went around the set that the production ran out of money and that everyone was going to get stiffed on Friday. I wasn't horribly worried since the only thing the production company needs from the set is film and audio. I had the audio, so I had a bargaining chip. If the production went on hold, I had cards to play that would ensure my boom operator and I would be paid.

Friday ended up being a super-long day. It was obvious that the production was going into hibernation and they were rushing to cram everything they could into the last day. When the day wrapped, I swapped out the production DATs with blank tapes, just in case things got hairy. After all, I was working in downtown Detroit where bad things can happen. The producer knew they had a song and dance to perform in order to get me to release the tapes. Unfortunately for them, I wasn't in the mood for music.

The rest of the crew had not yet been informed that the production was broke. So, the producer pulled me aside and handed me a check. Since up until that point, all payments were made in cash, I knew that things were going downhill. He asked for the tapes. Of course, I reminded him of our agreement that my boom operator and I were to be paid in cash before the tapes were released. Immediately, the producer got irate. He raised his voice and threatened me. After an exchange of words, I took the check and agreed to release the tapes the next day, after the check was cashed. With sweat on his forehead and panic in his eyes, he agreed.

The next day the bank told me there were insufficient funds in the production company's account to cover the check. I was not surprised. So, I held on to the tapes. In the months that followed, I received several angry phone calls from the producer, who demanded that I release the tapes to him so that his editor could start cutting the film. I refused. Of course, I wondered how he was paying an editor without any money. Then again, the editor probably had no idea that he was going to be stiffed, too. The threatening phone calls continued for months and months. The film was dead in the water without the sound and we both knew it. He had no choice but to raise money to pay my boom operator and me. And so he did.

I got paid exactly 365 days after the final day of shooting. It went down like a drug deal. We met at night in a public parking lot. He jumped in my car and handed me cash in an envelope. I counted it, then reached under my seat and handed him the DAT tapes. It was a done deal. We kept the meeting short and sweet with very little small talk. We've never spoken since. I think we're both happier that way. The last I heard, there were many crewmembers who never got paid.

It should be noted that I refused to release the tapes until my boom operator was paid as well. At one point, the producer wanted to pay only me. That wouldn't be fair to my boom operator, who trusted me to handle the business agreements. He was my teammate and good sound mixers always take care of their team.

FIRING A CLIENT

Clients that are constantly late or refuse to pay for overtime that they agreed to should be avoided. They're not good for business. Never tell a client that you don't want to work for them. This is a bad business practice. Instead, when they call to book you, tell them that you are unavailable. After a few calls, they'll take you off their list of usual suspects and start bothering other sound mixers.

I've had my share of late clients. One, a rather large production company, was notoriously late paying invoices. After several forty-five-to-sixty day late payments, I was starting to feel a little mistreated. The final straw was a payment that was approaching sixty days overdue. By sixty days overdue, I mean that with a thirty-day net term, nearly ninety days had passed since the date of the job and I still had not received payment.

I called their billing department for the second time and got the usual runaround. "I have your check sitting right here on my desk, Mr. Viers. It's going in the mail today," is what the accountant said. I called her bluff and told them that I was going to be in their neighborhood that afternoon and I would be happy to save them postage by stopping by to pick up the check. There was silence on the end of the phone. After a long pause the accountant, now as agitated as I was, told me that it would be against their policy and that the manager had to approve and sign the check. Then, she hung up on me. It was still a couple of weeks before I got paid. Apparently, it took a really long time for the ink from the manager's signature on the check to dry. I never worked for them again. I didn't want to. They called to book me, but I always seemed to be too busy. I essentially fired the client.

Hopefully, your career will be filled with tons of cool memories and stories. These help sugarcoat the bad experiences and billing issues that you'll have to deal with. It's a roller coaster of a ride! Be sure to keep your hands and feet inside the cart at all times.

CHAPTER EXERCISE Do some research of the film/television industry in your town. Make a list of local production companies to send resumes and speak with freelancers and rental houses to get a sense of the going rates in the area. The notes you take will help you get started once you're done reading this book. Don't worry. You're nearly finished!

CHAPTER 21

THAT'S A WRAP!

This book can be summed up with the following statement: **Gather clean, consistent, and intelligible dialog by selecting the right microphones, placing those microphones in the best position, recording them at the right levels, and treating unwanted background noise and reverb.** If you keep this statement in the front of your mind each time you walk onto a set, you'll walk away with the best possible sound every time.

You will face countless problems. This book has tried to cover the most common challenges, but understand that no two situations are the same. There will always be new challenges to overcome. By understanding your goal, your gear, and your role in the production, you will quickly become more proficient at your craft and as a result you'll be an in-demand sound mixer.

Adam Grabowski at the end of a long shoot day

Some sound mixers might agree with everything in this book, but that probably won't be the case. In all of my years in production, I have learned there is always more than one way to tackle a problem. If you asked ten different sound mixers how to record the same scene, you will undoubtedly get ten different answers. All of which may be solid and plausible solutions. The bottom line is don't stress over the process; rather, focus on the results. Is the result of your techniques clean, consistent, and intelligible dialog? If not, rethink your process.

Now, before you hurry off to power up some cool gear, here are some parting thoughts to help you on your way.

There is a culture to filmmaking that can't be learned from a book or in a classroom. No matter how much information I try to pack into this book, I can't explain the rhythm or non-spoken language of a film set. There is a vibe — a flow to the work. It's an understood feeling among the crew, kind of like playing in a band on stage that starts to jam to a part of the song that wasn't rehearsed. You can learn the song by reading the guitar tabs, but it's not until the other members of the band start playing that you feel the song come alive. This is filmmaking. It's less Top 40 and more jazz. It's a marriage of art and science. You can learn the science in this book, but you have to get your fingers on the knobs and your hands on a boom pole with other crewmembers before you can truly understand the art of filmmaking. Practice is the only way to improve your craft. Reading this book is not enough.

When in doubt, ask questions! This is very helpful when starting your career. If you don't understand a term or one of the seemingly countless acronyms used on a set, just ask. One of the methods I used for understanding things and asking questions is to ask different people. You'll be surprised to find out how many people really don't know what they're talking about. Ask around and get a general consensus from other crewmembers. Take notes on new things you've learned and make a list of things you don't know. Research online blogs and join Facebook groups for sound mixers.

Stay focused on techniques and not the technology. Technology changes; techniques don't. Avoid getting caught up in the latest box with flashing lights, knobs, and buttons. Any artist can paint the Sistine Chapel if he has the right time and paint. But, filmmaking is more akin to painting the Sistine Chapel in only a few days using cheap paint from the local hardware store. Use the tips and tricks in this book to get started. You can begin to make great production tracks now by using whatever tools you have available! Jump in and be ready to learn from your mistakes.

Remember, there is no such thing as a bad experience. It is all just experience. Start referring to difficult gigs as "learning lessons." You will make mistakes. Things will go wrong because of bad calls you made. Directors will treat you like dirt (sorry, my publisher wouldn't let me use profane language). A DP might even call you nasty names. This is all part of the fun! Hold your chin up and move on to the next location where even more fun and excitement awaits!

The workdays of a sound mixer are long and tedious. The personal sacrifices to work in this industry can be great. You'll have an unpredictable schedule and family time will be at a premium. Your fellow crewmembers can quickly become your family away from family. There will be times when you'll have to fight to get paid. But, there are other times when the money will flow like water. Your work may live on in a blockbuster film that makes history or a television show that is adored by fans for decades to come.

If you are a free spirit like Captain Jack Sparrow, you'll be happy to know that production work is "never the same day twice." There are exotic places to travel to, amazing people to meet, stars to schmooze with, and plenty of friends to make. One day you might find yourself in the middle of a breaking news story that is being watched by millions, sometimes even hundreds of millions of people. And there are days where you will spend countless hours in the back office of an industrial park listening to a business owner ramble on about the importance of a specific screw that is necessary to mount a steering column to the dashboard of a mediocre car. This is the life of a sound mixer — take it or leave it. If you choose to travel down this road, learn to enjoy every minute of it, including those moments when you're gathering room tone....

CHAPTER EXERCISE Before you start contacting local production companies for work, get your feet wet working on a few indie projects. Volunteering is fine at first, but don't make it a lifestyle. Remember, it's show *business*!

INDEX

ABOUT THE AUTHOR

Ric Viers has worked in the film and television industry for more than fifteen years. His location sound credits include hundreds of productions for nearly every major television network, Universal Studios, *Dateline*, *Good Morning America*, Disney, and many others. Known as the "Rock and Roll Professor of Sound," Viers has hosted several video series like *Rode University*, *Rode Rage*, and *The Detroit Chop Shop Video Diaries*. His sound design work has been used in major motion pictures, television shows, radio programs, and video games. In 2007, Viers launched his own label, Blastwave FX, to celebrate the release of his 100th sound effects library. Viers is the author of *The Sound Effects Bible* and is considered to be the world's largest independent provider of sound effects, with over 250,000 sounds and more than 600 sound effects libraries to his credit. He has produced sound libraries for numerous publishers, including Adobe, Apple, Blastwave FX, Sony, Sound Ideas, and The Hollywood Edge. For more information visit *www.ricviers.com*.

Visit *www.locationsoundbible.com* for resources, articles, tutorial vids, and more!

THE MYTH OF MWP

In a dark time, a light bringer came along, leading the curious and the frustrated to clarity and empowerment. It took the well-guarded secrets out of the hands of the few and made them available to all. It spread a spirit of openness and creative freedom, and built a storehouse of knowledge dedicated to the betterment of the arts.

The essence of the Michael Wiese Productions (MWP) is empowering people who have the burning desire to express themselves creatively. We help them realize their dreams by putting the tools in their hands. We demystify the sometimes secretive worlds of screenwriting, directing, acting, producing, film financing, and other media crafts.

By doing so, we hope to bring forth a realization of 'conscious media' which we define as being positively charged, emphasizing hope and affirming positive values like trust, cooperation, self-empowerment, freedom, and love. Grounded in the deep roots of myth, it aims to be healing both for those who make the art and those who encounter it. It hopes to be transformative for people, opening doors to new possibilities and pulling back veils to reveal hidden worlds.

MWP has built a storehouse of knowledge unequaled in the world, for no other publisher has so many titles on the media arts. Please visit www.mwp.com where you will find many free resources and a 25% discount on our books. Sign up and become part of the wider creative community!

Onward and upward,

Michael Wiese
Publisher/Filmmaker

INDEPENDENT FILMMAKERS
SCREENWRITERS
MEDIA PROFESSIONALS
MICHAEL WIESE PRODUCTIONS
GIVES YOU
INSTANT ACCESS
TO THE BEST BOOKS
AND INSTRUCTORS
IN THE WORLD
FOR THE LATEST UPDATES
AND DISCOUNTS,
CONNECT WITH US ON
WWW.MWP.COM
JOIN US ON FACEBOOK
FOLLOW US ON TWITTER
VIEW US ON YOUTUBE